M000305141

NELSON AND THE NILE

Nelson and the Nile

The Naval War against Bonaparte 1798

BRIAN LAVERY

CAXTON EDITIONS

Frontispiece
Nelson after the battle of the Nile,
painted in Naples by Leonardo Guzzardi.
(National Maritime Museum, London: BHC1895)

Approved by the Official Nelson Celebrations Committee

Copyright © Brian Lavery 1998

First published in Great Britain in 1998 by
Chatham Publishing,

Chatham Publishing is an imprint of
Gerald Duckworth & Co Ltd

This edition published 2003 by Caxton Editions an imprint of The Caxton Publishing Group

British Library Cataloguing in Publication Data
A catalogue record for this book is available from the British Library

ISBN 1 84067 5225

All rights reserved. No part of this publication may be reproduced
or transmitted in any form or by any means, electronic or
mechanical, including photocopying, recording, or any information
storage and retrieval system, without either prior permission in
writing from the publisher or a licence permitting restricted
copying.
The right of Brian Lavery to be identified as the author of this
work has been asserted by him in accordance with the Copyrights,
Designs and Patents Act 1988.

Typeset by Dorwyn Ltd, Rowlands Castle, Hants

Printed and bound in Dubai

Contents

Colour Plates

Foreword

This is an account of the great naval campaign in the Mediterranean 200 years ago; and, of course, it is also about Nelson. The Battle of the Nile was arguably the most decisive naval victory of its age, and its story is one worth telling in all its detail. Trafalgar looms far larger in the Nelson legend because of the death of the hero, the numerous personal accounts written of it, and the victory against numerical odds. However, it occurred at a time when the consistent failures of the French and Spanish fleets had already convinced them of their inferiority and when Napoleon's planned invasion of Britain had been abandoned. The Nile, on the other hand, was fought at a time when the opposing forces were far more delicately balanced.

The campaign is also a classic tale of the 'man alone', as found in much of modern fiction, including the naval commander as presented in C S Forrester's Hornblower novels; for Nelson, despite the legendary 'Band of Brothers', was very much alone during these three months. With his fleet's ups and downs, the mystery about the intentions of the French, his ultimate triumph and even his ambiguous position as hero at the end, it provides a plot that few novelists could better.

But Nelson's career, though essential, is only part of the story. The Mediterranean campaign of 1798 was the only one in which he and Napoleon Bonaparte were directly opposed to one another, though in the event they never met in combat. Bonaparte's Egyptian expedition was daring in conception and execution and had important cultural effects. More immediately, the defeat of his fleet in Aboukir Bay had enormous strategic consequences. Why and how did the destruction and capture of a dozen warships have such world-wide repercussions?

Contrary to what many believe, there is more to be said about Nelson's life and campaigns. Although virtually all his known letters have been published, the letters *to* him have not, nor have his log and signal books, which often reveal more about what was really happening. Furthermore, Nelson's successes depended entirely on the ships and men under him; on the fact that the Royal Navy, despite its ramshackle structure and numerous faults, was the best in the world, largely due to the quality of its seamen.

I am grateful to the Nelson and naval scholars with whom I have discussed such matters over the years: Robert Gardiner, Roger Knight, Roger Morriss, Tom Pocock, Nicholas Rodger, Colin White and many others. I am also grateful to students on my courses at Madingley Hall, Cambridge, and on the Open Museum courses at Greenwich, who have questioned many of my ideas and helped me refine them. I am particularly grateful to many past and present colleagues at the National Maritime Museum, especially Pieter van der Merwe for editorial support and David Lyon for reading and commenting on the text. In giving me time to write the book and the resources to illustrate it, the Museum as a whole has seen the importance of this subject in the bicentennial 'Nelson Decade' to 2005, and as part of a modern reconsideration of Nelson and his era.

Brian Lavery
Greenwich
January 1998

CHAPTER 1

'To drive the English from all their oriental possessions'

IT WAS FEBRUARY 1798, or 'Pluviôse', the 'rainy month' as the French Revolutionaries had aptly renamed it in their new, secular calendar, when General Napoleon Bonaparte left Paris by coach, to begin an eight-day tour of northern France. Just 28 years old, Bonaparte had recently been appointed General-in-Chief of the optimistically-named 'Army of England', and charged with organising an invasion which would finally overthrow the last great enemy of the French Revolution.

He spent many hours in the coach with his aides Lannes and Sulkowski, his secretary Louis Bourrienne and a courier by the name of Moustache. They travelled nearly 300 miles by night and day along the muddy roads of Normandy and Flanders, visiting the ports of Étaples, Boulogne, Ambleteuse, Calais, Dunkirk, Furnes, Nieuport, Antwerp and the Dutch island of Walcheren. Bonaparte was already famous in France and Europe so he travelled incognito, using the name of one of his aides. At each port he asked many questions of the officers he met and astonished them with the depth of his interrogation. The young man was short, with intense eyes in a lean face fringed with long, straight, unadorned hair in a style that the Revolution had made fashionable. His uniform, trimmed with an extravagant amount of gold lace, seemed to dominate his body but his extraordinary intelligence and personality were more impressive than his stature or the trappings.

La Manche, or the English Channel as his enemies preferred to call it, was not familiar territory to Bonaparte. He was a man of the Mediterranean, brought up on the island of Corsica, where his father was a lawyer of Italian stock with connections to the aristocracy. He had been born there in 1769, soon after the island was incorporated permanently into France, and on coming to the mainland in 1778, his accent made him an outsider at the military colleges in Autun and Brienne. A young lieutenant of artillery at the start of the Revolution in 1789, he first saw action in his native Corsica in support of an attempt to gain independence from France. He had a rapid rise through the ranks, because many officers fled when the Revolution against the absolutist monarchy of Louis XVI had itself turned to violence and repression in 1792. He first came to fame at Toulon, the great French naval base on

Napoleon Bonaparte in 1796 at the Battle of Arcola in northern Italy, where he defeated the Austrians. A print after the portrait by Baron Gros. (Scottish National Portrait Gallery, Edinburgh)

the Mediterranean. Early in 1793 it had been betrayed by Royalists in the city and occupied by the British and Spanish. Bonaparte organised the capture of a key position which dominated both the inner and outer harbour and the counter-revolutionaries, with their British and Spanish allies, were driven out. Stationed in Paris in 1795, he commanded troops against a Royalist rising and dispersed it with 'a whiff of grapeshot'. In the following year, soon after his marriage to Josephine de Beauharnais, he took command of the French army in Italy, where he won a series of striking victories against the Revolution's greatest continental enemy, Austria, and brought the northern part of Italy under French rule. Because of this he was known to the public as *L'Italique*.

There was nothing in the chilly coastal towns of north-west Europe that could charm Bonaparte. Calais and Boulogne were small harbours, much affected by the strong tides of the Channel. In later years it would take much dredging and civil engineering work to make them into great ferry ports but for the present they dried out with every fall of the tide and were only usable for six hours in every twelve. Ambleteuse and Étaples were fishing villages with tiny river ports, for they had not yet begun to develop as summer resorts for well-off Parisians. Antwerp was a great seaport but too far up the River Scheldt to be useful. Walcheren was a flat Dutch island and its main town, Vlissingen (Flushing), offered only a medium-sized harbour.

The weather was dark and cloudy on 10 February when Bonaparte arrived on the coast. On the 12th and 13th it was clear enough for him to look across the Channel to the white cliffs of Dover and perhaps he caught his first glimpse of his great enemy, Britain. From the 15th to the 18th the British ships patrolling the 20 miles of wintry sea recorded gales with snow and sleet, and north-easterly winds were to predominate for the rest of Bonaparte's trip. It was the 26th, after he was back in Paris, before the weather turned 'moderate and pleasant'.[1]

There was nothing to inspire Bonaparte's confidence in the operation. Thirty thousand troops were needed for the first wave of the landings – a small enough spearhead for the force which was intended to overthrow British power, though not unreasonable in view of the state of the British army and militia at the time. Barges and fishing boats were being converted at all the ports, while other small transport craft were being built to carry infantry, cavalry and artillery. Boulogne was the biggest of the French invasion ports and could hold a large number of barges but only a small number could be got out on any one tide. Calais was equally difficult.

Bonaparte kept his own counsel during the trip, at least in the presence of his secretary. But on the way back to Paris Bourrienne asked, 'Well general, what do you think of our journey?'. Bonaparte answered 'It is too great a chance. I will not hazard it. I would not thus sport with the fate of my beloved France'.[2] Bourrienne, according to his own account, could already read the general's mind. He knew that he had a plan which would take him in a very different direction.

On 23 February Bonaparte wrote his report to the government of France, the Directory.

> Whatever efforts we make, we will not, within a period of several years, gain the superiority of the seas. To perform a descent on England without being master of the seas is a very daring operation and very difficult to put into effect. If it is possible, it would be by surprise, by escaping from the squadrons blockading Brest or the Texel [at the mouth of the Zuyder Zee], then arriving in small boats, during the night and after a crossing of seven or eight hours, at daybreak on the coast of Kent or Sussex. For such an operation, we would need the long nights of winter. After the month of April, it would be increasingly impossible.

He went on to outline the faults in the preparations so far. There were not enough small boats to ferry the troops over. The French navy was firmly blockaded in Brest. There were not enough seamen with real operational experience. There was not enough money. Bonaparte recommended postponement but suggested attacks in other directions. King George's ancestral kingdom of Hanover was vulnerable and its seizure could be combined with an advance through the tiny states of western Germany. Another possibility suggested itself: 'We could well make an expedition to the Levant which would menace the commerce of the Indies.' But if none of these plans was considered feasible, then it would be as well to make peace with Britain, as there was no other way of damaging her by war.[3]

★

It was more than 8 years since the people of Paris had stormed the prison-fortress of the Bastille and begun the greatest revolution the world had yet seen. The old monarchy, the *ancien régime*, had bankrupted itself both financially and politically. Its antiquated system of taxation and internal customs duties could no longer cope after a long series of wars with Britain. In the late 1780s it realised it could only raise extra revenue by conceding some power to the people but, like many another absolutist regime, it found its greatest danger came when it began to reform itself. In 1788 the French assembly, the *États Général*, was summoned for the first time since 1614, but in contrast to Britain where power had in effect passed to an elected assembly a century earlier, there was no established tradition on which to build. Taking fright at the increasingly anti-royalist sentiment, Louis XVI and his queen, Marie Antoinette, attempted to flee the country in June 1791 but were stopped at Varennes. In August 1792 they were stripped of all power and the following January the King was executed by the newly-invented guillotine. Control passed into the hands of an extreme political clique called the Jacobins and the Reign of Terror began. In a period of 18 months, more than 16,000 people were executed, about half in the Vendée in western France after a royalist revolt was defeated. The image of the French Revolution, for the general public outside France at least, was established forever. As their property was confiscated and their lives threatened, the old clergy and the aristocracy largely fled the country. Religion was discouraged and even a new calendar was instituted.

Events in France rapidly attracted the attention of foreign powers. Britain had a parliamentary system (though it was far from democratic) and there the revolution of 1789 was welcomed in its early stages, as either leading to a constitutional monarchy or to a weakening of Britain's traditional enemy through internal divisions. But most of Europe had absolutist monarchies, very like the one which was undermined and then overthrown in France. Of the other great powers of Europe, Austria was the most hostile to the Revolution. France was provoked into declaring war on her in April 1792 and soon Prussia joined the anti-revolutionary campaign. The conservative powers expected a quick victory against the French rabble, but at Valmy in September 1792 their march on Paris was halted. France declared war on Great Britain and the Netherlands in February 1793, soon after the execution of the King and Queen, and conflict broke out with Spain in the following month. The new French armies, reorganised by the Jacobin military expert Carnot, were victorious on several fronts. Spain was driven out of the war in 1795 and forced into alliance with France in the following year. Prussia made a separate peace, and the Netherlands were occupied and transformed into the Batavian Republic, a 'sister republic' and in effect a puppet state of France. Bonaparte's campaign in Italy drove the Austrians out of the war, gave France control of northern Italy and forced the British fleet to abandon the Mediterranean in 1796. After Austria signed the Treaty of Campo Formio on 17 October 1797, only Britain remained in opposition to France, with the rather lukewarm support of Portugal.

Europe in 1798, showing France with her allies and satellites dominating Spain, northern Italy and the Netherlands ▶

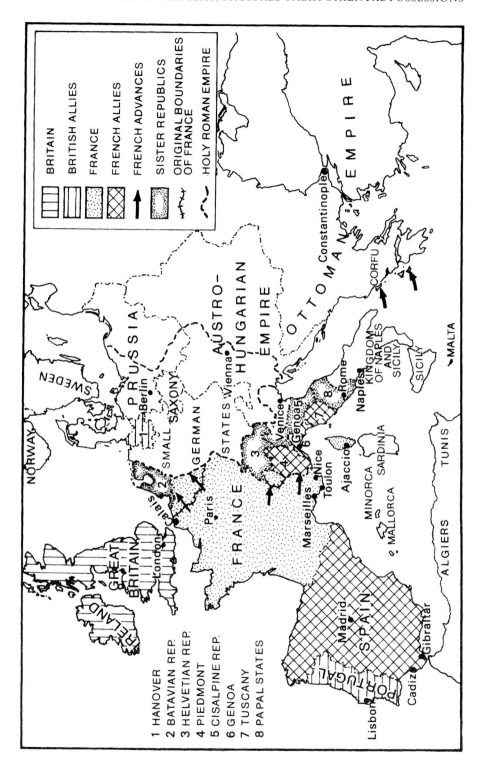

The Jacobins were overthrown by a coup on 9 Thermidor, or 27 July, 1794. A new, more moderate government took power in 1795. It was headed by a Directory of five members, elected by a Council of 500. But warfare continued and began to dominate French life. Wars kept ambitious generals, such as Bonaparte, out of the way. They provided a focus of national unity and could even raise revenue, to a certain extent, by means of plunder. With Bonaparte's campaigns in Italy, France was no longer merely defending her own territory against counter-revolution; she was an imperialist power in her own right, threatening the security of Europe by military as much as political means.

There was no single factor that made the French army superior to those of the *ancien régime*. It often fought in columns rather than line, creating a manoeuvrable force which could be easily deployed, but that was partly a development of older practices and the army relied on tactical flexibility rather than any single approach. Its troops, the product of the conscription of the *levée en masse*, were more numerous and far better motivated than the drilled automatons of Bourbon France, while the officers were chosen for tactical skill and zeal in battle rather than blue blood. The army learned to live off the country rather than rely on enormous trains of stores and supplies, so its movements were fast enough to outwit its cumbersome opponents. It abandoned many of the conventions of pre-revolutionary warfare, ignoring the complicated manoeuvres and the exaggerated respect for fortifications which had dominated old thinking. Initially the Republic was a regime fighting for its own survival, not for control of a distant colony or in support of a claim to a faraway throne, so its wars and battles were fought to a finish, not settled by a compromise peace treaty. If these tactical advantages were not enough, the army produced Napoleon Bonaparte, one of the greatest generals the world has ever seen.

★

Of the three propositions put forward by Bonaparte in February – a landing in England, an attack on Hanover and a move towards the eastern Mediterranean – only the last seemed both feasible and attractive. The attack on England had been a dream of French war policy for more than a century but the Royal Navy had always stood in the way, while an attack on Hanover would yield few material benefits and would do no fatal damage to British interests (as distinct from those of the King himself).

Certainly the idea of an expedition to Egypt had many attractions. To the politicians of the Directory, it would satisfy the need for perpetual warfare, for the Revolution seemed to have become addicted to fighting and there was no real enemy left on mainland European soil. It would remove Bonaparte from Paris for some time at least and divert his attention and ambitions away from national politics. On a geo-political scale, it could be seen as a culmination of a natural movement of France across the Mediterranean. She had taken Corsica in 1768 and Corfu in 1797. With Malta and Egypt in her possession, she would fulfil her natural destiny as the great power of the Mediterranean. France having recently lost her Caribbean empire, this would conjure up a new one in a different direction. It would balance the British capture of the Cape of Good Hope, by threatening to develop a new route to India. It would exploit the French navy's apparent control of the Mediterranean, using the fleet in an offensive operation for once, in a sea which had been vacated by the British. By threatening India it would deal a blow to the British without the risks of a strike across the English Channel, because a smaller army would be needed, the risks from the weather were far less and there was no hostile fleet in the area. Against this, certain flaws in the plan were apparent. It was not necessary in any real strategic or political sense, it would take about a tenth of the French army, including some of the best and most seasoned troops, out of the main area of conflict, and it would launch unprovoked attacks on Malta and Egypt, giving the world a warning of French ruthlessness.

★

Everyone with the slightest education was aware of Biblical and Classical Egypt, from Joseph and Moses to Anthony and Cleopatra, but modern Egypt was outside the experience of most Europeans, to a degree which is difficult to realise today. It was well beyond the range of the Grand Tour, in which the sons of rich families spent a year or two visiting France, Germany and Italy in search of cultural enlightenment. The French had maintained a steady trade with Egypt, which had expanded over the last 50 years, though their merchants rarely penetrated beyond the port of Alexandria. The educated Frenchman might have read recent works on the country, by Claude Savary and Constantin-François Volney. Savary had been in Egypt from 1776 to 1779 but had never got beyond Cairo. His *Letters Written from Egypt* gave an alluring account of the country, with a striking description of the Great Pyramid. Volney arrived in Alexandria in 1782. He too wrote about the antiquities of Egypt and a key passage in his *Journey in Syria and Egypt* gave an intellectual justification for Bonaparte's expedition.

> If Egypt had been in the hands of a nation kindly disposed towards the fine arts, it would yield material further to our knowledge of antiquity such as the rest of the world can no longer offer. In point of fact, there are no interesting ruins left in the Nile Delta, because the inhabitants have destroyed everything, either out of necessity or superstition. But in the less populous Said [upper Egypt] and at the less frequented edges of the desert, a few monuments remain intact.[4]

Coming from a land in which absolute monarchy was already being questioned, Volney was interested in alternative forms of government. Egypt provided no model for France or any other country but it certainly offered him scope for the kind of political and social observation he was interested in, for it had one of the strangest forms of government in the world. The Mamelukes had ruled the country for centuries. They were soldiers, bought as boy slaves in Georgia and the Caucasus and brought up and trained as elite cavalry. They had originally been the palace guard of the Caliphs but took power themselves in 1250. They were allowed to marry and have children but their power could not be inherited and their sons could not rise to high rank in the army, for it was believed that hereditary transmission would lead eventually to degeneracy. Instead, new entrants to the class continued to be purchased and brought into the country. The Mamelukes provided up to 10,000

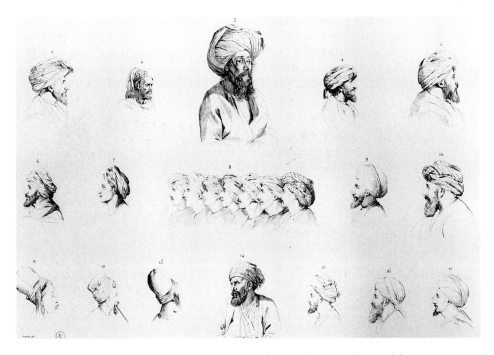

Various Egyptians, as drawn by Vivant-Denon. The group of seven in the centre are Mamelukes, with a much more European appearance. (Jean-Loup Charmet, Paris)

cavalry, which formed the core of the army, supported by native infantry. Government was under the control of the Mamelukes but much of the administration was carried out by Egyptian-born bureaucrats, while Christians and Jews dominated the financial world. The peasants, the *fellahin*, lived in poverty while the semi-nomadic Bedouins were in a constant state of revolt against the rulers.

In 1517 the Mamelukes were conquered by the Turks and Egypt became part of the Ottoman Empire. They were kept out of power at first but after a century they became the real rulers of the country again. By the seventeenth century power was in the hands of the Emirs or Beys, the leaders of the Mamelukes, and Turkish rule was largely nominal. The Beys tended to feud with one another but were still the rulers of the country in 1798.[5] But Turkish sovereignty, though it meant little in Egypt itself, was still highly valued in Constantinople. Assuming the Mamelukes could be defeated (which Bonaparte never doubted), how far was the Sublime Porte likely to resist? It was an important question, for the Porte ruled, in name at least, the whole of North Africa, Syria, Palestine and Arabia as well as Christian Greece and Macedonia. Turkish power had been driven back in central Europe, by Austria and Russia, but it still had a large army and a modest navy. Outdated as these were, they could put up a fierce resistance against the French if they were roused to action.

This was no great problem to Charles Maurice de Talleyrand, the French Foreign Minister. Languid, intelligent and cynical, Talleyrand made an ideal complement to Bonaparte – the diplomat and the man of action, both extremely competent, ambitious and uninhibited by any strong morality or ideology. Now in his forties, Talleyrand had been made Bishop of Autun just before the start of the Revolution but he had paid little attention to his vows of chastity. He had served briefly as ambassador to Britain in the months before the war broke out but parted company with the Revolution with the execution of the King and Queen in 1793 and went into exile in America. He returned home in 1795, after the fall of the Jacobins and the rise of the more moderate Directory. He became Foreign Minister 2 years later.

By the time Bonaparte had rejected the idea of a landing in England, Talleyrand had already considered the possibility of an expedition to Egypt and reported his conclusions to the Directory. He described the history and government of the country, concluding that the Ottoman Porte had no real authority and that the Pasha who represented the Sultan in Egypt was really the slave of the Mameluke Beys; that the Porte received very little revenue from Egypt and that the Mamelukes were in effective control. He also made a list of grievances, some spurious, that the French had against the Beys: that they had insulted French consuls, charged ruinous prices for provisions and extorted expensive presents from French visitors and traders. Things had allegedly got worse since 1793, for they had consistently insulted the revolutionary government. They were tyrants over their own people and Talleyrand was convinced that the French were liberators who could count on the support of the oppressed Egyptians and the Bedouin tribes.

Talleyrand produced a favourable report of the produce and commerce of Egypt. With a sub-tropical sun and the waters of the Nile, it had 'the most fortunate climate on the globe'. It produced grain, vegetables, rice, linen and cotton. The growth of sugar and indigo could supplant that of the island colonies which France had recently lost in the Caribbean. Only agricultural reform was needed to make Egypt prosperous and desirable. It was at the centre of the world, having good sea and land communications with India, Africa and Europe.

Talleyrand's final assessment was compelling:

1. That the conquest of Egypt is nothing more than a just reprisal for the wrongs done to us by the Porte and the insults we have had to endure there.
2. That it will be easy and even infallible.
3. That it will involve only modest expenditure, for which the Republic will soon be reimbursed.
4. Finally, that it presents innumerable advantages for the Republic.[6]

Bonaparte and Talleyrand made a powerful combination, not for the last time. According to Jean-Baptiste Barras, one of the members of the Directory, the debates on the expedition were long and intense. Bonaparte offered imaginative perspectives of advances in Africa and towards India, but Barras regarded these as 'sophisms given birth by his vivid imagination'. However, he persisted and won over the Directors one by one. Some at least were attracted by the need to find employment for the army, to prevent it interfering in politics. At last only Barras himself held out, but he accepted a majority decision of 5 March.[7]

However, the preparations for the invasion of England were to be kept up in the Channel ports. In Talleyrand's plan, it was important that the British should not be allowed to relax their defences, or they would be able to re-enter the Mediterranean. Perhaps there was also a feeling that if they did send forces against Bonaparte, a new opportunity of cross-channel invasion might open up.

★

From the beginning of the Revolution, the French navy was sandwiched between two opposing political forces. To the left, the crews of the ships supported the principles of the Revolution, while at the same time establishing their own right to fair treatment and an elimination of the excessive punishments of the old regime. On the right, the officer corps was even more aristocratic than that of the army and many of its members were horrified by mutinies in Brest in 1790-91. Large numbers fled in 1791-92, even before the Revolutionary War began. Of the remainder, many continued to support the Royalists and even went to the length of surrendering Toulon, the great Mediterranean base, to the British and Spanish in 1793. It was necessary to build a new officer corps, suitable for the navy of the Republic.

Unlike army officers, commanders of sailing warships could not be improvised in an emergency. The sea is not man's natural environment and even to survive on it requires a good deal of skill. To make a sailing ship progress safely over the oceans needs even more, but to fight a skilled enemy in battle took a perfect understanding of the capabilities of the complex machine that was one's home, vehicle and weapon, an understanding of the wind and weather, an ability to instil confidence in one's men and an instinct for the weaknesses of the enemy. A competent naval officer of any nation needed to have four main characteristics: seamanship, fighting ability, leadership and zeal for the state. Every admiral and captain, not to mention lieutenants and midshipmen, needed to combine these qualities in a single person, for any ship might find itself isolated and in action with the enemy at a moment's notice. To train such individuals would be the work of many years and to train a whole corps of such officers, to build up an ethos which could lead to victory, took decades or centuries. Under the old French regime a naval officer was expected to study mathematics, hydrography, languages, shipbuilding, fencing and dancing ashore. He would spend at least 2½ years at sea as a midshipman before reaching commissioned rank and then an at least 4 years before becoming eligible for promotion to *capitaine de frégate*. It would take perhaps 20 years of command, in normal circumstances, to become an admiral in charge of a squadron or fleet. With the British navy threatening France, there was no time to go through this process from scratch.

There were three ways of finding naval officers in a hurry. One was to promote petty officers – the naval equivalents of sergeants and corporals. This rarely worked, because few of them had the education and the background to take on their new role. A commissioned officer needed mathematics to navigate his ship, a good level of literacy to send and receive orders and letters and an elementary understanding of world affairs when on detached service away from the main fleet. The second way was to take on merchant ship captains. This too had its difficulties, for their culture and training were very different. The merchant ship captain was brought up to get his cargo from A to B with the minimum cost, damage and delay. He was naturally cautious and had none of the daring that was highly prized in a naval officer.

The third possibility was to use Revolutionary officials to supervise the other groups, to make sure that they used their energies and that their loyalties remained in the right place – 'political commissars' as a future revolution would call them. Such men were inevitably few in number but one such was Jean Bon de St André, a former Protestant pastor who was appointed to supervise the navy in Brest in 1793. He has been much mocked by later naval historians, especially for his conduct in the Battle of the 'Glorious First of June' 1794, the first great fleet action of the war. St André withdrew from the deck leaving the admiral, Villaret-Joyeuse, to take charge. But he had already achieved much in the chaos of the Revolutionary dockyards and naval bases by fitting out the fleet and sending it to sea. His job was essentially done when the fleet entered battle and it could be argued that he was wise to get out of the way.

With only limited success from other means of recruitment, the navy found some relief as the more extreme phase of the Revolution came to an end and officers from minor aristocratic backgrounds were lured back into the service. Other loyal officers were rapidly promoted, while new entrants were gradually trained up to become useful. The new Republican Navy, or *Marine Nationale*, was beginning to create its own spirit; mutiny and political divisions were no longer serious issues as they had been in 1789-94. The navy already had a large fleet of well-designed ships, built in the last years of the monarchy.

Even under the old regime, the senior officers of the French navy had suffered from a lack of tactical confidence. Since its defeat at Barfleur in 1692 it had always been recognised that the French fleet would never be numerically equal to the British. To make up for this, French strategists developed very different ideas. A large part of the campaign against Britain would be conducted by privateers, privately-owned warships whose operators hoped to make a profit by raiding commerce. Warships and fleets did not leave port except on particular missions, perhaps to attack or reinforce a distant colony, to support rebels in Scotland or Ireland or even to attempt an invasion across the Channel to southern England. Such a fleet should evade battle rather than seek it, for the mission was far more important than the abstract concept of 'control of the sea', as sought by the British.

Recently this doctrine had had some success. In the American War of Independence (1775-83), the presence of the French fleet off Chesapeake Bay had prevented the British from reinforcing their besieged forces at Yorktown, leading to a great victory by the Americans and eventually to their independence. But in the same war the French had missed some important chances. Combined with the Spanish and later the Dutch, they outnumbered the British but did not force this to a conclusion in the English Channel.

France needed a navy, not just to defend her shores but to protect her commerce on the high seas and especially to maintain her overseas empire, which was in many ways the most profitable and dynamic sector of the economy. In 1789, nearly 90 per cent of West Indian sugar and coffee brought to France was re-exported and, overall, West Indian business amounted to about a third of her foreign trade.[8] Before the war it had brought great prosperity to Bordeaux but the effects of this spread all through the country. It was reckoned that 3½ million individuals were directly or indirectly dependent on the trade. But the islands had been lost, to a revolt of the slaves and free blacks in St Domingue (later Haiti) in 1791 and to the British invasion of Martinique and Guadeloupe in 1794 (though Guadeloupe was soon recaptured).

The British empire was also triumphant elsewhere. In 1795, Admiral Elphinstone (later Lord Keith) had taken the Dutch colony of the Cape of Good Hope, providing a station for ships on the way to India and a naval base to harass any French ships in the area. Though the French East India Company had largely been driven out of the sub-continent in the Seven Years War of 1756-63, the Indian Ocean islands of Mauritius and Reunion were still held and provided a base on the way to India, almost as valuable as the British one at the Cape. But it was the situation in India itself which was attracting the attention of French strategists. Tippoo Sahib, the Sultan of Mysore in the south of the sub-continent, was a Francophile who had been educated and influenced by French officers in the service of his father, Hyder Ali. Since taking power himself in 1783, he had waged several wars against British power, treating his captives with great cruelty. He had been defeated in 1792 and forced to give up half his dominions but naturally this still rankled. Like Bonaparte himself he was a soldier, an indefatigable worker and a reformer who introduced a new calendar, weights and measures and a new currency. If the French could find a way to send an army to support him, then a campaign against the British in India had every hope of success.

Though the traditional sea route by the Cape of Good Hope was increasingly difficult for the French, another route via the Mediterranean seemed possible. The British fleet had been forced to evacuate the area because of Bonaparte's victories in Italy, while the base in Corsica was abandoned because of the Spanish threat to the lines of communication. France now had an important base in the Greek island of Corfu, and had taken over most of the ships of the conquered Venetians, so her land and sea power in the Mediterranean seemed secure. To Bonaparte and Talleyrand, it seemed only natural that this should be exploited.

★

On 12 April the Directory issued the formal orders that would give Bonaparte the authority and resources to prepare his expedition. As Commander-in-Chief of the Army of the East, he would 'lead the land and sea forces under his command to Egypt and will take possession of that country'. He was also to 'drive the English from all their oriental possessions which he can reach'. There was no specific mention of India but settlements in the Red Sea were to be attacked if possible. He was also to 'cause the isthmus of Suez to be cut through' and to 'take all necessary measures to ensure the French Republic the free and exclusive use' of the Red Sea.[9] The move towards India was obvious as a long-term objective but it would take some months or years to get there according to the Directory's perspective.

Bonaparte directed the organisation from Paris, but it was the subordinate generals in the ports of southern France, western Italy and Corsica who had to carry the great burden of assembling the troops, finding ships to carry them, and keeping them supplied with food, drink and all the necessities of war. At his right hand was General Louis Berthier, his chief of staff. At 44, Berthier was relatively old for the Revolutionary army and had served with the French forces in America from 1780 to 1783. Unlike Bonaparte he was a strictly non-political general, though he had been suspended by the Revolutionaries in 1792. In 1795 he was reinstated as a brigadier-general and became Chief of Staff of the Army of Italy, in which capacity he served under Bonaparte for the first time. He was short and stout with an oversized head – despite his service under the *ancien régime* he was regarded as rather uncouth, but no-one doubted his ability to organise the navy, army and political leadership for the Egyptian expedition.[10] Bonaparte's former aide from the trip to the Channel Ports, Jean Lannes, was stationed in Lyons, co-ordinating the movement of troops from the interior to Toulon and Marseilles, and organising the shipment of gold from Switzerland to finance the expedition.

At 45, Jean-Baptiste Kléber was one of the oldest of Bonaparte's generals. He was from a relatively humble background in Strasbourg but had served the Austrians, for whom he had been an inspector of fortifications. He volunteered for the French army after the Revolution and his experience earned him quick promotion to general. He retired after winning a series of victories in Germany in 1795-96 but Bonaparte recalled him for the new campaign, to take command of the forces to be assembled in the great French naval base at Toulon.

The scene of Bonaparte's first triumph in 1794, Toulon was arguably France's premier naval port, superior in natural advantages to the Atlantic harbours of Brest and Rochefort. It was also the most important naval base belonging to any nation in the Mediterranean and the focus of activity for both the French and the British navies over many years of war. It was surrounded by ranges of rugged hills up to 1800ft in height, with fortresses dominating their key points. Down below there were two main anchorages, the inner and outer road. The outer road was the larger, though it did not compare with the British anchorage at Spithead off Portsmouth, and it was subject to rough seas in easterly winds. The inner road was rather smaller, with space for only two or three ships of the line at a time, in rather foul and rocky ground. Further in was the inner harbour, created by building two jetties which provided space for thirty ships of the line closely berthed in tiers, along with many frigates and smaller vessels. Linked to that harbour was the great naval arsenal or dockyard, strongly fortified and fully equipped with storehouses, ropewalks, mast houses, ordnance stores, smitheries, offices, barracks, hospitals and all the facilities of a major naval base. The arsenal had slips for building ships and the best repair facility in the Mediterranean, a large dry-dock in which ships could be cleaned and have their decayed planking and timber renewed. It was difficult to operate such a dock

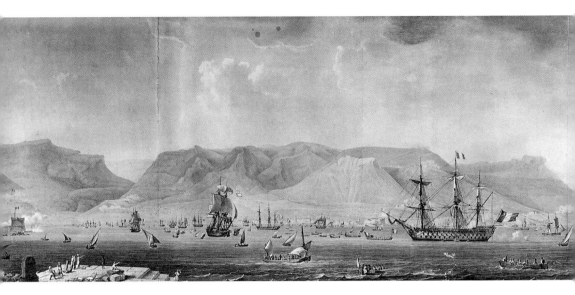

The anchorage at Toulon, with warships in the foreground and the town and dockyard at the foot of the hills. (Musée de la Marine, Paris)

in a tideless sea, so hundreds of convicts were needed to pump the water out when the dock was emptied.[11]

As in other ports, an embargo was put on merchant shipping leaving Toulon, so that both the ships and their crews could be taken up for service in the expedition. Small forces were also assembled in Nice and Antibes and sent to Toulon when ready. Kléber collected a force of seventy-one transports and began to embark his men on 7 May.[12]

*

At Genoa, the commanding general was Louis Baraguey D'Hilliers, 33 years old. In 1791, as a lieutenant of the regiment of Alsace, he had refused to serve the Revolution, but he soon changed his mind and in 1792 he gained great distinction as an aide to General Crillon, before suffering imprisonment when his patron fell from grace. Released in 1795, he commanded a division in Bonaparte's Italian campaign. In February 1798 he had been stationed at Mantua when a revolt broke out among the troops of the garrison. Despite this, his division was ordered to march to Genoa, where it was to embark for Egypt. The Genoa convoy was to be the largest of all, with 14,755 tons of shipping, comprising 72 vessels of which only 40 were French. The others were Ligurian (north Italian) and Spanish, with one Maltese and one Turkish vessel. The convoy was escorted by the frigate *Sérieuse*. Because so many of the ships had Italian-speaking crews, D'Hilliers decreed that each should carry one French seaman as a signalman and two others in charge of the distribution of victuals.[13]

Another division, commanded by Louis Desaix, was to sail from Civitavecchia, on the Italian coast north of Rome. In his thirtieth year, Desaix was close to Bonaparte and shared a similar background. A professional soldier from the minor aristocracy, he had survived the purges of the Terror. He was a supremely competent soldier, though instead of the ambition and bombast of Bonaparte he was noted for his idealism and humanity. There were difficulties at Civitavecchia and early in April it was reported that preparations were less advanced than elsewhere.[14] From Rome, Desaix reported on 12 April on his efforts to find provisions for his men. So far he had assembled 4500 tons of shipping out of about 8000 needed, mostly in small ships of 150 to 350 tons. He had found enough provisions, in the form of biscuit, meat, wine and brandy to supply his 8000 men for 2 months, as ordered. The crews would be fed at the expense of the captains of their ships but there was difficulty in finding suitable food for the officers. In a revolutionary army it was normal for the officers to eat the same food as the men; but Desaix felt they should have some dignity in neutral transport ships and gave each lieutenant a sum of 60 livres to buy his own food before setting off, with 30 livres extra for each step in rank above that.[15] The frigate *Courageuse* was sent to Civitavecchia and arrived on 26 April. However because of the weak condition of her hull she was armed *en flûte*, that is she was fitted only with light guns, and was intended to carry 600 men as a troopship.[16] Desaix, wary of British naval forces in the area, asked for an escort of a few frigates or ships of the line.[17]

In Bonaparte's home island of Corsica, General Vaubois was to organise a force of 4500 men. An artilleryman like Bonaparte, he too had served in the Italian campaign. He was instructed to find supplies for the voyage on the mountainous island. He pointed out that 'we have some wheat, but no flour, and the mills are without water and are unable to make any'. No biscuit had been received from Genoa or Livorno, for they had shortages of their own.[18]

At Marseilles, where General Reynier was in command, there was a shortage of funds and an ancient commission of thirty-one businessmen and accountants was revived to buy provisions for the army and fleet as the money became available.[19] Reynier looked with horror at the tiny ships which were to carry his troops and complained,

> The vessels which have been designated for the transport of the division I command are very small and can carry 100 to 200 men each. They are overloaded with artillery and equipment, some of which encumbers the decks already set aside for the billeting of the number of men which have to be put there. The officers must board the same ships as the troops they command.[20]

Individual ships were found to lack suitable accommodation. 'Le Juste; missing a galley stove for the troops, mats and hammocks for the officers . . . L'Antoine; missing a galley stove, mess tins, cans etc for the troops . . .'[21] Some of these problems would be solved, but the troops got ready for a crowded, uncomfortable voyage. They began to embark on 5 May and the operation was completed on the following day. The force then sailed for Toulon and arrived the same day to join the ships assembling there. Gunner Bricard was impressed to see the three-decker *L'Orient*, the flagship of the expedition, for the first time. 'I could not stop staring at this vessel. It was a great surprise for me to see its height and its length.'[22]

Vice-Admiral Brueys, the commander of the
French naval forces in the Mediterranean.
(National Maritime Museum, London: A3314)

To protect the great force of transports against any enemy force that might enter the conflict, Bonaparte began to assemble warships at Toulon. Rear-Admiral Brueys, in command of a force of eleven ships of the line, five frigates and three smaller vessels, was recalled from Corfu and on 2 April, after a long voyage in light winds, he arrived at Toulon to join the warships already there.[23] Eleven days later he was promoted to vice-admiral and given orders to take command of the fleet under General Bonaparte. He suggested that, since the invasion of England had been abandoned, the Brest squadron might escape from the blockade and join him. This was overruled, because the threat of invasion had to be kept up to divert British forces.[24] Meanwhile the dockyard workers toiled to get more warships ready to put to sea and according to a report of 7 March by the Minister of Marine, they were 'happy and zealous' in their work, constantly exclaiming 'Long live the Republic and may England perish' in the hearing of the Minister.[25]

Some of the warships were less than satisfactory. The old 74-gun ship *Conquérant* was in dry-dock and was found to be very weak in her structure: she was therefore to carry only 18- and 12-pounder guns instead of 36-pounders. Like the frigate *Courageuse* she was to be armed *en flûte* and to serve mainly as a troop transport.[26] It was decided not to use the six ships of the line from the former Venetian Navy, seized when Bonaparte had extinguished the 'Serene Republic' in 1797. Armed with 64 guns each, they were regarded as obsolete and an uneconomic use of scarce seamen.

'The ships of Venetian construction need as many sailors as a good 74 gun ship, and sailors are our weakest part.'[27] Two of the Venetian ships were surveyed and rejected because of their 'feebleness'. They also lacked cables, rigging and sails.[28] Nevertheless the French were able to muster twelve ships of the line, or thirteen if the underarmed *Conquérant* was counted; the British were convinced that they could find no more than ten for such an expedition.[29]

Brueys found that his captains paid a great deal of attention to the symbolism of the decoration of their ships, which of course had mainly been built in the days of the monarchy. A cap of liberty was often put on the figurehead and red, white and blue bands were painted on the sides of the poop. Brueys felt it was ridiculous to show one's patriotism in this way, to waste time when there was work to be done and to sacrifice the chance of leading an enemy into a trap by flying false colours.[30]

On 22 April Bonaparte divided the thirteen ships of the line into three squadrons, one led by Brueys himself and the others by Rear-Admirals Blanquet and Villeneuve. Another rear-admiral, Decrès, was to take charge of the convoy of merchant ships while a fourth, Ganteaume, was to serve as Brueys's chief of staff, with Commodore Casabianca as the flag captain in *L'Orient*. Each of the squadrons was to have a frigate and a corvette attached to it, while the warships which were armed *en flûte* were to be part of the transport convoy rather than counted among the naval escort.[31]

One of the greatest difficulties was to find crews to man the warships and merchant vessels. For more than a century the French had used the *Inscription Maritime* to conscript crews for their navy. The professional seamen of each coastal district were divided into *classes*, liable to be called out for naval service for one year in three, four or five according to circumstances. By the 1780s, seamen were supposed to be accommodated in barracks ashore and issued with uniforms. In theory it was far more efficient than the British press gang, but in practice it never worked well. The base of merchant seamen remained at 50-60,000 men throughout the eighteenth century, about half the size of the British merchant marine in the 1790s. The financial difficulties of successive governments often meant that the men were unpaid, which caused them to desert or avoid conscription. Shortages were created by capture in wartime and mortality on long voyages, so other means had to be used to find men. During the preparations for the Egyptian expedition, an order was issued to conscript fishing-boat skippers who were less than 40 years old and masters of small coasters who had been less than 3 months in command. Much of the new levy fell on the Mediterranean coasts of France, particularly Nice and Languedoc, causing great resentment. There was much resistance to the maritime conscription and at Narbonne, west of Toulon, the general commanding the area asked for 600 soldiers 'to put down the sailors of eastern Pyrenees, who absolutely do not want to serve the Republic in the warships'.[32] Enough men were eventually raised to sail the ships, but as a whole the crews of the warships were 2000 men, or 16 per cent, short of their full fighting complement.[33] Throughout the campaign it was necessary to deploy soldiers among the gun crews.

The total military force was to consist of 5403 men of the light infantry, 19,669 line infantry, 2810 cavalrymen and 3245 artillerymen and engineers – a total of over 31,000 men, about half being veterans of the Army of Italy. One hundred and seventy-one cannon were to be embarked for the army, with their full equipment and ammunition.[34] The transport of horses was a problem for any amphibious operation, especially one carried out over such a long range. They had to be hoisted on board the ships, kept in a very confined space, and fed for the duration of the voyage. Bonaparte was to take more than 2800 cavalrymen, and horses would also be needed for the artillery, supply trains and for the senior officers. He decided to take only 1230 horses with him, believing that Egypt would furnish enough to provide for the army's needs.[35] By an order of 9 April, 2 months supply of food was to be provided for the troops on board ship.[36] The army was organised into five divisions, with Bonaparte as commander-in-chief.

This was more than just a military operation, for occupied Egypt would have to be governed when it had been conquered. Bonaparte already had great and justified confidence in his own administrative skills, so he could take on the government. He took a small number of administrative staff with him, including Jean-Baptiste Poussielgue as Treasurer of the Army, but a French general of the period was expected to take civil administration in his stride. In the meantime, Poussielgue was sent to Malta on an espionage mission. Scientific and archaeological inquiry was also an aim of the expedition and the fleet carried 167 *savants*, including astronomers, mathematicians, engineers, architects, draughtsmen, scribes, painters and musicians.

On the night of 3-4 May, Bonaparte left Paris for Toulon. He arrived in the port on 10 May and addressed three *demi-brigades* of his troops on the eve of their embarkation, reminding them of past triumphs:

> Officers and soldiers,
> Two years ago I came to take command of you. At that time you were on the Ligurian Coast, in the greatest want, lacking everything, having sold even your watches to provide for your needs. There all was given you in abundance. Have I not kept my word? [shouts of 'Yes'] Well, let me tell you that I have not done enough yet for the fatherland, nor the fatherland for you. I shall now lead you into a country where by your future deeds you will surpass even those that are now astonishing your admirers and you will render to the republic such services as she has a right to expect from an invincible army. I promise every soldier that upon his return to France he shall have enough to buy himself six acres of land.

The soldiers, according to one account, cheered loudly and shouted 'Long live the immortal republic.'[37] But the 'six acres of land' would be heard of again, in less happy circumstances.

CHAPTER 2

'We have no Relaxation in Port'

BY EARLY 1798, BRITAIN'S five-year war with Revolutionary France had already gone through some dark days. The armies of the French Revolution, despised in the early stages of the war, had soon turned the tables and after the battles of Valmy in 1792 and Tourcoing in 1794 they had inflicted one defeat after another on Britain's continental allies. The Netherlands and Spain were transformed from British allies into enemies, while Austria withdrew from the war, in circumstances which still caused a great deal of rancour between her and Britain. In 1796, ringed by hostile forces on land, the British fleet had been withdrawn from the Mediterranean, partly to allow it to support her last ally, Portugal.

There was a serious financial crisis early in 1797. The Bank of England's bullion reserves fell to a very low point, causing the government to extend the use of paper money and impose new taxes. At almost the same time the country's main strength, the Royal Navy, had shown signs of crumbling. It was not stress of war or fear of battle which had caused two great mutinies at the anchorages of Spithead and the Nore in April and June 1797, but poor pay, bad victuals, friction between regular seamen and landsmen raised by the Quota Acts (see Chapter 3), and perhaps the effects of two political developments on shore; the rise of the United Irishmen and the growth of radical thought and agitation, inspired by the French Revolution and earlier developments in America. The mutinies had been settled before the French had got wind of them – Spithead by concession, the Nore by repression – but the shock to Britain's government and navy was immense, as great as any single event of the whole of the eighteenth century.

Amid all these bleak prospects, there were still some rays of hope. Early in 1797 the Spanish navy had been beaten in a decisive action off Cape St Vincent, while the Dutch were defeated off their own coast, at Camperdown, later in the year. In 1798 the Prime Minister was perhaps the first to see signs of recovery in the nation's fortunes. The son of William Pitt the Elder, Earl of Chatham, who had led Britain to its great victory in the Seven Years War, William Pitt the Younger was born in 1759, the 'Year of Victories' when General Wolfe took Quebec from the French. In 1783, at the age of 24, he became Britain's youngest-ever Prime Minister. His opponents laughed at his lack of experience but he proved to be a great political leader, who modernised the financial system of the government and stabilised the country after the defeats of the war in America. He favoured political reform, even bringing in an unsuccessful bill to widen the parliamentary franchise in 1785. But the growing radicalism and tyranny of the French Revolution, combined with the threat of revolt at home, caused him to turn to repression after 1793. Radicals were imprisoned or sentenced to transportation to Australia (at least in Scotland, where juries could be persuaded to convict them), habeas corpus was suspended, the press was restricted and meetings of more than fifty people needed official permission.

Yet Pitt was less effective as a war leader. The common view[1] was that he failed to understand that this was a new kind of conflict, an ideological war in which the capture of enemy colonies was not the key to victory, as it had been in his father's day. He himself admitted his ignorance of military affairs, when he confided to his Foreign Secretary. 'I distrust extremely any ideas of my own on military subjects.'[2] Britain's first bachelor Prime Minister, he was a remote figure who managed to keep much of his private life out of the glare of publicity. He was respected rather than loved by his colleagues.

★

The war made a greater impact on society than any since the Civil War a century and a half ago, but it was not 'total' in the modern sense: the British people were not subjected to mass conscription, direction of labour, bombing of cities or food rationing. Nevertheless, the average citizen of London could not be unaware of it as he walked the streets or went about his daily business.

London in the early nineteenth century, by William Daniell. In the foreground, watermen's steps with wherries waiting for custom. To the right, the Tower of London with the Customs House just upstream of it. In the background, London and Blackfriars Bridges and the dome of St Paul's Cathedral. On the left, the river is typically crowded with shipping. (National Maritime Museum, London: 5316)

Britain's capital had expanded in the last century, and had almost doubled its population to 900,000. Much of the new building had taken place in the 'West End', especially between Piccadilly and Oxford Street, where elegant terraces and squares were designed by great architects such as William Chambers and Robert Adam. Building had spread as far west as the gallows at Tyburn, now Marble Arch, and criminals were now hanged outside Newgate Prison, where the Old Bailey now stands, eliminating the grand parade of the condemned through the streets of the city. Meanwhile the poor were beginning to congregate in the east, where they might find work loading and unloading the ships that thronged the Port of London. The city was now too big to feed itself and the agricultural land around London had been taken over for building. Some supplies arrived by cart, and livestock was driven to Smithfield Market by road, passing down the length of what is now Oxford Street. Some food was home-produced, for thousands of Londoners kept animals for their personal use. Otherwise it came by sea, as barges brought grain for the bakeries and hay for horses and domestic animals such as pigs and chickens. Small fishing boats took their catch to market at Billingsgate, but the biggest trade in London, and perhaps in the world, was the transport of coal. Over 4000 colliers arrived in the port every year, carrying a volume of nearly half a million chaldrons, equal to 23 million cubic feet and valued at £1.8 million.

In the north of England was another world of coal mines, iron works and cotton mills. Industry was largely rural, for steam was only just beginning to replace water power as the main propellant of the Industrial Revolution, and rural cotton mills such as Robert Owen's famous New Lanark in Scotland were at their height. In the countryside the new field systems, with hedgerows and new crops such as turnips, were increasingly seen in almost every county. But the effects of the new economy showed in the shops, warehouses and mansions of London. The new farmers provided the bread for the poor of the growing slums, while the great meat market at Smithfield sold thousands of cattle and sheep every year, largely for the upper and middle classes or to make into salt beef to feed the army and navy. The cotton mills provided cheap cloth for home consumption and export. The export market created wealth for the landowners and merchants who were moving into the new suburbs of Mayfair and Bloomsbury. The same wealth helped to finance the Royal Navy through taxation and loans and provided financial subsidies with which the government hoped to tempt new or old allies into the struggle against the abominable Revolution.

If he was an active patriot, the citizen might well spend his evenings training with one of the volunteer companies of amateur soldiers in the city. There were at least 1400 such companies in Britain, consisting of nearly 123,000 men in 1798,[3] almost three times the strength of the regular army on home stations. The military effectiveness of these bodies was doubtful, but they were certainly a force for social cohesion and influential in forging a sense of national identity. Like their descendants of 1940 they expressed the spirit of a nation preparing for invasion, in which everyone had to feel he was playing his part in the resistance.

London had not yet turned its back on the sea as it would do in the late twentieth century; indeed its great enclosed dock systems had not yet been built.

The River Thames was only bridged at three points. The ancient London Bridge no longer had shops and houses on top of it, but the piers were largely the same ones which had supported it since 1209. They were so thick that they acted as a dam, restricting the flow of the river and allowing it to freeze in a hard winter, so that Frost Fairs could be held on the ice. The more modern bridges at Westminster (1750) and Blackfriars (1769) helped to ease the traffic flow between the city and the semi-rural south bank.

To travel eastwards, a Londoner might well hire a wherry from one of dozens of steps leading down to the river, on which a Thames waterman, as carefully licensed as a London taxi driver today, would row him to the steps nearest his destination. As he passed downstream through the arches of London Bridge, the wherry passenger could not be unaware that he was entering the greatest port in the world. A third of British trade came to London by sea. Despite the depredations of French privateers, the Pool of London, between the Tower and London Bridge, was so crowded with shipping that more than 700 ships at a time might be found moored there in a busy period. Already Parliament was debating ways of raising money to build enclosed docks downstream from the city itself.

In the area round the Pool, particularly near the main naval 'rendezvous' on Tower Hill and in taverns such as the 'Rotterdam Arms' and the 'Two Dutch Skippers' at St Katherine's-by-the-Tower, a Londoner might see the work of the press gang. Contrary to popular myth it could only take experienced seamen into the navy, but its methods were often brutal enough. 'He gave a whistle and in a moment I was in the hands of six or eight ruffians who I immediately dreaded and soon found to be a press gang. They dragged me hurriedly along through several streets amid bitter execrations bestowed on them, expressions of sympathy directed towards me and landed me in one of their houses of rendezvous.' Thus one young seamen wrote of his experiences.[4] But most the gang's effort was hidden from Londoners, as men from homecoming merchant ships were conscripted off Falmouth, Dover or Gravesend.

London was no longer quite as grotesque and squalid as it had been portrayed by William Hogarth in the middle of the century. His most famously critical image, of the poverty and degradation of 'Gin Lane' had at least been modified by legislation of 1751 which restricted the sale of strong liquors. Political life was still caricatured by the great cartoonist, James Gillray, whose image of a lean, arrogant, boyish William Pitt was complemented by more savage satires on the Parliamentary opposition and the French. Thomas Rowlandson, the favourite caricaturist of the latter part of the century, was uninterested in politics and gentler in his social satire than Hogarth, reflecting some improvements in city life. Sanitation in the city had improved in the last few decades but crime was still prevalent – the magistrate Patrick Colquhoun estimated that 11,000 people made their living from theft from shipping alone, organised in specialist gangs with colourful descriptions such as 'mudlarks', 'heavy horsemen' and 'scuffle hunters'. Hanging was the normal punishment for over 200 offences, though in practice many sentences were commuted to transportation to the colonies in Australia. All the same, nearly 200 people were publicly hanged every year in London, watched by immense crowds. It had little effect in stopping crime and the potential victims of the rope joked about 'dancing on nothing', 'riding a horse foaled by an acorn' and 'going up the ladder to bed'. But in one sense London was more peaceful than before; civil disturbances were no longer common since the anti-Catholic Gordon Riots of 1780 had torn the city apart for several days.

London was not self-consciously an imperial city as it was to become under Queen Victoria, but there were certain buildings which reflected the importance of trade and empire in national prosperity. East India House in Leadenhall Street, built in 1726, was the headquarters of the company which traded with and ruled much of India. South Sea House, in the same street, was a monument to a less successful company, whose shares had boomed and then collapsed in the famous 'Bubble' of 1720 but the company continued trading in a much smaller way from this office, 'a large handsome brick structure, decorated with stone copings, rustic quoins and window-axes'.[5] Less exotic trade was carried on from the Coal Exchange in Thames Street, near Billingsgate Dock. Meanwhile at the Royal Exchange, between Threadneedle Street and Cornhill, the insurance market was controlled from Lloyd's, which operated two coffee houses, two meeting rooms and a 'subscription room' within the building.

The Custom House, on the banks of the Thames just up river from the Tower of London, was a magnificent brick and stone building, its upper floor dominated by the 172ft Long Room, in which dozens of clerks worked at their desks. At the Board of Trade offices in Whitehall, built in 1733-36, clerks computed very useful statistics on home and foreign shipping and trade. The main function of the Board, however, was to act as a consultative body, especially in disputes between traders, and in regulating the commerce of the colonies, except India.[6]

The war with France was now one of the strongest unifying factors in a country which still had many divisions of class and religion. Naval victories, such as those at Cape St Vincent and Camperdown in 1797, provided unique opportunities for celebration, since land victories were unknown in these years. All classes could unite to illuminate the town, let off fireworks and hold balls and fairs. Every intelligent Londoner knew that events in Bombay, Martinique or the Cape of Good Hope could have an effect on his pocket, his standard of living and his national pride. Communication across the world was slow and a return message from India would take a year, but Londoners realised that they lived in a world economy, albeit one that was heavily weighted towards the wealthier classes of western Europe; they knew that a defeat or victory in a distant part of the world was not a remote event. But the war had to be paid for. Pitt had not yet gone so far as to introduce income tax, knowing full well that it would involve a bureaucracy and an infringement of privacy that the public would barely tolerate. He increased old, easily-collected taxes on land, carriages, servants and even windows. Indeed the tax on certain luxury items had recently been increased threefold, a scheme which was known the 'triple assessment'.

On going to the theatre, as increasing numbers did in this age of growing public entertainment, a Londoner could hardly fail to be aware of Britain's naval triumphs, or the hardships endured by her seamen. He might have seen Sheridan's musical entertainment of 1794, in which the phrase *The Glorious First of June* entered the language to describe the naval victory of that year. He could have attended entertainments entitled *The Fall of Martinique, Naples Bay or the British Sailors at Anchor, Netley Abbey or Yardarm to Yardarm* or *A Trip to Plymouth Dock or the Launch of the Caesar.* More recently he could have seen an operetta on Sir Sidney Smith's escape from captivity in France, or a celebration of the surrender of Trinidad.[7]

In his newspaper too, a Londoner would see the effects of the war and of Britain's naval and maritime efforts. If he had a particular interest in shipping, which many did through ownership of shares in merchant vessels or stock in great trading organisations such as the East India Company, he would read the specialist *Lloyd's List*, giving details of shipping movements. Even a man of more general interests, reading his *Times* in the middle of March 1798, would see much about trade and war at sea. On some days, when a batch of dispatches was released to the press, four or five news columns out of perhaps eight in the whole paper would be about naval exploits great and small – major battles such as Cape St Vincent and Camperdown, the capture of individual frigates or privateers, 'cutting-out expeditions' in which seamen in boats raided enemy ports, and occasionally the capture of colonies such as the Cape of Good Hope.

On a more typical day, even the small advertisements on the front page, though dominated by house sales and quack medicines, would have much to say about maritime war and trade. The navy was constantly advertising for surgeon's mates to join ships at sea, while the 'Commissioners for taking Care of Sick and Wounded Seamen' needed merchants to supply them with many different goods, including hospital bread, salt butter, candles and coal. Merchants were invited to inspect warehouses which were 'well adapted for the West India trade, having an immediate communication with Fresh Wharf, from whence goods may be landed and housed without any expense of cartage or trucking'. Several meetings of the East India merchants were reported, with objections raised against a Mr Charnock who had brought home 'rice and rough goods from India', while one David Scott was to be 'disengaged from every interest in a House of Agency which can preclude him from being a Director'. Thus the East India Company protected its monopoly of trade. In Parliament, the holidays of the Customs House were discussed, while the shipping column reported on the movements of several vessels, mainly naval. At Southdown near Portsmouth, two Frenchmen were detected trying to escape from a prison hulk in barrels, while at Deptford, on the River Thames, a man fell under a tea chest being unloaded from a small vessel, a hoy, and was killed. The army was represented by several items of news, mostly deaths of officers, courts martial and a review on Blackheath near London. At this the King and several foreign dignitaries had inspected the 17th Regiment of Light Dragoons, who had 'made a fine appearance and went through their military evolutions, particularly the broadsword, with great credit to themselves and much satisfaction to their officers'.[8]

★

But despite its fine appearance, the British army was at one of the lowest points in its history. In the past it had tasted greatness under generals such as Cromwell,

Fairfax, Marlborough and Wolfe. It had not had much success in European warfare for many years, though it had done better at colonial warfare, especially with Wolfe's capture of Quebec in 1759. In America from 1775 to 1783, it had done its best in the impossible task of controlling a continent with inadequate resources, but had to surrender major forces at Saratoga and Yorktown. In 1793 the army sent to Holland under the 'Grand Old Duke of York' had been obliged to retreat and its commander has ever since been ridiculed in the famous nursery rhyme. Morale and discipline were so low that the officers were accused of abandoning their allies and even their own men, in order to save their personal baggage. In the West Indies the army had achieved many of its aims in capturing French sugar islands but had been ravaged by disease and lost 19,000 men in 2 years. At home it suffered from a complicated system of administration, born in the days (not entirely over) when any kind of professional military force was feared as a potential instrument of despotism. With no less than four departments responsible for running it, the army's reputation for competence was not high, though the same Duke of York, a failure as a field commander, was beginning to show his abilities as a military reformer. The officers, members of the upper and upper middle classes, purchased their commissions and a proportion of them were more interested in social rather than military duties. The rank and file were recruited, without conscription, from the lowest classes of society; later the Duke of Wellington would describe them as 'the scum of the earth'.[9] A great general could shape them into an effective fighting force, but that was still in the future.

In 1798 the regular army had 102,563 men below the rank of sergeant, plus 137,000 militia, who were recruited by selective conscription and could not be ordered to serve outside Britain. Since more than half the regular army was stationed in India and the colonies, only 48,609 men were theoretically available. Most of these were needed at home for defence against invasion, so there were virtually none available as a striking force against the enemy. An admiral like the Earl of St Vincent might see the army as unnecessary, to be replaced some day by an expanded marine force. There were politicians like Henry Dundas who believed that Britain would be better off without European entanglements. But realists, including the Prime Minister, were well aware that the French could not be defeated by sea power alone, however triumphant, and that the war could not be won without Continental allies and an effective British army.

★

The greatest fleet in the world, over 700 ships of all types, was controlled from the Admiralty office in Whitehall. The architecture of the building was un-distinguished, redeemed only by the screen in front of it, erected by Robert Adam in 1760 to protect the office from rioting seamen. The First Lord of the Admiralty, a member of the cabinet and His Majesty's Privy Council, lived in a large house on the premises and many of his subordinates were also accommodated in a street behind the office. The nerve centre was the Board Room, in the front of the building on the first floor. There was an elegant chair covered in red velvet for the

The Admiralty Board Room about 1808, the room drawn by Augustus Charles Pugin, the figures (which are far too small) by Thomas Rowlandson. (National Maritime Museum, London: 2802)

First Lord, at the head of a rectangular oak table topped with green baize. Under the table was a Persian carpet. Down each side were seats for the junior lords. At the other end sat the Secretary, Evan Neapean, who supervised the clerks and kept the office running. Beside him was the Reader, who read out every incoming letter taken from a large pile, to save the fatigue of copying it out several times for Their Lordships. Down the centre of the table were the reference books which the Lords needed to conduct their business. Bell-pulls hung from the ceiling, so that they could call servants for refreshment, or clerks to prepare urgent messages.

The Admiralty clerks were on duty all morning, having opened the incoming letters by 10am and sorted them out in order. At noon each weekday, the Lords of the Admiralty arrived for their daily meeting, in which fleets would be ordered to assemble or sail, admirals, captains, boatswains and cooks appointed to ships, and the dockyards given instructions on which ships to repair. George, Earl Spencer, the First Lord, was nearly 40. As a son of the aristocracy his political rise was not difficult and was aided by his membership of a family which had supported the party in power for many years. In 1794 Pitt sent him to Vienna as Ambassador Extraordinary and on his return at the end of the year he was appointed to the Admiralty. He was married to Lavinia Bingham, the daughter of the Earl of Lucan, one of the most beautiful and brilliant women in the country and the doyenne of London society. Lord Spencer's own interests were mainly in the arts and sciences. He was president of the Royal Institution and a trustee of the British Museum. He revived the ancestral library in his home at Althorp House in Northamptonshire, collecting rare volumes from the time of Caxton onwards and making it perhaps the finest private collection in Europe.[10]

Some members of the Board were political appointees. Charles Perceval, Lord Arden, was a son of the Earl of Egmont who, unlike some of his colleagues on the Board, spoke regularly in Parliament. Thomas Wallace, the son of a barrister, was on the first rung of a governmental career which would take him, very slowly, to high office as President of the Board of Trade. Sir Phillip Stephens had started as an Admiralty clerk himself and risen to become Secretary of the Admiralty before resigning and standing for Parliament. Elected for the Admiralty-controlled borough of Sandwich, he was almost silent in the House of Commons and was in effect a civil servant in a different guise.

Three members of this board were naval officers, for Spencer was aware of his own lack of experience in maritime affairs and relied heavily on his professional advisers. Rear-Admiral Lord Hugh Seymour was present at meetings for most of the winter but he was part-time and still flew his flag from the 80-gun ship *Sans Pareil* as part of the Channel Fleet. Fifth son of the Marquis of Hertford, he had once been a member of the circle of the Prince of Wales, sharing a lifestyle that could euphemistically be described as 'convivial'. The letter-writer and gossip Horace Walpole described him as 'one of the most amiable men in England'.[11] Rear-Admiral James Gambier was very different. He was one of the most religious officers in the service, an evangelical whose attempts to control the morals of his men earned him the nickname of 'Preaching Jemmy'. He had distinguished himself at the Battle of the Glorious First of June in 1794 and a fellow captain, seeing the devastation aboard Gambier's ship the *Defence*, had hailed him, 'never mind, Jimmy, whom the Lord loveth, he chastiseth'. But Gambier had not had much sea experience and was not a great strategist, his appointment to the Board having more to do with his kinship with the Pitt family. Rear-Admiral William Young had begun his career in 1761, served all through the American War and had taken part in operations in the Mediterranean in the present conflict. He had helped to mediate with the mutineers at Spithead but he never gained any great distinction in a long career.

If any of the political Lords were inclined to forget the real purpose of their daily meeting, there was much in the room to remind them. Above a marbled fireplace were rolled-up maps of the oceans of the world, ready to be pulled down for reference. Under the high oak-panelled ceiling was a cabinet supported by Corinthian pilasters, perhaps the work of Grinling Gibbons. In the centre of them, between two bookcases, was a large globe which could be brought out to help them to plan operations on a world scale. Above that was a wind indicator, linked to a vane on the roof. Perhaps its importance was more symbolic than real, for the nearest fleets were more than 50 miles away at Portsmouth or the Nore; but it reminded even the least seamanlike politician that everything depended on natural forces, that no officer on active service could neglect the wind strength and direction for a moment, and that battles and campaigns would be won by the commander who knew how to use these forces to his advantage.

On the roof of the building was a mechanical telegraph which in good weather could convey a message to Deal or Portsmouth in a few minutes, by passing it from stations on hilltops on the way. But once it had got there, communication with a fleet at was as slow and unreliable as it had ever been. Beyond the visibility of the telegraph station, it relied on the speed of a dispatch cutter, which depended on wind, weather and enemy action. In any case, the Admiralty preferred to do its business by formal letter whenever possible, and these were laboriously copied out by its staff of sixteen clerks, paid between £200 and £90 per annum according to seniority. They filed everything meticulously and kept an index in enormous volumes, with such headings as 'Alterations in the fittings of ships', 'Complaints on persons in civil situations', 'Dockyards and naval establishments at home; artificers and workmen; employment and attendance' and 'Riots on the Impress Service'. Now known as class 'Adm 12' in the Public Record Office at Kew, it forms a bulky but invaluable aid to researchers.

★

In the cold London air of 16 March 1798, the Board sat down to consider its business. It had no system of delegation or of sifting out less important items by means of sub-committees and executive officers. That morning it issued orders to the Ordnance Board to transfer some 18-pounder guns from the frigate *Seahorse* to the *Dryad*; to the Navy Board to have the crews of the *Tromp* and *Phoenix* paid as soon as possible and for a convoy to be assembled at South Shields to escort several ships to Hull. HM Ship *Hebe* was to be got ready for sea, while the *Plumper*, gunboat, was to go into dry-dock. Orders on minor matters were issued to Admiral Lutwidge at the Nore, Admiral Peyton at the Downs and Admiral Lord Duncan in Edinburgh. Amid the trivia, the Board made one decision which would be remembered; Rear-Admiral Sir Horatio Nelson was to go back to active service and was to hoist his flag on board the *Vanguard*, 74 guns, at Spithead.[12]

But Their Lordships' minds were increasingly directed towards the more congenial climate of the Mediterranean. They all knew that British ships had barely operated in that sea for more than a year and a half. Reports of the launching, fitting out and movements of enemy ships were collated in a book, begun in 1794 after the comment of Sir Charles Middelton that 'there is no method whatever observed in arranging and collecting information and which is of the utmost consequence in judging of the enemies' intentions'.[13] One Robert Maxwell was employed as Translator of the French and Spanish Languages to interpret them. Most reports came from the Channel and North Sea ports and dealt with the preparations for invasion, the state of the fleet at Brest and movements of privateers and other raiders. They consisted of reports by officers on blockade outside the ports, by captains of merchantmen who saw enemy movements, and of the interrogation of prisoners, who seem to have been quite talkative in this age.

The Admiralty was naturally somewhat short of information from the Mediterranean, as it had no fleet there. It received reports from Consul Brame and from

Captain Day in Genoa, from Consul Foreste in Corfu and from a Mr Jackson in Turin. These of course took several weeks to reach London, usually through Vienna. A surprisingly good source was the French newspapers, which could be acquired by cross-Channel smugglers and were often in London a day or two after they were printed. The official newspaper, *Le Moniteur*, was generally tight-lipped, but *L'Echo* was as loquacious as any prisoner of war.

By the beginning of April 1798 the Admiralty had gleaned that the warships in Toulon were being brought forward for service. The 74-gun ship *Spartiate* had been docked and sheathed in copper. A new 84 was being built, and several other ships of the line were moving from the inner to the outer basin. Meanwhile the enemy squadron at Corfu, consisting according to Consul Brame of six French ships of the line, a frigate and eight captured Venetian warships, was ready to depart for Toulon, 'deeply laden with plunder and badly manned'.[14] As yet there was no concern in London, for it was reported that good seamen were also scarce in Toulon. Perhaps eyebrows were raised when *L'Echo* of 27 March reported that 500 seamen had just reached the city from local levies and another 800 were expected from Bordeaux. On 6 April the *Moniteur* reported that four frigates had recently arrived, joining seventeen ships of the line and ten frigates which were already there, with troops and artillery on board for an amphibious campaign. General Bonaparte was expected soon, and it was presumed that the expedition was intended for Naples or Sicily. This was seen as significant and a copy of the *Moniteur* was sent to Earl St Vincent off Cadiz, though not until near the end of the month.[15]

★

Why was the Mediterranean so important in British strategy? Britain had no colonies there and no ambitions to acquire any. Until the Suez Canal was built 70 years later, it was a dead-end for shipping, although the land route to India, from Alexandria to Suez across the Egyptian desert, was important for carrying dispatches. British trade in the area was certainly quite valuable and in 1792, the last year of peace, it had accounted for £1.3 million of British imports and £1.4 million of exports. It was overshadowed by the West Indies, from which £4 million worth of goods, mainly sugar, were imported to Britain every year and largely re-exported at considerable profit. Neither did it offer the great profits of the East Indies, from which Britain gained by £2.7 million of imports and £2.4 million of exports.[16] Thousands of loads of shipbuilding timber were brought in from the Baltic every year, for both the Royal Navy and the mercantile marine, along with hemp for ropemaking, and tar. The Mediterranean was much less important as a supplier of strategic goods – only a tiny quantity of sulphur, which was necessary in the making of gunpowder and was found near the volcanoes of southern Italy.

But the political and military considerations of the Mediterranean were far more important than the economic. Militarily, it allowed access to the southern flank of France. At her great naval base at Toulon France kept one of her strongest fleets, which could soon be got ready to sail to any destination in the Mediterranean or beyond. Such a fleet would allow the French to range freely around the sea and

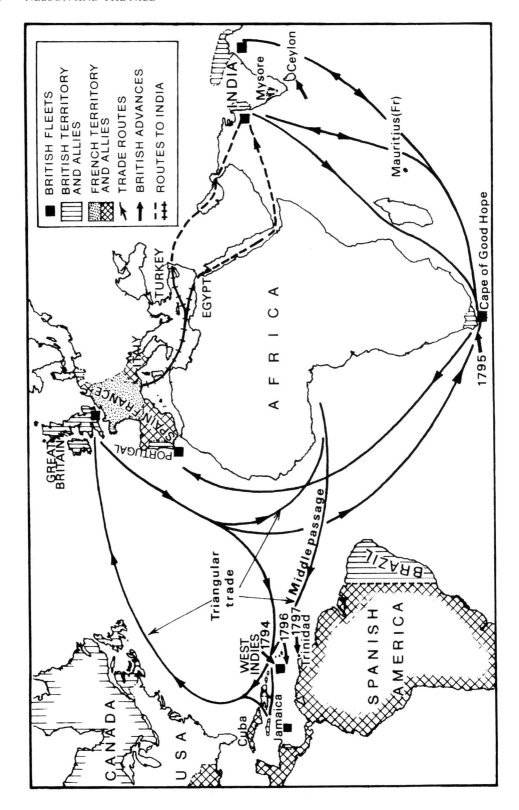

with its support they had recently expanded into the Greek islands, while their army had gained them the ships of the Venetian navy. Uninhibited by a British Mediterranean presence, the French could continue to build up their strength on both land and sea. Furthermore, they could break out of the Mediterranean and threaten British power anywhere in the world, while the British base at Gibraltar could do little to stop them: its largely unimproved harbour was too open for large numbers of ships to be stationed there, and the Rock provided few sources of supply. It was likely to be isolated and perhaps besieged at any time – memories of the Great Siege of 1779-82, which had paralysed the naval base, were still fresh.

Politically, the Mediterranean also offered a way to link up with potential allies against France. The war was already in its 'elephant and whale' stage in which the French were supreme on land and the British at sea, but neither was able to do any crushing damage to the other. Only an ally in continental Europe could mount a real attack on France, with the help of British seapower and cash subsidies. The other powers in the area – Russia, Turkey and especially Austria – had many reasons to hate and fear the French Revolution, but only a British fleet in the area could give them encouragement and real support. Such a fleet, according to professional opinion, could not operate without a secure base. Which was to come first, the chicken or the egg?

It was Britain's Mediterranean Commander-in-Chief Sir John Jervis, later Earl St Vincent, who had demanded the withdrawal from the sea in 1796. The French had gained control of northern Italy and he decided to evacuate Corsica. The Spanish were entering the war against Britain and from their bases at Cartagena and Minorca they could disrupt supply lines to Corsica, or to a new base being developed on Elba. Even seemingly trivial needs could cripple a great sailing fleet and Jervis wrote in August 1796:

> We need a great supply of nails, elm and oak board, lead and leather, but above all we are in the greatest distress for sewing twine, our only resource now being in drawing threads from new canvas or in converting the breechings and tackles in the great cabins of the three decked ships into white oakum and afterwards spinning it into twine.[17]

Jervis decided that his priority was no longer in the Mediterranean and left it to station his ships in the Atlantic, off the Spanish port of Cadiz. From there, within reach of Gibraltar, he could watch the Spanish and at the same time give some support to Portugal, Britain's last and increasingly reluctant ally.

Henry Dundas, the Secretary at War, was also a member of the Board of the East India Company and was constantly concerned about any threats in the east. On first hearing the plans for withdrawal he wrote to Spencer: 'Your letter of yesterday . . . has alarmed me beyond expression, as it seems to announce an intention to abandon the Mediterranean because Spain has declared war against us . . . Spain having declared war against us should in my poor judgement have led to a very

◀ The world in 1798, showing areas dominated by the British and French and the main intercontinental trade routes.

different conclusion.' A British fleet in the Mediterranean was 'so essentially connected with the present and future naval strength and glory of this country that it ought to be preferred to every other service whatever . . .'[18]

Spencer attempted conciliation and reassurance in his reply but offered no concessions.

> The general idea is this: to divide our European fleet into two principal parts (I leave the North Sea for the present out of the question), one of which shall remain as hitherto for the Channel service and consist of about thirty sail of the line; the other, of about the present extent of our Mediterranean fleet, be stationed from Cape Finisterre to Gibraltar, and taking every opportunity of annoying the enemy at Cadiz or elsewhere that offered.[19]

★

In his flagship *Ville de Paris* at anchor off Cadiz, St Vincent kept a strict eye on the Spanish fleet within the port and an equally severe one on the officers and crews of his own ships. He had been born 63 years before and it was almost half a century since he had first gone to sea. He took command of the Mediterranean fleet in 1795, after a successful period in the West Indies. On St Valentine's Day 1797 the Spanish had emerged from Cadiz, only to be intercepted by Jervis's fleet off Cape St Vincent. The British attack was spearheaded by the young Commodore Nelson, technically in breach of his orders. However, four Spanish ships were captured, a Spanish attempt to join forces with the French was foiled and the battle was judged to be a great success. Jervis became an earl, taking his title from the site of the battle.

There were few who could match St Vincent's strength of character and Spencer was often accused of deferring too much to his professional opinions. To his subordinates of all ranks, St Vincent was a fierce disciplinarian. His opinions of his immediate juniors were colourful and clear-cut. Captain Sir Charles Knowles was 'feeble' and 'totally incompetent', Captain Sotherby, in command of the *Victory* during 1797, had 'neither nerves nor experience for so great a charge'. But he was equally vociferous in expressing his high opinion of his favourite officers, such as Nelson and Troubridge.

Rigid discipline among the junior officers was also a part of the St Vincent system, according to his order books. They were to be given no preference over the men in the distribution of lemons, which were recognised as effective against scurvy; they were to take the tongues and heads of slaughtered oxen while the men had the better cuts; they were to turn out when called by beat of drum and the captains were to be on deck during important manoeuvres in the night; they were to show a high standard of formal discipline, to avoid flippancy when coming on to the quarterdeck or receiving orders from a superior and to avoid 'vain conceits and supercilious conduct'.[20] The Admiral also interfered in their private lives. When Captain Devonshire fell in love with the daughter of a naval storekeeper at Gibraltar, St Vincent disapproved of the match and asked Spencer to send him to the East or West Indies. His crude and often cruel sense of humour was well-known. He delighted in making a semi-literate officer read to him in bed, suppressing his giggles with the sheets.

The Earl of St Vincent in about 1800, engraved from a portrait by J Keenan. (National Maritime Museum, London: B84)

To counterbalance his ruthlessness in keeping order, St Vincent demonstrated great concern for the welfare of his crews and often showed small acts of kindness to loyal sailors. When a 'splendid seaman' called Roger Odell lost his savings of £70 while bathing, St Vincent made it up from his own pocket.[21] Occasionally he remitted punishments, being 'anxiously solicitous . . . to mix clemency with the wholesome rigour of the law whenever it can be administered without injury to my King and country'. He was greatly concerned about health and his orders of May 1798 set the pattern for the rest of the navy by moving the ship's sick berth from its old position among the hammocks on the lower deck, to a new and more suitable one under the forecastle.[22]

The blockading force off Cadiz was fully exposed to the storms and swell of the Atlantic, but it had one advantage over the fleet doing similar duty off the great French base at Brest: the water was shallow enough for the ships to spend most of their time at anchor, avoiding the fatigue and wear and tear of constant manoeuvre under sail. Even so, St Vincent's regime was hard enough.

> We have no relaxation in port, where we never go without positive necessity; the officers are all kept to their duty; no sleeping ashore, nor rambling about the country; and when at sea we do not make snug for the night, as in the Western Squadron, but are working incessantly by the lead to keep our position, insomuch both mind and body are constantly upon the stretch.[23]

St Vincent established an inshore squadron to patrol much closer to the enemy, keeping the Spanish on the alert and preventing any surprise attack on the main fleet, or sudden exit by an expeditionary force. This squadron, composed mainly of

74-gun ships which combined high gun-power with good sailing, was the post of honour of the fleet.

Ever since the withdrawal more than a year earlier, St Vincent had been under constant pressure to make some kind of return to the Mediterranean. Alternatives to a permanent fleet were considered – raiding forces of various sizes, from a single ship to a full fleet, operating for up to 3 months at a time – but there was a danger of weakening the main fleet if such forces were too large. In March 1797 Lord Grenville, the Foreign Secretary, had told Spencer that:

> I receive so many and such pressing representations about the possibility of having a fleet (at least of frigates) in the Mediterranean to co-operate with the Austrian army in the next campaign, that I am under the necessity of begging you to take the subject into serious consideration.[24]

Spencer was obliged to agree.

> If a naval war alone was the sole object to which we have now to look, we might undoubtedly rest well satisfied in having got ourselves clear of the Mediterranean as well as we have done . . . But it is most essential in the actual state of Europe, that we should enable our ally, the Emperor of Germany [ie the Holy Roman Emperor, also Emperor of Austria] to act with as much vigour against the French . . . it becomes incumbent on us to co-operate with them in the only manner now remaining open to us, by sending a squadron into that sea.[25]

However, on this occasion Austria made peace before anything could be done to support her.

Again in January 1798, St Vincent wrote, 'In respect of an active squadron taking a range round the Mediterranean, I do not perceive any great obstacle.' However, he went on to point out that any support from Sardinia, Tuscany or Naples would bring the wrath of the French down on their heads and lead to further French invasions of Italy. St Vincent could not see any worthwhile objective which would balance such an increase in French power.[26] He remained firm in his belief that the blockade of Cadiz and defence of Portugal were the most valuable aims for his fleet.

St Vincent had his own sources of information, mostly from Mediterranean consuls and often overlapping with that received in London. Late in March he heard from Consul Udney in Leghorn that the French and the former Venetian fleet from Corfu, consisting in all of thirteen ships of the line, had passed that way for Toulon. He was also told that a body of French troops would soon arrive in Genoa to embark.[27] A few weeks later he received a letter from Captain Day in Genoa, with a much clearer picture of French movements. Day wrote, 'Your lordship may be a party concerned in the event of the expedition now preparing at this and other ports of the Mediterranean by the French.' General Berthier had arrived in Genoa and demanded ships to carry a large body of troops. He had ordered numbers to be painted on their sterns, so that they could be identified in a large convoy. Day expected 10,000 men to pass through the port and 15,000 each

St Vincent's fleet at anchor off Cadiz, with the city in the distance. From Cooper Willyams's
Voyage up the Mediterranean. (National Maritime Museum, London: D8132-B)

to be embarked at Toulon and Marseilles. The most common story was that the
expedition was to go against Naples and Sicily, but Day's sources also suggested
'that it is destined against Portugal and is to be landed at Malaga'. Another
possibility was to send it to Cadiz to drive St Vincent away, allowing the French
and Spanish fleets to unite and perhaps try again to take control of the English
Channel.[28]

Whatever the truth, and however much St Vincent wanted to keep out of
Mediterranean affairs, the French preparations raised issues which could not be
ignored. It was not necessary to abandon his obsession with the defence of
Portugal, for the Toulon Armament might well be designed to transport an army
to Spain, where it would march on Lisbon. It was therefore on his own initiative,
rather than because of prompting from Spencer and the Cabinet, that he resolved
to send a small force off Toulon to make an armed reconnaissance of the area and
to find out what it could about French preparations and intentions. But at the
back of his mind he must have been aware that pressure to send a squadron into
the Mediterranean would come soon and he perhaps preferred to keep the
initiative on what level of force to send.

St Vincent already had some idea who he wanted to command the
reconnaissance. Rear-Admiral Sir Horatio Nelson was his favourite officer since
his part in the Battle of Cape St Vincent a year earlier. He was also the general
public's latest naval hero. In this role he had several advantages over other naval
heroes both past and present. Almost a century ago, commanders like Rooke and
Shovell had gained considerable success but had been heavily involved in politics,
to such an extent that support for one or the other was a matter of faction as much
as anything else. George Anson had captured a Spanish treasure galleon in 1743

and defeated a French fleet 4 years later, but he was far too taciturn to be popular, even before he had become involved in the scandal surrounding the notorious execution of Admiral Byng 'to encourage the others' in 1756. Hawke and Boscawen had done well in the Seven Years War but were largely forgotten. George Rodney had won a great victory at the Saintes in 1782 but in character he had been completely unreliable, arrogant and a compulsive gambler. Howe, the victor of the Glorious First of June in 1794, was old and aloof, Duncan of Camperdown did nothing to court publicity, while St Vincent himself was unpopular with many of his own officers and was not a man to seek public acclaim. Nelson was not without character defects of his own, as time would show, but he was relatively young, of charming disposition and actually available in England at the moment, where he was an ornament to the society of London, Bath and Norfolk. He bore very obvious scars of battle and his courage and leadership abilities were equally apparent. He was not a cautious, elderly commander-in-chief like Howe or St Vincent, but a daring young officer.

CHAPTER 3

The *Vanguard* goes to sea

AT THIS TIME Nelson was a Rear-Admiral of the Blue, 39 years old, a married man of 10 years standing with no children of his own but with a stepson from his wife's previous marriage. He was unfit for military service by any modern standards. Never very healthy at the best of times, he had lost the sight of his right eye in 1794 and his right arm above the elbow in 1797. The son of a clergyman in Norfolk, he came from a middle-class background like many naval officers of the period, but he had two great assets in his early career. One was the support of his uncle Captain Maurice Suckling, the Controller of the Navy. The other was his great ability, obvious even when he was a young man. He was promoted lieutenant in 1777 at the age of 18, though the regulations stated he should have been at least 20. Two years later he became a full captain and having attained that rank any further promotion was by seniority alone. In 1797, having reached the head of the captain's list, he was promoted again to become the youngest rear-admiral in modern times, at 38.

As a young man Nelson saw many kinds of service in different parts of the world. He made a voyage to the West Indies in a merchant ship, then took part in a polar expedition. During the War of American Independence (1775-83) he served mainly in frigates, escorting convoys, capturing enemy merchantmen and taking part in several amphibious operations including a landing in Nicaragua in 1780. After the war he took charge of a small squadron patrolling the West Indies with Prince William, the future King William IV, under his command. His usual zeal was applied to the task of stopping smuggling between the islands and the newly independent United States; but tact would perhaps have been more useful in such a situation and he became unpopular in many quarters. It was during this period that he married the widowed Frances Nisbet on the island of Nevis, Prince William giving the bride away.

Nelson was 'on the beach' at his home in Norfolk for 5½ years until 1793, when the outbreak of war with revolutionary France brought him the command of the 64-gun ship of the line *Agamemmnon*. This was a happy period for him: the ship became a favourite of his because of her good sailing qualities, while many of the friendships formed at that time were to remain important throughout his life. Sent to the Mediterranean, he continued to take part in amphibious operations. When

Nelson late in 1797, wearing the undress (*ie* informal) uniform of a rear-admiral, after his triumph at St Vincent and the loss of his arm; painted by Lemuel Abbott. (National Maritime Museum, London: BHC2887)

Toulon was captured in 1793 with the help of French Royalists, Nelson was sent to Naples to contact the British Ambassador, Sir William Hamilton, and became acquainted with him and his wife Emma. When Toulon had to be abandoned, Corsica was attacked and occupied with a view to setting up a British base. It was there, during the siege of Calvi, that he lost the sight of his eye.

Service in a fleet action was the main aim of every naval officer worth his salt, for it was in a great battle that fame, fortune and promotion might be won. Nelson saw no such action until 1795, when he was under the command of Admiral Hotham. An indecisive battle was fought with the French in the Gulf of Genoa and two of their ships were taken, almost entirely due to Nelson's efforts. He raged at his admiral when he refused to pursue the enemy and wrote to his wife, 'had we taken ten sail and allowed the eleventh to escape when it had been possible to have got at her, I could never call it well done.'[1] This minor affair was soon forgotten but the elements of Nelson's tactical doctrine were already in place – ruthless determination in pursuit of victory, total fearlessness, an almost perfect eye for enemy weaknesses and a belief that hierarchy and subordination were only means to an end.

In February 1797 Nelson had a much more satisfying experience when the fleet, now commanded by Jervis, met a Spanish force of almost double its strength coming out of Cadiz. Jervis's approach to battle, though determined, was too slow and might well have allowed the Spanish a chance to escape. Seeing an opportunity, but against the letter of Jervis's orders, Nelson took his ship the *Captain* out of the line and attacked the Spanish more directly, supported by Cuthbert Collingwood in the *Excellent* and Thomas Troubridge in the *Culloden*. Seeing two Spaniards become entangled with each other in the confusion, he personally led a boarding party onto the 80-gun *San Nicolas* and then over to the 114-gun *San Josef* – 'Nelson's Patent Bridge for Boarding First Rates' as the fleet soon dubbed it. Two other Spanish ships were captured and Nelson was knighted for his key role in the victory.

In July he set out on yet another action against enemy shore positions. Two Spanish treasure ships were sheltering in the harbour of Santa Cruz in Tenerife. Nelson landed with about 1100 men but his force was greatly outnumbered and lost almost a quarter of its strength. The attack was a disaster, Nelson was wounded by grape shot and aboard his flagship, the *Theseus*, the surgeon Robert Tainsh amputated his right arm. On 27 July, two days after the amputation, he wrote to St Vincent, 'I am become a burden to my friends and useless to my country' and asked for a frigate to 'convey the remains of my carcase to England'. Back in London for the first time since the Battle of Cape St Vincent he reported 'I had a very miserable passage home, and this day I am not the least better than when I left good Dr Weir.'[2] He asked for a pension of £1000 a year for the loss of his arm, couched as custom demanded in a petition to the King outlining his services in the navy. He regained his spirits when he found he had become an object of public adulation and found domestic bliss with his wife, who slowly nursed him back to health. By 6 October, though his arm had not improved, he was assuring St Vincent that he would again offer him his services as soon as he was better. On 8 December he placed a paper in St George's Church in London: 'An officer desires to return thanks to Almighty God for his perfect recovery from a severe wound, and also for the many mercies bestowed upon him.'[3] Five days later he was pronounced fit for service.

Already quite famous, Nelson's abilities had attracted attention in the highest quarters in the navy and in society. Most who met him remarked on the contrast between his undistinguished appearance and his charm in conversation. The latest was Lady Spencer, the wife of the First Lord of the Admiralty. At first she thought him 'a most uncouth creature' with the appearance 'of an idiot' but soon 'his wonderful mind broke forth'.[4]

★

By the time he became fit for service, Nelson had been told that the new 80-gun ship *Foudroyant*, completing in Plymouth Dockyard, was intended as his flagship. She was delayed in construction and he was given the 10-year-old *Vanguard* instead. Her story had begun in December 1779, when the Admiralty ordered a new ship of 74 guns to be built in the Royal Dockyard at Deptford near London. Ships of the line were in great demand, for the War of American Independence was at its height and France and Spain had recently allied themselves against Britain. The 74-gun ship was already established as a standard class of warship by this time. She was a two-decker in that she carried her main armament on two complete decks of guns, with lighter ones above on the quarterdeck and forecastle. She was a ship of the line in that she was regarded as strong and powerful enough to take her place in the line of battle, where she might be opposed to an enemy of up to 120 guns. She was also called a Third Rate, but that indicated the number of guns rather than the quality of the ship. First Rates were three-deckers of 100 guns or more, frigates of 32 to 38 guns were Fifth Rates, while the Third Rate included all ships of 60 to 80 guns. By a further order of April 1780, the new ship was to be named the *Vanguard* – already a traditional name in the Royal Navy. The first had been built in 1586 and had served with Drake against the Spanish Armada. The fourth and most recent had been scrapped in 1780.

The 74-gun ship had originated in France around 1740 but several French examples, including the *Invincible* of 1744, had been captured by the British. This helped inspire a re-think of British ship design. Experience showed that the two-decker 70-gun ship was too small for the tasks demanded of her, while the 80-gun ship was unsatisfactory. If the latter carried all her guns on two decks there was an alarming tendency for the hull to 'hog' – to sag at the ends and bend out of shape. If she had three decks she was too high and dangerously unstable. If a ship was to fight in the line of battle she needed at least two decks of guns but if she was too short she would be ill-proportioned and leewardly, while if she was too long she would tend to hog. The '74' was the smallest ship which could carry an effective battery of 32-pounder guns on her lower deck, and that size of gun had proved to be the most efficient in service. The first true British 74s were the *Dublin* class of 1755, designed by Sir Thomas Slade, the newly-appointed Surveyor of the Navy and were 165ft long on the gun deck. The design had expanded over the next 2 years but not very much: the *Bellona*, designed in 1757 and launched in 1760, was 168ft long on the gundeck, and this was to remain the standard size of 74 for the next 20 years.

When the *Vanguard* was ordered, there was a tendency to look back to the old days of ship design. Slade's successor as Surveyor of the Navy, Sir John Williams, was ageing and had never been such a good designer as Slade in any case. Twenty-one out of thirty-four 74s begun during the American War were to Slade's designs, though he had died in 1771. The *Vanguard* was one of fourteen ships built to the plans of the *Arrogant*, first drawn in 1758, and nine of these were begun after war broke out in America in 1775. Six of them were to serve under Nelson at the Nile. Slade was a taciturn man who is best known today for drawing the plans of HMS *Victory* but his work on the 74-gun ship was at least as important.

The Royal Dockyards had to give priority to the repair of existing ships and there were great problems with the supply of timber. As a result, the construction of the *Vanguard* did not begin until October 1782. A 74-gun ship normally took about 2½ years to build, but the *Vanguard* took 4½. The rate of building slowed down after the end of the war in 1783, for the dockyard labour force was cut and the navy was already well supplied with new ships. By 6 March 1787 she was ready to launch.

A visitor to Deptford Yard that morning would have stood under the wooden hull and gazed upwards in admiration at the great wooden structure towering more than 50ft above him. The lines of the hull were not nearly as sharp as a nineteenth-century clipper ship but the curves were beautiful in a slightly Rubensesque way. The lower hull was not yet covered in copper sheeting, as that would be fitted later in dry-dock, so the 4in planks of the bottom were still visible, with the 'caulking' of

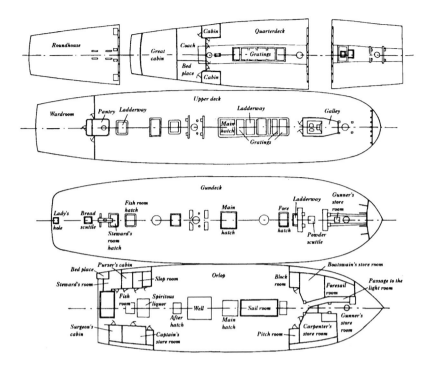

The deck plans of a 74-gun ship. The captain's (or admiral's) quarters on the quarterdeck consisted of the great cabin, coach and roundhouse. The officers' cabins in the wardroom and gunroom are not shown, since they were temporary canvas structures.

oakum and tar which would keep the water from entering the gaps between them. Under the planking, invisible to the spectator, was a massive skeleton of about 120 individual ribs, up to 15½in thick in places. The upper hull was difficult to see from the ground, but it was decorated with friezes and carvings along the side, a figurehead in the bows and even more extensive carvings on the stern. More functionally, it was pierced with gunports on each side and on each deck. A ship of this type would consume the equivalent of about 3000 trees, perhaps 70 acres of forest. The *Vanguard*'s hull had cost the government just over £33,000 and her rigging and stores £6000.[5]

For the launch, the most privileged guests would be on board the ship itself. They might be impressed by the 168ft-long main gun deck, and admire the great timber knees which linked the deck beams to the sides of the hull. But visitors who were familiar with the navy knew that this deck would soon be the dormitory and dining room for more than 500 seaman and marines, as well as carrying twenty-eight 32-pounder guns and their carriages. The ship which looked so massive from below would seem tiny and fragile when tossed about by an ocean swell. Her sides, nearly 30in thick in places through frames and two layers of planking, would feel all too thin when enemy cannonballs battered against them. Her great masts, up to a yard in diameter but not yet in place, could snap like twigs an a storm. But for the moment there was celebration. The *Vanguard* was decked out with enormous flags and watched by a crowd of cheering spectators on shore and in boats as she slid into the waters of the River Thames at high tide.

She had reached middle-age by 1797, for the average ship could be expected to last about 20 years in this period. She had seen some service in the West Indies and in July of that year she arrived at Chatham for a substantial repair. The work on the hull cost £10,752, nearly a third of her original cost, and she was floated out of the dock on 18 December. Her rigging must have been even more extensively repaired, for that was work valued at £8369 – more than the original spars and cordage had cost in 1787.

★

Perhaps remembering the day 26 years earlier when he had joined his first ship there as a boy of twelve, Nelson was in Chatham when the *Vanguard* was floated out of the dry dock but he left the next day to attend a memorial service in St Paul's Cathedral. He arrived in Bath on 1 January 1798, leaving his prospective flag captain, Edward Berry, to enlist the crew and supervise the hard work of fitting out the ship, though Nelson continued to take in interest from afar.

Nelson had given much thought to what officers and crew the *Vanguard* should have, although theoretically that was the responsibility of her captain, not the admiral, and in any case Nelson had not yet been formally appointed to the ship. He went to considerable lengths to find places for old comrades and the sons and nephews of family and service friends. In this he was given unusual indulgence by the Admiralty, who were already beginning to appreciate his merits. Berry, the captain, was just the kind of fighting sailor that was dear to Nelson's heart. Also a Norfolk man but 10 years younger than the Admiral, he already had a reputation for gallantry when he was appointed lieutenant in Nelson's *Agamemmnon* in 1796. He followed him to the *Captain* and as first lieutenant he earned Nelson's 'fullest approbation' by taking charge of the ship when the captain was on shore on operations. At the Battle of Cape St Vincent he was the first to board the Spanish 80-ship *San Nicolas*, the famous 'Patent Bridge'. He was promoted captain in March 1797 and the *Vanguard* was his first command.

It was not unusual for a flag-captain to be very junior in those days, because he was constantly under the eye of the admiral, but despite this Nelson placed great trust in Berry. When Nelson was invested with the order of the Bath in September the King exclaimed 'You have lost your right arm!' and Nelson turned an embarrassing situation to his advantage by bringing Berry forward and saying 'But not my right hand.'[6] Berry was 'a perfect gentleman in all his ideas, and one of the best and most gallant officers in our service'.[7] He was married shortly before his appointment to the *Vanguard*, with Nelson's encouragement. 'If you mean to marry, I would recommend you doing it speedily, or the to be Mrs Berry will have very little of your company.'[8]

Captain Edward Berry, painted by John Singleton
Copley. (National Maritime Museum, London:
BHC2554)

Besides the admiral, his retinue and the captain, a 74-gun ship like the *Vanguard* needed forty-three commissioned and warrant officers. A dozen of the most senior lived and ate together in the wardroom aft on the upper deck. This was about 35ft long and 16-18ft wide, with windows which looked out over the stern. Eight of the officers had cabins down the sides of the ship in the wardroom itself, often shared with an 18-pounder gun. There was little privacy, for the canvas sides were rolled up in the daytime. The other wardroom officers had cabins below, in the gun-room or on the orlop deck, below the water line of the ship, where there was little air and natural light.

A 74-gun ship was allowed five lieutenants. They were the only commissioned sea officers under the captain, and they could hope to become captains themselves one day, if they distinguished themselves in action or attracted the attention of a the Admiralty or a Commander-in-Chief. Each lieutenant, in theory at least, was over 20 years old, had served at least 6 years at sea, half of these as a midshipman, and had passed a fairly stiff oral examination in seamanship and navigation. In practice the rules could be bent by means of false musters, lying about one's age, and by acquaintances among the examining board who asked very easy questions. But a lieutenant was obliged to carry out his duties aboard ship under the eyes of the seamen and incompetence could not long be concealed.

Because of the great expansion in the navy over the last 5 years, some of the lieutenants had been commissioned from the ranks and Midshipman Elliot of the *Goliath* commented, perhaps with an element of snobbery: 'I suspect I was equal to at least two of the lieutenants, who had just been made from common seamen, and were neither used to nor very fit for command. Four out of our five lieutenants were made in that way, the distress for officers was so great – two were efficient, one very good, and the other two very much otherwise.'[9]

A lieutenant would take control of the ship for 4 hours during a watch, calling the captain if any important decision had to be made. He would take charge of a division of seamen for health and welfare purposes, and perhaps command half a deck of guns in action. There was no formal specialisation within the rank but one lieutenant in each ship might be responsible for signals and by custom the junior one trained the seamen in the use of muskets and pistols.

The First Lieutenant was normally the most senior and had different duties from the rest. He was the captain's right hand, to whom most of the detailed administration of the ship was delegated. He was responsible for drawing up the innumerable lists of the crew for various purposes such as manning the guns, raising anchor, setting sails, manoeuvring the ship, manning boats, sleeping, eating and welfare. Unlike the others he stood no watches – he was allowed to sleep throughout the night, unless an event of major importance brought him on deck. His job required hard work and administrative skills but it was the best way to promotion for a man without political influence; if the ship distinguished itself in action the First Lieutenant would be promoted to commander or even captain. Service under Nelson was already seen as a guarantee of an active life, so a post on his flagship was to be valued. He was determined to have Edward Galwey, who was already under orders to sail with the frigate *Arethusa*. Such was Nelson's standing at the Admiralty that Galwey was immediately released and appointed to the *Vanguard*. He had first been commissioned in 1793 and in the frigate *Seahorse* had taken part in Nelson's ill-fated attack on Tenerife, where he had attracted attention by his administrative ability. After Nelson was sent home wounded, Galwey looked after his belongings and accompanied them to England.[10] He wrote to Nelson, 'The numerous company at your apartments this morning prevented me from taking the liberty to say that I think myself highly favoured at the obliging offer you was so kind as to make to me of being one of your officers when employed.'[11] According to Nelson he had 'no friends', that is, no-one with political influence to help him in his career.

Nelson decided to have Nathaniel Vassal as the Second Lieutenant. This was highly unusual, as Vassal was senior to Galwey by 2 years. Nelson commented: 'If they do not choose to stand as I like in my ship, they may stay away; and so I have told Mr Vassal.'[12] He was persuaded to take the appointment but the Admiralty persisted in listing Vassal in the senior position in the ship. Three other lieutenants, Parkinson, Compton and Adye (possibly a relative of a court official of the Leewards Islands whom Nelson and his wife had known in 1786[13]), came on board as the ship was commissioned on 24 December.

As a flagship the *Vanguard* was also allowed an extra lieutenant, the Honourable Thomas Bladen Capel, who did not actually join until the following April. As his title suggests he was from the aristocracy, being the youngest son of the Earl of Essex. Like Nelson he combined ability with good connections, though Capel had less of the former and more of the latter; he had been recommended by Lady Spencer, the wife of the First Lord, who later wrote to Nelson: 'What shall I say to you for your attention to me and your behaviour to Captain Capel!'[14] He was 20 years old when he joined and had been commissioned less than a year. Nelson chose Capel as his flag lieutenant – his staff officer on operational matters and his signal officer.

Wales Clodd, the Master of the *Vanguard*, was technically a warrant officer, holding a warrant from the Navy Board rather than a commission from the Admiralty. It was rare for a master to be promoted to commissioned rank but in other respects he was treated as the equal of the lieutenants and indeed he had more responsibility than most of them. He was in charge of the navigation of the ship in the broadest sense – position fixing and setting courses, but also manoeuvring the ship in difficult situations. Clodd had first reached the rank in 1783 in the *Alarm* frigate and his appointment to the *Vanguard* in December 1797 was his first position on a large ship of the line. The master had three mates, who were in effect senior midshipmen, in line for promotion to lieutenant and living in the midshipmen's berth until they qualified for the wardroom.

The surgeon, Michael Jefferson, had served with Nelson before, as the surgeon's first mate in the *Agamemnon* in 1793. He had treated his right eye when it was injured at Calvi and was especially trusted by the admiral. He was of course a qualified medical practitioner, only recently certificated as a full ship's surgeon by the Surgeon's Company. However, in those days a surgeon had far less status than a physician and was skilled mainly at amputation and bleeding, with some general medical knowledge. He was allowed three mates, all qualified, who lived in the midshipman's berth and ranked with the master's mates in the ship's hierarchy.

Alexander Sheppard, the Purser, was the supply officer of the ship, responsible for issuing the men with food and drink, providing necessities such as coal and candles, and selling clothing and tobacco. He was equal in status to the surgeon but paid was much less; indeed he had to provide a surety of £800 for the goods in his charge. In return he expected to make a profit on some of his transactions and it is not surprising that pursers as a class were generally suspected of cheating and robbing the crews of their ships.

Religion was important to Nelson, and to his old chaplain the Reverend Morris of the *Theseus* he wrote; 'I am determined not to go to sea again without a chaplain.'[15] Morris was unable to get himself sent home from Lisbon in time, so Stephen George Comyn was appointed to the ship and had arrived on board by 25 February, when Berry assured Nelson that he would pay the clergyman 'every attention to him in my power'.[16]

A 74-gun ship was allowed sixteen midshipmen, who were training to become commissioned officers. Most were between 15 and 20 years of age, though some, consistent failures in the examination and without friends and influence, might be much older. Each would serve under a lieutenant to assist in his watch-keeping and welfare duties, perhaps take command of one of the ship's boats, and a group of guns in battle. He would be expected to learn navigation under the eye of the master and seamanship as part of his watch duties. Thomas Meek, a relative of Nelson's neighbours, the famous Cokes of Holkham in Norfolk, had been pressed as a seaman and was serving on the receiving ship *Zealand* at the Nore. Nelson wrote 'there ought to be the greatest difference between made between a forced man and the man who voluntarily offers his life to preserve his country',[17] but agreed to appoint him as one of the midshipmen, because he was recommended by his cousin William Suckling. He soon became a competent and active young officer.[18] Another was John Henry Kremer, from George III's other kingdom of Hanover. He towered above everyone else on the *Vanguard* and he had to be rescued from some financial trouble in Portsmouth, when he was arrested for a debt of £60.[19] Edward Naylor was nominated by Phillip Rumsey, a relative of Nelson's aunt. He was late on board and his patron apologised. 'He used all expedition he could, but did not set off for Sheerness until Saturday morning and on his arrival there had the mortification to see the *Vanguard* get under way without being able to get on board.'[20] He finally joined the ship at Portsmouth. Despite the foibles of the midshipmen, Berry agreed that 'Upon the whole the ship is well officered – The quarterdeck looks respectable.'[21]

Before being rated as a midshipman a young man had to serve 3 years at sea, probably between the ages of 12 and 16. In the past such youths had held the ratings of Able Seaman or Captain's Servant, but the Admiralty had recently established the designation of Volunteer First Class for them. Many officers, including Nelson and his flag lieutenant Thomas Capel, had spent some fictitious sea-time on the books of ships commanded by relatives or family friends. Family connections were still vital in getting a start to a naval career, and on the *Vanguard* the young volunteers included William, the 14-year-old son of Thomas Faddy, the Captain of Marines, who despite ill-health was promoted to midshipman in April 1798. Francis Collier, the son of the late Commodore Sir Francis Collier, was taken on at his mother's request and Nelson wrote to her, 'I shall have much pleasure in having so very fine a lad under my wing; and indeed it is our duty to be useful to the children of our brethren.'[22]

The carpenter, boatswain and gunner were the Standing Officers, so called because they stayed with the ship even when she was out of commission, and their only avenue of promotion was to a higher rate of ship. They were quite well paid and were vital in the ship, but in one important sense they were on the opposite side of the great divide from the wardroom officers, midshipmen and volunteers first class: they were not gentlemen and therefore did not have the right to take their recreation on the quarterdeck. Each was responsible, in his respective department, for maintenance of the ship's hull, her rigging and her armament. The boatswain also had disciplinary duties in mustering and punishing the crew.

Berry was clearly unhappy with the standing officers of the *Vanguard* when he came on board. The boatswain was 'old, infirm and unable to go aloft'. With the Navy Board's agreement he was replaced by Michael Austin of the *Monmouth*. The old carpenter was due for superannuation and Berry asked for William Cork of the *Circe* as a replacement; the Navy Board pointed out that he could not be promoted direct from a Sixth Rate to a Third Rate, so John Cooper of the *Nassau* got the job on the recommendation of Captain O'Brien.[23] At 25 he was young for the job but Berry was assured that he knew his business.[24]

The ship had a number of junior warrant officers, appointed by the Navy Board in London and responsible for maintenance and discipline. Their status aboard ship was little above that of the common seamen but their warrants at least protected them from disrating. They included the master-at-arms, who acted as a kind of police chief; the cooper, caulker, sailmaker and armourer, who were skilled artisans; and the cook, who was generally a disabled seaman from Greenwich Hospital and who had absolutely no training in his culinary role. Again it was Berry rather than Nelson who concerned himself with these appointments. He found that an experienced sailmaker, John Rees, was already part of the crew and had him warranted by the Navy Board. He asked for a caulker's warrant for Edward Cogan, who had been recommended by Captain Peard of the *St George* and was accepted by the Navy Board on condition that he pass the examination first.[25]

The Marines (who did not become Royal until 1802) had their own officers, and an organisation which resembled that of the army rather than the navy, though they were recruited, paid and controlled by the Admiralty. They too had commissioned officers, a Captain and two Lieutenants in the case of a 74-gun ship. Captain Faddy, who appeared to Nelson to be 'a good kind of man' was recommended by his old friend and former captain, William Locker, the Lieutenant-Governor of Greenwich Hospital.[26] The Marine officers were definitely gentlemen and lived in the wardroom.

In addition to the officers, a 74-gun ship of this time was allowed two sergeants, three corporals, a drummer and seventy 'private marines'. The rank and file were trained in drill and musketry in the barracks at the main naval ports and sent on board ship with virtually no nautical knowledge. The *Vanguard*'s first draft from the barracks at Chatham consisted of a lieutenant, a sergeant, two corporals and forty privates and arrived on 1 January 1798.

★

Marines could be sent from barracks but seamen were a problem for all captains, for the navy was going through a severe manning crisis. In the last peacetime year of 1792, Parliament had voted for a navy of 16,000 men. By the second year of war this had gone up to 85,000 and the difference had been made up by the usual means of recruiting, the press gang and cash bounties for volunteer seamen. In 1795 the pressure of war demanded 100,000, and by 1797 the unprecedented figure of 120,000. Desperate measures were needed and new ideas had to be tried.

The navy did little to train its own seamen and recruited the great bulk of its experienced men from the merchant service, so there was inevitably a shortage in wartime. The strategic value of a good seamen was immense. When Captain Davidge Gould of the *Audacious* decreed that in his ship 'the men are never to go into their hammocks with their wet clothes on, nor to sleep anywhere without their clothes on, as there can be nothing more prejudicial to their health', he justified it on the grounds that 'a seaman in the Kings's service is too much consequence to his country to be allowed to risk his life by such means as saving himself a little trouble.'[27] The seamen resented being treated as a commodity in this way but took perverse pleasure in their value to the state. John Nicol of the *Goliath* left the navy after this war and spent the next one evading the press gang. When his friends mocked him for this he replied,

'Necessity had no law.' Could the government make perfect seamen as easily as they could soldiers, there would be no such thing as the pressing of seamen, and I was happy to be of more value than all of them put together, for they would not impress any of them, they were of so little value compared with me.[28]

In 1795 the two Quota Acts were passed by Parliament. These decreed that each local authority, whether inland county or seaport town, was to find a specified number of men for the navy, in proportion to its resources. Both seamen and landsmen were recruited, being offered bounties of up to £70, compared with an able seaman's annual pay of £14/12/6 (£14.63), and a landsman's of £10/11/6 (£10.57). A seaman counted as two landsmen towards the total and it seems that twice as many landsmen were recruited as seaman, so several thousand unskilled men entered the navy. Some at least were of low moral character, or were vagabonds or debtors taken from prison. One man with a dubious past was discovered by Lady Nelson.

> I forgot to mention a circumstance to you relative to a manservant which did live with Mr Gordon and is now on board the *Vanguard*. The man lived seven years with the gentleman that Mr Gordon had him from, brought a good character, lived with Mr G I think nearly two years, when there were several things missing such as tumblers, a few tablecloths and things of that sort. Suspicion falling on the man he confessed he had been the thief, but it was clearly the first offence therefore Mr G promised if he would enter on board a man of war he would not prosecute him.[29]

The problem did not end there. Mutiny was already a great problem in the Navy, and may or may not have been linked to movements ashore – the Corresponding Societies which favoured some of the principles of the French Revolution and the United Irishmen who fought for freedom for their homeland. Seamen had not had a pay increase for nearly 150 years, and the price of food was rising. Those most affected were 'men about the middle age, married and had children. Their families were daily claiming relief from them; provisions for the two preceding years, 1795 and 1796, had been enormously high, and they found themselves starving.' Moreover the pride of the seaman was offended by the bounties offered to landsmen. 'The true-bred seaman is a high-minded animal. In his lounge or forecastle walk he views the landsmen in the waist as an inferior animal, and the latter soon learns to know the depression of his species . . . "What," said they, "shall these tailors and cobblers be receiving their fifty pounds while we are doomed to take five?"'[30]

Why was the seaman so valuable? Certainly his level of skill was high but more important was his attitude. Thomas Trotter drew attention to 'the unparalleled hardships to which seamen are exposed from the nature of their employment. Toil and danger are their constant attendants. They suffer privations to which all other men are strangers.' They had 'unfailing fortitude' and matchless patience'. They could only be trained by years of service at sea.

> Nautical astronomy and all its auxiliary branches may be learned on shore. Even the manual duties of seamanship may be acquired in a short time, but there may still be wanting that soul of enterprise, that hardihood of frame that can mock danger and surmount difficulties in every

hideous form; that can submit to sickness, privation and famine without repining at their fate and can view even death itself in all its most horrid aspects, of a sinking ship, a lee shore or wounds in battle. Such are the requisites necessary to form the true-bred British seaman.

They could not be learned easily.

No person will have the hardihood to contend that a seaman's duty can be learned in less than seven years, or after 21 years of age. He must be accustomed to it from boyhood, for no adult can ever be brought to endure privation, dangers and hardships which are inseparable from a sea life.[31]

★

Several ships were being decommissioned at Chatham and Nelson was promised that the *Vanguard* would be 'choicely manned', which he accepted with a note of scepticism. 'This may not happen but it stands so today.'[32] The first large draft arrived on New Year's Day 1798 – 60 men each from the 90-gun *St George* and Nelson's future flagship the *Victory*, which was then being converted to a hospital aship for French and Dutch prisoners. There was no need for Berry to send out his own press gangs, and indeed the area round the dockyards at Chatham and Sheerness had been well scoured already during 5 years of war. Instead he relied on the goodwill of the port admiral, Skeffington Lutwidge, Nelson's old captain from his days of Arctic exploration. He was based in the receiving ship *Zealand* anchored at the Nore, at the junction of the Thames and Medway, where men pressed from passing merchant ships were kept until allocated to sea-going vessels. Berry was

Chatham Dockyard from across the River Medway. Towards the left is a sheer hulk, used for getting masts in and out. To the right, a three decker is being rigged. Ships are under construction on slipways and in dry-dock for repair. An engraving by Robert Dodd. (National Maritime Museum, London: 2413)

often frustrated in his dealings with Lutwidge and by the end of February he was still 'applying for more men, having frequently represented the want of them'.[33] The men were not all as choice as might have been hoped, and 212 landsmen had been entered by the time the ship sailed from the Nore.[34] There was at least one volunteer for the ship – Thomas Johnson of the *St George* had served with Nelson before and was said to be a good boatswain's mate. By early February Berry conceded that 'the ship's company on the whole are very tolerable'.[35]

On coming on board, each new man went before the First Lieutenant who rated him according to his experience and abilities. Boys were Third Class if under fifteen and Second Class if over that age. Landsmen had little or no seafaring experience, while Ordinary Seamen had spent at least 2 years at sea and had learned a great variety of knots and ropework, how to climb the mast to take in sail in the roughest of weather, to help at the guns in action, to row or sail a boat and look after themselves and their comrades aboard ship. An Able Seaman had to be reliable enough to steer the ship, cast the lead to find the depth of water, help the sailmaker or fit and reef sails. Other men, probably those with previous Royal Navy service, might become petty officers – the boatswain's mates who carried out much of the disciplinary work, or the more cerebral quartermasters, who supervised the steering of the ship and the stowage of the hold. Equal in status were men with certain technical skills, who might be appointed to the carpenter's crew or become quarter gunners – assistants in the gunner's department, who also served as an elite division of seamen.

The men were also given duties in various 'parts of ship' and this also depended on skill and experience. Topmen were allocated to each mast and worked aloft. They were usually young, fit and experienced, the most valuable seamen on board, though a few landsmen or boys might be attached for training. The forecastle men worked mainly on deck and were usually older, skilled at such work as raising anchors. The afterguard worked on the quarterdeck under the eyes of the officers and tended to be smart men, but less skilled. The waisters worked in the central part of the ship, and were the least skilled of all. Most of the technicians and servants were 'idlers'; they stood no watches but worked only in daylight hours, unless called in an emergency. Captain Davidge Gould, who was to command the *Audacious* under Nelson during the Nile Campaign, divided his men as follows:

Forecastle men	66
Foretopmen	40
Maintopmen	40
Mizzen topmen	16
Waisters	128
Afterguard	54
Marines	65
Gunner's crew	24
Carpenter's crew	10
Quartermasters	12
Boatswain's mates	6
Idlers	40
Boys	18

This made a total of 541. There were also 6 fictitious seamen called 'widow's men', whose wages were put into a fund for seamen's widows and orphans, and 43 officers of one kind or another, making a total of 590 on board a fully manned 74-gun ship.[36]

★

When floated out of the dry-dock the *Vanguard* was an empty shell and over the next few weeks Berry and his officers and men had to turn her into a fighting ship, with help from the Dockyard. On 30 December she was hauled alongside a kind of floating crane known as a sheer hulk and her lower masts were hoisted into place. More drafts of seamen arrived over the days and were set to the back-breaking work of fitting out the ship. Nearly 130 tons of iron ballast had to be hoisted out of a lighter into the hold, followed by 280 tons of shingle.[37] About 25 miles of rope, ranging from 18in to 1½in in circumference, had to be prepared and put in place. Of all the aspects of the seamen's work which were incomprehensible to the landsman, his work with rope was perhaps the most arcane. The *Vanguard*'s rigging was virtually all new according to the Dockyard accounts, so the able seamen of the ship had to spend the month of January making mouses and collars for the stays, puddings for the masts, strops for blocks, worming, parcelling and serving the shrouds and turning in the deadeyes with throat seizings. The topmasts were swayed up into place on 17 January and the yards, which would hold the upper edges of the sails, were raised two days later. As the masts and yards were hoisted into place by the less skilled men, the seamen began to gammon the bowsprit, set up the backstays and bend the sails to the yards.

Work was interrupted on the 29th when the captain, officers, seamen and marines were assembled and asked to volunteer to give 10 days' pay each to 'the exigencies of the war'. They agreed unanimously. Five days later the ship was fully rigged though not well manned. A team of riggers came on board from the Dockyard and the ropes which held her to the buoys off Chatham were cast off. The sails were set and Mr Atchison of the Dockyard took charge as pilot. The ship moved down river to Blackstakes near Sheerness, where she anchored in 10 fathoms of water.

Berry was still living on shore, though Chatham offered few attractions. Visitors to the area tended to notice the Dockyard itself or the medieval castle and cathedral in nearby Rochester, but were silent about Chatham. One exception was the local historian Edward Hasted who described it as 'a long, narrow, disagreeable, ill-built town'.[38] Berry found lodgings in the pleasant, modern suburb of Brompton, on the hill above the Dockyard. His new wife and his sister were there and often came on board. One night 'it blew so fresh we were necessitated to remain there all night. They behaved very well and liked the frolic'. He was bored with Dockyard life but satisfied with the performance of his crew. 'I shall be very glad to get into a better climate than this. It's very well on shore but not so at sea. We never look clean and the smallest accident puts a man on the [sick] lists. By the bye it is rather extraordinary not to have had one serious accident since the *Vanguard* has been commissioned.'[39]

A model of the 74-gun ship *Hercules*. Though slightly smaller and older than Nelson's ships at the Nile, she was very similar in appearance. The rigging of the model, though largely a modern restoration, is accurate for a ship of the late eighteenth century. (National Maritime Museum, London: C1669)

She was still unarmed, because the weight of the guns would have made her too deep to navigate the waters of the upper Medway estuary. On 11 February three small ships arrived alongside carrying the ship's guns and carriages from the Ordnance Depot at Upnor Castle opposite the Dockyard. The lower deck carriages were hoisted in first, followed by the 32-pounder guns of the lower deck. Each one, weighing 2½ tons, was slung from a tackle attached to the end of one of the yards and hoisted up until level with its gun port. It was hauled in with another tackle inside the ship, and then gently lowered onto the carriage. As the less skilled men moved on to the slightly lighter guns of the upper deck, the able seamen and gunner's crew began to rig the tackle of the 32-pounders. By 4 March the ship was fitted with her full complement of twenty-eight 32-pounders on the lower deck and the same number of 18-pounders on the upper deck. On her quarterdeck she had two conventional 24-pounder guns, with ten lighter, short range 24-pounder carronades. She had four 24-pounder carronades on her forecastle and two long guns, giving her a total armament of eighty-four guns, though she was still rated as a 74.

The anchor was raised, the sails were set and the ship proceeded out of the Medway to the great naval anchorage at the Nore, off Sheerness. More men were drafted in from the *Zealand*, and the ship's orders were changed. Instead of being equipped for the English Channel she was now to be fitted for foreign service, which meant she had to carry a much greater quantity of food and stores. As a town, nearby Sheerness was less attractive then Chatham. Swept by cold north-easterly winds, isolated from the rest of the country and surrounded by malarial marshes, it was already known as 'Sheer-nasty' by many naval officers. As a man of action, Berry chafed at the hard work and bureaucracy of fitting out. By early March he was 'provoked to madness owing to being detained here a day longer than I expected'.[40] The problem was that the crew had to be paid for their previous services before setting off on a foreign voyage. The seaman himself lived in an almost cashless society aboard ship, with all necessities supplied by the purser and paid for by credit against his wages. However, his wife and family had to be provided for and 300 women were actually on board the *Vanguard* at the Nore, living with their men until the ship sailed. The seaman also needed a little money for himself, for luxuries bought from shore boats and his occasional excursions on land. Ships were only paid in home waters, so the cash might have to last for a long time. Sending the ship to sea without paying the men could lead to mutiny, so Berry had to wait until Saturday 10 March when the Clerk of the Cheque of the Dockyard came alongside in the Dockyard yacht and issued a total of £10,000.[41]

When she weighed anchor from the Nore the next day she was fully rigged, manned, armed and stored, ready to sail the seas and do battle with the King's enemies, as a result of many thousands of man hours of both skilled and back-breaking labour. On top of 310 tons of iron and shingle ballast in the depths of her hold she carried 250 butts of water weighing nearly 200 tons, 90 casks of beer, 7 tons of wine and a similar amount of spirits. She carried 3234 pieces of beef of 8lbs each, contained in 62 butts weighing a total of 11½ tons. She had 12½ tons of pork, plus cheese, oatmeal, pease, flour, suet, raisins and molasses in wooden casks of various sizes. She carried 14 hundredweight of candles, nearly 40 tons of wood and coal for the ship's galley and three bales of slops to clothe the crew. The whole of her equipment and stores weighed 971 tons, plus an estimated 45 tons for the crew with their chests and bedding.[42]

Berry stopped at the anchorage in the Downs, off the east coast of Kent. He wrote to Nelson: 'It may be satisfactory to know we have got this far, in which we have been perfectly fortunate. Half an hour longer would have detained us longer than I know. The wind has been very scant.'[43] After dropping off 150 men intended for other ships he sailed for Portsmouth and anchored at Spithead on 15 March 1798.

CHAPTER 4

'The accidents which have happened to the *Vanguard*'

NELSON ARRIVED IN PORTSMOUTH at 5.30pm on 29 March and next day he was rowed out to the *Vanguard*, anchored outside the main harbour in the choppy but protected waters of Spithead. As he climbed up the side a blue flag was hoisted at the mizzen mast and fifteen guns fired in salute, showing that a rear-admiral was on board. He brought with him his secretary John Campbell and his servant Tom Allen, from his home village of Burnham Thorpe, who was then 29 years old and had already served with him in various ships since the *Agamemnon* in 1793.

Nelson's tastes were simple so he did not bring his own cook. Anthony Leary, a 28-year-old Irishman from County Cork, was selected for the job from among the crew of the ship. His steward was Thomas Spencer, a 27-year-old seaman from Nottingham, likewise chosen from the crew.[1] Nelson joined with the wardroom officers in buying a stock of food to supplement the official rations and paid his first monthly subscription of £1/19/0 (£1.95p) on 30 April. The officers purchased sugar, tripe, rice, cheeses and oysters, and topped this up with tea and raisins in Gibraltar. They bought live sheep, pigs, geese, ducks and fowls and killed and ate them regularly throughout the voyage. They also purchased 420 bottles of wine.[2]

Nelson worried about his clothing and wrote petulantly to his wife: 'I have looked over my linen, and find it very different to your list as follows; thirteen silk pocket handkerchiefs: only six new, five old. Thirteen cambric ditto: I have sixteen. Twelve cravats: I have only eleven. Six Genoa velvet stocks: I have only three. You have put down thirty huckaback towels: I have only from 1 to 10.'[3]

The stern cabin of the *Vanguard*, 40ft long and about 30ft broad at its widest point, would be his home, office and headquarters for the next few months, perhaps years. It was divided into three separate cabins, one for sleeping, one as a lobby and perhaps an office and the largest, well-illuminated by the stern windows, where he would dine, receive guests and perhaps relax. He was fond of the open gallery on the stern of the ship, where he could walk in the fresh air unobserved by officers and crew. When the *Vanguard* was refitted at Chatham he had insisted on its being extended by a foot, by moving the bulkhead forward and reducing the size of the cabin. The Navy Board in London protested that this would weaken the structure but Nelson's standing at the Admiralty was such that he was given his way. This was the exact opposite of normal Admiralty policy, which was to abolish stern galleries altogether.

His furniture had been sent to Chatham to be put on board the ship and Berry advised him on making his cabin more comfortable. A floor covering of kersey cloth, probably painted in a black and white chequer pattern, and some curtains for the windows were provided by Chatham Dockyard, but it seems they were not suitable. Berry suggested that: 'If a floor cloth would not be too expensive and you thought it worthwhile, I think that one in the dining room would be comfortable where the table stands – 16ft in length and 13ft 5, 6 or 7ins broad. Also a carpet for the side of your cot if you use one. A looking glass I believe I mentioned, about two ft long in a gold frame.'[4] He strongly recommended curtains for the quarter galleries which, he joked, were *very necessary* – one of these galleries would have served as the admiral's toilet, or 'necessary house' and privacy was important. He left it to Nelson to judge whether curtains were also needed for the stern windows. In addition to this Nelson would have needed bedding, a table or two, several chairs and a chest with drawers. He wrote to his wife before sailing: 'My place is tolerably comfortable, but I do not shine in servants.'[5]

★

By Admiralty orders dated 27 March, Nelson was to escort a convoy to Lisbon and then join the Mediterranean fleet under St Vincent off Cadiz. On 1 April the *Vanguard* sailed with its convoy from Spithead, but the wind turned westerly and forced a return to St Helen's anchorage, off the Isle of Wight. Nelson regretted that he had 'lost the finest east wind that has blown this year'[6] and he had to wait another week before getting away. His status did not relieve him of the duty of escorting a convoy: all warships on the way to their stations were expected to protect merchant ships when required and in the days before torpedoes, aircraft and submarines a two-decker 74 could do this as well as any other warship. On 8 April the *Vanguard* left with eleven merchantmen loaded with naval stores for the base at Lisbon. On the 26th the convoy anchored there and Nelson was relieved of one responsibility. On the last day of April he reached St Vincent's fleet off Cadiz and saw eighteen ships of the line, two frigates and a brig anchored 10 or 12 miles east of the Spanish port. He dropped anchor in 21 fathoms of water and fired the appropriate salutes. The *Vanguard* was now part of St Vincent's fleet.

Nelson was immediately rowed on board the flagship *Ville de Paris* and had a warm welcome from the commander-in-chief. St Vincent wrote to Spencer that 'the arrival of Admiral Nelson has given me new life. You could not have gratified me more in sending him.'[7] Nelson found St Vincent 'everything I wished him; and his friends in England have done me justice for my zeal and affection to him.'[8] The commander-in-chief had already decided that Nelson would be sent into the Mediterranean with a small but powerful reconnaissance force, to cruise off Toulon and find out what the French were up to. He was to take the *Vanguard* and two other

74-gun ships, the *Orion* and *Alexander*, as well as three frigates for scouting purposes – 'as large a detachment as the continuance of the blockade [of Cadiz] would admit.'[9] It is not clear what St Vincent wanted from this force – too weak to be a battlefleet, but too strong for a normal reconnaissance. Did he hope that Nelson's force would deter the French from sailing, making his own position off Cadiz secure? Did he hope that Nelson, with his well-known predilection for action, would launch an attack on the French convoy, just enough to perhaps disrupt it and prevent it reaching its destination intact? Did he hope it would be enough to convince Spencer and the cabinet that he was doing something and alleviate pressure to do much more?

Nelson's orders were

> to proceed . . . up the Mediterranean and endeavour to ascertain by every means in your power, either upon the coast of Provence or Genoa, the object of the equipment . . . and in case of your receiving any information to communicate with me, you are to despatch the *Bonne Citoyenne* or *Terpsichore* with it; and continue on this service with the rest of the squadron as long as you may think necessary and your stock of water will enable you to do . . .[10]

St Vincent was not well supplied with frigates, the most efficient ships for reconnaissance. The navy as a whole had nearly 110 fully-fledged frigates, the 'Fifth Rates', in service in May 1798, but they were spread around the East Indies, the Cape of Good Hope, North America and the West Indies. Some were on convoy escort, some in port, eight off Ireland and thirty-nine more with the main fleets.[11] Technically there were ten under St Vincent's command at the beginning of May, plus seven smaller vessels which might serve if necessary, but only five were actually to hand at that moment; he made a considerable sacrifice by sending three of these with Nelson.[12]

The largest was the *Emerald* of 36 guns commanded by Thomas Waller, who had been present at the Santa Cruz disaster. She was the only one that was immediately available and soon joined Nelson. The *Terpsichore* of 32 guns was slightly smaller and was captained by William Gage. As her name suggests, the *Bonne Citoyenne* was one of many ships in the Royal Navy which had once flown the French flag. She had been built in 1794 and captured by the frigate *Phaeton* in 1796. She carried only 20 guns and was classed as a sloop, too small to be recognised by the rating system. However, she was a well-regarded ship, especially for her sailing qualities, and her design was copied several times by the British. She could go closer inshore than any of the other ships, and would perhaps be useful in chasing small enemy vessels.

The *Terpsichore* and *Bonne Citoyenne* were based at Gibraltar, where Nelson arrived on 4 May with the *Vanguard* and *Emerald*. He anchored in the shadow of the Rock, to find the other two frigates, along with the 74-gun ships *Orion* and *Alexander*, taking on stores and carrying out minor repairs to their masts and rigging. Rear-Admiral Sir John Orde, another of St Vincent's subordinates, was having a party on board his flagship the *Princess Royal*. An officer of the frigate *Alcmene* wrote 'I never saw anything neater in my life. The quarterdeck was neatly dressed with

Alexander John Ball, a miniature by an unknown artist.
(National Maritime Museum, London: 9168)

flags, and the bitts were covered with flowers.'[13] Nelson was already dedicated to his mission and commented 'I have no turn for such things.'[14] The *Vanguard* replenished her water and took on what stores she could find, though Gibraltar was not well supplied with foodstuffs.

Captain Sir James Saumarez of the *Orion* was already well known to Nelson, having served with him in Sir Peter Parker's squadron in the 1770s, and under him off Cadiz in 1797. Recently he had been doing Nelson's old job as commander of the Inshore Squadron. Nelson's acquaintance with Captain Alexander Ball of the *Alexander* was much slighter and less auspicious. In peacetime in 1783 Nelson had met Ball ashore at St Omer in France, wearing a very grand uniform with gold epaulettes, which were not then part of a naval officer's dress. Nelson wrote: 'Two noble captains are here – Ball and Shephard . . . they wear fine epaulettes, for which I think them great coxcombs; they have not visited me and I shall not, be assured, court their acquaintance.'[15] Now, 15 years later, Ball came on board the *Vanguard* to report to his new superior and Nelson said to him, 'What, are you come to have your bones broken?' If there was any lightness in Nelson's tone it was not appreciated by Ball, who answered pompously that 'he certainly had no wish to have his bones broken, unless his duty to his King and country required such a sacrifice, and then they should not be spared.'[16]

As darkness fell at 6pm on 8 May, Nelson hoisted the signal to weigh anchor, for he was anxious to conceal his movements from the watching Spanish. Winds were light and the squadron had to warp out of the harbour: an anchor was put under the ship's launch, rowed out ahead and dropped; it was then hauled in by men at the ship's capstan, pulling the ship slowly forward, at the same time as another anchor was laid out by another boat, for the laborious process to be repeated. It was well into the morning before the six ships reached the end of the Rock and got ready to set sail. The element of surprise was lost, for as the sun rose at 6am the squadron came under attack for the first time. The Spanish fort at Cape Carnero fired a few random shots and hit the *Alexander* on the port side under the main chains, doing no real damage.[17]

Nelson was now free of the more irksome duties of fitting out and convoy escort. He was in command of a fine squadron, with more responsibility and independence than most admirals with twice his seniority. His was the only substantial British force in the Mediterranean and the largest one in that sea for 19 months. He set course for Toulon, passing outside the Spanish islands of Majorca and Minorca, and made good progress in south-easterly winds, averaging about 85 miles a day. On the 17th, about 70 miles from Toulon, a strange sail was sighted on the horizon and the *Terpsichore* went in pursuit. She captured *La Pierre*, a small French warship of 6 guns carrying a crew of 65. The prisoners were interrogated one by one and Nelson gained his first real intelligence about enemy movements.

> We have separately examined the crew of this corvette and from the whole I believe the following may be depended on as near the truth – that Bonaparte arrived at Toulon last Friday and has examined the troops which are daily embarking in the numerous transports; that troops frequently arrive from Marseilles; it is not generally believed that Bonaparte is to embark, but no-one knows to what place the armament is destined. Fifteen sail of the line are apparently ready for sea, but nineteen are in the harbour . . . Reports say they are to sail in a few days, and others that they will not sail for a fortnight . . . The Admiral Brueys has his flag in *L'Orient*, 120 guns; *Le Formidable* and *Spartanade* [*Spartiate*] of 80 guns are also flagships . . .[18]

All this was accurate enough, except for the suggestion that Bonaparte was not to go with the expedition, but it did not answer the two most vital questions: when would the fleet sail and where was it going? Nelson wrote a report to St Vincent and sent it in the prize, now under the command of Charles Harford, a midshipman of the *Vanguard*, who was 'an intelligent young man . . . who has just served his time' and was therefore, he hinted, eligible for promotion to lieutenant.[19]

Nelson took up a position 75 miles south of Toulon, 'exactly in the situation for intercepting the enemy's ships bound into Marseilles, Toulon etc'.[20] In the morning of Saturday 19 May there was some bad weather, with gales from the northwest. All the ships began to furl some of their sails and then take down their upper yards and masts. By the next day the threat had passed, and the ships settled into normal routine. On the 20th the *Bonne Citoyenne* captured another prize, a French merchant brig carrying cotton from Syracuse to Marseilles, and took her in tow.[21]

Spirits were high among the officers on the evening of Sunday the 20th. Berry was 'elated beyond description at being so fortunate as to be the detached squadron in the Mediterranean . . . fine weather, and not discovered by the enemy though close to their ports, we thought ourselves in the height of glory; what more could we wish for?'[22] To Saumarez the capture of *La Pierre* 'appeared the forerunner of

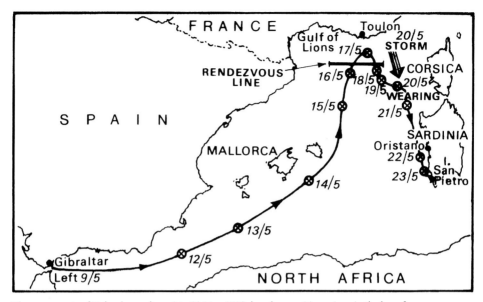

The movements of Nelson's squadron, 9 to 23 May 1798, based on positions given in the log of the *Alexander*.

our future good fortune, and we began to make exulting reflections on the advantages of our situation.'[23] Nelson had 'his squadron about him, who looked up to their chief to lead them to glory, and in whom this chief placed the firmest reliance, that the proudest ships in equal numbers belonging to France would have bowed their flags, and with a very rich prize lying by him.'[24]

According to one admiral who had many years of experience in the Mediterranean, the area south of Toulon was a 'notorious gulf, so proverbial for the treachery of sudden anemological changes'. The winds originated over the land but 'when a breeze springs up in the afternoon, and freshens as the sun goes down, it may be expected to blow strong at midnight'.[25] On board the *Vanguard* there was no premonition of trouble. The crew spent the afternoon of the 20th hauling up upper masts and yards, the topgallants and royals, and then setting up the rigging ready for some fair-weather sailing. Presumably this was done on Berry's initiative. Nelson according to his account was 'walking in his cabin', and had delegated the running of the ship to his flag captain, as was his privilege. He gave no orders for the other ships to reset their upper spars, which suggests that he was not involved in the decision on board the *Vanguard*. Saumarez in the *Orion* was slightly more cautious and set up only the topgallants, not the royals, while Ball in the *Alexander* seems to have kept them all down.

The wind began to increase to 'fresh breezes' at 8pm and the lower sails, the courses, were taken in. By 10pm there were 'heavy squalls of wind' and the ships began to reef the topsails on all three masts. Teams of fit young topmen were sent aloft in the wind and rain to reduce the area of sail. The men on deck hauled on tackles which pulled the highest part of the sail up to the yard, while the topmen climbed out on the yard, heedless of the violent rolling of the ship, and tied together

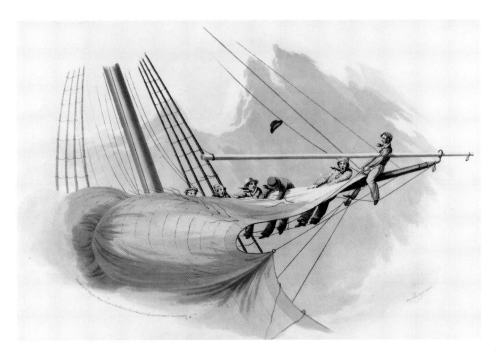

Seamen on a yard, reefing topsails in a storm. The stunsail yard has been lashed up to the shrouds to get it out of the way of the seamen. A print by Edward Duncan after W J Huggins. (National Maritime Museum, London: B54)

the reef points in the sails, preventing the unused portion from flapping about in the gale. By midnight even this small area of canvas had to be taken in and the *Vanguard* set only a special heavy-weather sail, a main storm staysail. The *Orion* kept her reefed topsails set, but at 1am on the 21st they were blown out by the wind. The *Alexander* had the same problem and all three of her topsails blew out during the night.

Sails had a kind of fail-safe system, in that they would simply tear in the worst of weather. The higher masts, however, if left up in gales, would break and cause great damage. Those of the *Vanguard* were under heavy pressure because the royal yards were still set, and perhaps because the rigging, being new, still had a tendency to stretch and did not support the masts as well as it might. Thus at 1.30am on the 21st the main topmast of the *Vanguard* groaned under the stress, gave a resounding crack and toppled over the side. The topsail yard was crowded with men balanced precariously on the footropes which were slung underneath it and with dread in his heart, above the noise of the wind and rain, Berry enquired how many men had been lost. By a miracle it was only two, one being swept away while the other fell to his death on the deck. The rest managed to cling to the wreckage and scramble back onto the ship.

By this time the ships were in conditions which Admiral Beaufort in his famous scale would have described as 'the air completely filled with foam and spray. Sea completely white with driving spray; visibility very seriously affected'. There was a great rolling motion, caused by the waves meeting the ship at right angles to its course. Even in a moderate form, this is perhaps the most uncomfortable movement of a ship, and in such a gale it was almost unbearable even for experienced seamen. The conditions in the Gulf of Lyons tended to accentuate it: 'One of the peculiarities of the Gulf is the sudden rising of its waves, and their attaining a size not at all proportionate to the strength of the winds.'[26] Keeping still on deck, braced against the motions of the ship, could be very tiring in itself. To move about the decks was even more so, and to climb the rigging, or do any kind of work, was positively exhausting. Anything not securely lashed or stowed, from the admiral's furniture to the ship's anchors and cannons, was likely to move violently and do damage to itself or whatever it met. The motion was worse because the *Vanguard* no longer had any sails to steady her, and half an hour after the loss of the main topmast the fore topmast also went over the side, without loss of life. Two hours later the rolling increased yet more and an even greater disaster occurred. The foremast broke just above the deck, damaging the bowsprit as it fell. The remains of the mast were still attached to the ship by the rigging and were beating against the bows. One of the anchors, 3½ tons of iron with sharp points, was mixed up with it too and was crashing against the hull, threatening to make a hole. At the same time the rigging of the main topmast was still attached, endangering the mainmast.

At daylight the *Alexander* and *Orion* sighted the *Vanguard* through the rain and spray. Soon their officers perceived 'the admiral to have lost his foremast, main and mizzen topmast'.[27] The two ships had done rather better during the night, having lost sails but no masts. They were also affected by the rolling and on the *Orion* Samaurez ordered extra breech ropes to be fitted to the guns; otherwise one of them might break free and become the proverbial 'loose cannon', 3 tons of wood and metal crashing about the deck, destroying everything it touched and perhaps smashing a hole in the side.

The *Vanguard* was sailing as close as she could to the wind on the port tack – that is, with the wind coming over her left or port side. With the wind coming from the north-west she might expect to sail two points, or 22½ degrees into it with all her sails set. With her damaged rig it is doubtful if she could sail into the wind at all and her bow was probably pointing at right angles to it, steering a course to the north-east. But this was not the whole story, for a ship in winds of such force could expect to make much leeway; to be pushed sideways by the wind to a large extent – at least six points or 67½ degrees in conditions like these.[28] The *Vanguard*, then, was heading east-south-east, straight towards the rocky, hostile coast of Corsica, which was 'not many leagues distant'.[29]

The only hope was to turn the ship around so that the wind came on her other side. Given the degree of danger, the only way to do this was to 'wear' the ship, by turning her stern through the wind. Normally the motive force would be provided by the foresails, with the after sails taken in or at least rendered ineffective. Otherwise the ship would settle with the wind directly behind her and be totally at the mercy of natural forces. But the *Vanguard* was without a foremast, and the remains of her main and mizzen were tending to make the operation more difficult because they operated aft of the centre of rotation. As a desperate expedient the remnants of

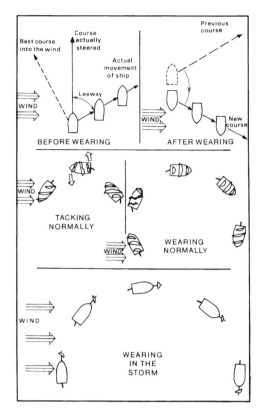

Top. The courses of the *Vanguard*, before and after wearing. Because of the great amount of leeway in such a wind, the effect was to alter course by only about 45 degrees.

Middle. Tacking and wearing in normal circumstances. Tacking is done by turning the head of the ship towards the wind, so ground is gained rather than lost and much less space is needed. However, it can only be done in light and moderate winds, and the foremast, which was missing in the *Vanguard*, is important because of its effect on turning the ship through the wind. Wearing is done by turning the head away from the wind

Bottom. Wearing using the 'small rag of a spritsail' which was all that was left on the *Vanguard*.

a spritsail were unfurled from the yard on which they hung under the bowsprit. Such sails were a remnant of an earlier period, seldom used by this time because they were difficult to control. Even the bowsprit was unreliable, for it was damaged in three places by the fall of the foremast and was itself ready to break.

Nelson waited for a favourable lull when the wind and waves were less severe, then gave the order to put the helm up. Slowly the *Vanguard* swung through 90 degrees until the wind was behind her. Even more slowly, and to the great relief of all on board, she began to turn into the wind on the other side, with the help of the 'small rag of a spritsail'. Her head was now pointing to the south-west. Because of leeway the true course was more like south-south-east and wearing had altered only it by about 45 degrees; but this was enough to keep her clear of Corsica for the moment.

That crisis being over by about 7am, the *Vanguard*'s men were set to work hacking away the wreckage on the bow and mainmast. Ropes were cut with axes and one of the main anchors, adrift but still held on by a cable 8in thick, was sacrificed for the safety of the ship. A large quantity of water was swirling about the lower deck adding to the instability of the ship, so holes were cut in the planking to allow it to drain into the hold, and eventually be pumped out. Fortunately there were no major leaks in the 10-year-old hull, so the dockyard had evidently done a good job on the repairs. One of the ship's boats, a cutter, was swept off the deck and Thomas Meek, the young man who had been reclaimed from the press gang and promoted midshipman, was lost. The gale continued, the *Vanguard* still 'rolled dreadfully'[30] and her captain had little control over her movements, but at least she was out of immediate danger.

The captains of the *Terpsichore* and *Bonne Citoyenne* had reacted differently to the storm. Instead of attempting to keep some control of their ships by setting trysails, they took in all sail and allowed the wind to carry them along – 'laying under bare poles' as it was called. The *Bonne Citoyenne* cast off her prize, which was carrying a petty officer and five of her seamen but stayed in sight of her until the morning of the 21st. Having no sail set, neither ship was able to wear with the admiral during the night but the two frigates remained in contact with one another until nightfall on the 21st. The *Emerald*, however, remained in touch with the *Vanguard*.

The gale continued throughout the afternoon and evening of Monday the 21st but at 4am on the 22nd it began to moderate, so that the *Alexander* was able to set more sail. As the second day broke it became clear that the *Emerald* too had lost contact but the three ships of the line were still together. At 6.45am Nelson, using what masts were available to him, hoisted the signal for the *Alexander* to take him in tow and this was repeated by the *Orion*.[31] It was not easy to manoeuvre vessels in close contact in these conditions and it was three in the afternoon before the *Alexander* got alongside the flagship. A light heaving line was tossed onto the forecastle of the *Vanguard* and a much stronger rope, perhaps an anchor cable, was hauled over and securely attached to both ships, probably to the anchor bitts on the lower deck. The *Alexander*, now with her topsails and courses set, began to tow the *Vanguard* towards the Gulf of Oristano, in the centre of the east coast of Sardinia, where it was hoped

The *Vanguard* under tow by the *Alexander* on the morning of 22 May, by Nicolas Pocock. (National Maritime Museum, London: PW5876)

shelter might be found, though no-one in the squadron knew the area or had charts. But the wind made it impossible to turn into Oristano, so the three ships continued down the coast towards the island of San Pietro, 30 miles away.

In the late afternoon the winds dropped almost to nothing, creating more dangers for ships drifting along a rocky coast. The *Orion* and *Alexander* set yet more sail, including the studding sails which extended the width of the normal sails, while the *Vanguard* set what she could on the remains of her masts. At 7pm the island of San Pietro was sighted 11 miles off and the ships began sounding with their lead-lines, to find the depth of water and the nature of the bottom. A skilled seaman stood on the channels which projected from the side of each ship, casting a lead weight attached to a line into the water. The lead had a hollow in its base, which was filled with tallow so that a sample of the sea bottom might be brought up. The *Orion* found 50½ fathoms with soft rocks and shells at 11pm, and 70 fathoms and muddy ground four hours later – far too deep to anchor in.

The wind was still very light and the danger was increasing as the ships drifted towards the shore. As Berry wrote to his brother,

> All this time there was a heavy swell driving in towards the shore, so that at midnight we were completely embayed. You may easily figure to yourself our situation and the feelings of those who knew the danger when I tell you I could easily distinguish the surf breaking on the rocky shore; still there was hope anchorage might be found, though we knew of none. We therefore bent our cables [*ie* attached them to the anchors] and prepared for the worst, anxiously waiting for daybreak, which at length arrived and we found ourselves about five miles from the shore, the western swell continuing to drive us in and no wind to enable us to get off.[32]

Nelson hailed Ball in the *Alexander* and ordered him to cast off the tow, so that his ship at least might be saved. Ball refused and Nelson, already perhaps feeling the stress of command, 'became impetuous and enforced his demand with passionate threats'. Ball remained calm and replied in his rather pompous manner: 'I feel confident that I can bring you in safe. I therefore must not and by the help of almighty God will not leave you.' It is difficult to be sure that all this was indeed said and heard over the waves but Ball persuaded the admiral to persevere despite the risks.

At 6am a breeze got up from the north-west, to fill the *Alexander*'s sails and allow the ships to avoid being driven onto the rocks at the north end of San Pietro. The *Orion* went ahead into the bay, sounding as she went and finding a route for the others. Both the *Vanguard* and *Orion* hoisted the signal for a pilot and the flagship drew attention to it by firing a gun but there was no reply from the shore, for reasons which were to become apparent later. But by 11am the *Vanguard* had found a safe anchorage and the *Alexander* at last cast off her tow. Half an hour later the two ships dropped their anchors and came to rest 'in six fathoms and fine smooth water'.[33] It was 'a very safe harbour, sheltered from any wind', but San Pietro was a very small town and the area was rough and uncultivated.[34]

The first feeling, of course, was of relief. To Berry it was 'a luxury to scarcely to be equalled, and if ever there was a satisfaction at being in distress, we felt it'.[35] Nelson experienced humility, which he interpreted in characteristic religious vein

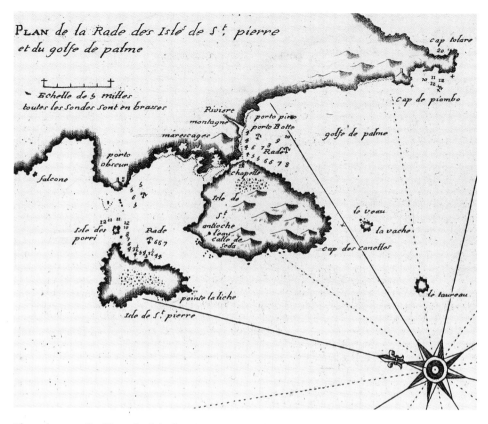

The anchorage at San Pietro, Sardinia, from Jacques Ayrouard's *Ports et Rades . . . de la Mer Méditerranée*, 1732–46. (National Maritime Museum, London: D8992)

in a letter to his wife: 'I ought not to call what happened to the *Vanguard* by the cold name of accident; I believe firmly that it was the Almighty's goodness to check my consummate vanity. I hope it has made me a better officer, as I feel confident it has made me a better man.'[36] He also felt gratitude to Ball, especially for the tow. He went on board the *Alexander* as soon as he could and embraced her captain, exclaiming 'A friend in need is a friend indeed!'[37] The old feud was forgotten and Ball was Nelson's most trusted confidant for the rest of the campaign.

Possibly the tempest was stronger when it struck the *Vanguard* than when it hit the other two ships of the line. But they were not very far apart, so it is also possible to believe that Berry was overconfident and negligent in setting too much sail. He was a junior captain with very little experience in command of vessels of any sort. Nelson never criticised Berry directly for the risks he brought on the *Vanguard* by setting the upper spars and failing to notice that a storm was on the way; it is only by his omissions that we can get a glimpse of his feelings. According to his report to St Vincent, Saumarez and Ball had been 'wonderful' during the storm, but there was no mention of Berry.[38] It was 'us' who got the upper masts and yards aloft; it was 'I' who decided to wear and steer for the Gulf of Oristano. However, Nelson did not try to evade his ultimate responsibility. When the gale began he believed that the ships were prepared for a storm and later wrote 'my mind was easy'.[39] He had spent a dozen years at sea as captain or admiral and had an almost perfect feel for shifts in wind and weather. It is difficult to believe that he would have made such a mistake while Saumarez and Ball got it right. He did not come on deck until the ship was already in danger, perhaps because he wanted to give Berry his head. It is difficult to blame him for this.

Having anchored in the bay, there was a great deal to be done. The first concern was for the immediate safety of the ships, and soon after anchoring three cutters were lowered from them and an officer went in each to take soundings round the bay, to make sure there was room to swing at anchor and to find a better site if one was available. Official reports had to be written even if there was no immediate prospect of sending them and Nelson's to St Vincent began, 'I am sorry to be obliged to inform you of the accidents which have happened to the *Vanguard*.'[40]

The officers had hoped for a friendly reception from the Sardinians, who were theoretically neutral in the war. At noon on 24 May the fort at San Pietro recognised Nelson's status as a rear-admiral by firing a six-gun salute. However, a boat soon arrived alongside the *Vanguard* and put on board a messenger from the governor, who 'very civilly informed us that by a late alliance with France he was not permitted to admit us to the port; at the same time observing that as he could not prevent it, we might do as we pleased, but he could not give us *pratique* [the right of contact with the shore]'.[41] Nelson wrote a letter of protest to the governor. His ship had suffered 'some trifling damage' and he was 'surprised to hear . . . that admittance was to be refused to the Flag of His Britannic Majesty into this port'. Sardinia and Britain were old allies, he wrote, but even the Muslims of North Africa were more helpful than fellow Christians.[42] Saumarez was sent to deal with the governor and had some success, despite the Sardinians' fear of French reprisals. To top up the supplies in the ships' holds he negotiated the purchase of 'oxen, sheep and as much poultry as can be procured . . . on moderate terms, which is a seasonable relief, as Gibraltar supplied us with nothing whatever excepting fowls.'[43] Berry paid £123 for 7403lbs of beef and sent the bill to the Victualling Office in London.[44]

In view of the damage to the *Vanguard*, Nelson had to decide whether to continue with his mission or to abandon it and go to either Naples or Gibraltar for repairs. The loss of his frigates did not weigh on his mind for the moment, for he assumed that they would soon be found, waiting at one of the rendezvous he had set. The damage to the *Vanguard* might have been considered more serious, but a determination to press on with his mission was one of Nelson's outstanding characteristics. There is no indication that he met with Saumarez, Ball and Berry to consider abandonment, and of the frigate captain who apparently assumed that he would have taken his ships in for repair he wrote 'I thought Hope would have known me better'.[45] Another possibility was to transfer his flag to the *Alexander* or *Orion*, but there is no sign that he considered this either. If the *Vanguard* was sent home, then a third of the remaining strength would be lost. If she stayed with the squadron with his flag on another ship, then the *Vanguard* would have difficulty in keeping up with him. It was quite common for the admiral to sail on the slowest ship and leave chasing to others.

Repair work to the *Vanguard* began almost instantly on arrival at San Pietro, despite the exhaustion of the seamen. Each ship carried a number of spare topmasts, topgallant masts and yards and these were put to good use. The carpenters of the *Orion* went to work making a new mizzen topmast for the *Vanguard*, presumably by converting one of their own spars, and delivered it within 24 hours of anchoring. Meanwhile the seamen drew rope from the boatswain's storeroom in the bows of the ship and made shrouds to support her new masts. Work was interrupted in the afternoon of the 24th when a squall struck the *Orion* and caused her anchor to drag; the ship had to alter her position and lay out another. The following morning it had to be raised again and the captain recalled from duty on shore, for at 10am a strange sail was spotted off the island and the *Orion* was the only ship in a state to pursue. Even a small French warship might be a threat at this stage and Nelson noted that 'the meanest frigate out of France would have been a very unwelcome guest'.[46] A merchant ship, on the other hand, might offer prize money and information. The *Orion* chased her quarry until 5pm but to Saumarez's disappointment she was found to be a neutral brig from the port of Ragusa (Dubrovnik) carrying grain from Palermo. On the 27th the *Orion* was in chase again and captured a Spanish brig. It was planned to set her on fire and sacrifice the prize money but instead the crew were allowed to go on shore to try and raise money for a ransom. Eventually she was retained as a prize, for she could be manned and used to carry the admiral's dispatches to Gibraltar.

In the meantime repairs to the flagship continued. On the afternoon of the 24th the *Alexander* sent eighteen shipwrights and her spare fore topmast over, before being herself lashed in place alongside the *Vanguard*. The stump of the old foremast was hoisted out with blocks and tackles hung from the intact masts and yards of Ball's ship and the following day the new foremast was lowered into place. A spare topgallant mast was set up as a fore topmast, and 'consequently everything reduced in proportion'.[47] The bowsprit was 'fished' by lashing pieces of timber across the broken parts. Rigging and sails were replaced and at 6.30am on Sunday the 27th, less than four days after arriving at San Pietro, the three ships were ready to weigh anchor.

Nelson was pleased with the results, that the *Vanguard* was sailing 'as an English man-of-war' and not as an impotent wreck. The work, he claimed, would have taken months in the Royal Dockyard, but all naval officers loved to complain about their shore-based colleagues. According to Berry, whose pride in his ship perhaps led to some exaggeration, the *Vanguard* was as good as any other vessel despite the damage. 'By our superiority in sailing with other ships, we find the loss trifling to what it would have been to the generality of ships.'[48] Particular credit went to James Morrison, the carpenter of the *Alexander*, an 'old and faithful servant of the Crown who has been near thirty years a warranted carpenter',[49] and who advised on how the repairs were to be done.

Due to variable winds it was several days before the ships were able to get clear of San Pietro. On the 28th a vessel out of Marseilles was spoken to and gave vital and tantalising information. The French had sailed from Toulon on the 20th, as Nelson's squadron had been fighting the gale. Saumarez hoped that the French too had been damaged in the storm and Nelson decided to press on to the rendezvous off Toulon, where he hoped to meet his frigates and then go in pursuit.

After that the squadron found reasonably favourable winds and averaged about 50 miles a day. Off Toulon on 3 June, the officers were disappointed that the missing frigates were not to be found. However, they spoke to a ship which 'mentioned having seen eleven sail of the line a few days ago, supposed to be English.' Saumarez was 'at a loss what conjectures to put on this intelligence'.[50] Two days later the tiny British brig *Mutine* was sighted and made sail towards the *Vanguard*. Commander Thomas Masterman Hardy came on board with a piece of news that changed the whole picture and delighted the officers present. The report of English ships of the line was true; they were to join with Nelson's reconnaissance squadron, making it into a true fighting fleet. To Saumarez this was 'very interesting intelligence' causing 'great glee, inasmuch our proceedings are becoming of very great import'.[51] According to Berry it 'was received with universal joy throughout our little squadron', while Nelson observed that his new force would be 'a match for any hostile fleet in the Mediterranean'.[52]

CHAPTER 5

To the Gates of Valletta

AT 6AM ON THE 30 Floréal, or 19 May, the signal to weigh anchor was hoisted aboard the French flagship *L'Orient*. Getting such a fleet under weigh was a long operation and it took 8 hours for 22 warships and 130 merchantmen to pass out of the great anchorage of Toulon. Only two were left behind; the frigate *Carerre* went aground on a sandbank, while the flagship waited to be the last to leave. It was late that night before Bonaparte, as General-in-Chief, finished his last letter to the Directory and ordered Admiral Brueys to set sail.

Outside the harbour, Rear-Admiral Blanquet in the *Franklin* took charge of assembling the convoys and squadrons of the Armament. All the transports of the Toulon and Marseilles convoys were French merchant ships and between them they carried over 11,000 men. Some had the square rig of ships and brigs; there was a solitary fore-and-aft rigged schooner and many ships with the Mediterranean rigs known as polacres and tartanes, which combined fore-and-aft and square sails. Square riggers would sail best with the wind astern or across their beam, fore-and-aft rigged vessels could perform better into the wind. They varied in size from 44 to 290 tons. Larger ships would be able to keep their speed up in rough seas, smaller ones would not. The average merchant ship had a crew of eight or nine men or 16 tons for every seaman. This compared with about 2 tons per seaman on a well-manned warship of the period, so the merchant ship would respond far more slowly to changes in wind and to orders from the fleet commanders. With such variety in size, type and rig, the convoy was a slow, unwieldy assembly. In all navies, officers complained that merchant captains lacked any discipline and sense of order, but this was an exceptionally difficult convoy even by these standards.

On board the merchantmen, the soldiers settled down for a long voyage in uncomfortable conditions. All were overcrowded. The *Égalité* of 122 tons, for example, carried 9 officers and 111 men of the 1st and 2nd companies of the Grenadier *demi-brigade*. This was approximately one man per ton, which was twice as many as would be allowed for on a British transport of the period.

When the convoy was in some kind of order, the *Franklin* led the fleet towards Cape Corse, the northern point of Corsica. *L'Orient* overtook the convoy in

The voyages of the different French convoys. ▶

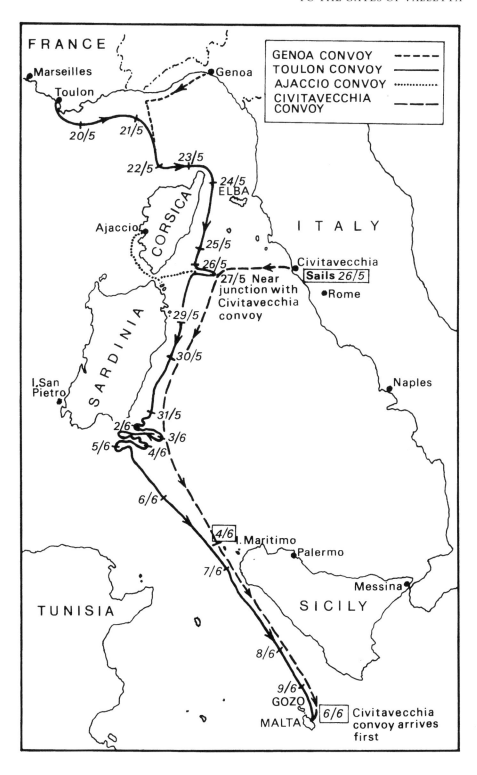

FRANCE

Marseilles

Toulon

20/5   21/5

22/5   23/5

24/5
ELBA

CORSICA

Ajaccio

25/5

26/5

27/5 Near
junction with
Civitavecchia
convoy

ITALY

Civitavecchia
Sails 26/5

Rome

29/5

SARDINIA

30/5

I.San
Pietro

Naples

31/5

2/6

3/6

5/6   4/6

6/6

4/6 .Maritimo

Palermo

7/6

TUNISIA

Messina

SICILY

8/6

9/6
GOZO

MALTA

6/6 Civitavecchia
convoy arrives
first

GENOA CONVOY   ------
TOULON CONVOY   ———
AJACCIO CONVOY   ....
CIVITAVECCHIA
CONVOY   – – –

the night, unseen from any ship, and could be seen at the head of the Armament at midday on the 20th. The progress of the unwieldy convoy was slow and the winds were not helpful. On the 19th the fleet encountered violent gusts and at midnight on the 20th it was on the edge of the storm that devastated Nelson's squadron, 50 miles away.[1] But for most of the time the winds were light and the fleet would average only 37 miles per day over 20 days.

Meanwhile the other convoys were setting sail. That from Genoa met the main force on the 21st. On the 23rd the whole force reached Cape Corse and passed round it overnight, with the convoy spread over a distance of 12 miles. It then headed down the east side of the island, slowing down even further because Bonaparte hoped to meet the twenty-two ships of the Corsican convoy at the southern end of the island. The wind was from the north-west, so the sailors in the fleet feared that this would stop the Corsican vessels from getting out of the harbour at Ajaccio, on the east coast. However, this convoy had actually left port on the 15th, four days before Bonaparte sailed from Toulon. It quickly reached the Maddalena Islands off northern Sardinia and was met by three ships loaded with money to support the expedition. On 28 May the main fleet arrived to find the Corsican ships already there. The vessels of this part of the force were particularly small, averaging only 110 tons; the rest had to slow down to allow them to keep up.

At Civitavecchia north-east of Rome on 26 May the ships' boats belonging to the convoy were recalled from the shore and had an exciting race to their parent ships, watched by Colonel Savary on the poop of the frigate *Courageuse*. The fortress at the harbour mouth fired a 100-gun salute and the Italian contingent got under way with a fair wind from the south-east. A Swedish ship called the *Jupiter* went aground but was got off by the efforts of her crew. The sea, quite violent in the morning, was now reducing and as night fell the last ships of the 56-strong Civitavecchia convoy left harbour. In one of the transports, General Belliard had already guessed the destination of the force.

> It is to be presumed that we will make sail for Egypt . . . We have embarked Arab interpreters and printers, with type and presses. Citizen Monge is already working to learn the language, and surely that is not to land on the coast of England. Perhaps at Malta we will take the funds that we need . . . I have taken ample supplies of victuals, of music and if the sea does not make me ill I hope I will not be bored.[2]

On being rowed to the *Courageuse* one evening after dinner, he found the society congenial – it was a 'chambre d'instruction' with Gaspard Monge, a mathematician who had served as Navy Minister in the early days of the Revolution, sharing his knowledge with all present in the great cabin. Hearing that the voyage might last 6 months, Belliard hoped for a transfer to the same ship as him.

Early in the morning of the 30th the Civitavecchia convoy was off Sardinia and in the distance it sighted seven men of war, some of the ships of the line of the Toulon Fleet. But the wind dropped and then it blew from different directions on the two convoys. The Civitavecchia ships were particularly difficult to keep together and many of them lacked even charts and compasses. They found themselves some way ahead of the main force and went on slowly down the side of Sardinia and then towards the western end of Sicily, making very slow progress in the light winds. Speed picked up over the next few days and on 4 June the *Courageuse* and her charges rounded Cape Maritimo, Sicily, and headed straight for Malta. On 6 June it was sighted from there, causing the Grand Master of the Knights of St John to mobilise his forces. The Civitavecchia convoy, however, remained out of gunshot from Malta, unable to do anything until the main force arrived.

★

On board *L'Orient*, Bonaparte had been convinced that the final junction of the convoys was about to be achieved on 27 May and he was disappointed that this did not happen. Among the army and civilian passengers, seasickness began with the first strong winds on the 19th, though on the 23rd Bonaparte reported proudly that he had suffered nothing so far. Some of the soldiers began to take an interest in the ships that were carrying them and in the *Peuple Souverain* Brigadier Laugier reported that she was a good sailer, though one of the oldest ships in the fleet. Her captain, Racord, was a good seaman, with 'uncommon activity, steady, and moreover very honest, as were all the officers by his side'. The captain took his meals with some of the senior army officers, who 'lived in very happy harmony and whenever the weather does not test those of us who are severely affected by sea-sickness, gaiety reigns in the great cabin and the fine band of the 12th *Demi-Brigade* entertains the whole crew'.[3] In the *Franklin*, Theviotte, a young officer of the military engineers, was less happy:

> Life on the ships is very uniform. I rise at 5 or 6 in the morning and read until 9 . . . We dine at 4 and go to bed at 11. The night is usually very peaceful, the space where we are shut up is very warm and little aired. The officers and captains [of the army?] sleep in the 36-pounder battery above the powder magazine. The other officers sleep in the great cabin . . . some in hammocks, others in frames, suspended or not suspended.[4]

On board the flagship, Bonaparte spent much of his time on a bed 'swinging on a kind of castors', designed to alleviate the effects of seasickness.[5] Unfortunately the design seems to have been lost. He seldom rose before 10am, but found time to hold meetings with the *savants*. A large proportion of them were on board *L'Orient* and Bonaparte amused himself by stirring up discussions on questions of philosophy, science and religion. General Caffarelli argued for a fundamental redistribution of property within society and sparked a fierce debate, while subjects like the age of the Earth and the interpretation of dreams attracted a different audience, or caused some officers to fall asleep. The great cabin of the flagship became known as the council chamber, though many of the debates were also held while walking on deck.

In an unusual example of inter-service co-operation, the troops aboard the warships were allocated to the gun crews. In *L'Orient*, carrying the general staff of the army, generals found themselves taking on the role of naval lieutenants and commanding batteries. Thus General Caffarelli was to command the guns on the quarterdeck and forecastle, with six army artillerymen, six naval gunners, twenty landsmen and boys and eighty soldiers. General Dommartin was in charge of the middle deck battery of 24-pounders, with 30 army artillerymen, 19 naval gunners, 40 boys and 200 soldiers. General Lannes, like a captain of marines, was to command a party of grenadiers who would do guard duty and fight with muskets in action.[6] On board the other warships the battery commanders were of humbler rank but the integration of the army and the navy was similar.

Bonaparte ensured that the mixed crews were trained in naval gunnery. Every morning the ships were cleared for action and gun drill was carried out. It was noted that the soldiers took to it with skill and enthusiasm but there was a feeling, in the *Peuple Souverain* at least, that such crews might fight better by running close to the enemy and either boarding him or driving him from the decks by musketry.[7] It was only by chance that Nelson's squadron was not encountered at this stage in the campaign and that a naval battle did not take place between it and Bonaparte's mixed force. Conventional naval wisdom suggests that seamen would always prevail over landsmen in such circumstances. But was an overwhelming British victory inevitable? Would the French soldiers have risen to the occasion, as they always did under the inspired leadership of their great general? Despite the co-operation on the gundecks, relations between soldiers and sailors were uneasy. In the *Franklin* the soldiers devoted themselves to gambling, which caused dissension and was a threat to good order. It was banned by order of General Kléber.[8]

There were reports of British ships in the area. When the French had sailed from Toulon, Bonaparte was aware of 'several English flotillas' in the Mediterranean but thought they were no threat.[9] On 27 May he informed the Directory that the crew of a passing ship had reported seeing a squadron, though he thought it could be no more than five or six ships of the line.[10] On 2 June he received news that a privateer had heard that three British ships, under the command of Admiral Nelson, had taken shelter at San Pietro in Sardinia and that Nelson's ship was dismasted.[11] This was reassuring, and reports from neutral vessels gave no cause for alarm. The crew of a Swedish ship, interrogated in detail on the 4th, had seen no British fleet since Cadiz and only individual frigates off Gibraltar. Another ship, presumably Danish, had actually been convoyed by a British frigate for part of the way but knew nothing of Nelson being in the area.[12] However, Bonaparte remained cautious and refused to split his fleet. When Brueys suggested sending four ships of the line and three frigates to look for the Civitavecchia convoy the General-in-Chief replied, 'If, 24 hours after this separation, ten English ships of the line are signalled, I will have only nine ships of the line instead of thirteen.'[13]

★

The ruling elite of Malta had much in common with that of Egypt. Like the Mamelukes, the individual Knights of St John were born outside the country they ruled. As warrior-monks they had no official offspring, so their wealth and power were not transmitted by heredity. They too had an ancient origin, which could be traced back more than 700 years to the early Middle Ages and the First Crusade against the Mohammedan occupation of the Holy Land. The principal difference was that the Knights, far from being bought as slaves, came from the aristocratic families of Catholic Europe.

A bird's eye view of Valletta. In the left foreground is Floriana, with the crowned hornwork projecting from it. Behind that is Valletta proper. To the right is the Grand Harbour with the two heavily populated promontories of Senglea and Vittoriosa. Behind them, fronting the sea, is Fort Ricasoli. On the other side of Valletta is Manoel Island with its fort. Fort Tigne can just be seen on the tip of the peninsula behind that. (National Maritime Museum, London: A1427)

The Knights of St John had begun as hospitallers in Jerusalem but had evolved into a fighting force during the twelfth century. Dedicated to the struggle against the rising power of Islam in the Holy Land, they were driven out to Rhodes where they carried on the fight on the sea, developing a powerful galley force. They had to abandon Rhodes in 1522 and in 1530 they were granted the sovereignty of Malta. Even there they were not safe from Muslim advances and in 1565 they endured a great siege by the forces of Suleyman the Magnificent, the Sultan of Turkey. After being relieved, they founded the city of Valletta in the centre of a group of natural harbours. Funded by kings and princes throughout Europe, the defences of Malta were built up and became magnificent and strong, far beyond the resources of a small and not particularly productive island.

Valletta itself stood on a tongue of land 1½ miles long and half a mile broad and was the strongest point on the island. The tip of the tongue was guarded by Fort St Elmo, while the city, built on a regular grid pattern, was protected by high walls on each side. A series of great bastions, surmounted by even higher works known as 'cavaliers', guarded the landward side. Beyond that was the suburb of Floriana, which had its own defensive wall and bastions and a large projecting fortification known as the crowned hornwork. To the west of the tongue of land was the Grand Harbour, open to the north but otherwise well sheltered and with enough depth of water for the greatest ships of the day. Several smaller, more sheltered harbours led off to the east and the 'three cities' of Senglea, Vittoriosa and Cospicua were sited on the peninsulas between them, each protected by its own fortifications and by the massive Cottonera Lines round the whole conurbation. The most northerly of the peninsulas on this side was protected by Fort Ricasoli. East of Valletta was Marsamxett Harbour, slightly smaller but almost as useful. It was guarded by Fort Manoel on an island on its western side and the recently completed Fort Tigne at its entrance. As Admiral Keith was to write a few years later, 'Malta has this advantage over all the other ports that I have mentioned, that the whole harbour is covered by its wonderful fortifications . . . At Malta all the arsenals, hospitals, storehouses etc, are on a grand scale.'[14]

By 1798 the rationale of the Knights had long disappeared. The Crusade against the infidel was irrelevant to modern Europe. The old aristocracies which had supplied their younger sons as knights were now in decline and threatened by the French Revolution, if not already overthrown. For many decades the order had come to rely heavily on recruitment from France. It consisted of eight groups known as *Langues* or tongues, based on the national origins of the members and each living communally in an *auberge* or inn. The three most flourishing of these – France, Auvergne and Languedoc – were French, and in practice two-thirds of the 300 Knights remaining in the Order were of French origin.

As rulers of Malta, the Knights had little credibility with the ordinary people. There was no route for a native Maltese to enter the ruling class, so even wealthy middle-class elements were denied the prospect of political power. The Knights' vows of celibacy were often broken among the women of the island, so the people had no faith in them as religious leaders. They had accumulated wealth for themselves on the island but their possessions in France had been confiscated by the revolutionaries. They had not fought a military campaign since 1718, and that had been unsuccessful. Bonaparte judged correctly that the order was weak, discredited and demoralised.

According to a report by the French spy Poussielgue, the effective forces of Malta, in addition to the Knights themselves, consisted of 2210 men including 800 chasseurs or light infantry who were barely organised and badly trained.[15] Another report suggests that the Knights controlled two battalions of the Malta Regiment, totalling 500 men, 200 more in the Grand Master's guard, 250 marines from the galleys and an equal number from the sailing warships; and 200 gunners, making a total regular force of 1400 men. In addition there were auxiliary forces consisting of 800 light infantry, 200 military engineers recruited from the island's workmen, and 500 auxiliary gunners, the street-porters of the island. This force of 2900 men was reasonably effective and in theory it was backed up by the militia. Every man in the islands between 20 and 60 years of age was liable for service and on paper 10,000 more men could be produced. In practice the militia was untrained and morale was low or non-existent. Most of the Maltese knew of no reason to fear the French Revolution, which promised to liberate them from the arrogance and misrule of the Knights and few turned out to defend the island. As a result, Malta was defended by an effective force of perhaps 3000 men, a tenth of the French troops available.

★

Why did Bonaparte attack Malta? He had no *casus belli* of any kind and such an attack gave warning of French ruthlessness. It would certainly annoy the Russians, who believed they had a kind of protectorate over the island and had been on the brink of war with France for some time. It could be seen as a time-wasting diversion on the way to Egypt, for no matter how weak the resistance, several days would be needed to attack and secure the island and it was known that a British squadron was in the area. Unlike Egypt it offered no prospects of colonisation for its own sake, for it was tiny, had no natural resources and the land was rocky and not especially fertile. It was not essential to the plan. The island would offer no supplies except water, nor would it do much to secure the route from France to Egypt. There was no prospect that the Knights themselves would launch an attack on French communications.

In a sense Malta was a project left over from previous plans, for as early as September 1797 Bonaparte had written, 'Why should we not take possession of Malta? Admiral Brueys might easily anchor there and capture it.' He then went on to develop the idea of an attack on Egypt, without making it clear whether the two plans were directly linked. Talleyrand had responded favourably to the Malta project but was much more cautious about Egypt. He favoured an attack on Malta because of the danger that it might fall into other hands, in particular those of Austria.[16] Though defeated in northern Italy, Austria had gained a naval base in Venice through the Treaty of Campo Formio and now had the makings of a modern fleet. A base at Malta would allow her to dominate the Mediterranean, perhaps in alliance with the British. Talleyrand wrote:

> The possession of this island, joined to that of Istria and Dalmatia, would make Austria a maritime power capable of causing anxiety to France and the Cisalpine Republic, of which latter it is easy to believe she could not be other than her enemy. Malta from its geographical position would give her the means of troubling the navigation of the entire Mediterranean. There is also the danger that the island might fall into the possession of the English and the Russians.[17]

The acquisition of Malta might also be seen as a part of the general French eastward expansion, begun with Corsica and leading towards Egypt and India. Perhaps Bonaparte, with a landsman's eye, saw it as a position on his lines of communication which had to be reduced. Not least, Malta was filled with rich treasures in her churches and in the houses of her rulers. The French Directory needed a constant supply of such plunder to help pay for its incessant military operations.

★

On 9 June Bonaparte sent messengers ashore to the Grand Master, to demand rights for all his ships to enter harbour to take on water. At 6pm Hompesch, the Grand Master, presided at a meeting of the council during which it was pointed out that the regulations of the Order would forbid such an entrance: states which were at war with other Christian countries were only allowed to send in four warships at a time for any purpose. On receiving the news that night, Bonaparte was not disappointed, for the demand for watering was merely a pretext for invasion. 'Water is refused!' he said, 'Then we will go and take it.' An emissary was sent ashore again with a more aggressive message. 'The Commander in Chief, Bonaparte, is indignant to learn that you will not grant such permission except to four vessels at a time – for in effect, what length of time would be required under such circumstances to water and victual 500 to 600 sail? . . . General Bonaparte is resolved to obtain by force that which ought to have been accorded him by virtue of the principles of hospitality, the fundamental rule of your Order.'[18]

The warships were drawn up in a line before Valletta, while most of the convoy anchored in a group to the north-east of the channel between Malta and Gozo. At daybreak on the morning of the 10th, the plans for invasion were put in motion. Bonaparte ordered his men to land at four main points. The city of Valletta was of course the strongest point in the central Mediterranean and a direct attack on it in small boats would be suicidal, however weak the garrison of the city. Instead, the first landing was to take place 2½ miles west of the city.

At 6am on the 10th, the assault began. The men of General Vaubois's division, embarked in the warships, climbed into longboats, barges and cutters and were rowed to the leeward side of the flagship, where they had some shelter. The General-in-Chief got into one of *L'Orient*'s boats to go with them and Rear-Admiral Decrès supervised in the frigate *Diane*. Escorted by some of the smaller vessels of the fleet, the boats began to row towards the bays of St Julien and St George's, where they would be out of range of the guns of the city. The defences were weak there and the troops landed without too much difficulty, capturing some of the small forts which guarded that part of the coast.

The *Diane* began to engage the guns of Valletta; the Maltese batteries, though firing devastating balls of 36 or even 48lbs, were badly aimed and did no damage. The four galleys of the Maltese navy came out of the harbour to meet the frigate. Though armed only with a feeble 3-pounder gun each, they put up a fierce fire. The French troops cannonaded the galleys from the captured forts on shore, doing some damage. Meanwhile French gunboats, under the command of Lieutenant Jouan of the *Peuple Souverain*, arrived and forced the galleys to retreat.[19]

On shore, the troops advanced towards the Wignacourt Aqueduct which brought water to Valletta, where they would rendezvous with the division which was landing at St Paul's bay. They encountered some resistance and the ground was broken up by walls and houses, with the main party of Maltese behind the aqueduct, but the French suffered few casualties.

The second landing was in St Paul's Bay, named after the Apostle's famous shipwreck in Biblical times. The division led by General Baraguey d'Hilliers, consisting of troops from the Genoa convoy of transports, landed on the peninsula which formed the western side of the bay, virtually unopposed.

The bay of Marsaxlokk, on the eastern side of the island, was better defended. A reconnaissance party was sent under General Donzelot and on the beaches it found many rocks which would impede the landings. At 7.30am, 900 men of General Desaix's division, from the Civitavecchia convoy, were put into the boats

The French landings on Malta. Based on a drawing of 1800, reproduced in de la Jonquière's *Expedition d'Egypte*, vol 1.

▶

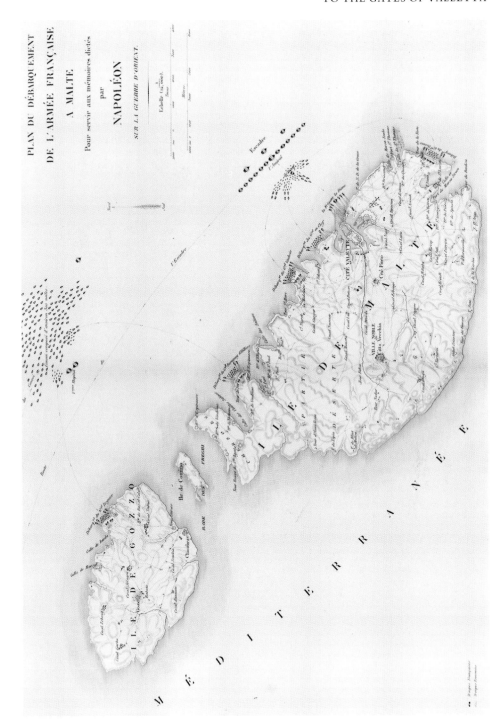

PLAN DU DÉBARQUEMENT
DE L'ARMÉE FRANÇAISE
A MALTE
Pour servir aux mémoires dictés
par
NAPOLÉON
SUR LA GUERRE D'ORIENT.

Echelle (1/12,000).

The French fleet bombarding Valletta with *L'Orient* (the second large ship from the left with the boats at her stern) opposite Fort Ricasoli. (Musée de la Marine, Paris)

belonging to the warships of Blanquet's division. The *Franklin*, carrying Rear-Admiral Blanquet, was sent round to cover the landing but the winds were very light and the great 80-gun ship made very slow progress. At midday, while the force was still some way from its destination, the command group got into the *Franklin*'s longboat, which was armed with a 12-pounder gun. But the force still had 4 hours of rowing before it reached Point Tombarelles, a triangle of land which formed the eastern side of the bay. With gunboats guarding their flanks, they began to head towards the beach. As they approached they were fired on by two Maltese guns and the *Franklin*'s boat found itself dangerously far ahead of the rest and exposed to Maltese fire. She fell back into the protection of the others and the assault floundered for a moment. General Belliard rallied the stragglers, the gunboats fired on the Maltese artillery and Martinet's boat again took the lead. The landing took place in front of the Maltese battery, which was soon captured.[20] After the 900 men of the first wave were landed, the boats went back to fetch 400 more. There was much to do, for the Maltese still held Fort Rohan (St Lucian's Tower), on a tongue of land in the centre of the bay. It was manned by 160 men who kept up a fierce fire and did not surrender until daybreak the next morning. Then the division was able to begin its march inland. It joined the other two in besieging Valletta and the three cities.

The attack on Gozo was perhaps the least necessary of the four. There was no reason why the smaller island could have been expected to hold out after the main one had fallen. Even if it had somehow fallen into the hands of the British it would have mattered little, for it had no natural harbours. It is ironic, then, that this attack cost the French the greatest casualties. The coasts of the island were quite well defended, though not nearly as strong as Valletta. It had a militia of over 1100 men, divided into 280 gunners, 800 infantry and 30 cavalry and most of these seem to have turned out when summoned by church bells. The French transports came within a mile of the coast and the soldiers went into the boats to be rowed ashore. On landing, the men had to climb the heights of the rocky island to attack the forts. This took all day but the last forts were taken during the night of the 10th.[21]

Despite some opposition, the French assaults were all completely successful: three men were killed and five or six wounded.[22] Only the city of Valletta still held out.

★

To be successful, the defences of Valletta relied on two factors. They needed a substantial force to man the guns and ramparts, and they needed some hope of relief. The Knights had been besieged before and eventually relieved by forces organised by their fellow Catholics. This time they had no knowledge of any likely relief. As far as they knew the French, now godless revolutionaries rather than faithful Catholics, were the only power that counted in the Mediterranean. They knew nothing of Nelson's foray. Rescue by a Protestant fleet from Britain would have been a new experience for them but not in itself unwelcome. They were not a particularly sectarian order and were dedicated to the struggle of Christianity as a whole against the Muslims. Certainly Nelson, as the representative of conservative, Christian forces, would have seemed preferable to Bonaparte. Had they known that Nelson was on the coast of Italy at this very moment, things might have been very different.

Rescue by Nelson would perhaps not have disorientated the Knights but attack by France certainly did. The 200 Frenchmen inside Valletta had to think where their loyalties lay. Their natural tendency, perhaps, would have been towards the *ancien régime* and the émigrés who continued to support it. But such forces had manifestly failed to make any impact on the Revolutionaries, and former monarchists, such as Admiral Brueys in command of this very fleet, were beginning to make their peace with the Republic now that the extreme days of the Jacobins were over. The French Knights had to choose between loyalty to their country, however it might have changed since they had left it, and loyalty to their church and order. This view was articulated most clearly by Bosredan Ransijat, the Secretary of the Treasury. On 10 June he wrote to the Grand Master, 'when I became by vow a member of our institution, I did not contract any other military obligation beyond that of warring against the Turks, our constitutional enemies. I could never contemplate fighting against my native country.'[23] He was locked up in the castle of St Angelo for his treachery.

However, Ransijat was simply more honest than others of his countrymen. Hompesch's secretary, as he walked around the besieged city, found much doubt among the defenders. A lawyer, acting as a sentinel, said, 'I fear very much that the Grand Master knows not what he is doing. They are firing away; but to what purpose? It can only alarm women and children. It would be far better if the council would consider and verify whether we have sufficient forces to resist the assault which the French are capable of attempting this very night.' More threateningly he went on to ask, 'What? Sacrifice ourself for a handful of degenerate and panic-stricken knights, who do not know how to defend, govern or command us!'[24]

Those who remained loyal began to see treason everywhere. As the guns of Valletta failed to do any damage to the attacking French gunboats, Father Vie

Cesarini noted, 'The bullets fell without force at the feet of an enemy who seemed to defy them and laugh at us that the perfidious Tousard had mixed up the calibres, impaired the powder, suborned the gunners.'[25] Meanwhile there was disorder in the streets of Valletta and the outer forts at Tigne and Ricasoli hoisted the white flag of surrender.

In the circumstances, the Knights soon gave up the struggle. In the morning of 12 June an emissary was rowed out to *L'Orient* to ask for a truce; a 24-hour cease-fire was agreed. Late that night, Bonaparte was wakened from his bed by a new delegation which came on board and signed a convention between the Knights and Bonaparte, as representative of the French Republic. The Knights would abandon the forts and give up sovereignty of the island, but in return the French government would do its best to secure Grand Master Hompesch a petty principality, perhaps in Germany, where he could live out his days. In the meantime he would have a pension of 300,000 francs to keep him in some style. The French Knights would be allowed to return home with full rights of citizenship and arrangements would be made for Knights from other countries with their home governments.

Then and subsequently, there were many rumours that treason had been the reason for the Order's downfall. But was it realistic for the Knights to hold out much longer? They evidently knew nothing of Nelson's fleet and even Bonaparte, with his much greater sources of intelligence, did not know that it had been reinforced from three ships to thirteen. It was 200 miles away, off Toulon, when the French had arrived at Malta. The distance narrowed during the three days before the surrender, though not by much; it was 172 miles away, at Elba, at noon on the 13th. By the 18th, Bonaparte's last day on the island, it was less than 100 miles away and already knew of the French attack. If the Knights had known of this and had held out for a few more days they might have found relief.

★

As they walked through the Porte des Bombes and into the city of Valletta, General Caffarelli looked up at the magnificent fortifications and remarked to his leader, 'Upon my word General, it is lucky there is someone in town to open the gates for us.'[26] Bonaparte appointed a council to govern Malta, headed by the same Bosredan Ransijat who had recently been locked up for supporting the French. He issued a proclamation giving an *ex post facto* justification for an unprovoked attack on a peaceful state. The Knights, he said, had supported French émigrés against the Revolution, had allowed the Spanish to recruit men on the island while they were at war with France and had aided the British in similar ways, while denying help to French frigates.[27] He now began a series of reforms of Maltese life and government. Slavery was abolished and arrangements were made for 600 Turks and 1400 Moors to be repatriated. Maltese men were to wear the revolutionary tricolour cockade and were given the opportunity to earn French citizenship. Some boys from the wealthier families were to be educated in Paris. With his usual administrative zeal and skill, he reorganised the posts and hospitals and followed the practices of the Revolution in restricting the powers of the clergy and cutting down the number of

Bonaparte leaving *L'Orient* to land on Malta. A rather crude and retrospective view, from a
German publication. (National Maritime Museum, London: PAD5599)

monasteries. This was the beginning of an attack on the church which was to prove
fatal to the French cause, for the Maltese, though disillusioned with the Knights,
were devoutly Catholic and immensely proud of their beautiful and rich Baroque
churches.

The Maltese navy had once been a considerable force in the Mediterranean and
its fleet of galleys had taken part in the great Christian victory against the Turks at
Lepanto in 1571. It had declined greatly since then, though the Knights still relied
on galleys, manned by slaves and prisoners of war, as part of their fighting force.
Four of them were found intact in the harbour of Valletta. Since 1701 the Knights had
also invested in sailing warships and a 64-gun ship and two frigates were also found,
one of the latter being unserviceable.[28] The galleys were incorporated in the French
fleet and taken on to Egypt.

Apart from ships and a forward naval base, Malta might also provide two of the
commodities for which Bonaparte and his armies had an insatiable appetite – troops
and money. Some of the Turkish ex-slaves were recruited to his ships. Over 900 men
of the Maltese army were mustered on the 14th and General Dugua asked for
volunteers to serve with the French: only 24 offered to go.

The French were much more successful at finding money and treasure. Immediately after the surrender, General Berthollet and two officials were ordered to:

remove all the gold, silver and precious stones which may be found in the church of St John and other places, dependencies of the order of Malta, silver plate at the Inns, and that of the Grand Master. They will cause to be melted down in the course of tomorrow all the gold into ingots, which will be placed in the military chest following the army.

An early report suggested that 1185 livres were found in this way.[29] But such conduct was close to plunder in the eyes of the Maltese and any credit the French might have had as liberators soon began to evaporate.

On 14 June Bonaparte decided to send the frigate *Sensible* home with dispatches, including a letter asking for reinforcements to be sent in the frigate *Badine*. She also took General Baraguay D'Hilliers, going home because of ill health, and some of the trophies of the conquest, including a silver model of a galley with 'some curiosity value because of its antiquity' and a silken altar cloth from China. It took some time to find a suitable crew, for the *Sensible* had originally been armed *en flûte* to carry troops, with a reduced number of seamen. She was re-armed and 62 freed Turkish galley slaves were used to make up the numbers of her crew to 284. Because of the delays, she did not sail until the 18th.[30]

Bonaparte had never intended to spend long in Malta and soon began preparations to leave. By the 18th, most of the men had been re-embarked on their ships, leaving 3000 men of Vaubois's division behind as the garrison of the island.

CHAPTER 6

A Very Different Plan of Operations

By THE BEGINNING of April 1798, even before Nelson left England, the British government was coming to the conclusion that a substantial naval force must sent into the Mediterranean. It was not just the fear of the Armament at Toulon, though that was real enough. Pitt's morale was recovering from the defeats of previous years and on the 7th he wrote to the Foreign Secretary: 'I think I see many symptoms of the spirit of the country awakening so much on the idea of meeting and defeating invasion.'[1] Potential alliances were beginning to appear on the horizon and the Prime Minister and Foreign Secretary were keen to build a new coalition against France. The eastern powers of Austria, Russia and Prussia were no longer engaged in partitioning Poland among themselves and the first two at least had begun to turn their eyes elsewhere.

The Austrians were the most consistent opponents of the French Revolution. They had been the first to go to war with the Revolutionaries in April 1792, 11 weeks before Prussia and Sardinia and 10 months before Britain. Their army, though made up of a combination of Germans, Magyars, Czechs, Italians, Slovaks, Flemings, Serbs, Poles and Croats, was efficient by the standards of the *ancien régime*, if not by the new parameters set by the Revolutionaries. Marie-Antoinette, executed by the Revolutionaries in October 1793, was a member of their royal family. The Austrians had been defeated by Bonaparte's campaigns in Italy and they had panicked when the French army was only 90 miles from Vienna, but they had not been destroyed. They were now disillusioned with the Peace of Campio Formio which they had signed with France in October 1797, and were beginning to suggest a new alliance against France.

The Foreign Secretary, Lord Grenville, had been negotiating with the Austrian Ambassador, Count Starhemberg, for several months. The Austrians wanted guarantees that neither side would make a separate peace with the enemy and that the British were capable of carrying on the war into 1799. They wanted a financial subsidy from Britain to cover the costs of their great army and the amount and terms of this were to provide plenty of causes for dispute between the two powers. Furthermore, the Austrians demanded that a British fleet should re-enter the Mediterranean, a point which, on the 1 April 1798, they 'pressed with peculiar earnestness'.[2]

The most immediate reason for this demand was to protect their allies and kinsmen in the Kingdom of Naples, comprising the whole of Italy south of Rome, then trembling in fear of a further French invasion. The Queen of Naples, Maria-Carolina, was a daughter of the great Austrian Empress Maria Theresa and a sister of the executed Marie-Antoinette. The system of government was akin to that of Austria, with a powerful, if dissolute, monarchy. Yet Austria, as a major land power which was new to the exercise of sea power, perhaps had exaggerated ideas of what a naval force could do. Wiser statesmen were well aware that a fleet could not stop the French marching south from Rome and the best it might achieve was to protect the other part of the kingdom, Sicily.

Grenville wrote immediately to the Prime Minister about his meeting with Starhemberg.

> I told him as to the Mediterranean Fleet that we wished it ourselves, but that no minister would ever advise sending a fleet there without a port to which a ship could look in case of accident or distress of any kind; that to use the ports of Naples or Sicily for that purpose would only bring the thing to an issue between France and Naples, possibly before Austria or Naples were prepared for it; but that, whenever those two powers expressed their readiness, the one to receive and supply our ships, the other to support this resolution, there would not probably be much difficulty in doing whatever might be found necessary to assert our naval supremacy in the Mediterranean as elsewhere.[3]

Spencer at the Admiralty was asked his views but was cautious and largely guided by St Vincent's pessimism. Asked if a fleet could be based at Naples or

Earl Spencer in 1801; an engraving after a painting by J S Copley. (National Maritime Museum, London: B2672)

Messina he replied: 'The fleet might be supplied with fresh meat, bread and wine and probably many other articles of victuals, but the salted provisions must come from home.' He refused to estimate the extra cost of such a fleet except that 'it must be very considerable'. He did not think it possible to find 70 sail of the line to share between the Channel and Mediterranean Fleets unless he could be given 6000 more men 'of which there is not the least prospect'.[4] Grenville was disappointed. 'Your letter . . . has very much spoiled all the dreams in which I was indulging myself of Austrian succour, of France driven within her ancient frontier, and of Europe saved.'[5] But the Prime Minister was less easily put off. Spencer was summoned to Downing Street on 5 April with accounts of the dispositions of ships but Pitt remained 'by no means satisfied . . . that we may not send a fleet into the Mediterranean'.[6]

The Cabinet met several times during the rest of the month and Spencer began to find himself increasingly isolated. Pitt was enthusiastic about the prospects of an alliance. The King was in favour and said so to Grenville.[7] The Foreign Secretary was keen. As the Secretary of War in charge of army operations, Dundas was always suspicious of the way in which Spencer was led by his subordinates; in January he had written to him 'Exercise your understanding and if your Board don't support your opinions and your measures, send them to sea and find others in their place.'[8] Windham, the Secretary at War (who was responsible for finance and troop

Henry Dundas in 1798, engraved after a portrait by George Romney. (National Maritime Museum, London: A4902)

movements and is not to be confused with the Secretary for War and the Colonies, in charge of military operations overseas), was also in favour of the Austrian alliance and disappointed with the slow progress. After a Cabinet meeting on 11 April he noted, 'Does not go far enough, in my opinion, in the terms on which we are willing to engage.' After the next meeting on the 18th he regretted a 'decision to take tardier course, which will not bring the fleet there till 1st of June, before which, I am afraid, the fate of the country in question will be decided.' A plan had been put forward to send a large fleet to Naples, but not for 2 months. On the possibility of advancing this Spencer remained pessimistic and wrote to Grenville on the 26th: 'I am so far from seeing any prospect of sending sooner than we talked of, that I confess I have still very great apprehension of our ability even to fulfil our present stipulation. The last accounts state the force at Brest to be in a greater state of forwardness than we had reckoned upon.'[9] Meanwhile the government had received reports of a riot in Vienna against the French ambassador, who had refused to remove the tricolour from his embassy. He was forced to leave the city. At a decisive meeting on the 28th, Pitt's government 'resolved on sending ships immediately to Mediterranean'.[10] It was a momentous and risky decision, with far-reaching consequences.

Spencer wrote to St Vincent the next day, in terms which might be considered defensive.

> You will by the present conveyance receive a letter from Nepean [the Secretary of the Admiralty] preparing you for orders to act upon a plan of operations very different from what we have hitherto adopted, and which I have no doubt will appear to be attended with a considerable degree of risk. You will easily conceive that such an instruction would not have been in contemplation if the circumstances in which we find now ourselves did not in a manner oblige us to take a measure of a more decided and hazardous complexion than we should otherwise have thought ourselves justified in taking; but when you have apprised that the appearance of a British squadron in the Mediterranean is a condition on which the fate of Europe may at this moment be stated to depend, you will not be surprised that we are disposed to strain every nerve and incur considerable hazard in effecting it.[11]

Unlike his colleagues in the Cabinet, Spencer emphasised the Toulon Armament as the reason for the change in policy and barely mentioned the prospective alliance with Austria. It was 'represented as being very extensive, and is very probably in the first instance intended for Naples'. However, still pandering to St Vincent's obsessions, Spencer pointed out that it was 'in truth more likely either for Portugal or Ireland', perhaps in the former case convoying troops to Spain where they could march to an attack on Britain's last remaining ally. But destruction of Bonaparte's expedition would not be easy. 'Unless the force which goes into the Mediterranean should chance exactly to hit upon the moment when the Armament is at sea, it will be difficult, if not impossible; but in case of finding them in port, the appearance of such a force cannot fail to check their proceedings.'[12]

St Vincent was left with a choice in one key matter – whether to take his whole fleet into the Mediterranean or to send a detachment. Spencer could see the 'great advantage which has hitherto been obtained from the constant check which you have kept on the Spanish fleet at Cadiz' and his hints that this should be kept up accorded with St Vincent's opinion of the importance of that station. If he should decide on a detachment, Spencer had little doubt about who should lead it. 'I think it almost unnecessary to suggest to you the propriety of putting it under the command of Sir H Nelson, whose acquaintance with that part of the world, as well as his activity and disposition, seem to qualify him in a peculiar manner for that service.' In this decision Spencer may or may not have been influenced by Lord Minto, the former Viceroy of Corsica. He had gone to see the First Lord on 24 April and wrote to Nelson:

> That everybody knew you as an officer and his lordship was probably apprised that you were well acquainted with the Mediterranean as he was with the room we were sitting in; but that I had had the best opportunities of knowing other points which qualified you particularly for the command in that sea; that you had proved yourself quick and sharp with the enemy where you had just cause of offence; but that on the other hand you possessed the spirit of conciliation with all friendly or neutral powers in a no less remarkable degree.

Spencer thanked Minto for the advice and commented that 'his opinion was exactly the same with mine'.[13]

★

Besides placating St Vincent, Spencer had a more material problem. Where were the ships to be found without perhaps fatally weakening some other vital sector? Spencer now had some small advantages, despite his fears about over-commitment. In 1795 the navy had been allowed some money for shipbuilding and a few new ships of the line had been ordered. Some of these were just becoming available and in the first five months of 1798, one 80-gun ship and six new 74s were launched. If men could be found to crew them, each of these could be sent to sea within a few weeks and become a real addition to the strength of the British fleet. Ships which were nearly ready were brought forward at the expense of those needing more extensive repairs. The Admiralty ordered that the *Foudroyant* should have as much of her fitting-out as possible done before her launch, so that she could get to sea more quickly. The *Belliqueux*, an old 64 launched in 1780, was to be sent to sea after minor repairs though she was not likely to last more than a year or two in that condition. To help with the urgent work in the yards, the carpenters and their crews from ships in harbour were to be sent ashore to work in the dockyards and paid at civilian rates.[14] As a result of various measures, the number of ships in first-line service began to creep up. The navy had 108 ships of the line in commission in the first three months of 1798, 111 in April and May and 113 on 1 June.

Secondly, the Dutch fleet was no longer a threat since its defeat at Camperdown in 1797 and, indeed, several captured ships were added to the British navy. This was not such an advantage as it might have been, because the ships made available were small, usually of 64 guns. Such vessels were useful in the North Sea because the Dutch rarely built bigger ships, being constrained by the shallowness of their harbours. They were outclassed by the 74, used in large numbers by the French and Spanish. However, Duncan's fleet in the North Sea was allowed to decline from

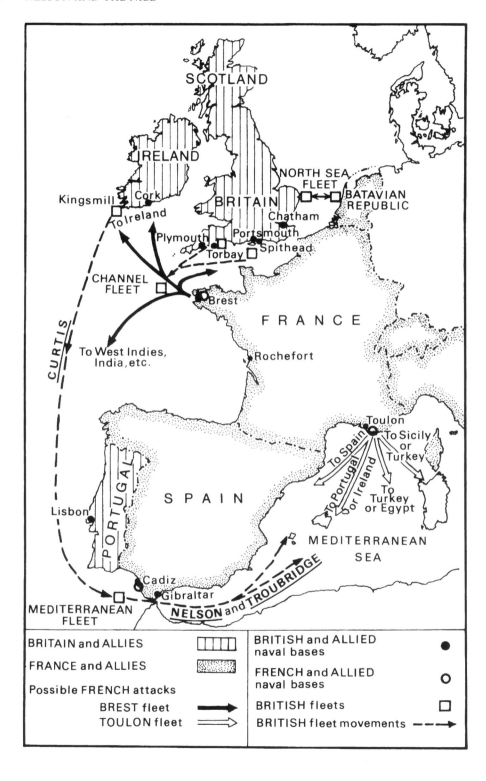

fifteen ships to eleven, freeing men for service elsewhere.[15]

New ships were useless unless they could be manned with a proportion of experienced seamen. The government had already scraped the bottom of the barrel of naval manning by the Quota Acts of 1795 and had been thoroughly frightened by the great mutinies of 1797 which appeared to result from them. The same number of men (120,000) was voted by Parliament in 1798 as in 1797, but it was mainly a question of finding them, to replace men lost by death or desertion. Ships in home waters were stripped to meet new commitments overseas and desperate measures were needed to replace the men. On the 25 and 26 May 1798, while Nelson was completing his repairs at San Pietro in Sardinia, an act was rushed through Parliament suspending for 5 months all the protections from the press gang which had been granted to seamen in coastal and river trades.[16] Even the vital coal trade to London had its protections withdrawn for a month. Again it was a desperate, short-term measure; merchant shipping could not be squeezed any more without real danger to the country's commercial and military interests.

Looking at the world strategic chessboard, the Admiralty began to consider ways of moving more ships to the Mediterranean without leaving gaps elsewhere. It would take several months to recall ships from the overseas fleets, so three of the line remained in the East Indies, six at the Cape of Good Hope, seven at Jamaica, four in the Leeward Islands and two off Nova Scotia.[17] As always the main French fleet was based at Brest. From there it could move out to attack distant colonies or up the Channel to support an invasion of England. The British Channel Fleet under Lord Bridport had the task of countering this. For decades the main strategic debate had centred on the question of whether to use close or distant blockade of Brest. In the Seven Years War, George Anson had kept a strong fleet bottling the French up. The advantages were obvious but it was expensive and needed a fleet which was clearly superior in numbers or quality to the enemy. Perhaps a third or a quarter of the fleet would be away at any given moment for repair and replenishment, so the blockading squadron needed that margin of superiority. Furthermore, Brest was a much more difficult station than Cadiz. Far from waiting at anchor off the port, the British had to spend their time patrolling back and forth on a hazardous oceanic coastline, negotiating strong tides and difficult currents, dangerous rocks and Atlantic gales. This bred skills and hardihood among the officers and men, but even so they often had to return to the bases in southern England during winter storms.

Blockade had proved impossible during the American War because of British numerical inferiority against France and Spain. When war with France recommenced in 1793, Lord Howe had favoured distant or 'open' blockade. The main fleet would remain at anchor at Spithead or Torbay in southern England while frigates would watch out for the French. If they sailed for India, the West Indies or the Mediterranean there was time to catch up with them, or at least to disrupt a landing at their destination. If they sailed to support a cross-Channel invasion in the

◀ Possible French movements from Toulon and Brest, showing British fleet movements designed to counteract them.

Straits of Dover, the Channel Fleet was there to block them, or cut them off.

The weakest point in this system was Ireland, which could be reached from Brest before a fleet at Spithead or Torbay could react. The majority Catholic population had many causes of grievance, including poverty and religious repression. Even the Protestants of the north were dissatisfied, for they had few real political rights. In March 1798 the government attempted to forestall a rebellion by arresting the leaders of the United Irishmen and it discovered ample evidence that a revolt was planned. With material support from France this would become far more dangerous to British interests. No great French force might be needed in Ireland, just supplies of guns and ammunition for rebels plus a hard core of seasoned troops. A successful French invasion of Ireland would be more than just a blow to British confidence and prestige. A new French privateer campaign could be launched against the great ports of Bristol, Liverpool and the Clyde. New invasion routes might be opened up in northern England or southern Scotland, close to the new industrial centres of the United Kingdom. Britain would be surrounded and isolated and far more vulnerable.

A special force was therefore needed in the south of Ireland, based at Cork. Vice-Admiral Robert Kingsmill commanded a squadron which included four ships of the line. As reports of Irish rebellion began to intensify at the Admiralty, this was given priority for expansion and was increased when Rear-Admiral Roger Curtis, with his force of four ships of the line and a frigate, was ordered to go to Cork instead of Brest and to make as much show as possible. According to Kingsmill's orders, 'as the appearance of the said squadron off the coast of Ireland under an impression of its being likely to continue there some time may in the present state of affairs be productive of the most beneficial consequences, to recommend it to you not to let the time of its probable continuance on the coast be known.'[18]

By the middle of April the Admiralty had intelligence that a French expedition to Ireland was expected soon, and Curtis was to continue there another 2 weeks. But the Armament at Toulon was still high on the Admiralty's agenda and Curtis's squadron might hold the key. If the blockade of Brest was tightened so that the French could be stopped outside that port, rather than on the coasts of Ireland, then the Irish squadron could be reduced to a patrol force of frigates and sloops. Bridport was ordered to 'exert the utmost diligence in preventing the sailing of the enemy's fleet from Brest and there furnishing the rebels from thence [Ireland] with any supplies'. He was to keep a force of frigates as close to Brest as possible.[19] Under orders from the Admiralty, Bridport would move far nearer to the system of close blockade during the summer of 1798, keeping a force of at least ten ships of the line off the port when the weather allowed. His flagship, the *Royal George*, would spend up to 11 weeks continually at sea, alternating with the second-in-command, Sir Alan Gardner. Thus Curtis's force of eight ships of the line could be sent to meet St Vincent and the latter could be ordered to detach a substantial force to join Nelson in the Mediterranean.

In Spencer's private letter of 29 April the size of the Mediterranean force was left to St Vincent. It was to be 'sufficiently strong' to 'the defeat of the purpose (whatever it may be) of the Toulon Armament' but to allow the remaining ships to keep up the blockade of Cadiz.[20] However, the formal orders of 19 May were much more explicit about the numbers. 'Having been joined by the Rear Admiral [Curtis] and the ships above mentioned, your lordship is to lose no time in detaching from your fleet a squadron consisting of twelve sail of the line and a competent number of frigates under the command of some discreet flag officer.'[21]

How was the size of this force decided? Lord Minto's letter of 25 April mentions just this figure. 'Twelve sail of the line I understand are thought of for this squadron; but I have not this from Lord Spencer.'[22] It was probably based on some calculations that St Vincent and Spencer had made at the beginning of April. The Venetian navy was rightly discounted, being only six ships of the line, 'three of which are very bad indeed'. The French were reckoned to be able to muster six ships of the line of their own at Corfu 'ready for sea and weakly manned'. They also had three more ships at Toulon, with one or two more getting ready but with 'little prospect of their being able to equip more than ten sail of the line in the whole'.[23]

Thus Nelson would be given a force of twelve ships of the line (after Saumarez's *Orion* had been sent home) and several frigates, more than enough to defeat any likely French force, according to Spencer's calculation. On 26 April however, he was stunned by reports that the French had up to seventeen ships available. 'If the force there is really what the last accounts from Turin describe it, our detachment to the Mediterranean will be of no avail; for the whole of that plan proceeded on the supposition of their not having more than about ten sail of the line effective.'[24] Presumably he was reassured in cabinet before issuing the orders on 19 May, but in fact the French had thirteen ships of the line at sea, some larger than any of the British ones.

On 2 May the Admiralty issued new orders to Kingsmill, Curtis, and St Vincent. Kingsmill was informed that he would lose the services of Curtis and his squadron, and would have to do his best with frigates and sloops. Curtis was ordered to take eight ships of the line, a frigate and a fireship 60 miles south from Cape Clear and there open his sealed orders, which in turn would order him to join St Vincent off Cadiz. St Vincent was to take this force under his command, but he was to send twelve ships on into the Mediterranean immediately.

In effect the Admiralty was adopting a more aggressive policy on several fronts: a much more continuous blockade of Brest and a squadron, if not a fleet, in the Mediterranean. The new strategy had originated with politicians rather than naval officers, though aggressive commanders such as Nelson were brought to the fore as a result of it. The immediate reason was the hope of an Austrian alliance combined with fear of Bonaparte's expedition. Beyond that, it was a symptom of increasing confidence in government circles. At Cape St Vincent and Camperdown the British fleet had shown that numerical disadvantage did not necessarily prevent victory. The worst of the naval mutinies were over and there was to be no repetition of such events on the scale of Spithead and the Nore. In Ireland several potential leaders of the threatened rebellion had been arrested and when it actually broke out it proved to be less dangerous than it might have been. At home the threat of the radicals

Thomas Troubridge. A portrait showing him after his promotion to rear-admiral in 1804, by Sir Thomas Beechey. (National Maritime Museum, London: BHC3168)

was decreasing. The excesses of the French Revolution made it seem less and less attractive to them as an example, while repression was taking its toll of the radical leaders in Britain. The government had no cause for complacency in any field or front but it had some reason to hope for the best.

Curtis sailed on 9 May. St Vincent's orders were sent out with him, with a duplicate sent on 2 May by fast lugger, being received on the 19th. St Vincent had already gone some way towards providing such a Mediterranean force, by sending three ships of the line under Nelson, who was 'discrete' as defined as 'separate, detached from the others, distinct'.[25] He also had a competent force of frigates, though St Vincent was not to know that he would soon lose contact with them; in any case he had no spare ones to send.

It is not likely that St Vincent ever seriously considered taking his whole fleet into the Mediterranean, for that was very far from his inclinations. Nor was there any question of sending Curtis's force on the Mediterranean. Curtis was senior to Nelson but was much less distinguished and had never shown any particular promise. His ships had been hurriedly sent out from home waters and did not have the full range of stores needed for long-term service so far from the dockyards. Despite his exhaustion, St Vincent wasted no time in selecting the ships to join Nelson: those of the inshore squadron under Captain Sir Thomas Troubridge. They were all 74s and no three-decker was included, perhaps because such a ship would slow the squadron down in any chase of the French. Furthermore, Nelson would probably feel obliged to use it as his flagship, wasting more time in transferring his goods and staff from one ship to another. One captain who was not chosen to go was Cuthbert Collingwood of the *Excellent*, an old friend who had backed Nelson up at the Battle of Cape St Vincent. This annoyed Collingwood, who was already aggrieved with the Commander-in-Chief. St Vincent, he wrote, had caused him 'great mortification', for he 'knew our friendship; for many, many years we had served together, lived together and all that every happened to us strengthened the bond of our amity.'[26]

On 22 May the small brig *Mutine*, commanded by Thomas Hardy, left St Vincent's fleet to take dispatches to Nelson off Toulon and inform him of the change of plan. Troubridge's ships were allowed to complete their stores by taking them from other vessels and then they were collected together. Thus on the afternoon of 24 May, as Curtis's eight ships were sighted from the masthead of the flagship, St Vincent hoisted the signal for the detached squadron to weigh anchor. By 9pm they were under weigh, more than 12 hours before their replacements were at anchor off Cadiz.[27]

Although St Vincent was thus giving Nelson a powerful force, it was not a fleet in the fullest sense of the term. When St Vincent's fleet had been active in the Mediterranean in September 1796, it had blockaded the ports of Toulon and Cadiz, escorted convoys throughout the area, sent ships to conduct diplomatic negotiations with Algiers, defended naval bases at Corsica and Elba, sent dispatches home and to ambassadors and other fleets and attempted to give support to Austria, Britain's main ally at the time.[28] In contrast, Nelson's detachment was to have a single role, to find and destroy the Toulon Armament. In modern terms, it was a task-force rather than a fleet. In this sense, both Spencer and St Vincent had tended to modify the intentions of the Cabinet on 28 April. The alliance with Austria demanded a permanent force, perhaps headed by a senior admiral with a large staff in a three-decker flagship, supported by supply vessels and maintained by a shore organisation. But Nelson had no supply organisation at all and could not be expected to remain in the Mediterranean for more than about 3 months.

★

Meanwhile in London, speculation continued about the destination of the French and eyes were turning increasingly to the east. At the beginning of May, reports from Genoa suggested that the French were buying up '4,000 casks of a very large size with ten iron hoops each, without any bung holes'. These, it was suggested, might be lashed to the sides of ships to raise them in shallow waters. Spencer suggested that they could be used to take Bonaparte's fleet through the Dardanelles, in an operation directed against Turkey or Russia or both.[29] Meanwhile the Foreign Secretary received intelligence reports that the ships at Toulon were embarking printing machines, scientific instruments and great quantities of books on voyages to Egypt, Persia, India, Turkey, the Black Sea and the Caspian. The writer, the Intendant of Mines in France, conjectured that Egypt was their target and that they might try to cut across Suez and move towards India, or that they might try to cross Persia.[30]

On 9 June Dundas's mind began to turn towards Egypt and India, perhaps inspired by a letter of 25 April, from a former Chief Engineer of Bengal, who had visited Egypt and wrote to him:

> I have long foreseen that so soon as the French government could disengage itself from its more pressing European concerns, their views would be directed to the possession of Egypt, not only as a great and important national object to France, but one which, at the same time that it gratified the vanity of the people, would afford the means of providing for a large body of those officers and soldiers whose return to their own country is so much dreaded; and whilst it opened to their ambition the rich spoils of India, held out to them the glory of driving from India their rivals, who alone dared prescribe bounds to their rapine and insatiable ambition.[31]

Dundas wrote to Spencer: 'Did the instructions to Lord St Vincent mention that Egypt might be in the contemplation of Bonaparte's expedition? It may be whimsical, but I cannot help having a fancy of my own on that subject.'[32] He lay awake all night worrying about it, for as a long-standing member of the East India Board of Control he had a direct interest. The fate of the empire might turn upon this expedition and he urged Spencer to find a force to send to the Red Sea, to block the French should they succeed in Egypt. 'A small active squadron at the mouth of the Red Sea is fatal to their project. That squadron coming an hour too late is good for nothing. It is *impossible* that any other service can be equally pressing.'[33]

This was taken seriously at the Admiralty and by the middle of June experts were being consulted about the navigation of the Red Sea. They were asked what was the shortest possible time for a frigate or a sloop of war to get there and answered that it would take at least 3 months at that time of year. Dr Marsden, the orientalist, reported that ships from Bombay could get there in an average of 18 days but that it might take as long as 66, or as little as 13. However, it was agreed 'the navigation of the Red Sea is attended with no difficulty at a proper season'.[34] A force of small ships could therefore be effective there if it could be got round in time. Bonaparte would not be able to take his great ships across the isthmus so he would have to rely on what transports he could find locally and any French warships from their bases in the Indian Ocean. A group of frigates and sloops could play havoc with such forces, so orders were sent to Commodore John Blankett, already on his way to India in the 50-gun ship *Leopard*, to take charge of a small squadron in the Red Sea. According to Windham there was 'fear that Blankett will be too late and not in force sufficient. Reports from the officers of the [French] frigate lately taken that light transports had been sent to Europe, to the Mauritius and thence with some other force ordered to the Red Sea. Thinks that the expedition from Toulon will very possibly go on, Bonaparte succeeding or not in giving Nelson the slip.'[35]

But there was still no certainty that the French had gone to Egypt. At the end of July another rumour in Dundas's circle suggested that they were mainly interested in material gains.

> Your friend Mr Gilpin thinks, however, that Bonaparte is not bound for Alexandria but Constantinople and this is the opinion of the best informed circles in Paris, founded on the

knowledge they have of the character of the government, who seek for plunder wherever it is to be found . . . The robbery of all the factories in the Levant and the spoils of the Porte will be a considerable object to them.[36]

★

Alone as she had been for most of the last 5 years, Lady Nelson made the best of Nelson's friends and family. She interrogated the servants about Nelson's missing clothing and towels and claimed, quite accurately as it turned out, that everything was there in Nelson's trunks, if he looked for them. 'Another time I will take more care and hope we shall have proper servants. Can't Allen find the keys in his trunk?' She sympathised with her husband's difficulties – in Bath her own servants consisted of 'An old Catholic cook near 60 years of age, a girl of fourteen and Will'.

She departed from Bath on 3 May, as Nelson left St Vincent's fleet. She spent 2 weeks in Kentish Town, just north of London, and went to the Royal Academy as part of a 'strong party', though she was already aware that her husband's portrait by Lemuel Abbot was not on display there. On 20 May, while her husband was battling with storms off Toulon, she arrived at their new home at Round Wood, near Ipswich, consisting of 'a small hall, 2 genteel parlours, a dressing room, kitchen, back kitchen, dairy, cellar, 3 wine vaults, 4 good bedchambers, 2 dressing rooms and 2 servants' chambers; also a large barn, stables, cow-house and other offices'[37] and wrote 'the satisfaction I felt was very great in being under your own roof'. A large part of her life was devoted to getting the property in order. She found the

Lady Nelson just after the Battle of the Nile, by Daniel Orme. (National Maritime Museum, London: A94)

water supply in reasonable condition but planned some alterations to the house. 'A closet taken down in the eating parlour to admit a sideboard and a window in the damp dressing room thrown out to the east . . . are the only expenses which are necessary besides the fixtures until I have the happiness of seeing you.' She found the house needed more furniture than could be expected for such a small dwelling but she had succeeded in eliminating damp and making the walls dry.

She saw a great deal of the new Mrs Berry, who came from Norwich. They went to races and balls together and Lady Nelson found her companion 'a very pleasant young woman. Not in the least gay.' The balls were 'well attended by the county families. Lord and Lady Broom, Lord and Lady Rouse, the Rowleys, Sir Harry and Lady Parker. Admiral Reeve introduced them to me. I found Lady P a very proud woman and Sir H a very great man'. These were families which could afford to 'drive four horses and still live in great style'. But she did not find herself completely accepted. 'The Middletons are the only country family who have been attentive. Admiral Reeve told me country families always wished to know how long newcomers intended staying before they made any advances to be acquainted.' She did better with the naval families in the area. Vice-Admiral Samuel Reeve gave her 'a handsome dinner, two courses, everything in season. He requested I would do him the honour of going to the promenade, which I consented to, provided it was not in the fields. It was a weekly meeting in the Assembly Rooms . . . I stayed till 10 o'clock, having had quite enough for my shilling.'

Lady Nelson was far from her husband's war but its effects could be felt nearer home. Before she left Bath there were reports that St Vincent had been in action again. 'One day he was beat, the next day he had taken twelve sail of the line.' She had letters from Nelson's father who lamented the bad morals caused by military camps about the country. 'The general indecorum besides pillage the constant attendant of large encampments with many other inconveniences.' But Lady Nelson had no trouble. 'The military does not incommode us. We often see them exercising their horses on the Woodbridge Road, and that is all we can say of them.' In the middle of June a fleet of merchantmen becalmed off the Suffolk coast was mistaken for the French and the local troops were put in readiness. Early in July she read newspaper reports that Malta was in the possession of the French, and that the Maltese had risen up against them. When asked where her husband was she answered that she did not know but the newspapers said he had gone into the Mediterranean. She continued to worry and felt 'extreme anxiety . . . no one period of the war have I felt more than I do at this moment.'

Her love for her husband was sincere enough but not demonstrative or passionate. She tended to sign off with phrases such as 'Love attend you,' 'Believe me your faithful wife' or 'God bless you my dear husband'. Her letters to Nelson were long, detailed and domestic, but were not received until long after the issues were resolved in the Mediterranean. Perhaps this was fortunate, for Nelson was completely obsessed with finding the French and had no interest in domestic matters. Lady Nelson for her part had little understanding of her husband's life at sea. She hoped he was getting an adequate supply of newspapers to inform him of world events. When she finally received news of the storm of 20 May (nearly 4 months later) she commented characteristically, 'What a storm. On that very Sunday May the 20th it blew a storm at Ipswich'.[38]

★

When St Vincent gave Nelson the job as commander of the Mediterranean squadron, he caused a bitter controversy among his senior officers. Sir John Orde, the third in command, was also a rear-admiral, but several years senior to Nelson. He was incensed at being passed over and wrote to St Vincent,

> Sir Horatio Nelson, a junior officer and just arrived from England, is detached from the fleet in which we serve up the Mediterranean with the command of twelve sail of the line . . . I must not say I am surprised at these measures, although very different from what I had hoped to have experienced; but I cannot conceal from your lordship how much I feel hurt . . .[39]

After that relations between St Vincent and Orde could only get worse. When a boat from Orde's flagship was captured on patrol off Cadiz, St Vincent issued an order that a 'lieutenant of approved firmness' should be put in charge of each boat. When St Vincent inspected Orde's ship and found some slackness among the marines, Orde took this as an affront to his authority. When there was a misunderstanding and Orde was wrongly accused of sending a letter of complaint to St Vincent, relations worsened. Orde was supported, among others, by Captain Collingwood, who complained of St Vincent whose 'impetuous conduct towards several others on trifling occasions, shut the door to the few comforts that were to be found there.'[40] Finally St Vincent resolved to exceed his powers and send Orde home. This he believed had a 'wonderful effect' on the squadron but he was rebuked by the Admiralty. Orde's request for a court martial on St Vincent was refused but he remained obsessed with the incident, though maintaining 'the difference with Lord St Vincent did not originate in Admiral Nelson's appointment as has in various ways been falsely reported, nor had they the smallest connection with each other.'[41] Orde challenged the admiral to a duel in the following year, after both had returned to England. St Vincent failed to turn up and Orde was arrested and held in custody until he gave a surety of £2000 to keep the peace.

★

As Troubridge sailed from St Vincent's fleet on 24 May, he had nine sail of the line and the cutter *Earl of St Vincent* under his command. At Gibraltar he sent his boat ashore, expecting to find his remaining 74, the *Audacious*, and the *Leander* of 50 guns. To his fury the ships were still in Tangier, across the Strait, taking in stores. He sent the cutter out to find them and was equally surprised to find that Hardy's *Mutine* had failed to make any progress in taking dispatches to Nelson. She had been delayed by unfavourable winds and had then chased a French privateer and run her ashore. Troubridge lectured Hardy that 'he will have to account to you [St Vincent] for the delay.'[42] It was 5am on the 27th before the missing ships were found and the fleet was able to head north-east into the Mediterranean.

Troubridge sent the *Earl of St Vincent* away because her mast was in bad condition and, in his erratic handwriting, complained of the dockyard workers who had repaired her: 'I really think these people ought not to be paid for the time they idle away.'[43] He now had a fleet of ten 74-gun ships of the line plus the *Leander* and the *Mutine*. He decided to pass outside the Spanish islands of Majorca, Minora and Ibiza, sending the *Mutine* to the westward of them in order to have the best chance of finding Nelson, should he have been forced to return. She was also to look into Cartagena and report on Spanish preparations there.

On 2 June, off Barcelona, Hardy sighted the frigate *Alcmene*, Captain George Hope, which had been in contact with the ships that had parted from Nelson in the storm of 20 May. They remained in company for 2 hours and Hope told Hardy what he knew of the damage to Nelson's ships, especially the *Vanguard*. Hope believed that Nelson must now return to a dockyard for repairs. Hardy knew he had not gone to Gibraltar, unless he was travelling outside the islands, where he would meet Troubridge. He decided to press on to Toulon with the *Mutine*, while Hope implemented his own plans for finding the missing squadron.[44] Thus it was the *Mutine* which sighted the *Vanguard* and her two companions off Toulon on 5 June and Hardy was soon on board the flagship.

CHAPTER 7

'A Match for any Hostile Fleet'

IT TOOK SEVERAL DAYS to get Nelson's new squadron together. On the morning of 7 June the *Alexander* and *Orion* chased two suspicious vessels, leaving the *Vanguard* and *Mutine* to await the reinforcements. The *Orion* captured her chase, which proved to be 'a Spanish vessel from Genoa, not very valuable'.[1] She found herself alone with the prize and Saumarez experienced 'deep distress' at finding himself parted, 'knowing how important and very material it was for the good of the service we were upon that the squadron should not be separated'.[2] The *Alexander* caught up with her prize at 7am on the 8th and boarded her; she too was Spanish, and more valuable than the *Orion*'s prize, though neither ship provided worthwhile information.

At 1.10pm on the 7th, soon after the *Alexander* and *Orion* had parted company, the lookout at the masthead of the *Vanguard* sighted the topsails of Troubridge's squadron. Nelson wrote that he:

> . . . discovered a strange fleet, E by N, which I supposed to be the squadron under Captain Troubridge. After I made the private signal, I observed it was answered by the *Culloden* showing her distinguishing pennants, by which I was satisfied the ships in sight were the squadron sent to join me. 30 minutes past 6, the undermentioned ships having joined me, I hove to the fleet.[3]

The masts were braced round so that the effect of the sails on the main masts cancelled those on the fore and mizzen masts and the ships were stationary in the water. Boats were lowered so that Nelson could communicate with Troubridge, and the other ships awaited the arrival of the missing *Alexander* and *Orion*.

Nelson sent the *Leander* and *Mutine* north to find them. They sighted the *Orion* during the afternoon of the 8th. The latter ship cleared for action on 'finding the strange vessel not to be the admiral',[4] but private signals were exchanged and Saumarez was relieved of 'the most acute anxiety I have ever suffered' at being separated from the fleet.[5] Saumarez decided that his Spanish prize was too big to be manned from his crew. Having taken eight Swiss volunteers on board the *Orion* and enlisted them as marines, he allowed it to be ransomed for 10,000 Spanish dollars. It was a poor bargain, for Saumarez commented 'no captured vessel ever gave so much uneasiness as she has caused me and I have often wished we had never seen her, even had she been worth a million of money.'[6] Soon afterwards he heard the signal guns of Nelson's fleet in the distance and fired one gun in reply. As dawn broke on the morning of the 9th he rejoined the admiral.[7] Meanwhile the *Leander* and *Mutine* had found the *Alexander* and she too was in sight of the fleet by midday. The force was fully united by the morning of Sunday the 10th and the ships held divine service as required by Admiralty regulations, no doubt with an extra feeling of thanksgiving.

★

In many ways Nelson's fleet was a very effective one. The officers and men were hardened by 5 years of war and morale was high among the captains and officers. His force of thirteen 74-gun ships was perhaps the most efficient that could have been found for such a service. The 74 combined the advantages of speed and gun power as no other ship did.

> The 74-gun ship . . . contains the properties of the First Rate and the frigate. She will not shrink from an encounter with a First Rate, nor abandon the chase of a frigate on account of swiftness. The union of these qualities has therefore, with justice, made the 74-gun ship the principal object of maritime attention, and given her so distinguished a pre-eminence in our line of battle.[8]

Normally a squadron of this size would have had a three-decker of 98 or more guns, such as the *Victory*, as a flagship. This would have given more gun power, an imposing vessel to impress friend and enemy alike, and an extra deck to accommodate the admiral and his staff. But Nelson's squadron had been formed with speed in

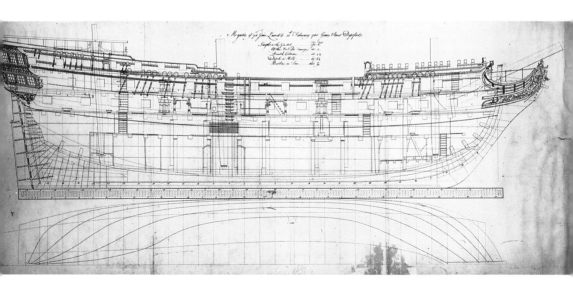

Profile of the *Majestic*, drawn at Deptford in 1785 as the ship was completed. (National Maritime Museum, London: 813A)

mind, for pursuing the French. Even the *Victory*, one of the best of the three-deckers in service, was generally about a knot slower than a typical 74 in any wind condition.[9] Furthermore a three-decker had higher sides and would make more leeway in strong winds.[10]

All his ships except the *Leander* and *Mutine* were, in the most important respects, identical to the *Vanguard*. The *Audacious*, *Bellerophon*, *Defence*, *Goliath* and *Zealous* had indeed been built to the same plans, drawn by Sir Thomas Slade. Two others, the *Swiftsure* and *Theseus*, had been built to slightly different designs by Slade. Two more, the *Majestic* and *Orion*, had been built to the plans of Slade's contemporary William Bateley. Only the *Alexander* had been designed by his successor, Sir John Williams, and only the *Culloden* by the current Surveyor of the Navy, Sir Edward Hunt. Despite the high reputation of French prizes among naval officers none of the ships were French-built, though the *Minotaur* was one of six ships in the navy copied from the French *Courageux*, built in 1753 and captured in 1761. All were 168 to 170ft long on the gundeck except the *Minotaur* which was slightly larger at 172ft 3in. The larger type of 74-gun ship was fashionable with the Admiralty in London at this time but the products of their new policy had not yet reached the fleet. Six of the ships had been built in the Royal Dockyards, the other seven in private yards – a fairly typical proportion for the time.

Superficially their hulls had some variety in their figureheads and carvings, and each captain had considerable control over the way in which the ship was painted. Five of the 74s had plain yellow sides with the wales in black. Another six, including the *Vanguard*, had a thick black line painted between the rows of gunports, while *Theseus* had her hammock cloths above the deck painted yellow, to give the impression that she was a three-decker. The *Culloden* had another variation, with two narrow stripes between the gunports instead of one broad one. The *Zealous* and *Minotaur* were gaudier, with red sides. The former had a small yellow stripe and the latter a thick black one between the gunports.

There were slight differences in their sailing qualities, because the underwater hull lines were different for each class. The *Alexander* and a sister ship had been heavily criticised when first built: 'Neither the *Alexander* or *Alfred* promise to be good ships; they neither sail nor carry sail . . . she [the *Alfred*] carries a lee helm and often misses stays.'[11] The *Orion*, one of the best sailers, could make 9 knots 'in a topgallant gale', a breeze in which only the royal sails, at the top of each mast, were not set. If she had to be reduced to reefed topsails she could still make 6 or 7 knots.[12] Most ships could make 11 or 12 knots in ideal conditions, with a strong beam wind which had not yet built up a heavy sea, but such perfection was rare. Despite the comments of the captains, there were only minor differences in the sailing qualities of the 74-gun ships in the squadron.

The two other ships, the *Leander* and *Mutine*, were odd vessels in any fleet of the 1790s. The *Leander* was a two-decker of 50 guns, a direct descendant of a type which had been popular a century earlier, when it was believed that they could serve in the line of battle, or as cruising frigates when needed. In fact they did neither job well but survived in large numbers until the middle of the eighteenth century, when the 'true frigate' evolved. The two-decker 50, however, revived in the early stages of the American War, before the French and Spanish had joined in the struggle. At that time British sea power was spread very thinly along the whole of the east coast of North America and the type proved very useful as flagships for small squadrons of frigates. The *Leander* had been ordered during that period, in 1777, and completed in 1780. The 50-gun ship was cheaper to build and man than the 74 – the hull of the *Leander* cost £20,731 compared with about £36,000 for an average 74, and she needed only 350 men compared with 590. In every other respect the advantages were with the larger ship. The *Leander* had only 24-pounders on her lower deck, the 74 had 32-pounders. The sides of a 50 were too thin to stand up against the guns of a line of battle ship. Her sailing qualities were poor, because her height was similar to that of a 74 but she was 22ft shorter, and therefore poorly proportioned. Nonetheless the *Leander* was considered good for a ship of this type. One of her captains offered faint praise: 'Never had any trial with good sailing ships but she appears in general . . . fast compared other ships of her description.'[13]

The *Mutine* had been captured from the French at Tenerife in the previous summer. She was a brig, in that she had only two masts instead of three, and was rated as a sloop, smaller even than a Sixth Rate. At 349 tons, she was about a fifth the size of a typical 74-gun ship, and was armed only with 6-pounder guns. She sailed well in light winds but was vulnerable in heavy weather, because of her small size and because her gunports were close to the waterline. She could carry out some of the duties of a frigate but she would have to flee from an enemy reconnaissance screen and so was not likely to get a good view of the French fleet. Her shallow draft was useful, however, for she could be sent into ports or shallow water where the others could not go.

★

Nelson seems to have taken a more direct part in the sailing of the *Vanguard* in the weeks after the storm, as the use of 'I' in the log indicates. This added yet more to his responsibilities, and was perhaps encouraged by the configuration of the ship. In a three-decker like the *Victory* the admiral lived aft on the upper deck while the captain was above him on the quarterdeck, close to the position where the ship was controlled. On a two-decker like the *Vanguard* there was no admiral's cabin as such, so Nelson took over the captain's accommodation, displacing Berry to the wardroom where two lieutenants' cabins would have been knocked together to accommodate him. Berry had no grounds for complaint. By the normal rules of seniority he would perhaps have commanded a 28-gun frigate, and was very lucky to be in a 74 at all. Nelson, however, was now living in the quarterdeck accommodation. His sleeping cabin would have been in the forward part, leaving the great cabin with its range of windows free for work, eating and entertaining. At night there would only be a thin wooden partition between him and the steering wheel. He would hear the shouted orders of the officer of the watch, the warnings of the lookouts, and be instantly aware of any crisis in the sailing of the ship. It is not surprising that he got little sleep at crucial stages in the campaign.

Aboard the ships, daily life and work continued as usual. Each captain had control of the 'internal economy' of his command, within the limits set by the Admiralty Regulations. Many wrote detailed orders for their officers and crew, but the only set which is known to have survived from the Nile campaign was that produced by Captain Davidge Gould of the *Audacious*.[14] The captain might vary the exact routine, having meals at slightly different times for example, but each ship followed a broadly similar pattern. Typically, the day began at 7 or 7.30am, when the boatswain's mates roused the sleeping men from their hammocks with cries and often blows. The hammocks were rolled up and lashed with the bedding inside and taken on deck where they were stowed in the hammock rails round the sides of the deck. Breakfast was at 8am. A few lookouts and helmsmen were left on duty while the rest of the men sat at mess tables between the guns, often with companions of their own choice. As with all meals it was one of the high points of the seamen's day, when friends might gather together and discipline was relaxed. After that all the men were on duty until noon, perhaps washing the decks, carrying out maintenance on the rigging or hull, or exercising with the sails or guns. There was some controversy among officers about how often the decks should be washed – too often might contribute to rheumatism among the crew. The lower deck of the *Vanguard* was washed twice a week and the odd corners of the orlop deck below the waterline were fumigated three times a week.[15]

From day to day the captains recorded some of the maintenance work and training carried out. 'Got up the best bower cable and washed its place with vinegar. Cleared out the gunner's store room . . . Employed clearing boatswain's stores . . . Washed lower deck . . . Gunners fitting new slings for main yard.' 'People making points and gaskets' on the *Vanguard*.[16] 'Great guns and small arms' were exercised regularly, though in the case of the former, mainly without actually firing them. The crews loaded and unloaded, set the sights and hauled the guns in and out through the gunports. The fleet was constantly in expectation of meeting the enemy and Berry commented, 'the decks of all the ships were kept perfectly clear night and day and every man was ready to start at his post at a moment's notice'.[17]

Noon was important for the officers because a sight of the sun had to be taken when possible, to help in fixing the position of the ship. Then the hands were piped to dinner, the main meal of the day. At least an hour was allowed, perhaps more. Care was taken not to interrupt this, except in case of absolute necessity. Alcohol was issued to the men in large quantities, usually in the form of wine or brandy in the Mediterranean.

In a few ships the men were divided into three watches, but most had only two, the starboard and larboard, so that at sea most of the crew would operate a routine of 4 hours on, 4 hours off, interrupted only by the dog-watches between four and eight in the afternoon which were only 2 hours each. During the night watches, only a few men were needed at any given moment. The rest stood by, to be called if sail needed to be taken in, the yards trimmed or any other work done. They could rest, but on most ships they were not allowed to sleep. If it was necessary to tack or

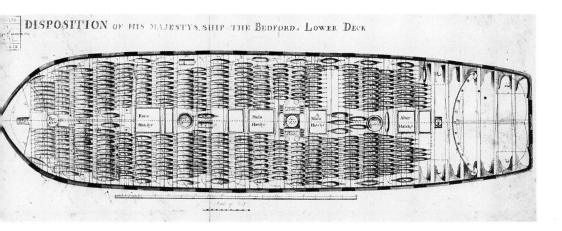

DISPOSITION OF HIS MAJESTY'S SHIP THE BEDFORD, LOWER DECK

The hammocks of the 74-gun ship *Bedford*, probably in the late 1790s. The last four rows, to the right, are shown in red instead of blue in the original and are for the marines. The space aft of them is useless for hammocks because of the rudder, but the dotted outlines of some of the officers cabins can be seen. (National Maritime Museum, London: 6579/67)

to take down sail on the onset of a storm then the other watch and perhaps the idlers would have to be called.

Below decks at night, conditions were less than comfortable. The bulk of the crew, about 500 men, lived in a space about 150ft long and 50ft broad, interrupted by guns, masts, capstans and other obstacles. The official allowance of space for each hammock was 14in, though petty officers were allowed up to 28in. The First Lieutenant took care that the men of the different watches were interspersed in the hammock bill, so that at sea each man at least had enough space to move. The hammocks were hung up for less than 12 hours each night, between 8pm and about 7.30am. With luck one watch might get nearly 7 hours of sleep, albeit interrupted. The other would only be allowed the 4 hours, so the seamen suffered from a regular lack of sleep during a long voyage. The *Vanguard* was one of the few ships to operate a three-watch system, which meant that seamen had the luxury of almost 8 hours in their hammocks every night, uninterrupted in two nights out of three.[18] Most captains had a prejudice against three watches, and there is a suspicion that had more men been on deck when the storm struck the *Vanguard*, less damage would have been done.

There was a little variety in the daily routine. Four days a week the men were served either beef or pork, boiled by the ship's cook and issued to the messes. On Mondays, Wednesdays and Fridays there was no meat issue but the men had oatmeal, butter and cheese instead, while stocks from home lasted. In the Mediterranean local produce had to be used, such as the poultry that were bought at San Pietro. 'Bread' or ship's biscuit was standard issue every day. Divine service was held on Sunday mornings, conducted by the Captain if the ship had no chaplain. The Articles of War were read to the crews monthly, promising that offenders against eight of its clauses 'shall suffer death', with the capital punishment as an option for eleven more. Two days, Monday and Friday in the case of the *Audacious,* were normally set aside for washing clothes, and they were inspected by divisional officers on a Saturday. There was no naval uniform except for officers and marines, but on a long voyage the crew would eventually be obliged to buy 'slops' from the purser, and without contact with the shore they would take on a certain uniformity of appearance. Seamen's clothes, consisting of loose trousers, checked shirt and short jacket, contrasted with the tight breeches, white shirt and long coat of the landsman. Captain Gould, like most captains, set minimum standards for his men and decreed that each should have a blue jacket, a waistcoat or undergarment (preferably white), a pair of shoes and a Dutch cap or round hat marked with his name and available to be worn for inspection.[19] The seamen could often make his own clothes and specific days (make and mend) were set aside for that.

★

Nelson was sailing away from a fleet which was in a state of some turmoil. The old paternalistic navy of the middle of the century was in decline and a new one, harsher and more class-conscious, had taken its place. As a leading modern historian has written, 'it is clear that the service that had suffered the mutinies of 1797 must have been very different from that of forty years before.'[20] It was only a year since the great fleet mutinies at Spithead and the Nore, the peak of a great wave of unrest which had perhaps begun with an outbreak on the *Janus* in 1783 and was to last for the rest of Nelson's lifetime. Of the ships in Nelson's squadron, the men of the *Culloden* had revolted against Troubridge in 1794 and barricaded themselves below decks. The *Majestic* and *Minotaur* had been involved in the Spithead mutiny. The crew of the *Defence* had at first resisted during that affair, until threatened by the guns of the *Pompee* and *Glory* but the ship was to have a major mutiny of her own later in the year. Of course not all these ships still had the same crews by 1798, but such traditions tended to linger aboard.

The state of discipline on the *Theseus* had been 'an abomination' according to St Vincent[21] when Nelson hoisted his flag in her in May 1797, with Ralph Willet Miller as flag captain. After a few weeks he found a note on the quarterdeck.

> Success attend Admiral Nelson! God bless Captain Miller! We thank them for the officers they have placed over us. We are happy and comfortable, and will shed every drop of blood in our veins to support them and the name of the *Theseus* will be immortalised as high as the *Captain*'s.
>
> Ship's Company.[22]

Off Cadiz St Vincent was ruthless in keeping his men in order, using marines and soldiers as a deterrent. When the ships were at anchor he decreed that 'the whole party of marines in their respective ships of the fleet is to be kept constantly at drill or parade under the direction of the commanding officer of marines, and not to be diverted therefrom by any of the ordinary duties of the ship'. When floggings took place the captains were directed to 'cause an officer's guard of marines to attend the punishment, with loaded arms and bayonets fixed'. When a man was hanged for mutiny or a similar offence, St Vincent insisted that the man's own shipmates haul on the rope which killed him. 'The sentence is to be carried into execution by the crew of the *St George* alone, and no part of the boat's crews of the other ships as is usual on similar occasions, is to assist in this painful service, in order to mark the high sense the commander-in-chief entertains of the loyalty, fidelity and subordination of the rest of the fleet.'[23] Men had recently been hanged on board the *Defence* and *Swiftsure* before these ships joined Nelson.

Nelson was aware of the disciplinary problem and supported St Vincent's measures, reminding his captains that the Commander-in-Chief's orders still applied to the detachment.[24] There was to be no serious unrest in the squadron and Nelson's leadership may have had some effect on this, as already shown in the *Theseus* affair in 1797. An equally important factor was that the squadron was continually on the move, unlike the fleet at Cadiz which spent most of its time at anchor. Seamen rarely mutinied under sail, except in rare and revolutionary cases such as the *Bounty* and *Hermione*. They were professionals and patriots, who would never willingly put their ship or their country in danger. The experienced seaman of the age was a being isolated from ordinary society, who valued the respect of his peers more than anything else. He was aware of his grievances, but immensely proud of the importance of the fleet in national defence and aware of the danger that could be caused by neglect of duty at sea.

If there was no actual mutiny, there was plenty of unrest among individuals, punished by some severe floggings. When accused of an offence too serious to be dealt with by the informal punishments of lieutenants or petty officers, a man was 'put in irons', with one or both of his ankles locked into iron stocks called 'bilboes' on the lower deck. In the morning he was brought before his captain and given a chance to state his case. If he was found guilty a grating was taken up from a hatchway and rigged almost vertically against the side of the ship. The man's wrists and ankles were lashed to it, the marines drawn up on the quarterdeck and the officers and crew assembled to witness punishment. A boatswain's mate picked up the 'cat of nine tails' made from pieces of light rope, and whipped the man on the back. In theory a captain could award only twelve strokes without the authority of a court martial, but this was certainly not observed during the Nile campaign. When Morris Kirk of the *Goliath* was given three dozen on 1 July it might have been justified in that it was given for three separate offenses of 'insolence, disobedience and neglect of duty'; but four weeks later his shipmate William Mason was given twenty-four lashes for theft alone.[25] St Vincent hoped that the marines were a force for law and order but they were just as likely as seamen to find themselves under the lash. On 5 June for example, Private Thomas Kew of the *Orion* was given twenty-four lashes for 'insolence to his superior officer and disobedience of orders'. Six weeks later Sergeant Cox was reduced to the ranks for 'drunkenness and riotous behaviour'.[26]

Men were flogged in all the ships during the campaign but more in some than others. Ball's *Alexander* had one of the best records. Between 10 June and 31 July only three men were flogged. The tiny *Mutine*, with a crew of less than 120, flogged men about twice a week on average, with up to 4 men being flogged on the same day.[27]

Seamen and marines relaxing below decks, from a drawing by Lieutenant Gabriel Bray done on board the frigate *Pallas* in 1775. (National Maritime Museum, London: 1991–3)

The *Vanguard* does not seem to have been any better than average; on 15 June Berry 'punished Henry Fields and Thomas Hayes, seamen, with two dozen lashes for drunkenness and Thomas Browning, marine, with one dozen lashes for insolence to his officer and Edward Williams, marine, with two dozen lashes for theft'.[28] Aboard the fleet many men were flogged for the venial offences of theft and drunkenness, caused by boredom, large beer and wine rations, and the bad character of many of the Quota men. Others were punished for disobedience, insolence and neglect of duty, offences which might or might not be linked to a general spirit of mutiny.

The only episode during the campaign which caused Nelson to call a court martial, however, involved an officer. Lieutenant Roberts of the *Orion* was accused of entertaining Midshipman Hill in his cabin late on the night of 15 June, in suspicious circumstances. The officers of the ship, too shocked to spell out the word in full, agreed that 'the dreadful crime of s——y' had not actually taken place but expelled him from the wardroom and reported him to the captain, who asked Nelson to assemble a court martial to try him for 'scandalous and infamous actions unbecoming the character of an officer and gentleman, in derogation of God's honour and corruption of good manners, in violation of the second Act of War'. The admiral agreed but Lieutenant Roberts left the ship in Sicily before the trial could take place.[29] Saumarez later said that he had 'found it necessary to send Mr — away at Syracuse'.[30]

On 20 July Nelson wrote to St Vincent: 'At the moment we have not one sick man in the fleet.'[31] This was something of an exaggeration, as the surgeon's journals from the *Theseus* and *Vanguard* show. On board the flagship Surgeon Michael Jefferson found that many of the men suffered from fevers during the first 4 months of the commission. After that ulcers became common and were 'very tedious of cure'. Many were old cases dating back many years but he dealt with fifteen new ones from 17 June to 31 July and eleven of these were still under treatment on 1 August. Individuals suffered from intermittent fever, acute rheumatism, 'hectic' (defined as 'appertaining to the habit or constitution') and a venereal ulcer in the groin. However, eight of the fifteen cases were of ulcerated legs, suggesting that scurvy was not far away.[32] Surgeon Robert Tainsh of the *Theseus* had found a similar problem on joining the ship in August 1797:

> there were amongst the ship's company a great disposition of ulcers of a foul tendency. I also understood the disposition had been of long standing but could not trace its origin unless from the ship's company having been a good deal on salt provisions.[33]

However, there were only five mild cases of scurvy during the year up to August 1798. The ship had no 'portable soup' such as Captain Cook had used to defeat scurvy on his circumnavigations but 'onion and lemons we have been very well supplied with, which of course has prevented scurvy'.[34] Such fruit was plentiful in Italy and Sicily. In June the *Mutine* picked up extra supplies of both during the brief visit to Naples and the *Vanguard* did the same at Syracuse.[35]

According to the Admiralty Regulations a ship was 'not to carry any woman to sea . . . without orders from the Admiralty', but this was rarely observed. On the *Goliath* four of the nineteen seamen and marines killed at the Battle of the Nile left widows on board.[36] If these numbers were extrapolated to the entire ship's company of 570 at the start of the action, that would suggest over 100 women on board. This is almost certainly an overestimate, but it suggests the proportion of women afloat was much higher than is usually supposed. On the same ship, John Nicol observed of the battle; 'The women behaved as well as the men, and got a present for their bravery from the Grand Signior.'[37] Foley seems to have had a particularly liberal attitude on this issue, but there were certainly women aboard other ships. Some 40 years later, Ann Hopping and Mary Ann Riley were refused the Naval General Service Medal for taking part in the action, solely on the grounds of sex,[38] while Christina White of the *Majestic* petitioned for a pension on the grounds that she had acted as a dresser and nurse during the campaign.[39] In the *Orion*, Ann Hopping, who had a husband and brother on board, was to work in the magazine in battle, helping make up flannel cartridges. She was to recount her adventures many years later at the age of 93.[40] Captain Berry of the *Vanguard* was at the opposite extreme to Foley. Before sailing from England the ship had 300 women on board but he was determined that '*All* the females go on shore tomorrow . . . I have set my face against taking *one* to sea.'[41] There is no evidence of any women in the ship after that.

Nelson's force was almost self-contained, for a few months at least. In 1796 St

Vincent had worried about the lack of bases in the Mediterranean but Nelson was soon to show how far a fleet could go without them. His ships were well-manned and in good condition. Even the damage to the *Vanguard* was to the masts and rigging rather than the hull, and showed that a certain amount of repair work could be carried out with only a primitive harbour and without the co-operation of the government of the area – though a series of disasters on this scale would eventually have crippled the fleet as the stock of spare parts diminished. A warship carried food for 6 months and water for 3; the latter could always be replenished by sending boats ashore to fill casks in neutral or even hostile territory. The store rooms in the bows of the ship were crammed with spare canvas, timber, rigging blocks, tar, rope, gun carriage parts and everything needed to keep the ship afloat, sailing and fighting. There were enough craftsmen on board to carry out running repairs. As the ships had not seen action, the magazines were full of gunpowder and the shot-lockers of round and chain shot.

★

The one thing that Nelson desperately needed was information about the movements of the enemy. From the cross-trees near the masthead of the *Vanguard*, a lookout might see a horizon 12 miles away in perfect visibility and perhaps the topsails of an enemy fleet for 10 miles beyond that. He could cover 1400 square miles in a sea of 960,000 square miles. To known anything from outside that area Nelson needed to obtain, evaluate and process as much information as he could find.

His first source was the British diplomatic representatives in the area, for despite Napoleonic advances there were still ambassadors in Constantinople, Turin, Naples and Florence. There were also nine consuls in Italy and one each in Malta, Morocco, Algiers, Tripoli, Tunis and Egypt. By far the most important of these representatives was Sir William Hamilton in Naples. Diplomatic information was generally reliable, and it gave Nelson his first indication that the French had taken Malta, for example. The problem, of course, was that the fleet was only rarely in touch with such sources: it had contact with Hamilton on 17 June but at the end of the month it failed to find the British consul in Egypt. Hamilton managed to get a few letters to him during the campaign, but Nelson was generally disappointed with the amount of diplomatic information he received.

The second and more extensive source of intelligence was from ships met at sea, whether friendly, neutral or enemy. British merchant ships had been driven from the Mediterranean, so none were encountered during the campaign. Neutral and enemy ships posed several problems. In the first place they were likely to take fright at the sight of a great fleet in a war zone, and ships would have to be detached to chase them. Secondly, on boarding a ship there was always the problem of language. The ships stopped by the fleet over the next two months hailed from Spain, France, Italy, Germany, Greece, Sweden, Turkey and Ragusa (Dubrovnik) and their crews spoke at least nine different languages. Certainly some of Nelson's officers spoke French and Italian and his crews came from many nationalities. Nelson, Ball and

A seaman casting the lead to find the depth of water, showing a typical sailor's dress of the period. By J A Atkinson, 1807. (National Maritime Museum, London: PU7765)

Hood had spent time in France in the 1780s and Saumarez, as a Channel Islander, spoke the language as a native. There was some kind of lingua franca among seamen and much could be communicated by sign language. There were plenty of opportunities for mistakes and misunderstandings, however, and one of these may have had a decisive effect on the campaign.

Usually it was necessary to stop a passing ship and either interrogate the captain through a speaking trumpet, or more likely send a party on board. A book of the period suggested how the lieutenant in charge of such a party might organise boarding.

> You are always to take a midshipman and a man who understands the language with you; and the midshipman is to continue in the boat to prevent the boat's crew from asking questions or giving answers; and not one of the boat's crew to be suffered to come out of the boat . . .
>
> Questions to be asked of strange ships.
>
> Have you been spoken with by any ship since you sailed? If you have, when and by what ships? If by ships of war, by what nation? What questions did they ask and answers did you give? If they were enemies, in what latitude and longitude? and how were they steering after they parted from you? Have you heard any guns? If you have, tell the circumstances. If the ship has lately left the land, how does it bear?[42]

Nelson was keen that such activities, though very necessary, should not interfere with the progress of the squadron. 'When the signal is made for any ship to examine a strange sail the captains are particularly desired to give directions to the officers who are sent to board them, to oblige the master of the vessel to lay her head in that direction which may cause least delay.'[43]

Having obtained the intelligence, Nelson and his officers had to evaluate and interpret it. At least forty-one vessels were stopped between 8 May and 1 August and some of these yielded no information at all.[44] They ranged in size from a 400-ton Genoese ship stopped by the *Vanguard* on 27 May, to a tiny fishing boat from Stromboli which was spoken to by the *Leander* on 18 June. Much of the information received was second- or third-hand and had been translated through several languages, but it was surprisingly accurate nonetheless. The great French Armament could not pass unnoticed and the *Alexander* was informed by a Tunisian warship that she had 'spoke to a Greek who informed him that on the 4th of this month he had seen the French fleet, consisting of a great number of which many were large ships of war, the others merchant vessels (number not known) off Trapania in the island of Sicily.' A Dutch ship told the *Orion* on 15 July: 'Last Thursday spoke a Greek ship off Malta that informed him he had heard from another vessel that the French fleet had taken Malta and that they were laying there.' There were tantalising glimpses of Nelson's missing frigates, for example when a Genoese ship reported that it had been boarded 2 days before by a British frigate which sounded very like the *Terpsichore*.

★

The great weakness of Nelson's force, as he reminded St Vincent and Hamilton in almost every communication he sent to them, was his lack of frigates. The type is rather difficult to define exactly but essentially it was a ship with a single deck of guns (apart from the usual ones on the forecastle and quarterdeck) with good sailing qualities and enough gun power to defend itself and escape from a more powerful enemy. By the most common definition, frigates carried 28 to 44 guns, though smaller ships of 24 guns might also be included in the category. These, the smallest ships, carried only 9-pounders; some of the older ships of 32 guns had 12-pounders, but the most numerous and popular types, carrying 32, 36 or 38 guns, had 18-pounders on the gun deck.

Compared with a ship of the line the frigate was smaller, rarely more than 150ft in length, and had no poop deck aft, above the quarterdeck. Essentially her lower deck was unarmed and therefore was not pierced with gunports. This deck would be at almost the same level as the water outside, while the deck above, carrying the main armament, was well clear of the waterline. A frigate could afford to heel quite substantially in a wind, and could carry more sail than a ship of the line in certain circumstances. Her hull lines were finer, because the underwater body did not have to support the great weight of guns on two or more decks of a ship of the line.

Throughout the campaign Nelson was consistent, almost obsessive, in his desire to keep his ships of the line close together. On 7 May, with only three large ships under his command, he gave 'positive orders that no temptation is to induce a line of battle ship to separate from me except in the almost certainty of bringing a line of battle ship of the enemy to action'.[45] On 8 June, now that he had a battle fleet rather than a reconnaissance force, his orders enjoined the commanders of divisions to 'keep their ships in the closest order possible, and on no account whatsoever to risk the separation of one of their ships . . . the ships are to be kept in that order that the whole squadron may act as a single ship'.[46] On 11 June he kept up the same policy. He reinforced this a week later with instructions that the fleet should be in the *'closest order possible*, and on no account *whatever* to risk the separation of their ships'. He did not expect his ships to sail in any particular formation except at the approach of battle and they might, for example, come close to one another to exchange information by hailing; but clearly he expected them to be within a radius of a mile or two of the flagship. This could cause problems and on 3 July the *Culloden* failed to give way to the *Vanguard* and forced her to alter course, risking collision with the *Zealous* and *Alexander*. Nelson drafted a letter of rebuke to Troubridge but thought twice about sending it.[47] The opposite problems sometimes occurred during the night, especially in light winds; at dawn on 7 July Nelson found 'the *Orion* missing and *Mutine* not in sight'.[48] The fleet was put in close order next day, with the ships no more than 200 yards apart but that did not last and open order was resumed.

Nelson had, however, made plans to fight a battle in the open sea. By an order of 8 June he divided the fleet into three sub-squadrons – six ships led by the admiral himself and four each under Saumarez and Troubridge. If the French were met at sea, two of these were to engage the enemy ships of the line while the other was to 'pursue the transports and to sink and destroy as many as it could'.[49]

Apart from keeping his fleet in close contact, what other tactics were available to Nelson? In theory it might be possible to spread them in line abreast by day, with each ship perhaps 20 miles apart from its neighbour, allowing them to communicate along the line on sighting of the enemy. Such a disposition would have allowed the fleet to be spread over perhaps 200 miles and would certainly have avoided the problems that were to occur with Nelson's fleet on 22 June, but Nelson's knowledge of the weather in the Mediterranean made him aware that it was too risky. Having made such a disposition, there was no guarantee that the fleet could re-concentrate in time to fight the enemy. 'It is very necessary in fine weather in the Mediterranean for the ships of the squadron to keep as close together as possible, for the winds are often so variable and in contrary directions in the space of four or five miles, that an opportunity of bringing the enemy to battle may be lost.'[50]

There is no sign that Nelson feared defeat by a section of his fleet being cut off, for his ships were fast enough to escape from a superior force, and he trusted his captains and crews to fight it out in any circumstances, should they be cut off by some mischance. But he did fear the escape of the enemy in an indecisive battle, which was likely if he was not able to concentrate his forces in time. On 18 June he told his captains 'the destruction of the enemy's armament is the sole object'.

Between the total concentration of the fleet demanded by Nelson and its dispersal over a broad front, was there a compromise solution? Supposing he had treated three or four of his 74-gun ships as frigates and made them into a reconnaissance screen, thus widening the fleet's field of vision? Of course he would have risked losing contact with these three or four scouts, leaving him only nine or ten in his line of battle against the French thirteen; but British ships had prevailed against greater odds in the past and would do so again, mostly under Nelson's leadership or inspiration. There was little in the sailing performance of a 74 that stopped her from acting as a frigate on occasion, and many did. True, she was much bigger than a frigate, but in moderate or strong winds a 74 would sail at least as fast, though perhaps slightly slower in light winds. When sailing into the wind a 74 might make slightly more leeway but this would not have been a problem in practice, as most of the chase was carried out with the wind behind. Because of her unarmed lower deck a frigate could cope with heeling better and could therefore carry more sail, but the difference was not great. A 74 should not 'abandon the chase of a frigate on account of swiftness'.[51] The 74 had a greater draught of water, but the *Mutine* was available to reconnoitre small harbours, and there was no problem in open waters, for the Mediterranean is a deep sea, with few underwater obstacles.

Nelson's ships, seamen and junior officers carried with them the traditions and skills of more than a century of shipbuilding, naval warfare and seamanship. They were hand-picked to a limited extent, in that St Vincent had detailed the best ships available to him; but in most respects they were quite ordinary, a cross-section of the navy of the time, with all its faults and virtues. Nelson's leadership, and that of his captains, would be needed to make them into a victorious fighting force.

CHAPTER 8

To the Fountain of Arethusa

By 10 June Nelson had a powerful and efficient squadron, but no information on the French except that they had sailed from Toulon 3 weeks ago. He speculated that they might rendezvous with the forces from Genoa in Telamon Bay, on the west coast of Italy. It took 2 days to get there in light winds but on the 12th the squadron stationed itself between the islands of Monte Cristo and Giglio while Hardy took the *Mutine* inshore to investigate. He found nothing and Nelson sailed south-east to try his luck in other Italian ports.

On the 13th he met a Tunisian warship which gave him second-hand information that the French had been seen off Sicily on the 4th. If this was true, which it was, then Ireland and Portugal could be ruled out as the enemy destination. The most likely target was Sicily itself, though the germ of another idea was already beginning to form in Nelson's mind. On the 15th he wrote to Spencer suggesting that 'If they pass Sicily, I shall believe they are going on their scheme of possessing Alexandria and getting troops to India – a plan concerted with Tippoo Saib, by no means so difficult as might at first view be imagined.'[1] He decided to head for the neutral kingdom and port of Naples, which ruled Sicily and therefore might feel under threat from the French expedition. His friend Sir William Hamilton was there, the senior British diplomat in the Mediterranean. There he might find moral and military support, and, above all, information.

★

Sir William Hamilton, British ambassador and envoy plenipotentiary to the court of Their Sicilian Majesties, was then 67 years old. He had been sent to Naples 34 years earlier, after trying his hand in the army and Parliament. A man of great sensibility, a collector of paintings and classical antiquities, an early student of vulcanology and archaeologist of the ancient city of Herculaneum, he was one of the world's first art historians and an eighteenth-century gentleman of the best kind. He met his second wife, the former Emma Hart, during a period of leave in England in 1783-84. She was one of the most beautiful women of her day, a former servant girl and mistress of Hamilton's nephew. Their marriage in 1791, after her 5 years as Hamilton's mistress in Italy, was frowned on by London society but Emma's charm was enough to give her a place in Naples, where she had become an intimate friend of the Queen.

Sir William Hamilton in a caricature of 1801 by
James Gillray, showing him pursuing his
antiquarian interests, but with an element of satire
on his wife's infidelity. (National Maritime
Museum, London: A239)

   The Kingdoms of Naples and Sicily, or the Two Sicilies, consisted of the almost
whole of Italy south of Rome. Naples was the second largest city in Europe, after
Paris. It was a beautiful, romantic, impoverished and violent land, ruled by King
Ferdinand IV since he had succeeded to the throne in 1759, at the age of 8. He was
13 when Hamilton arrived at his court and the two were to grow together, though
it is doubtful if Ferdinand ever reached what might be called maturity. In 1768 he
married Maria-Carolina, daughter of the Empress Maria Theresa, the benevolent
despot of Austria-Hungary. As well as giving him many children she came increasingly to dominate the King's life. General Sir John Acton, born in France to an
English father, rose to power after in Naples 1780 with the support of the Queen
and was *de facto* prime minister. The King was easily bored with the business of
government but jealous of his power. He was devoted to the pleasures of hunting,
sailing, fishing and adultery. The Queen in contrast 'gives up the greater part of her
time in daily looking into every paper and in preparing matters for the despatch of
business when she meets the King in council at night.'[2] She was as despotic as her
mother but not benevolent. Hamilton accepted that Acton had made things better
in the kingdom but believed that 'no great change can be effected during this
corrupt and bigoted generation, unless good faith and better education were univer-
sally introduced.'[3] The country was noted for sexual immorality among the ruling
class, the poverty of the common people and the strange, oppressive, yet fundamen-
tally weak government. Since Bonaparte's campaigns in northern Italy and the
Treaty of Campo Formio in 1797, the Kingdom of the Two Sicilies had lain in
terror of a further French invasion of its dominions.

On 28 May Hamilton had picked up a prime piece of intelligence, which could have had a decisive effect on the campaign. Acton told him that the French ambassador 'had assured him seriously that the grand expedition from Toulon which was commanded by General Bonaparte was really destined for Egypt, that they were to establish a colony and build a city on the spot where stood ancient Berenice'. There was even a plan to build a canal through the isthmus of Suez.[4] Hamilton reported this to London, which of course did not receive it until much later. But there is no sign that he passed it on to Nelson, perhaps because he thought the idea too fantastic, a piece of disinformation intended to give false assurance to the Neapolitans and at the same time mislead the British. Certainly he did not pass it in writing, which proved to be a great mistake.

Hamilton had heard of Nelson's presence in the Mediterranean and on the King's birthday on 4 June he gave a dinner for the British in Naples, at which he toasted 'the speedy arrival of a British squadron in the Mediterranean'. This delighted the assembled company. 'Now we considered ourselves perfectly safe under the protecting shield of a British admiral, and that admiral a Nelson with a Troubridge for second in command, and under his orders a Saumarez, a Hood and others who had so gallantly distinguished themselves as to be commonly called "the fire eaters"' wrote Miss Cornelia Knight.[5]

On arrival off Naples, Nelson's ships stayed well offshore with their hulls out of sight, though their masts and sails were observed from the shore. A battle with the French might be imminent so Nelson could not leave the fleet, nor could he detach a ship of the line. Troubridge was called to the flagship and instructed to go on board the tiny *Mutine* which would take him into the harbour. Another British vessel, the 12-gun brig *Transfer*, could already be seen there, for she had brought dispatches from St Vincent to Hamilton.

Troubridge arrived at Naples in the '*Lutine*', as Hamilton persisted in calling her, at 5am on 17 June. He was rowed ashore with Hardy and met by Hamilton who took him straight to a meeting with Acton. On the face of it this had some success. Troubridge lacked diplomatic skills and he cut out the pleasantries and got to the heart of the matter. Hamilton commented,

> We did more business in half an hour than should have been done in a week in the official way here. Captain Troubridge went straight to his point and put strong questions to the general, who answered them fairly and to the satisfaction of the captain. As no time was to be lost the admiral now being informed of the position and strength of the enemy and desirous of attacking them as soon as possible, I prevailed upon General Acton to write himself an order in the name of His Sicilian Majesty, directed to the governors of every port in Sicily to supply the King's ships with all sorts of provisions . . . When Captain Troubridge had received this order from the General and put it in his pocket his face brightened up and he seemed perfectly happy.'[6]

The difficulty with this kind of meeting was that it allowed no chance to discuss the information about the French going to Egypt. The Neapolitan leadership was uncertain whether to resist the French or placate them. If Acton favoured resistance, his hand would be weakened by a suggestion that the French were no immediate threat. Hamilton believed his duty was to persuade the Neapolitans that their best defence lay in co-operating with Nelson, offering him full facilities for stores and repairs and perhaps even a squadron of frigates to sail with his fleet. The suggestion that Bonaparte was not interested in Naples would not be helpful. Though Hamilton now knew that the French were attacking Malta, he believed that this was a flanking move against Sicily. The information about Egypt could not emerge from a meeting between Acton, Hamilton and Troubridge, and Hamilton did not see fit to include it in his letters to Nelson. Indeed a few weeks later he was to write: 'M. Garrat [the French envoy] tells this government that Bonaparte writes his word that he is gone to the Levant and for that reason I should think he may have taken quite another direction.'[7]

After less than 2 hours on shore, Troubridge was back on the *Mutine* and under weigh with the *Transfer* by 11 that morning. On rejoining the squadron, Troubridge came on board the flagship to report, while the *Transfer* was sent to the fleet off Cadiz with Nelson's dispatches. Nelson was less used than Hamilton to the ways of Ferdinand's court and unsatisfied with Acton's support. He wrote: 'I find plenty of goodwill towards us, with every hatred towards the French, but no assistance for us . . . *no co-operation*, though we are come to their assistance.'[8] He had hoped for a guarantee of all kinds of help: for supplies including ammunition and new masts, full rights to enter all ports in southern Italy and Sicily, and above all the use of a squadron of Neapolitan frigates. All he had was some information about the French attacking Malta, and a vague promise of assistance.

Nelson was prepared to believe the French were at Malta, probably in advance of an attack on Sicily – 'If the enemy have Malta, it is only as a safe harbour for their fleet and Sicily will fall the moment the King's fleet withdraws from the coast of Sicily.'[9] He wrote a goodbye letter to Hamilton: 'I would not lose one moment of the breeze in answering your letter. The best sight (as an Irishman would say) was to see me out of sight.'[10] He set sail for Malta through the Straits of Messina, between Sicily and the toe of Italy, arriving at the Straits on the 20th. Pilots came on board and Saumarez commented that the one who took charge of the *Orion* 'reminds me more of the poet's description of old Charon than of a modern human being. I hope he is not come to ferry us across the Styx. The whole of the [pilot boat] crew have the same grotesque appearance.'[11] Chaplain Willyams also had a Classical education and he was happy to believe that the squadron was the first modern European fleet to pass between the rock of Scylla and the whirlpool of Charybdis – not quite true, as Admiral George Byng (later Lord Torrington), for example, had taken a British fleet there in 1718. Willyams wrote: 'the noise occasioned by the tumult of the waves gave rise to the fictions of poets, who likened it to a voracious monster roaring for its prey. . . . But we found none of these difficulties. Perhaps the constant friction of the waters has worn away the rocks and shoals that obstructed the passage and given more ample room to the current, which however is now extremely rapid.'[12] Saumarez found his Stygian pilot perfectly competent and all the ships got through safely.

If there were doubts about the support of the rulers of the Two Sicilies, there was no question about popular feeling on the island. At Messina, Nelson's squadron was seen as a saviour from the French. Cheering multitudes lined the shore and 'hailed our arrival with acclamations of joy and gratitude'. Boats came out to the fleet carrying 'many of the principal people of this city and neighbourhood . . . who expressed their joy at seeing a British fleet, when they discovered the object of their pursuit'.[13] 'A vast number of boats came off and rowed round it with the sincerest exultation, as the Sicilians had been apprehensive that the French fleet was destined to act against them . . .'[14] Among the boats was one carrying the British consul for Sicily, James Tough, bringing a note. Two Spanish 74s and a 40-gun frigate were in Palermo harbour, afraid to leave because of the British fleet. They were not relevant to the campaign and the squadron went on its way.

★

In the early morning of 22 June, as the ships passed the south eastern tip of Sicily, both the *Leander* and *Mutine* came upon vital pieces of information. At 4.20am the *Defence* spotted four ships to the east-south-east and the *Leander* was sent to look at them. At about the same time Hardy stopped a Ragusan brig and at 5.25am he signalled that he wanted to speak to Nelson. An hour later, according to Nelson's journal,

> Captain Hardy came on board with intelligence that he had spoke a vessel that had left Malta yesterday. The master reported that the French had taken Malta on Friday last, that their fleet had sailed from there on Saturday leaving a garrison of their troops, but could not give any information of the destination of their fleet.'[15]

Nelson needed only a short time to digest this. There was disappointment that the French would not be caught in a blockade of Malta, where they might be defeated at sea. As Nelson wrote later: 'It would have been my delight to have tried Bonaparte upon a wind, for he commands the fleet as well as the army.'[16] But there was still hope of catching them, wherever they were going. Nelson reasoned that it had to be Egypt. If the French had left Malta on 16 June to attack Sicily they must have landed several days ago, and the people of Messina would have been aware of it, not to mention the British Consul. The westerly wind, and their route via Malta, ruled out anywhere outside the Mediterranean. They could only be heading east, and the only place of any significance was Egypt. An attack elsewhere on the Ottoman empire would yield little of value to the French, and would be no great threat to Britain.

In deciding to go east, Nelson was conscious of coming to a daring and surprising conclusion, as indeed was every Briton on first conceiving the idea. In London Henry Dundas had first thought of it on 9 June, and felt it necessary to defend the notion against being 'whimsical' and having 'a fancy of my own'.[17] Hamilton had clearly regarded it as incredible. Even the fifth lieutenant of the *Goliath* wrote later to his family, 'Pray did you ever expect to receive a letter from the land of Egypt?'[18] The British navy had always operated in the western Mediterranean and barely

The inshore squadron of St Vincent's fleet off Cadiz in 1798, with the Spanish fleet at anchor to the left. A watercolour by Thomas Buttersworth. (National Maritime Museum, London: PAH9505)

Naples as seen from Hamilton's window in the Palazzo Sessa, painted by Giovanni Lusieri in 1791.
(J Paul Getty Museum, Los Angeles, California)

knew the area east of Sicily. None of the thirty rendezvous nominated by Nelson and St Vincent were east of Malta. The fleet had very few charts of the area; most had been produced by Frenchmen and Spaniards so were not available to many British navigators. Such charts as existed were often vague and inaccurate, with many gaps in the coverage.

Between 7 and 7.15am Nelson signalled for 'those captains in whom I place great confidence'[19] – Saumarez, Troubridge, Darby and his new friend Ball – to come on board the flagship. He was clearly agonizing about his decision to go to Egypt and needed support but he did not go to the length of calling a formal council of war, which would have covered him legally against any misjudgment. Such a council would have involved the most senior officers but Nelson did not summon Louis and Peyton, who were senior to Ball. In the cabin of the *Vanguard* Nelson put a series of rather loaded questions to those present.

> The vessel we spoke with this morning is from Malta one day, she says the two frigates in sight are French, that the French colours and garrison are in Malta, that the fleet and transports left it six days today, but they did not know where they were going, some said to Sicily.
>
> With this information what is your opinion? Do you believe under all circumstances which we know that Sicily is their destination? Do you think we had better stand for Malta, or steer for Sicily?
>
> Should the armament be gone for Alexandria and get safe there our possessions in India are probably lost. Do you think we had better push for that place?'[20]

Berry, the most junior, answered in the affirmative to the last question but produced no arguments in support. Darby, the least distinguished, produced argument but no real conclusion – given the state of the wind it was likely that they had gone to the east and it would be difficult for Nelson's squadron to go back to Sicily in the circumstances; however, he made no mention of Egypt. Ball agreed that the French had gone towards Alexandria, while Troubridge and Saumarez raised the most urgent point – that the capture of Alexandria would be a serious threat to British interests in India.[21] Saumarez felt privately that this was 'the merest conjecture only'[22] but Nelson had his mandate to act and at 9am, after the captains had returned to their ships, he made the signal for the fleet to 'prepare to bear up and sail large', that is to go to the eastward with the wind behind it.[23]

Meanwhile the investigation of the four strange ships continued. At 5.30am, as Hardy was coming on board the flagship, the *Culloden* reported that the ships, now east-by-north of the fleet, were running with the wind behind them. At 6.46am the *Leander* reported 'strange ships are frigates' – the biggest warlike force that the squadron had yet found. The *Orion* repeated the signal so that the flagship could see it but within half an hour, even as the four captains were being called on board, the flagship replied with signal number 9 to the *Leander* – 'To call in chasing ships'. According to Saumarez the frigates were 'not considered of sufficient importance to run the risk of separating the squadron in chasing them'.[24] One can sense a note of incredulity when *Leander* signalled again at 8.29am – 'Ships seen are frigates.'[25] But Nelson was adamant, they must press on to Egypt and the squadron must be kept together at all costs, especially on the eve of battle. He was unaware that he had just seen some of the

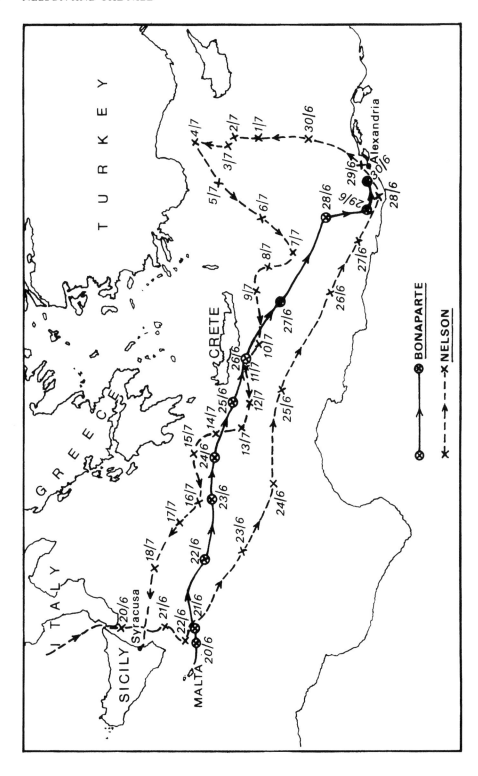

outlying ships of Napoleon's great fleet and missed an opportunity which might have changed the course of history. The Ragusan's information was only half true; the French had indeed taken Malta and had sailed; but on the 19th, not the 16th.

★

Nelson sailed south-east to Alexandria, keeping well clear of the shoal waters off Libya. On the 26th, while still 230 miles from Egypt, he called Hardy on board the flagship and gave him orders to sail on ahead in the *Mutine*, to warn the British Consul of what was happening and see what he could find out about the French. With a strong following breeze from the north-west, passages of 100 or 150 miles a day were recorded and by the afternoon of 28 June the squadron had the city in sight. Nelson made the signal to prepare for battle in anticipation of meeting the French but then cancelled it when no enemy ships were to be seen. By sunset the squadron was 3 miles from Alexandria and held its position off shore, constantly sounding with the lead in the shallowing waters. They could see nothing ashore except 'one Turkish ship of the line, four frigates, about twelve other Turkish vessels in the old port and about 50 sail of different nations' vessels in the Frank's port'.[26]

On landing in Alexandria, Hardy failed to find the consul, George Baldwin, who was on leave of absence and had not been there for nearly three months. His deputy was 'a stupid vice-consul, not an Englishman',[27] who had accepted the dispatches but could give no further help. At first Hardy was taken for a Frenchman by the Egyptians but eventually the military commandant of the city was called to speak to him. The Egyptian refused to accept that there was any danger.

> It is impossible that the French should come to our country. They have no business here and we are not at war with them . . . In any event you cannot stay in our waters and we have no plausible reason to authorise you to do so. Water and victual your ships if you have to, but go away. If the French really think of invading our country as you pretend, we shall thwart their undertaking.[28]

At 11am on the 29th Hardy arrived back and had his boat rowed out to the *Vanguard*. He hailed Nelson and told him the news from the city. Desperately disappointed, Nelson had to decide what to do. Suffering greatly from the stress of the voyage, he was nevertheless impatient to get on. According to his flag captain, 'His anxious and active mind . . . would not permit him to rest a moment in the same place.'[29] He was now convinced that the French must have gone elsewhere and decided to look round the Eastern Mediterranean. The squadron sailed from Alexandria at 10am on 30 June, heading north towards Turkey. By 11 am on the following day, 25 hours after Nelson left, the French fleet was anchoring off Alexandria and preparing to land its troops.

Why did Nelson not wait for a few days at least, to see if the French would arrive? On the way to Egypt Saumarez had noted in his diary 'the wind continues

◀ The courses of the French and British fleets in June and July, with the noon position marked for each day, showing the near miss on the morning of 22 June, and how Nelson overtook the French on the 24th and 25th.

Alexandria on 29 June 1798, from a drawing by Lieutenant Davis in the *Swiftsure*. The vessel in the centre is presuambly the *Mutine*, with a boat on the way to bring news to the fleet. (National Maritime Museum, London: D8795)

favourable, we hope to arrive in Alexandria before the French'.[30] The possibility of this must have occurred to Nelson and, if not, it must have been pointed out by Saumarez when he came on board the *Vanguard* on the 26th and the 29th. Furthermore, the *Mutine*'s intelligence from Alexandria appeared to show that the Egyptians were expecting the French, and indeed had mistaken Nelson's fleet for an anticipated invasion. Nelson acknowledged this when he wrote that the Turks were 'preparing to resist them'.[31] Clearly he placed too much reliance on the information from the Ragusan brig, though he must have been aware of the possibility of misunderstanding or disinformation. His conviction was reinforced by the fact that he had not met the French between Sicily and Alexandria and he neglected to take the sighting of the French frigates on the morning of the 22nd into account. A few years later he was to blame the decision on the absence of the British consul, who might perhaps have negotiated an anchorage and some supplies for him. He wrote to George Baldwin: 'With respect to my opinion of what would have been the consequences had I found you at Alexandria, there can be no doubt but that I should have been off Alexandria when the French fleet arrived . . . I believe if you had been there to explain between me and the Turkish governor that I should have remained a few days to get some water and refreshments.' However, the need to replenish the fleet was not urgent and he spent the next 3 weeks sailing round the Levant before seeking shelter and supplies.

Nelson had no hard evidence that the French were going to Egypt, and was always anxious about his own supposition that this was the case. He had asked his captains to sign letters agreeing with him about Bonaparte's course and after the event he wrote to St Vincent:

I am before your Lordship's judgement (which in the present case I feel is the tribunal of my country) and if under all circumstances it is decided that I am wrong, I ought for the sake of our country to be superseded . . . However erroneous my judgement may be, I feel conscious of my honest intentions.

The terms were so defensive that Ball advised him not to send the letter. 'I felt a regret that your too anxious zeal should make you start an idea that your judgement was impeachable because you have not yet fallen in with the French fleet, as it might induce a suspicion that you are not satisfied with your own conduct.'[32] Sir William Hamilton's failure to pass on his information from Acton was crucial here. Had Nelson had just one piece of hard evidence he might have stayed a little longer, defeated the French army as well as the fleet, and the rise of Bonaparte would have been abruptly halted, perhaps for ever.

★

From leaving Gibraltar on 8 May until the aftermath of the Battle of the Nile 3 months later, there is no sign that Nelson thought about anything other than the campaign against the French. Seamen and junior officers with the fleet barely mention the chase round the Mediterranean in their autobiographies,[33] and perhaps they had little conception of the difficulties that their leaders were under. To the rank and file in any war, sudden and apparently pointless movements are soon taken for granted. Lieutenant Wilkes of the *Goliath* had more insight than some and he wrote: 'Words will give but a faint idea of the chagrins and difficulties poor Nelson and we all felt . . . We were at a day's warning . . . we expected to find them at Naples, afterwards at Malta . . . away we hasted for Egypt . . . poor disappointed us . . . come all this way for nothing.'[34]

The captains were fully aware of the problems but still found time to think about other matters, especially the perennial one of how wealthy they would be from prize money after the voyage. Hardy wrote to his brother, 'We have been fortunate enough to have two neutral vessels condemned, it is supposed [worth] ten thousand pounds. However if half I shall be satisfied.'[35] Ball was concerned about a captured ship laden with cotton, oil, sugar and grain and wrote to his agent in Gibraltar to 'beg that you will thoroughly inform yourself of the prices these articles bear so that everything may be disposed of to the best advantage for the benefit of the captors'.[36] Saumarez had higher interests; he was in tune with the Romantic sensibilities of his age in that he found beauty in the natural landscape and in his serial letters to his family he waxed lyrical about the Bay of Naples, Stromboli and the Straits of Messina:

We can now discern the famous Etna disgorging columns of smoke. Some distance below its summit it appears covered with snow, whilst here we are melting with heat. It has indeed a most stately appearance, and the whole country of Sicily appears everything it has been reported of for its fertility as well as for the varied beauty of its scene.[37]

Nelson showed no interest in these matters. Up to 4 May he wrote many letters to his wife, discussing among other things his clothes, the passengers on his ship and the affairs of friends. He wrote only three letters to her after leaving Gibraltar and all deal entirely with the events of the voyage, with no reference to other interests or family concerns – he even described the damage to the *Vanguard* in detail, as if writing an official report. Apart from that his comments were brief: 'You must be content with short letters,' he wrote from off Naples in June.[38] His letters to St Vincent and Sir William Hamilton were formal and betrayed few signs of the friendship he felt for both men. Aboard the *Vanguard* he had a few close friends but an inadequate staff and no-one to delegate to. If he had been an admiral in command of a squadron of twenty ships or more he would have been allowed a 'captain of the fleet', an experienced officer with the status of a rear-admiral, who might have taken much of the load. Captain Berry was a Nelson protégé, but his accounts of the voyage show no great intimacy with the admiral and he may have been under a cloud after the events off Toulon. Nelson's secretary, John Campbell, had 'not enough activity' to please his master.[39] His flag-lieutenant, Thomas Bladen Capel, was only 21 and could not be expected to serve as a mature, experienced adviser. His servant Tom Allen was an old friend but his relationship with his master was never easy. He was 'clumsy, ill-formed, illiterate and vulgar, his very appearance created laughter at the situation he held; but his affectionate, bold heart made up for all his deficiencies; and . . . Tom Allen possessed the greatest influence with his heroic master.'[40] John Sykes, the coxswain of his boat in the *Agamemmnon* and *Theseus*, would perhaps have been a better confidant. He saved Nelson's life twice during an attack on Spanish gunboats in 1797 and according to Captain Miller, 'His manners and conduct are so entirely above his situation, that nature certainly intended him for a gentleman.'[41] But Sykes had stayed on board the *Theseus* when Nelson went home wounded in 1797 and soon, as a fine seaman, he was promoted to be Gunner of the frigate *Andromache*.[42]

Despite the legend of the 'Band of Brothers', Nelson appears remote and isolated throughout the campaign. He had not yet developed the lightness of touch, the flamboyance which would allow him to make grand gestures. There was no putting the telescope to his blind eye, no encouraging signal on the eve of battle. His charisma had already shown itself on many occasions and his self-confidence allowed him to delegate a great deal to his more trusted captains. But the most important characteristics of his leadership in this campaign were his determination and single-mindedness, which he conveyed to his senior captains. Even Saumarez, who was not entirely satisfied with Nelson's leadership, had to admit that 'did the chief responsibility rest with me, I fear it would be more than my too irritable nerves would bear. They have already been put to the trial in two or three instances this voyage.'[43]

No doubt Nelson found companionship among the junior officers of the flagship, as he was wont to do. In his earliest days as a captain a woman passenger noted 'his attention to the young gentlemen who had the happiness of being on his quarterdeck . . . The timid he never rebuked but always wished to show them he desired nothing of them that he would not instantly do himself . . . How wise and kind in such a proceeding! In like manner he went every day into the school room and saw them do their nautical business, and at 12 o'clock he was first upon deck with his quadrant.'[44] He continued this practice in later life, even on the eve of Trafalgar, so it can be assumed that during the Nile campaign he took an equal interest in Mr Kremer of Hanover, young Edward Naylor, and before his death William Meek of Norfolk. Unfortunately none of them left an account describing it. He must have been similarly close to the wardroom officers, especially since many of them were old friends from previous commissions; but again, only Captain Berry wrote anything down.

It was not that his duties were particularly onerous in themselves. An admiral had no particular working routine or hours of work, so could normally spend the night in his bunk. There was no need to interfere in the running of individual ships and Nelson had no inclination to do so. Apart from the threat of storms, the navigation of the Mediterranean was not especially difficult. There were few sand-banks or hidden rocks, no fogs and no tides. The ships were rarely far enough from the shore to need much celestial navigation. Of course intelligence had to be collected and collated but it tended to come in at a very slow rate, with an average of one merchant ship stopped for every 2 days at sea. Few reports had to be made to superior officers and no instructions had to be issued to detached forces. Yet all this merely increased Nelson's sense of isolation and allowed him time to brood over what needed to be done and what might go wrong.

Nelson of course was subject to stresses that are almost inconceivable in today's world. He was almost completely out of contact with higher authority for several months and forced to make every decision on his own. In itself this was not unique for a naval officer; George Anson had relied on his own resources for nearly 4 years during his great circumnavigation of 1740-44, raiding Spanish possessions and ships in the Pacific. Captain Cook had undertaken voyages of about 3 years each, during which he was forced to make all his own decisions. William Bligh was much less successful in this lonely and isolated type of command and was overthrown from the *Bounty* in 1789. But none of these officers had the great responsibilities of Nelson. Anson's expedition was heavily depleted by weather and disease but was never in danger from the enemy. It was offensive rather than defensive and the country's safety would never have been threatened by its failure. Cook and Bligh were explorers pursuing long-term aims with few and small ships. Nelson was charged with finding and defeating the mysterious Toulon expedition, which might threaten vital British interests anywhere – in Portugal, Ireland, the West Indies, Italy or even in India. He genuinely and perhaps accurately believed that his failure would be a national disaster and the responsibility weighed very heavily. He had never commanded a fleet in battle and he had very little information on where the enemy could be found. He had several strokes of bad luck, beginning when the gale struck the *Vanguard* off Toulon and ending when he failed to find the French at Alexandria. He was alone in a great sea, where every government was either hostile or at best neutral and too afraid of French power to give him much help. If some of his decisions can be criticised with hindsight, it is only because he was human, subject to the fatigue, doubt and anxiety of all mortals.

Nelson's mental condition was noticed by his officers. According to Saumarez the dismasting of the *Vanguard* caused him 'a most anxious night'.[45] After the failure at Alexandria Berry noted that: 'It has now become a subject of deep and anxious deliberation with the admiral, what could possibly have been the course of the enemy.'[46] Nelson's letter to Hamilton reporting the failure was slightly garbled under stress, causing him to write that he had carried out the expedition 'with a single ship' – which Hamilton, in replying, corrected to 'with a crippled ship and without a single frigate'.[47] The admiral reassured his wife in every letter that he was in perfect health but he was aware how much his problems were bearing down on him. The want of frigates caused him real distress. His failure to find the French, he told Sir William Hamilton, Lady Nelson and the Earl of St Vincent, caused him 'great mortification' and he lamented 'What a situation I am placed in!'. His squadron was in 'a wretched state' and he felt that 'to be unsuccessful hurts me most sensibly'.[48] By the end of June he was showing clear signs of exhaustion.

★

With a certain air of hopelessness the squadron sailed round the Eastern Mediterranean. After going north towards Turkey they turned east on 2 July, to head back to Sicily and Naples, for Nelson was beginning to fear he might have been duped into leaving that area. The winds were unfavourable and the ships had to tack, making slow progress. There was little trade in the region, so no ships were met and no new information received. In the first week of July the officers of the flagship had some heavy drinking sessions and alcohol consumption peaked; apart from their private stocks, the admiral, perhaps the captain and twelve or thirteen officers consumed twelve bottles of port, nine of sherry, six of claret and twenty of porter.[49]

On 12 July Nelson made a mysterious comment in a letter to St Vincent. 'Both Sir William Hamilton and General Acton, *I now know* said they believed Egypt was their object; for that when the French minister at Naples was pressed on the armament appearing off Sicily, he declared that Egypt was their object.'[50] This is not quite fair to Hamilton, who had the information but did not believe it. But much more important, how had Nelson suddenly found this out? Certainly Hamilton had written letters to Nelson since the squadron was at Naples and they included hints of what the French ambassador had said. But none of these had yet been received and, indeed, in the same letter quoted above, Nelson was complaining of the lack of contact: 'I own I fully expected to have found dispatches off this end of Candia [Crete].'[51] It is not the kind of material that would be picked up by casual contact with a merchant ship and we can be certain that Nelson had not known it on 29 June, when he wrote to St Vincent with a detailed justification of his reasons for going to Alexandria.

Is it possible that Hamilton had in fact mentioned it casually to Troubridge, perhaps on the way to the meeting with Acton, and the latter had failed to tell Nelson? It may be that both men had discounted it at the time and that for the same reason Troubridge had not mentioned it to Nelson when he came on board the flagship afterwards. It is more difficult to believe that he had failed to mention it at

Bellin's chart of Syracuse from his *Petit Atlas Maritime* of 1764, showing the old city, the two rivers described by Cooper Willyams and the Fountain of Arethusa. (National Maritime Museum, London: D8804)

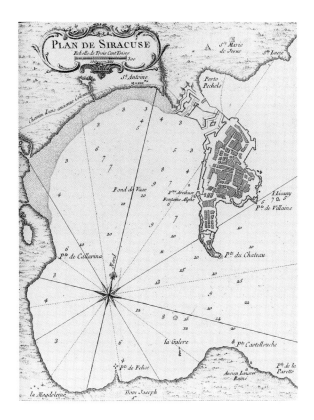

the meeting on 22 June, when he was asked to state in writing why he agreed with Nelson's decision to go to Egypt. Was he too embarrassed or ashamed to admit his mistake? If so, why had he evidently confessed it later? Or had Troubridge or Hamilton also mentioned it to Hardy at some stage in Naples, and then Hardy eventually let it slip to Nelson, assuming Troubridge had already told him? It is a great mystery, but only an explanation of this sort seems to explain the circumstances. It also underlines how unlikely everyone thought an attack on Egypt to be – obvious as it may appear with hindsight.

★

At last, on 20 July, Sicily was in sight. Nelson had 'been off Malta, to Alexandria in Egypt, Syria, into Asia'[52] and was 'as ignorant of the situation of the enemy as I was 27 days ago'.[53] At 3.30pm the squadron anchored in Syracuse Bay. Nelson wrote to his wife, his commander-in-chief and to Sir William Hamilton. 'It is an old saying "The Devil's children have the Devil's luck". I cannot find, or to this moment learn, beyond vague conjecture where the French fleet are gone to.'[54]

Boats were hoisted out and parties of men sent on shore under officers, to make contact with the authorities and seek food and drink for the squadron. Troubridge was put in charge of the watering and soon encountered some difficulties. Two small rivers discharged fresh water into the bay, and the boats headed for one of them. The crews soon found that the mud and weeds at the entrance made it very difficult to approach and they ran aground some distance from the shore, affronting the dignity of Chaplain Willyams of the *Swiftsure* who was obliged to wade ashore.[55] A more serious problem was that the people used the river to steep hemp, which made the water unhealthy and unpleasant. Empty water casks had to be rolled a quarter of a mile across the fields to a bridge, where they could be filled up and floated down river. A more convenient source was eventually found in the city, which was supplied by an aqueduct leading to the legendary Fountain of Arethusa in the centre of the old town.

Each 74-gun ship carried a launch, a broad, strong boat, 31ft long and 10ft broad, rowed by a crew of fourteen men, usually with a midshipman and a coxswain in command. As well as its work in lifting heavy items such as anchors, it was designed to carry twelve large casks of water, called butts, holding 108 gallons each. These boats were fully employed bringing water and other goods on board the squadron. While the launches and their crews did the heavy work, the ships' barges and pinnaces ferried officers around the harbour. These boats were designed mainly for fast rowing and were much lighter and narrower than the launches. They were needed because, yet again, there were difficulties with the local authorities, and Nelson's promise from Acton was not quite as effective as he wished. 'Our treatment is scandalous for a great nation to put up with, and the King's flag is insulted at every friendly port we look at.' However, he added for Hamilton's benefit, 'You will observe that I feel as a public man, and write as such. I have no complaint to make of private attention, quite the contrary. Every body of persons have been on board to offer me civilities.'[56] Part of Nelson's protest was intended to reassure the French in Naples that the British were not being helped unduly, for he believed that his letters were being opened. In any case the Governor's attitude appears to have softened over the days. Lady Hamilton later claimed that her influence on the Queen helped here.[57]

There was much routine work which could be done at anchor. When stores of any kind were found to be unsuitable, regulations decreed that a survey should be done by three warrant officers of the respective department of other ships before they were condemned. Committees were assembled on the *Bellerophon* to look at her anchor cables and a cask of butter, on the *Orion* to examine butter, salt, beef and raisins and to evaluate the boatswain's stores. A quantity of rice was condemned on board the *Culloden* and ordered to be thrown over the side.[58]

The presence of the fleet attracted the attention of the Sicilian population, who were as friendly as they had been a month ago. As Willyams reported

> In the afternoon the landing place at the gate of the city was a scene of much gaiety and show; the boats from the fleet pulling in towards the shore, the crowds that lined the strand, the long range of carriages in which the principal nobility of the place came to view the British fleet, the gaudy liveries of their servants with the variety of dresses, which everywhere presented themselves in the appearance of the several orders of the people, formed so pleasing an assemblage.[59]

Syracuse, with the local population on the waterfront and a captain's barge and other naval boats approaching the landing place. From Cooper Willyams' *Voyage up the Mediterranean*. (National Maritime Museum, London: D8806-A)

The Chaplain went ashore with some of his colleagues to see the sights and his comments combine curiosity and liberalism with prejudice.

> The convent of Monte Virginis is appropriated to females of noble family only. As Englishmen we could not but lament that so many lovely women should, by superstition, be thus secluded from the world, where otherwise they might have contributed by their presence to adorn, as by their social virtues to have added to the general stock of human happiness.[60]

At the Monastery of the Capuchins he saw the mummified bodies of past monks in the crypt.

> Our attention was immediately called off from other matters by an assemblage of venerable personages arranged along the wall in niches formed for the purpose. They were all dressed in the habit of St Francis and at first sight had the appearance of life; but on close examination their skin appeared dry, shrivelled and as hard as wood. Some of them had been dead for near two centuries.[61]

Lieutenant Thomas Wilkes of the *Goliath* also found time to go ashore and wrote to his cousins;

> Syracuse, once a most superb city far beyond our modern conceptions, the remains of its theatre and amphitheatre, catacombs etc leave no doubt of its ancient grandeur and population. Nor does that stupendous and astonishing work cut out of the solid rock called the Tyrant's Ear leave us any doubt of the craft and cruelty of Dionysus the tyrant.[62]

Purser Samuel Grant of the *Goliath* was not fully satisfied. He had his linen washed, 'but not so well as I have been used to' and lamented the lack of social contact.

The better sort of people here extremely attentive and polite to you, but no sort of domestic hospitality shown. I do not think during the five days we have been here that one person of any description whatever has been asked to dine at a private home, and so scarce a commodity money appears to be, that even the English consul (who is an Italian) told a Purser whom I was at his house with today that he had it not in his power to give him the change of a 40 guinea bill.'[63]

Meanwhile the officers had found supplies of food and drink. Each ship was ordered to send a launch to the landing place in the town on the first morning, to receive fresh beef and vegetables. On the following day it was decided that each ship should be issued with two bullocks every evening, to be killed on board. The crews laboured under oppressive temperatures and Nelson ordered that boats should not carry too many casks of wine at once to prevent them being damaged by heat. It was to be preserved by mixing it with 2 gallons of brandy for every 140 of wine. On the 24th, as the ships were getting ready to sail, each sent a boat on shore to receive eight bullocks. These were to be kept alive until needed and straw was purchased to feed them. The *Vanguard* took on a supply of lemons, a local product, and distributed them among the other ships. Bread was more difficult to find. The *Alexander* and *Orion* were running short and the other ships sent them supplies from their own stores. It was not enough and by the 27th all the ships were on two-thirds of their normal bread allowance.[64]

Despite all the difficulties and hard work, the mood in the fleet was much improved by four days at Syracuse. Captain Hood commented 'from the extraordinary good watering place we found, added to the attention of the Governor and Naples, we obtained every refreshment.'[65] Nelson's spirits were beginning to recover and as his ships raised their anchors he wrote and 'the fleet is unmoored, and the moment the wind comes off the land shall go out of this delightful harbour where our present wants have been most amply supplied and where every attention has been paid to us . . . Surely watering at the fountain of Arethusa, we must have victory.'[66]

CHAPTER 9

A Formidable Position

ON 18 JUNE THE French Armament was ready to sail from Malta. The ships of the convoy began to tack out of their anchorages at Valletta, Marsaxlokk, St Paul's Bay and Gozo. They were followed by the warships and next day the whole force set course to the south-east. The winds were poor and contrary so the ships sailed only 33 miles on the first day and 12 on the second. By the 21st they had begun to increase and speed went up to 60 or 80 miles a day.[1]

Only forty of the senior officers knew the true destination of the Armament; among the rest, speculation was as intense as it was in Nelson's fleet. Sicily, Portugal, Greece and even the Crimea were all mentioned.[2] There was an increasing awareness of the enemy presence at sea, for the frigate *Justice* reported seeing sixteen British ships heading west down the coast of Italy. Naval officers knew that the Armament, as then constituted, would suffer heavily if it met strong opposition, for 'the ships of the line were encumbered with baggage and they had the troublesome task of defending an immense and incoherent convoy, which twenty days of sailing had shown was quite incapable of organising itself except to run away'.[3] Yet on the morning of the 22nd no-one seems to have known that Nelson's fleet was only 20 miles away and that the *Leander* had been recalled from investigating some frigates on the horizon.

The French set course for Egypt via the south coast of Crete, which was sighted on the 26th. Sailing close to the coast was perfectly normal in the Mediterranean, where the tradition of 'cabotage' or coasting was still strong among merchant sailors. This might explain why many of the transports were found to be without compass or charts. Seamen would use their knowledge of coasts and headlands and go across the open sea only for short distances, and when it was absolutely necessary. This system was alien to a thorough seaman like Nelson, who saw the coast as a source of danger and shipwreck and preferred to have sea-room to manoeuvre. It was more natural to Brueys, to the merchant captains who made up the bulk of his fleet and to the landsman Bonaparte who associated the sea with danger and the land with safety. Thus, by chance, the Armament was overtaken by Nelson's squadron, which had set a straight course for Egypt.

Bonaparte had less time for his philosophical discussions or 'Institutions' in this part of the voyage and was more preoccupied with preparations for the landing in Egypt. He reorganised the convoy to integrate the section from Civitavecchia. The ships from Genoa would go in front and the *Sérieuse*, carrying General Menou, would sail ahead of them. The Civitavecchia ships would be next, with the frigate *Alceste* in the rear, followed by the Marseilles convoy. The bulk of the warships would be split into two groups. Seven ships of the line, five frigates, a Maltese galley and eleven of the Toulon merchantmen carrying the cavalry (but not their horses) formed one group; the other six ships of the line, including the flagship, formed the other, with five frigates escorting the Corsican convoy.[4] The individual soldiers were briefed and equipped for the landing. Each was to carry four musket flints and sixty rounds of ammunition, with victuals for four days. On the 22nd he issued a proclamation to the troops, which managed to combine historical imagination, grand strategy, religious liberalism and a fear of the excesses of his own men.

> Soldiers,
>
> You are going to undertake a conquest whose effects on civilisation will be incalculable. You will strike the surest and most painful stroke possible against England until you can deal her the final death blow. We shall undergo tiring marches; we shall fight several battles; we shall succeed in all our enterprises; Destiny is with us.
>
> The Mameluke Beys, who favour English trade exclusively, who have covered our merchants with insults and tyrannise over the unfortunate inhabitants of the Nile, will have ceased to exist in a few days after our arrival. The people amongst whom you are going to live are Mohammedans. The first article of their faith is 'There is no other God but God and Mahomet is his prophet'. Do not argue with them. Behave towards them as we behaved towards the Jews and Italians. Show respect to their muftis and imans as you have to rabbis and bishops . . .
>
> The people amongst whom we are going treat women differently from us; but in every country he who commits rape is a monster. Pillage enriches but a few. It dishonours us, it destroys our resources, it makes enemies of the people it is our interest to have as friends.
>
> The first city we are going to meet with was built by Alexander. At each step we shall find memories worthy to excite emulation.[5]

At 9pm on 27 June, as the fleet was 250 miles from its destination, the frigate *Junon* was signalled to come alongside *L'Orient*. Her captain was summoned on board and General Bonaparte ordered him to make all speed to Alexandria, to seek out the French consul and warn him of the approach of the Armament and to instruct him to gather French expatriates under his protection. The *Junon* set all sail and, despite calms on that and the following night, found fair winds at other times. Pompey's Pillar was sighted from 15 miles away and at 9 miles there was a complete view of the city, including the French tricolour flying over the consulate by the harbourside. At 1pm on the 30th a lieutenant was rowed ashore. He found the consul, who was already under threat from Egyptian retaliation. A British fleet of fourteen ships of the line had been there and had left only the previous evening – indeed they had been mistaken for the French, for the Egyptians had been in a state of alert since the news of the capture of Malta had made them aware of Bonaparte's ambitions in that area. The forts were manned and a Bedouin army was being assembled.

The *Junon* took the beleaguered consul back to the fleet, meeting it at 7pm.

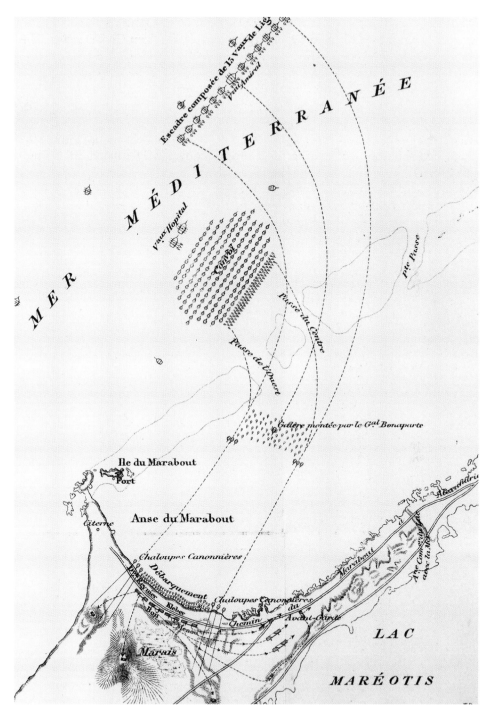

The French landings at Marabout, near Alexandria, based on a plan in de la Jonquière's *Expedition d'Egypte*. In practice the affair was far more chaotic than the drawing suggests. (Chatham Collection)

Bonaparte was warned of the watchfulness of the Egyptians and the danger from the British squadron and this spurred him on.[6] The landing had to be executed as quickly as possible, despite rather rough seas. In Malta he had landed in four places to take a small island; in Egypt he planned to land all his force at a single point, for the threat of serious retaliation was much greater and he needed to keep his strength concentrated, in the short term at least.

★

From the sea the city of Alexandria seemed well fortified and defended, with a rocky shore on its northern coast to make a landing there difficult. There was little time for reconnaissance. The possible landing place at Aboukir Bay, 12 miles to the east of Alexandria, was apparently not considered. Bonaparte chose the bay of Marabout, which was visible from off Alexandria and was only about 7 miles away. It had a curved beach facing to the north-east, nearly a mile long, sheltered from westerly winds and partly protected by sandbanks running parallel to the shore from the tip of a peninsula. This would reduce the amount of surf on the beach but it also prevented even the smaller merchant ships from coming close inshore; the ships' boats would have another long row, this time in rough water.

At 8am on 1 July, Bonaparte signalled for his ships to prepare to anchor and to get the troops ready for a landing. The great convoy of transports went in close as possible in the shallow water, forming a group about a mile in diameter, with its closest point about a mile and a half from Marabout. This was not done without difficulty. The frigate *Alceste* tried to anchor with them but in the heavy sea she was driven onto the ships anchored behind. She raised her anchor and tried again. The ships from Marseilles had no clear orders about where to anchor and were in some confusion. Captain Barre had to send to the flagship for instructions and all this caused long delays.[7]

The ships of the line anchored further out than the merchantmen. They were bigger and needed deeper water; moreover they had a duty to protect the transports from the British squadron, should it reappear. They were ordered to anchor about a mile north of the transports, forming a line of battle running from the north-east, with the flagship in the centre. The manoeuvre began at 10.45am when the *Franklin* dropped her anchor in 20 fathoms of water, in a bottom of mud and sand, and the other ships formed line ahead and astern of her.

In the original plan, General Menou's division on board the transports was to form the left wing of the second wave. However, in the morning of the day of landing, an aide arrived with orders that Menou was to take the first party ashore, perhaps because the distance of the transports from the shore was much shorter than that from the warships. By midday Menou had assembled a miscellaneous collection of 250 ship's boats round the frigate *Sérieuse* and at 1pm he himself got into the frigate's launch to lead the *avant-garde*. By that time, Bonaparte had signalled for the warships' boats to be lowered into the water and the troops of Kléber's and Bon's divisions began to climb down the high sides of the ships of the line and into them. There is no sign that any specially-designed landing craft had been prepared for the expedition, so ordinary ships' boats were used – a typical 74 of the period carried a longboat 36ft long, a barge of 32ft and a cutter of 26ft. Bonaparte called for the captured Maltese galley *Negresse* to come under the stern of *L'Orient*, for he intended to use the captured Maltese vessel for his personal transport during the landing. Getting the troops into the boats took more than 2 hours, but then there was a diversion as a strange vessel was sighted to the north-east. It might have been a frigate from the British squadron and the frigate *Diane* was sent to investigate; it found the French frigate *Justice* arriving from Malta.

Brueys was beginning to have doubts. The sea was rough and night would fall soon. He advised Bonaparte to delay the landing. The General-in-Chief replied: 'Admiral, we have no time to lose; Fortune has given me three days; if I do not profit from it, we are lost.'[8] Nelson believed his destiny was controlled by God but Bonaparte placed his face in a vaguer concept of 'fortune'. Brueys helped him down the side of *L'Orient* into the waiting galley and according to one account the admiral said aloud: 'Fortune has abandoned me. These words are prophetic.'

At 6.20pm Bonaparte gave the signal and the *Negresse* began its journey towards the beach at Marabout, 5 miles away. About 100 ships' boats, each carrying 30 or 40 soldiers and manned by perhaps a dozen sailors, formed up round the galley, with General Kléber's division to Bonaparte's right and Bon's to the left – the nautical terms of port and starboard are perhaps less appropriate here, for the force had now taken up its military formation, under the command of its General. Meanwhile the rest of the troops aboard the convoy of transports were preparing for their landing. They were to form up round the frigate *Courageuse* and then follow the orders of Captain Motard, the adjutant-general of the fleet, who would lead them in the galley *Amoureuse*. The divisions of Desaix and Reynier were to form this, the third wave of the assault.

After struggling with a heavy sea, Menou's boat from the transport ships was the first to arrive on the coast of Egypt, just east of the fort of Marabout and he led his division ashore. Since they did not have the flat bottoms of landing craft, the boats had to disembark their men some yards from the shore, leaving them to wade the rest of the distance. Some of the heavily-loaded troops discarded their weighty ration packs. Several boats capsized in the surf, but there was no loss of life at this stage. Apart from the French soldiers, the beach was deserted – no people, no animals. Menou planted the French flag and led his troops to the top of a sand dune. From there he found time to admire the ruins of Roman Alexandria.[9]

If Bonaparte had planned his trip ashore in the galley as a triumphal procession, he was disappointed. It was a long row from the warship anchorage to the beach and the regular order of the boats carrying Kléber's and Bon's divisions was soon disrupted. The *Negresse* lost sight of them in the night. With a relatively deep draught, she had to stop more than a mile from the beach. The conqueror of Italy got into a small boat and was rowed the rest of the way, arriving at 11pm.

Kléber's men had arrived a little earlier and the troops, thirsty after long hours in the boats, ran towards the streams of fresh water which they found behind the beach. It was brackish, but delicious compared with their supplies on board the

Vivant-Denon's on-the-spot drawing of the landings, showing Bonaparte's galley to the left, and the tower at Marabout. (Jean-Loup Charmet, Paris)

Franklin. Also unopposed, they found time for an hour's rest while more men landed.[10] There was a brief attack on Menou's division by a small party of Mameluke cavalry and a Captain Moreau was killed, but the French still had more to fear from the sea than from such activity.[11] About twenty men were lost in the landing, due to rough seas and reefs, according to Bonaparte.[12]

Just after midnight, when Bonaparte mustered his troops and reviewed them: 1800 to 2000 men of Menou's division had landed, 1200 to 1500 from Bon's and 900 to 1000 from Kléber's, with a few, perhaps as many as 600, from Desaix's men of the third wave.[13] Reynier's group was still in difficulties. The ships had not found their proper anchorages until late in the afternoon and by that time the sea had got worse; some of the masters of the transports had refused to launch their boats. The ships were mixed up and it was difficult to assemble the men in coherent units. Some were apparently landed but the rest of the division had to wait until daylight when the operation resumed.[14] No artillery or horses were disembarked with any part of the army. It would have been impossible to take horses in ships' boats at the best of times and certainly not in such a rough sea. Artillery could have been landed with some difficulty but it would have taken a large proportion of the available boats and, without horses to move it, would have been largely useless ashore.

It was important to capture Alexandria quickly, for it offered supplies in the middle of desert country and a port where the horses and artillery could be landed. The troops had been issued with food and water but many seasick soldiers had neglected to take them ashore, while others abandoned them in the scramble through the surf. Food and water could be obtained in the city. Bonaparte left

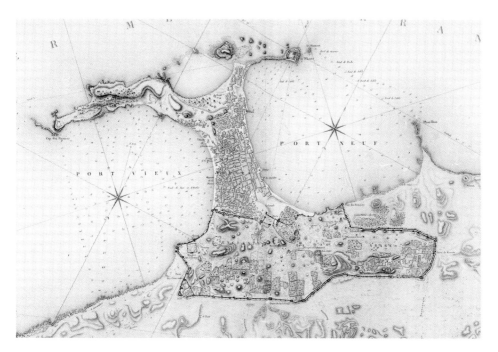

Vivant-Denon's map of Alexandria, showing the walled and largely derelict old city to the south, the more recent Arab Town forming the vertical of the T and the Old and New Ports on each side. (Jean-Loup Charmet, Paris)

Desaix's men to guard the beachhead and marched off early in the morning of 2 July. There was no road as such but the route to the city lay along a neck of land, often only a few hundred yards wide, which separated Lake Mareotis from the sea. The march was unopposed until a force of about 300 cavalry was seen at 8am when the troops were a mile and a half from Alexandria. The Bedouin decided against a suicidal attack on vastly superior forces and headed down the Cairo road.

Alexander the Great's city was based on a T-shaped peninsula with a harbour on each side; the modern city was on the upright of the T and Alexander's old town was a walled enclosure on the land just to the south, 2 miles long and about half a mile broad. The assault on the walled town began at 10am. Menou's division, forming the left of the army, had marched along the beach. It now took station to the west of the city, opposite the short stretch of wall and the Triangular Fort which formed its corner. Menou led the storming of the wall himself and was the first to enter the city, suffering seven wounds on the way. Meanwhile, Kléber's men attacked the western end of the long south wall. He too was wounded while showing his men where to climb the wall. He survived despite being hit in the face and his men also entered the city. Bon's division attacked the Rosetta gate on the eastern side of the walls. The battle continued with the Egyptian forces retreating to the Triangular Fort and the more modern city to the north, on the neck of the peninsula, but the walls were ruinous and the Egyptian garrison was tiny. They surrendered before the end of the day, leaving Bonaparte and his army in control.[15] Accounts of French casualties vary; from 15 to 40 killed and from 60 to 100 wounded according to which figures are used.[16]

Every effort was to be made to placate the ordinary people, to divide them from the Turks and the Mamelukes and to present the invasion as a liberation. On 2 July Bonaparte proclaimed,

> The beys who govern Egypt have long insulted the French nation and injured its merchants; the hour of their punishment has arrived. For too long this rabble of slaves bought in Georgia and Caucasia have tyrannised over the most beautiful part of the world; but God, from whom all depends, has ordered that their empire shall cease . . . The Egyptians will be called upon to hold all offices; the wisest and most learned and most virtuous will govern and the people will be happy.

He called on the 'Cadis, sheiks, imans' to 'tell the people that we are friends of the true Moslems'. In translation this was rendered as 'we are true Moslems'. It was also mentioned that the French Revolutionaries had made war on the Pope and overthrown the Knights of Malta, long-standing enemies of Islam.[17]

Bonaparte wrote to his masters in Paris, 'This country is not at all inferior to the picture painted by travellers; it is calm, proud and brave.'[18] Not everyone agreed and most were bitterly disappointed with the obvious decay they saw around them. The city had declined from a population of 300,000 in Roman times to 6000 now. To Commissary Jaubert of the fleet it was 'a heap of ruins, where you see a paltry hovel of mud and straw against the magnificent fragments of a granite column. The streets are not paved.' Only the so-called Pompey's Pillar (actually erected by Severus more than 300 years after Pompey) and 'Cleopatra's Needle' (which had nothing to do with Antony's queen) stood out in the 'image of desolation'.[19] To Laugier, there was 'no trace of its ancient splendour or the genius of its founder. Everything carries the stamp of despotism which always knows how to destroy and never to conserve.'[20] Unconsciously they echoed Mark Wood of the East India Company who had visited in 1779. 'The appearance of Alexandria from the sea is very beautiful and conveys some idea of the former grandeur, but which on landing quickly vanishes . . . this mighty city dwindles into obscure houses and narrow dirty streets, amidst heaps of ruins.'[21] To men who had seen the glories of Italy and had been promised new delights in Egypt, this was a grave disappointment. To soldiers who had seen Rome, her former rival as the greatest city of the Mediterranean looked like a decayed, crumbling backwater. Seeing the desert shores, one soldier joked, 'There are the six acres of land they promised us.'

This attitude among his troops inspired Bonaparte to accelerate his campaign, to try and inflict crushing defeats on the Mamelukes before demoralisation became total. Within two days of taking Alexandria he sent columns of troops to secure the rest of the western part of the Nile delta by seizing the towns of Rosetta and Damanhour. Having done that the columns reunited at Rahmaniya on the Nile on 11 July. They marched south and on the 21st they met the main Mameluke force at Embade, 10 miles from the Great Pyramid. Bonaparte had 25,000 men but hardly any cavalry. The Egyptian forces consisted of 6000 Mameluke cavalry, 8000 Bedouin and 15,000 fellahin who fought on foot. Forming his infantry into squares against the charges of the Mamelukes, Bonaparte inflicted a crushing defeat and became master of the country. The following day he entered Cairo but the capital of modern Egypt was no less of a disappointment to his men.

★

The fleet under Brueys had no reason to feel greatly inferior to Nelson's force. The British admiral's name was not yet well known in France, though some accounts of his actions at Cape St Vincent had reached Paris and Toulon. Reports of Royal Navy movements in the Mediterranean were often received by Brueys but they referred to 'la flotte Anglaise' or 'l'escadre Anglaise', rarely to Nelson by name. The French navy could look back over the last few years with a certain amount of satisfaction. It had weathered the storms of the early 1790s, when it had been disrupted by mutiny from revolutionary sailors and betrayal by Royalist officers and dockyard officials. Now, it seemed, the British were the ones most prone to mutiny.

Nor was the French fleet's performance in battle to be despised. In the last war it had drawn with the British off Ushant in 1779 and in America it had forced them to withdraw from the Chesapeake in 1781, making way for the Franco-American victory at Yorktown which had secured American independence. It had been defeated in the West Indies at Battle of the Saintes in 1782 and had lost six ships in the Glorious First of June, or 13 Prairial as the Revolutionary calendar called it. That affair was nevertheless regarded in as a victory in France, for a vital grain convoy had escaped and reached Brest. France's allies had been beaten at Cape St Vincent and Camperdown; while these defeats might highlight the prowess of the British they did not necessarily reflect badly on the French themselves. For a totally crushing defeat, France had to look back almost 40 years to Quiberon Bay in 1759. The spirit of the new Revolutionary navy was recovering: its officers were gaining in experience and confidence; its men, by and large, were dedicated to the defence of the Republic and it was beginning to weld itself into a coherent fighting force.

Francois-Paul, Comte de Brueys d'Aigallieri, had been born in 1753 to an aristocratic family in Languedoc, in the south of France. It was peacetime when he joined the *Marine Royale* at the age of 13 but he served against Barbary corsairs in the Mediterranean. He first fought the British in 1780, as a lieutenant in De Grasse's fleet in the West Indies. After the war in 1784, he became captain of a small dispatch vessel in the West Indies, where he surveyed fortifications and sent home observations on the navigation and commerce of the area. He was one of the few officers not to flee when the Revolution began to put fear into the hearts of the old aristocracy. He was appointed captain of a 74-gun ship in 1792 and stood firm against the mutinous elements in his crew, but was retired from active service during the Jacobin period. The naval situation, and a change of government, caused his recall and promotion to rear-admiral in 1796. At the request of General Bonaparte, the Minister of the Marine put him in charge of a squadron at Corfu and from there he took part in the Italian campaigns. In 1798 he was promoted vice-admiral and put in charge of the naval side of the Egyptian expedition.

After the capture of Alexandria, the transports could be brought into the harbours on each side of the city and the remaining troops, along with the horses, artillery and stores, could be unloaded. Some of the soldiers were still on the warships and the healthy ones were disembarked by boat. Others, unable to march with the army because of lameness or age, were to be left on board as marines. Bonaparte believed that his victorious troops would stiffen the resistance of the seamen, as well as helping to compensate for their lack of numbers. French-born sailors in the transports were sent into the warships to augment their crews and Egyptian seamen were to be recruited in their places. Such instability in manning, however unavoidable, was bad for any ship and the new men in the crews were to have little time to integrate themselves in their new roles.

Bonaparte and Brueys had to consider what to do with thow that it had achieved its primary task by delivering the army and its supplies to Egypt. Its present anchorage off the city was clearly untenable. The bottom was not good holding

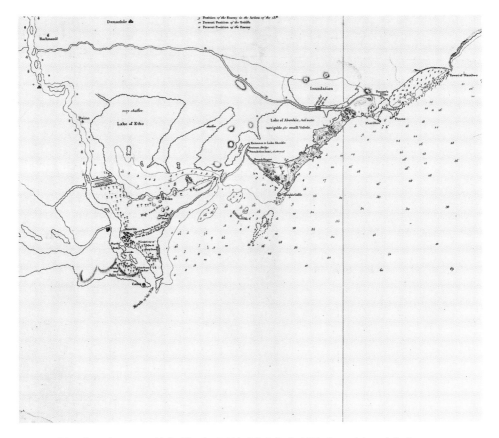

A chart of the Alexandria area, published by the British Admiralty in 1801. From right to left, the main features on the coast are: the Rosetta mouth of the Nile; Aboukir Bay; the Port and town of Alexandria; Marabout Bay. (National Maritime Museum, London: A8581)

ground for anchors, the area was strewn with rocks and the fleet had to be spread out, making it possible for an enemy to pick the ships off one by one.[22] One admiral claimed that he would not have waited 24 hours off Alexandria once the troops had been landed.[23] The ships still carried a certain amount of army artillery and heavy equipment which could not be landed easily by small boats, so it was important to find a more sheltered and suitable anchorage to put them ashore.

One possibility, favoured by Admiral Brueys, was to send the fleet to Corfu after the remaining stores and artillery had been landed. The harbour there was safe from natural disaster and enemy attack. The fleet would be in the rear of any British force which might threaten Egypt and Nelson would certainly not have been able to maintain an effective blockade at such a distance from his bases and with the French fleet on his lines of communication. Brueys's squadron would be a threat to both Austria and Sicily. It would be a 'fleet in being' which would dominate the Mediterranean by its very existence, without having to do very much.

Bonaparte, on the other hand, wanted the fleet to stay close to him, preferably in the harbour at Alexandria. It is never easy to interpret his long-term plans, because there was always an element of opportunism in them. Certainly, he was considering the possibility of a return to France quite soon: after he had inflicted a few defeats on the Mamelukes he would leave the command to one of his generals and go home. The idea of an invasion of England had not been abandoned and the Egyptian expedition was still in a sense seen as a diversion. As he had told his troops on 28 June, '[In Egypt] you will strike the surest and most painful stroke possible against England until you can deal her final death blow.' The officials at Toulon dockyard were also preparing for the return of the fleet[24] while, for himself, Bonaparte had asked his brother to find him a property in France, so he apparently contemplated a return by the winter.[25] On a higher strategic level, he may have considered the possibility of sending Brueys back to bring another convoy of troops and supplies. In any case, he wanted to keep the fleet close to him, where it would protect his rear and be ready to do his bidding. As an aggressive, active general the idea of a passive 'fleet in being' was alien to him. As commander-in-chief in Egypt, he felt he needed Brueys's force under his immediate command.

The coast of Egypt was notoriously short of good harbours and anchorages. The mouths of the Nile were too shallow for any but specially-designed local craft, known as 'djermes'. Apart from the large harbours at Alexandria and a partly sheltered anchorage at Aboukir, the straight, flat and featureless coast provided no places where a fleet could rest in any degree of safety. Bonaparte therefore urged Brueys to take it into harbour at Alexandria where it could be protected by forts and gun batteries on land. He wanted him to set up a naval base there and ordered him to land officers and workers, and recruit local employees to that end. However, he was aware that it might not be easy to get the fleet in. On 3 July he ordered Brueys to 'take his squadron into the Old Port of Alexandria tomorrow, if the weather permit and there is the necessary depth of water.'[26]

The city of Alexandria was built around two natural harbours, the Old Port to the west and the New Port to the east. No-one doubted that the New Port was too open and shallow for a fleet such as this, but the Old Port offered some prospects. Ships' boats were sent to carry out surveys under experienced officers and Ensign Lachadenede reported that three channels had been found into the harbour. The best one offered no more than 5 fathoms or 30ft at its minimum depth. A large vessel like *L'Orient* could be reduced to this draught by taking out guns and stores, but the ships would have to go in very slowly, with a calm sea and a favourable wind, for a north-westerly could create waves which would reduce the minimum depth by a quarter or a half. They might enter at the rate of two per day: but what would happen if the British arrived when half of them were in?[27] Even more important, as Brueys himself pointed out on 7 July, the ships could come out at only the same rate – in practice the Port of Alexandria could then be blocked by a single, determined enemy ship of the line.[28]

★

Thus the decision was made after nearly a week of vacillation: the fleet would go to Aboukir. At 5pm on 7 July Brueys signalled for his ships to raise their anchors for the move. After the short journey to the Bay, just 9 miles to the east, they had orders to put themselves in a line from the north-west to the south-east, more than 2 miles to the south-east of Aboukir Island. There were difficulties because the bottom was little known and inadequately surveyed, and the first position they took up certainly had grave faults. In fact the head of the line ran almost due west from the flagship in the centre, with the tail falling away from the south-east – '*s'embossé*' or humped, as Brueys had evidently intended it to be. At first the *Spartiate* was at the head of the line, anchored in 7 fathoms, but this was too far from the shore and Brueys ordered the *Guerrier* and *Conquérant* to take station ahead of her, anchoring in 5 fathoms.[29] The last ship was a peculiar choice, because of her weak hull and reduced armament. If her 50-year old structure was not strong enough to support 36-pounder guns, how could it be expected to stand British broadsides? However, she had to go somewhere unless the line was to be shortened and Brueys did not believe she would be in any great danger. He expected that the enemy would attack his centre and rear, not the northern end of the line. The ships at the head of the line, he believed, were partly protected by the fort and by the shoals around them. Moreover, their retreat would be cut off by a British force at the centre and rear, so he presumed they would be attacked last. A conventional naval attack would have seen the head of the British line making for the rear of the French, with one ship placing itself alongside each of the enemy. Brueys did not know that his opponent was not a conventional naval tactician.

On 7 July Brueys showed an unwonted confidence when he wrote of the possibility of setting up an '*inexpugnable*' position at Aboukir. This, however, depended on having strong forts or batteries on land at each end of the line of ships.[30] With a similar idea in mind, Brigadier Potevin of the army engineers surveyed the coasts round the bay and reported on the fort at the northern end on the mainland. It had twenty guns, mostly in poor condition, and was manned by fifty men. It would need considerable repair to make it effective and was a long way from the anchorage. Offshore was a small island that was slightly more promising, though no ship could anchor within about a mile and a half of it, well beyond the effective range of any guns of the time. Indeed as Potevin was writing his dispatch, the fleet came to anchor between 3 and 5 miles from this fort.[31] Nevertheless it was decided to strengthen the defensive and offensive power of the island. It was given two mortars for long-range fire and some 6-pounder guns for its own defence. However, it was found that the mortar shells could hardly reach the position at the north end of Brueys's line, far less be aimed accurately at such range.[32]

In choosing the disposition at Aboukir, Brueys may have been influenced by the Battle of St Kitts in 1782, in which he had served as an officer in De Grasse's fleet. Finding himself outnumbered, Admiral Samuel Hood (an elder cousin of the captain of the *Zealous*) had anchored his squadron of twenty-two ships in Frigate Bay, in an L-shaped formation, with the heel of the L facing in the direction of the prevailing north-easterly wind. De Grasse attacked from the south with twenty-eight ships but his approach was slow and difficult against the wind and Hood's formation was unshakeable. He abandoned the attack after a few days.

If Brueys's disposition was really based on Frigate Bay, then there was a fundamental difference. The north-east trades are constant in the West Indies outside the hurricane season, whereas winds are much more variable in the Mediterranean.

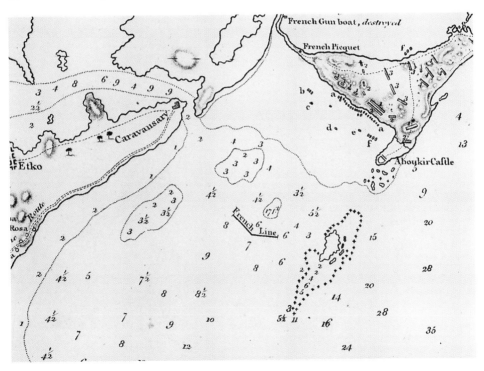

Detail from the Admiralty chart of 1801, showing the position of the French fleet in Aboukir Bay. Nelson's ships had to round Aboukir Island, which is shown but not named, and the dangerous shoals around it are clearly marked. Depths are in fathoms. (National Maritime Museum, London: A8581)

Inasmuch as the winds were predictable, they were not necessarily in the French favour. A south-westerly would make Brueys safe, for any fleet attacking him would have to make a long tack towards his position, all the time feeling the full force of the French guns. A westerly wind was more likely in July and August and it would be much less suitable, for it would allow a British force to attack any point on the French line after rounding the shoals at Aboukir. A north-west wind was equally likely and would be even worse. It would allow the British to attack with the wind broad on their beams, their best point of sailing, and then allow them to move down the enemy line at will with the wind behind them.

A better disposition might have been found, with the first ship anchored close to the shoal to the north and the line running south-west from there and then turning through about 90 degrees to run south-east. No ship could attack over the shoals and in a westerly wind any which attacked from either the east or the south would face a contrary wind, slowing their approach and making them vulnerable to raking fire while they could only make a feeble reply. But no formation would be completely safe in both a westerly and a north-westerly wind. In the latter case, an approach from the south would be impossible because of the shoals but one from the north-east would be relatively easy, with a beam wind.

Brueys's general plan could thus be faulted but its execution was even more flawed. It was necessary for the ships to be anchored close to each other and also close to the shoals at each end of the line. At St Kitts, Hood had ensured that his ships were anchored with their bowsprits and sterns almost touching and had taken a great deal of care in getting them into place: Brueys's whole line was nearly 2 miles long, with about 175 yards between ships. It was also important for each ship to have some control over its movement at anchor, either by anchoring bow and stern or by having springs on their cables. Without either of these, the ships would tend to face into the wind, and if the enemy attacked from that direction then the French would be bow on and unable to reply. Moreover, if the ships were left free to swing at anchor, then they would have to moor sufficiently clear of the shoals to allow for this. This, as it turned out, was what Brueys did and it proved to be the most serious flaw of all.

Brueys might well have found a stronger position inside the bay, but it would have depended on detailed surveys of the area and the officers most skilled in such tasks were fully occupied in surveying the entrances to Alexandria. Nonetheless he continued to try and improve the situation and on 13 July he wrote to Bonaparte that he was trying to put his squadron in 'a formidable position', in case he should have to fight at anchor. However, he was hampered by strong northerly winds and admitted that the anchorage was too open to allow a safe formation against an enemy of superior force. His surveyors continued to look at the possibility of entering Alexandria and the latest reports suggested that 27ft 6in of water was available there. This was enough for a ship of the line with a favourable wind and a calm sea; but how and when would they get out again?[33]

During his 3 weeks at Aboukir, Brueys's mind was preoccupied with another problem – the difficulty of keeping his ships supplied with food, water and even firewood. They had little chance to replenish from the scant resources of Malta and during the voyage they had been obliged to feed troops as well as their own crews. They had left Toulon 2 months ago and by the second half of July they were running short of everything. Most of the food which had come with the supply ships had been intended for the army and had been ordered ashore on 4 July.[34]

Ships' biscuit, the staple diet of seamen in all the European navies, was in short supply. Only 5 days' worth was left on the 6th, before Brueys sailed from Alexandria. French ships also carried flour and had furnaces and bakers on board to make it into bread, but only in small quantities.[35] Rice was a possible alternative but officers were sceptical about its nutritional value compared with biscuit and bread and they demanded 10 ounces per man compared with 6 ounces of bread. It was estimated that 2500 quintals (hundredweight) were needed for a month's supply. Brueys asked that some be sent before the bread ran out completely, so that the men could be accustomed gradually to the change of diet.[36] The naval victualler believed there were 5000 quintals at Rosetta for the use of the army but no-one had the authority to transfer it to the fleet, as Bonaparte was on the way to Cairo.

Firewood was equally important, for boiling rice or baking bread. One hundred and fifty tons were needed urgently but the coast of Egypt was not well provided with trees. Eighty cows and 150 sheep were required to complete the seamen's diet but were difficult to find in addition to the needs of the army. Commissary Poussielgue wrote of the 'great cries' from the fleet for more supplies.[37]

Water was also in short supply. Even the smallest craft of the French fleet, the 'avisos' or despatch vessels, were too deep draughted to enter the Nile to collect fresh water and Brueys asked for some of the local craft, the 'djermes'. These were,

the boats used for transporting merchandise from the Nile to Alexandria. They are strong built and draw little water . . . they are without decks and have two or three masts according to their size, with very large lateen sails. When the sailors wish to furl the sails, they are obliged to climb up the yard, which cannot be lowered, being made fast to the head of the mast.[38]

Ships' boats were too small to carry much and the voyage to Rosetta was long and difficult in an open boat. It was possible to send watering parties ashore at Aboukir but that too had its dangers. On 22 July a party was attacked by mounted Arabs who killed eleven and wounded four more. The French sailors barely had time to retreat to their boats. In future all landing parties at Aboukir would have to be large in number and well-armed[39] – a problem which was to have enormous consequences for the squadron. By 24 July Brueys could see the possibility of men dying of hunger and thirst.[40]

On 27 July Brueys received news of Bonaparte's victory over the Mamelukes at the Battle of the Pyramids and issued double rations to his crews in celebration. But he was rather more worried about the sightings of enemy ships. The British frigates *Terpsichore* and *Seahorse* had arrived on the 21st and sailed away again; Brueys was not to know that they had lost all contact with Nelson's force. He had reports that the latter squadron had been seen off Crete on the same day, sailing east. He commented, 'the movements of the English seem quite extraordinary. I can only attribute it to the want of victuals, that a force undoubtedly having orders to search for us should return without combat.'[41]

CHAPTER 10

The Band of Brothers

FIVE MONTHS AFTER the Battle of the Nile Nelson famously wrote to Lord Howe, 'I had the happiness to command a Band of Brothers,'[1] paraphrasing Shakespeare's 'We few, we happy few, we band of brothers' from *Henry V*.[2] In fact he had used the phrase earlier, in letters to St Vincent on 25 September and to his wife on 1 October, and there was an echo of it even in 1797, when Lady Spencer spoke of the admirals and captains, presumably of St Vincent's fleet, as 'a chosen band, they all can do the same great actions'.[3] Nelson's phrase rings down through naval history and it is not inaccurate, but it should not deter the historian from examining the dynamics of the group, and reporting on the strengths and weaknesses of the relationships.

Quite possibly Nelson intended it to mean, in modern business jargon, 'a flat management structure' in which all the captains were equal under the admiral. In Syracuse, for example, he did not automatically select his senior captains to meet the Governor, but wrote asking 'should any captains of the squadron wish to pay their respects to him at the same time, the admiral would be glad of their company'.[4] This sort of egalitarianism, even within a single rank, cut across a century of naval tradition in which seniority within a rank was almost as significant as the holding of a higher one.

How well could Nelson get to know and influence the captains under his command in the short space of about 7 weeks from 10 June to 1 August? He was, of course, seriously constrained by the fact that they were all in different ships and the means of communication between them were very limited. The most obvious method, and the only one likely to be available in battle or in strong winds, was by signal flags. This was a very restricted means, for the 'alphabet' code, in which words could actually be spelled out, was still a few years in the future. The flagship carried seventeen specialised flags and pennants and could also use ordinary flags, such as the Union Flag, as part of a signal. Some signals still relied on the movements of sails, as they had in the days before special signal flags came in. The way to indicate 'having discovered a strange fleet' was to have the main- and fore-topgallant sails hoisted but hanging loose, the topsail yards lowered down and to fire one gun. Altogether there were 179 prearranged messages in St Vincent's signal book of 1796, plus a few extra ones which were added by Nelson for his own squadron. Only the more common tactical and operational orders could be sent in this way. Indeed the tradition of centralisation was so strong in the navy that subordinate captains were expected to obey signals rather than send them and only selected ships carried a full set of flags. A few signals, such as the reporting of a strange sail in a certain direction, could be made by flags which all ships carried but there was no question of a tactical discussion between captains and admirals using signal flags.

Messages to individual ships and captains could be passed by hailing and signal No. 93 called for a named ship to pass within hail of the flagship. Nelson did this quite often, for example on 17 June when he hailed Saumarez to tell him the latest information about the French movements. The obvious snag of this method was highlighted by the fact that Saumarez 'could not distinguish at what place' the French had been seen.[5] Hailing was suitable for passing on gossip or for making arrangements to speak in more detail later but it too was unsuitable for detailed discussions.

If Nelson had general written orders to issue to the fleet he would signal for each ship to send a midshipman or lieutenant to the flagship in a boat. On receipt of the new instruction, each of these messengers would sign one of the two order books kept in the *Vanguard*. Most of these instructions were purely administrative or concerned with the order in which the fleet was to sail but Nelson did issue two important tactical orders on 8 June. He put the fleet into two divisions for action in the open sea and decreed that if the battle was fought inshore the ships should have an anchor ready at the stern. New combinations of flags were devised for these orders and added to the signal book.[6]

The final method of communication, the one which tradition has associated especially with Nelson's name, was to have his captains on board for a tactical conference. Historians have frequently conflated Nelson's 'band of brothers' comment with Captain Berry's statement that 'It had been his practice during the whole of the cruise, whenever the weather and circumstances would permit, to have his captains on board the *Vanguard* where he would fully develop to them his own ideas of the different and best modes of attack . . . With the masterly ideas of their admiral therefore on the subject of naval tactics, every one of the captains of his squadron was most thoroughly acquainted.'[7] This conjures up an image of a dozen captains round the table with their admiral, constantly discussing and exchanging ideas on how to annihilate the enemy. It may well be accurate for some of Nelson's campaigns, in which the captains were to spend some time under Nelson's command and get very used to his ways. It was much less so before the Nile: for the fleet only came together as a fighting formation on 10 June, less than 8 weeks before its great battle. Many of the officers already knew Nelson well before the fleet was formed, but thereafter they could not have had much opportunity jointly to discuss every tactical eventuality.

There were physical difficulties in transferring captains from one ship to another by boat and Berry agrees that it could only be done 'whenever the weather and circumstances would permit' – in calms, or light winds when the seas were not too rough and the boats could keep up with the pace of the ships. Furthermore, it was not desirable to have too many captains away from their ships at once, because Nelson was constantly concerned that the enemy might be sighted at any moment. There is in fact no evidence that all the captains were assembled together between 10 June and 1 August. Although Troubridge had made the signal for all his captains to come on board the *Culloden* on 4 June, that was before he made contact with the admiral.[8]

The evidence shows that Nelson was more likely to call for his captains in ones or twos. According to his signal log, Saumarez, nominally the second-in-command of the squadron, was on the *Vanguard* four times between 10 June and the arrival at Syracuse on 20 July.[9] He was on board on at least one more occasion according to his own diary, for dinner on 15 June, but presumably that invitation was extended by hailing, without any need for an entry in the signal log. Troubridge was called to the flagship rather more often; nine times according to the log. He often had to be briefed before being sent on detached missions, into Naples on 17 June for example, but this also gives some indication of his standing with Nelson. Hardy was called upon five times for briefing or debriefing, because the special qualities of his ship, the little *Mutine*, made her suitable for inshore reconnaissance. The maximum number of captains on board the *Vanguard* on any one occasion was five, including her own, Berry. This was on 22 June when the conference was held on the decision to steer for Egypt. Besides Nelson and Berry it involved the four most trusted captains, Saumarez, Troubridge, Darby and Ball. Foley, who would ultimately make one of the most important decisions of all, was not present and indeed he was invited on board the flagship only once, on 7 July with Troubridge and Ball. In all, Ball was summoned four times, Darby of the *Bellerophon* and Hallowell of the *Swiftsure* twice each, and Hood of the *Zealous* and Thompson of the *Leander* once each. Five captains – Miller, Louis, Gould, Peyton and Westcott – were evidently never called at all.

Of course there may have been a few other occasions when individuals were invited on board the flagship by hailing, but this method could not have been used for a general invitation and it is quite certain that Nelson never made such an invitation by signal during the period in question. Certainly he and his captains would have had some chances to get together while the fleet was at Syracuse in July, but their group discussions must have been limited, with so much work to do in repairing and storing their ships.

If only because he is one of the most important witnesses, we have to give some credence to Berry's evidence but the inference usually drawn from it, that Nelson had regular general conferences during the run-up to the Battle of the Nile is clearly wrong. For this Berry's phraseology, composed in the glow of hindsight, bears some of the blame but to be fair, he does not explicitly say that all the captains came at once or that they were included equally.

How, then, were tactical ideas communicated? Were they outlined to the senior captains, especially Saumarez and Troubridge as leaders of divisions, who then passed them to their subordinates? There is no evidence for this. Saumarez's papers give no hint of it and the ships' logs of the *Orion* and *Culloden* show no sign of junior captains being called on board. In fact, such communication may not have been necessary anyway. An analysis of the battle will show that the tactical ideas, such as they were, were contained in Nelson's orders of 8 June. Nelson's plans were essentially very simple and needed little elaboration. The 'Nelson touch' as it was called a few years later, relied on leadership, seamanship, instinct and controlled aggression, not on detailed tactical planning.

★

The date of his promotion to captain was perhaps the most vital stage in any naval officer's career. His commission as a lieutenant depended, in theory, on length of service, examination and a suitable vacancy. Promotion to commander was by selection and entitled the candidate to take charge of a small ship, too insignificant to be 'rated'. Promotion to captain was also by selection but from then on everything proceeded according to seniority. After about 20 years as captain an officer might be retired to become a 'yellow' admiral. Otherwise he would be promoted to the lowest grade of flag rank, rear-admiral of the blue, and would slowly progress through the nine grades of rear, vice and full admirals of the blue, white and red squadrons. If he was promoted young enough and lived long enough he would eventually become Admiral of the Fleet. Obviously there was the possibility that incompetent or senile officers would reach high rank but the naval administration could get round that by keeping them ashore on half pay. It could also accelerate the promotion of very deserving candidates but only by 'reaching down' the captains list. When the Admiralty determined to promote Nelson to flag rank in 1797 five officers above him in the list had to be promoted as well. Nelson disregarded the rules of seniority whenever he thought it necessary but most captains were obsessed with them and studied their relative position in each new edition of the Navy List to keep up to date on their chances of becoming an admiral. When considering the careers, abilities and attitudes of the 'Band of Brothers', it is useful to list them in order of seniority, because that is how they perceived themselves.

Sir James Saumarez was the second-in-command of the squadron according to the laws of seniority. He was slightly older than Nelson, having been born in 1757 to a well-established naval family in the Channel Islands. He had not enjoyed the same meteoric rise, but had been promoted captain in February 1782, about 2½ years behind his admiral. At the beginning of the war, in 1793, he fought a successful frigate action, then joined the 74-gun *Orion* in 1795. He fought in the Channel Fleet's action off the Ile de Groix later that year, and at Cape St Vincent with the Mediterranean Fleet in 1797.

Saumarez was well aware of the insecurity of his position in Nelson's squadron. Both St Vincent and Nelson had intended Thomas Troubridge as second-in-command and for the *Orion* to return to the fleet off Cadiz as soon as the junction between Nelson and Troubridge had been carried out. One day on the poop of St Vincent's flagship, Saumarez had 'expressed so very anxious and importunate desire to go [home]' that the Admiral did not intend to stand in the way of his wishes.[10] He ordered Nelson to 'take everything out of the *Orion* she can spare, consistently with her passage to Gibraltar, where you will direct her to proceed.' She was then to be sent home. Saumarez wanted the best of both worlds and wrote to his wife,

Sir James Saumarez in 1801, from a print engraved by R. Greatbach. (Chatham Collection)

'What a blessing if our present endeavours should be crowned with success and I have the good fortune to return to England immediately after.'[11] He was fortunate in one respect at least, for in the event Nelson decided to keep the *Orion*, at least until the missing frigates were found.

As we have seen, Nelson tended to confide in Troubridge rather than Saumarez and the latter, as second-in-command, was the one to suffer most from the 'flat management' of the 'Band of Brothers'. He always resented the fact that he was never singled out for praise in view of his special responsibility, while Nelson did everything possible to promote the interests of Troubridge, who was to play little part in the final outcome.

Saumarez was a highly competent and even distinguished officer. Unlike Troubridge, Ball and Hardy, however, he was never under the spell of Nelson and was critical of him on several occasions during the campaign. When Nelson refused to include one of his letters in the official mail, Saumarez wrote 'he is so full of mystery at this time that he seems unwilling any letter should be sent but those he writes to government'. He formally supported the decision to go to Egypt but wrote privately, 'it is very doubtful whether we shall fall in with [the French] at all, as we are proceeding on the merest conjecture only, and not on any positive information.' When Nelson decided not to investigate a report that two of his missing frigates had been seen off Crete he wrote 'I am rather surprised the admiral did not endeavour to fall in with them.' After the battle he was openly critical of Nelson's tactics.[12]

Saumarez was also capable of self-doubt and during a particularly difficult stage of the campaign he wrote, 'Fortunately I only act here *en second*; but did the chief responsibility rest with me, I fear it would be more than my too irritable nerves would bear.'[13] This might be taken as an admission of unfitness for high command;

Right: Thomas Masterman Hardy in 1801, by an unknown artist.
(National Maritime Museum, London: BHC2745)

Below: Pages from a signal book which was almost certainly used during the Nile campaign.
(National Maritime Museum, London: D8796)

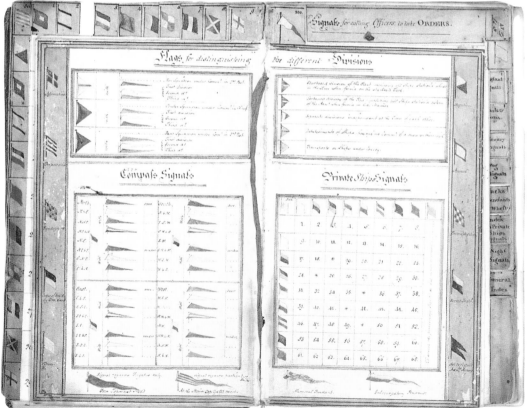

Nelson wounded during the battle, coming on deck to see *L'Orient* on fire. Artist unknown.
(National Maritime Museum, London: BHC2903)

more justly, it could be said to show that Nelson's responsibilities were beyond the normal demands on any commander and in the end Saumarez recognised this. He would go on to fight a great squadron action off Gibraltar in 1801, and to lead the Baltic Fleet with distinction from 1808 to 1812.

According to Lady Nelson, Saumarez's letters to his wife were 'so long that I verily believe he mentions what you give them to *eat*'.[14] The historian has to regret that this was not literally true and that so few of them have survived in manuscript. His marriage and home life were happy and he was religious in a very different way from Nelson. The Admiral was always conservative in his beliefs and practices, whereas Saumarez was much more evangelical and was a patron of the Sunday School movement during his spells on shore. He was aloof from his officers and crew, so he was regarded with less affection than some captains.

★

Thomas Troubridge was the most senior of four captains in the squadron who had all been promoted early in 1783. He was unusual in having no family naval connections. According to legend he was the son of a baker in the City of London, whose little sister had attracted the avuncular affections of Sir Charles Saunders, a member of the Board of Admiralty who had sailed with Anson and taken Wolfe's army to Quebec. Thomas Troubridge, it was said, began his career as a cabin-boy in the East India Company but before he died Saunders had him appointed midshipman on a frigate. Troubridge fought in several actions in India during the American War but became a prisoner early in the war of 1793, being released after the ship he was in was captured by the British at the Battle of the Glorious First of June. He took command of the *Culloden* in 1795 and at the Battle of Cape St Vincent he was at the head of the fleet and therefore able to support Nelson in his attack, his conduct being described by Jervis as 'masterly'. He was Nelson's second-in-command at Tenerife, taking over after the admiral was wounded and evacuating the troops to prevent an even greater disaster.

If St Vincent was forthright, Troubridge was more so. When the two men took office at the Board of Admiralty in 1800 they began a programme of dockyard reform. When St Vincent commented 'The artificers are all thieves', Troubridge went further and said 'All the master shipwrights should be hanged, every one of them, without exception'.[15] As a Member of Parliament he was accused of 'violence of party and scurrilous abuse of persons of the highest rank'. As a captain his views were equally decisive. When asked how to spot a potential mutineer he replied, 'Whenever I see a fellow look as if he was thinking, I say that's mutiny'.[16]

Troubridge was a highly effective leader, seaman and fighter. St Vincent considered him to be 'the greatest man in that walk that the English Navy has ever produced'.[17] During the Nile campaign Nelson sent him ashore to meet Sir William Hamilton at Naples, with a note saying 'Captain Troubridge is in full possession of my confidence . . . my honoured acquaintance of 25 years, and the very best sea officer in His Majesty's Service.'[18] This regard was fully reciprocated by Troubridge at the time.

★

Henry D'Esterre Darby of the *Bellerophon* was only two weeks behind Troubridge in seniority and was competent without being of outstanding ability. Of Irish origin, he was the nephew of the Vice-Admiral Darby who had commanded the Channel Fleet in 1780. Henry Darby had served continuously since the beginning of the war, largely in convoy escort and with the Channel Fleet, where he had seen little action and attracted no notice. Nelson called him to the meeting of 22 June on board the *Vanguard*, presumably because of seniority alone. His comments on that occasion were the most guarded of all the captains present, and he seems to have evaded the main issue without actually saying no to the admiral. In battle, however, he was to show a great deal of courage.

Thomas Louis knew Nelson only slightly, for he had only joined the Mediterranean fleet with the *Minotaur* at the end of 1797. Born in 1759 in Exeter, he had seen action as a lieutenant in the American War and spent some time commanding press gangs in Ireland. He was appointed to the *Minotaur* in 1794, since when she had served as flagship for several admirals, but he had not been in battle.

Captain John Peyton had attained his rank the day after Thomas Louis. He too was from a naval family; his grandfather was an admiral, his father an official at the Navy Office in London and he had three brothers in the navy. He had gained his promotion to captain after serving on his grandfather's flagship in the American War. He had joined the *Defence* only a few months ago after service in St Vincent's frigates. He suffered from ill health during the campaign and wrote to Nelson:

> The rapid decline of my health and bodily strength is such to place me in the most uncomfortable situation in looking to the long continuance of the hot weather that must take place. I feel but too strongly its operation on my constitution will make it very unjustifiable in me retaining a situation I shall not be equal to.

He asked to leave the ship as soon as it was in a suitable port.[19] But the *Defence* too was to serve well in battle.

★

Alexander John Ball was unique among the captains in two respects. In the first place he enjoyed the intimate and personal confidence of Nelson after the incident off Sardinia. In a single moment, by refusing to cast off the tow, he demonstrated the qualities that Nelson valued most – courage, seamanship and the refusal to be intimidated by a superior officer. He was called to the meeting on the 22nd over the heads of Louis and Peyton. Nelson showed him a delicate letter to St Vincent written on 29 June, and Ball wrote back 'I should recommend as a friend never to begin a defence of his conduct before he is accused of error.'[20] Not every captain could address his admiral in this way.

Secondly, Ball had intellectual interests far beyond the range of the average naval officer. Most had been 'round the world but never in it'; they knew the winds, tides and currents, whereas Ball could understand societies and cultures on land. If a naval officer went into politics he tended to become a purely departmental minister for the navy like Anson or St Vincent, or an outspoken critic of the naval administration like Vernon or Cochrane. Though he did not live long enough to enter national politics, Ball could understand and work with the aspirations and desires of people on shore. He wrote intelligently about the economy and society of Egypt and later became a great colonial administrator as governor of Malta, where his name was revered at the time and is still respected.

Ball was born in 1756, a younger son of a landowner in Gloucestershire. His family had political interest but no direct naval connections and it is said that the young Ball, like many other officers, was inspired by reading *Robinson Crusoe*. He was a lieutenant by 1778 and during the American War he attracted the attention of Admiral Rodney, the victor of the Battle of the Saintes, who ensured his promotion to commander and then captain. Like several of his colleagues he saw much service but little action in the first 5 years of war against the French Revolutionaries. His general knowledge was largely acquired by wide reading during periods of ill-health, and his background in the gentry gave him social graces. He was in Nelson's description 'the polite man', able to make sociable conversation even with a captured French admiral. His dealings with Nelson show a good deal of humourless pomposity but this was offset by his personal charm.

★

Like Saumarez and Peyton, Samuel Hood came from a famous naval family. His cousins, Lords Hood and Bridport, were admirals who had commanded major fleets and two of his brothers were also in the navy. He served under both of his naval cousins in the American War and the then Admiral Sir Samuel (later Lord) Hood advanced him to commander in 1782, at the age of 20. However, the war ended before he could make the crucial step to captain and he was not promoted until 1788. Like Nelson he served with Prince William, the future William IV, in the West Indies where he had to keep up with the Prince's heavy drinking habits. His high connections gave him the duty of attending the King with the frigate *Juno* during his visits to Weymouth. He commanded the same ship in wartime in the Mediterranean and was lucky to avoid capture in 1794. Promoted to the *Zealous* in 1796, he served under Nelson and Troubridge at Tenerife. After it was clear that the expedition had failed he was sent to negotiate with the Spanish. He bluffed their commander into believing that the British would set fire to the town and the remains of the force were allowed to retreat in peace.

Hood was a very tall man of rather gangling appearance. His manners were ungraceful and awkward but charming at the same time. He was single-minded and unusually fond of life at sea. Like Ball, he was a well-rounded man who studied many subjects, though perhaps with a more practical approach. 'He was intimately versed in astronomy, as concerned with navigation and geography; in shipbuilding, in fortification and all the branches of mechanical philosophy. He studied without any exception the language, laws and customs of every country he visited.' He was motivated by 'the belief that those acquisitions of knowledge might one day be useful to his country'.[21] There is no sign that Nelson paid any great attention to

Samuel Hood in 1808, engraved from a portrait by John Hoppner. (National Maritime Museum, London: 1264)

Hood during the voyage round the Mediterranean and he was only called on board the flagship once, on 3 July, with Troubridge and Hardy. But on the approach to battle Nelson was to hail him to confer on a vital matter and his advice might have had a decisive effect on the outcome.

★

Davidge Gould of the *Audacious* was perhaps the least distinguished of the 'Band'. He supported Nelson during the indecisive skirmish known as 'Hotham's Action' in 1795 but otherwise had seen little action. He was meticulous in ship organisation, as his instructions to the officers and crew of the *Audacious* show,[22] and in battle he was to do his duty but little more. Even the eulogist James Ralfe had difficulty with Gould in his *Naval Biography*, though he took part in several fleet actions including the Nile. 'It is not pretended that any pre-eminent share of merit was attached to him on that occasion; such an assertion would be unjust, and tend to deprecate the characters of those who were his colleagues.'[23]

Thomas Foley was very different. He was from a landowning family in Wales but had an uncle who had sailed in Anson's great circumnavigation of 1740-44 – a flying start to any naval career in that period. He became a captain in 1790 and during the war that followed he served mainly as a flag-captain under three successive admirals. In that position he was present at the Battle of Cape St Vincent in 1797. Though his ship played no great part in the action he was appointed to the *Goliath* soon afterwards. Jervis considered him able but so far he had had little chance to show what he could do in his own right. He had few dealings with Nelson before joining him in June 1798, and little opportunity to develop contact, for he was called on board the flagship only once, with Troubridge and Ball on 7 July. At the Nile there is no doubt that he showed a great deal of initiative, though the exact amount remains controversial to this day. He was described as 'above six feet in height, of fine presence and figure, with light brown hair, blue eyes of a gentle expression, and a mouth combining firmness with good humour'.[24]

George Blagden Westcott of the *Majestic* was by far the oldest of the captains, having been born around 1745. His origins were as humble as Troubridge's: his father was said to be a baker from Honiton, Devon and his brother a tailor. His early service is obscure but he probably rose from the lower deck or was recruited from the merchant service and he first appears as a master's mate on board the frigate *Solebay* in 1768. He was over 30 when commissioned as a lieutenant in 1777 and around 45 when promoted captain in 1790. He had no strong links with Nelson and was never invited on board the flagship during the campaign. He was described by Nelson's friend Collingwood as 'a good officer and a worthy man'.[25]

Benjamin Hallowell of the *Swiftsure* and Ralph Willet Miller of the *Theseus* were both well known to Nelson and were of North American origin. Hallowell originated in Boston, the son of a customs official who later served in Canada. Born in 1760, he became an acting lieutenant at the age of 21 and a full lieutenant 2 years later. Promoted captain in 1793, he served as a volunteer at Calvi in 1794 where Nelson praised his 'indefatigable zeal, activity and ability'. He was often unlucky. His first ship of the line, the 74-gun *Courageux*, was lost while he was attending a court martial, but he was present, again as a volunteer, at the Battle of Cape St Vincent. He was appointed to the *Swiftsure* in January 1798 and soon helped in the capture of three French privateers.

Miller had even closer associations with Nelson. He was born in New York in 1762, the son of an American who had remained loyal to the British crown. He was sent to England and joined the Royal Navy to fight against the American rebels. He became a commander in 1794 and he too fought at Calvi, where he was noticed by Nelson. He was soon promoted and Nelson asked him to be his flag-captain on the 74-gun ship *Captain*, in which he was with him at Cape St Vincent. He moved with Nelson into the *Theseus* in 1797 and shared with him the credit for bringing that ship into good order and discipline, being equally praised by her crew (see Chapter 7). He commanded a small-arms party at Tenerife and stayed with the *Theseus* after Nelson went home wounded. Nelson had great respect for his moral character, describing him as the only truly virtuous man he ever knew. However, there is no sign that he relied on his advice at any stage during the campaign.

Thomas Boulden Thompson of the *Leander* was actually senior to Hallowell, Miller and Berry, but he had never been a flag-captain like the last two, so he had to work his way up the rates of ship rather than being appointed quickly to a large one.

He remained in command of a 50-gun ship rather than a 74. He was the nephew of Commodore Edward Thompson, and even adopted his uncle's surname. He joined the *Leander* in 1796. He was another veteran of Tenerife, where he his local knowledge had been vital to the planning of the attack.

The name of Thomas Masterman Hardy is more closely associated with Nelson than that of any other officer, for he formed a friendship with the admiral that was to last until the very hour of Nelson's death. They first met in December 1796 when Hardy was a lieutenant in the frigate *Minerve* and Nelson served as Commodore aboard her. Put in charge of a prize ship, he created a diversion when the *Minerve* was attacked by three Spanish ships of the line. Three months later, again in the face of the enemy, he leapt into the sea to rescue a man and Nelson called out 'By God, I'll not lose Hardy! Back the mizzen topsail!'. In May 1797 he commanded the boats of the *Minerve* and *Lively* at the capture of a French brig, the *Mutine*, off Tenerife. He was promoted commander and put in charge of the prize. He was still in command of her when sent into the Mediterranean in May 1798 to find Nelson, and he was to play a vital role in intelligence-gathering during the campaign.

★

This then was the Band of Brothers – the 'elite of the Navy of England' as St Vincent described it – a rear-admiral, fourteen captains and one commander. It included intellectuals like Saumarez and Hood and men of action like Troubridge. Hood was the highest in the social scale as a cousin of two Viscounts (albeit recently ennobled because of their naval services rather than coming from the established aristocracy). Saumarez, Darby, Ball, Gould, Foley and Thompson came from the landed gentry; Troubridge and Westcott from the 'lower orders', and the rest mainly from merchant and professional middle class backgrounds. Oddly enough none was the son of a naval officer though Nelson, Saumarez, Hood and Foley all had cousins or uncles who held high rank in the navy and Peyton had a naval grandfather. Westcott was 53; Saumarez, Troubridge, Ball, Gould and Foley were in their early forties, Hardy was 29 and the rest were in their thirties, so it might be said that most of them were in their prime. All except Darby, Louis, Peyton, Ball and Westcott had seen substantial service with Nelson before and Saumarez, Troubridge, Miller, Berry and Hardy had come to know him intimately in the course of their recent naval service.

As a leader and seaman Nelson was already clearly in a class of his own. Among the rest, Saumarez and Troubridge were recognised of men of great ability, while Ball demonstrated his talents in the early stages of the campaign. Hood, Foley and Hardy had not yet had a chance to shine but had latent abilities. The others were men of average capacity, though Gould was perhaps a little below. None was incompetent, none would hold back in action and none would have a public dispute with his leader.

In assessing the 'Band of Brothers' it is important to look at what had gone before. Certainly relations between the leaders of detached forces had improved since Francis Drake's time more than 200 years earlier, when he hanged one of his

SAUMAREZ   THOURBRIDGE   DARBY   LOUIS   PEYTON   BALL   HOOD

GOULD   FOLEY   WESTCOTT   THOMPSON   HALLOWELL   MILLER   BERRY

Nelson's captains in order of seniority from top left to bottom right. From a commemorative print by Robert Smirke. (National Maritime Museum, London: 3563)

deputies on a dubious charge of conspiring against him. Disputes between naval officers, however, were rife throughout the eighteenth century. In 1744 Admiral Mathews failed to bring the French and Spanish to action off Toulon, largely because his second-in-command, Lestock, failed to support him. In the American War the indecisive Battle of Ushant in 1778 resulted in a dispute between Admiral Keppel and his second-in-command, leading to two politically-charged courts martial. Even the great victories in the present war had their taste of bitterness. After the Glorious First of June in 1794 several officers were accused of holding back and Captain Molloy of the *Caesar* was dismissed his ship for failing to bring her fully into the battle. At Camperdown in 1797 Captain Williams of the *Agincourt* was placed on permanent half pay for disobeying signals and failing to bring his ship into action. Taken in these terms, the 'Band of Brothers' was indeed a great success, and Saumarez's criticisms seem minor indeed.

However, Nelson required much more than a mere absence of conflict and the legend is one of absolute unanimity, harmony and co-operation. If we can reject the image of all the captains sitting round a table for discussions on tactics, we can still keep the idea of men working successfully together towards a common goal. But the real significance of the 'Band of Brothers' would only emerge in the test of battle. Nelson had to find the French, then defeat them. Had he failed at either, then his reputation would be lost and he would be lucky to get a second chance. His name would probably be long forgotten.

★

Leaving Sicily on 24 July, Nelson was still convinced that the French had gone east and he had outlined his intentions to Hamilton. 'I shall go to the Archipelago [the Greek islands] where if they are gone towards Constantinople I shall hear of them. I shall go to Cyprus and if they are gone to Alexandretta or any other part of Syria or Egypt, I shall get information.'[26] His determination had not been affected by the setbacks. Even at Syracuse a certain amount of news had been gathered from visiting ships. On the 22nd another Ragusan brig from Malta produced a mixed bag of second-hand information. Her crew reported that they had heard of the French being seen off Crete at least 3 weeks ago, that they had attacked Crete and been repulsed, and that a British frigate had been fired on from Malta. The third point was not surprising or new, the second was inaccurate, but the first confirmed that the French were going eastwards.

Nelson's squadron followed and on the 28th it arrived at the Gulf of Coron (Koroni) on the south-west corner of the Greek mainland. The *Culloden* was sent into the wide bay to seek information. According to the Master's log;

> Passed between Cape Gallio and the island of Venica near the Morea. Passed through about mid channel with 12 fathom water. When we had the rocks well open that lay to the eastward of Venica, hauled up for the town of Corona and passed alongshore about a mile distance . . .
>
> Fresh breezes and squally. Sent two boats away manned and armed to board three vessels at anchor in a Bay near Corona, one of which had French colours flying, about 3 miles from Corona. Made and shortened sail and tacked occasionally in the Bay of Coron. Backed and filled occasionally. At 2 the Captain returned from the town. Up boats, filled and made sail towards the French brig. Made the signal for her to slip. ½ past 2 took her in tow.'[27]

On returning to the fleet Troubridge made the signal for 'having gained intelligence and wishing to communicate' and hailed the flagship. He had spoken to the Turkish Governor who had heard, via his own government, that the French were in Egypt. He confirmed that Bonaparte's squadron had been seen off Crete a month ago. A new picture was beginning to emerge. It was clear that the French had been overtaken by Nelson during their passage east and the report of their going to Egypt no longer seemed unlikely. The French ambassador's alleged disinformation was now seen in a new context. 'This corresponding with the information of the other vessels and the French vessel from Limassol in Cyprus, we were sure they were at Alexandria,'[28] wrote Hood.

Yet again the trip to Egypt was blessed with favourable winds from the north and west. The *Culloden* was slowed down by having the French brig in tow, for the prize was loaded with wine which was in short supply in the fleet and there was no time to transfer the cargo. However, the ships set all the sail they could carry and on the 30th they covered 161 miles. Nelson was in an agony of suspense and ate and slept little during the voyage. On the 31st, while 75 miles from the city, the

Alexander and *Swiftsure* were sent a few miles ahead to look out. At 10am on 1 August the *Alexander* sighted the land around Alexandria.

By midday it was clear that the port was full of shipping, far more crowded than before, and the French tricolour was flying from the forts and the town: there could be no doubt that the French army had landed. Did the vessels in the harbour include the ships of the line? If so they would be unassailable and Nelson would have to prepare for a long, difficult blockade and criticism of his failure to find them a month ago. Or had the large ships gone off to some other anchorage such as Corfu? Then Nelson would have to choose whether to cut off the army in Egypt or to try to find the fleet. Neither alternative was wholly satisfactory.

Early in the afternoon the *Alexander* signalled that she could see 'two ships of the line and six frigates with the French colours hoisted' – that the main battlefleet was not present and the transports were safely protected in harbour. At this point Saumarez records that 'despondency nearly took possession of my mind, and I do not recollect ever to have felt so utterly hopeless or out of spirits as when we sat down to dinner'.[29] Nelson was keeping his own counsel. If he wrote anything after leaving Syracuse it has not survived and his thoughts are unrecorded, but the strain must have been almost unbearable.

Hood in the *Zealous* and Foley in the *Goliath* began to probe to the eastward, knowing that Aboukir Bay was the only spot on the coast where a group of ships could find shelter. At 2.30pm the masthead lookout of the *Zealous* spotted a ship and then a whole fleet at anchor. Hood sent a man with a telescope up to confirm it. Meanwhile in the *Goliath* George Elliot, the signal midshipman, was already up on the fore royal yard sweeping the horizon with his telescope. He saw the fleet at almost the same time as the man in the *Zealous* and decided to make his report in person to the captain. 'The *Zealous* was so close to us that had I hailed the deck they must have heard me; I therefore slid down by the backstay and reported what I had seen.' Desperate to have the honour of being the first to transmit the news to Nelson he began to hoist the appropriate signal flags but one of the ropes broke and the remaining flags gave the compass bearing but did not say what had been sighted. Meanwhile at 2.45pm the *Zealous* had confirmed the sighting and hoisted the flags to tell the admiral of '16 sail of the line at anchor bearing East by South'. On the deck of the *Goliath* Lieutenant Wilkes perceived 'thirteen sail of the line, four large frigates and eight or ten corvettes, all moored in a most masterly state of defence with the *Orient* of 130 guns in the centre, apparently expecting our approach, situated as they were in an unknown bay to us, and at anchor infinitely superior. But there was no hesitation or regret but want of daylight.'[30]

CHAPTER 11

Attack at Aboukir

IN ALL THE ships of Nelson's squadron, the sighting of the enemy after nearly 3 months of searching was greeted with enthusiasm among all ranks. According to Berry, 'The utmost joy seemed to animate every breast on board the squadron at the sight of the enemy; and the pleasure which the admiral himself felt was perhaps more heightened than that of any other man.'[1] Having eaten little for several days, Nelson sat down and enjoyed a hearty meal. On board the *Orion*, Saumarez and his officers were finishing a gloomy dinner when the officer of the watch came in with the message, 'Sir, a signal is just now made that the enemy is in Aboukir Bay, and moored in a line of battle.' The officers 'sprang from our seats and only staying to drink a *bumper* to our success, were in a moment on deck.' On the captain's appearance on the quarterdeck, the crew 'gave three hearty cheers'.[2]

An officer on one of the ships recorded the arcane conversation between two men in a gun crew.

> *Jack* There are thirteen sail of the line, and a whacking lot of frigates and small craft. I think we'll hammer the rust off ten of them, if not the whole boiling.
>
> *Tom* We took but four on the First of June, and I got seven pounds prize money. Now, if we knock up a dozen of those fellows (and why should not we?) d–n my eyes, messmate, we will have a bread-bag full of money to receive.
>
> *Jack* Aye, I'm glad we have twigged them at last. I want some new rigging d–bly for Sundays and mustering days.
>
> *Tom* So do I. I hope we'll touch enough for that, and a d–d good cruise among the girls besides.
>
> *Jack* Well, mind your eye, we'll be at it 'hammer and tongs' directly. I have rammed three shot besides a round of grape in my gun; damme, but I'll play hell, and turn up Jack amongst them.[3]

Nelson had a similar experience in the *Vanguard*. 'I heard two seamen quartered at a gun near me talking and one said to the other, "Damn them, look at them, there they are Jack, and if we don't beat them, they will beat us." '[4]

To Thomas Trotter, a leading naval physician, the British seaman seemed to know no fear, because he lived for the moment with no thoughts of the long-term future; 'he acquires no experience from his past misfortunes and is heedless of futurity.'[5]

That courage which distinguishes our seamen, though in some degree inherent in their natural constitutions, yet it is increased by their habits of life, and by associating with men who are familiarised to danger, and who, from natural prowess, consider themselves at sea as rulers by birthright. By these means, in all actions there is a general impulse among the crew of an English man of war either to grapple the enemy, or lay him close aboard: Frenchmen shudder at this attempt . . .[6]

But the seamen were perhaps less enthusiastic than the officers. As the *Goliath* entered the Battle of Cape St Vincent John Nicol observed 'A serious cast was to be perceived on every face; but not a shade of doubt or fear.' and he implies that the mood was similar at the Nile.[7]

The seaman was frustrated after many months cooped up on his ship, proud of his skill at gunnery and at everything else aboard, and longing for the end of the war. According to John Nicol, 'We rejoiced in a general action; not that we loved fighting, but we all wished to be free to return to our homes and follow our own pursuits. We knew there was no other way of obtaining this than by defeating the enemy. "The hotter the war the sooner the peace." '[8] The seaman was not quite as carefree as he seemed on the surface and he knew the risks of battle full well.

★

In view of his great efforts to keep his ships together and the effect this had on the campaign, is ironic that Nelson's fleet was strung out over several miles when the French were finally sighted. The *Alexander* and *Swiftsure* were 2 or 3 miles away from the main fleet, for they had been ordered to look into Alexandria. The *Culloden* was 7 miles behind it in the opposite direction, for she was still towing the brig captured off Koroni. The rest of the ships were bunched together within a circle about 3 miles in diameter, in no particular order; the *Zealous* and *Goliath* slightly to the east, where they had sighted the enemy in Aboukir Bay and the *Majestic* and *Leander* bringing up the rear of the main body. The whole squadron, then, was spread over about 10 or 12 miles. This did not matter as much as it might have done, because the French were at anchor and clearly had no intention of going anywhere.

Nelson now had to make his most important decision of the whole campaign – whether to fight the French now or to wait until morning. It was 2.30pm[9] when the enemy was sighted approximately 9 miles away. Nelson's ships were making about 5 knots, so it would take 2 hours to reach the enemy position even if all the sails were kept up, an hour and a half longer if all the ships were to be gathered together before the attack, and longer still if the fleet was to be formed up into regular line of battle. On 1 August in these latitudes, the sun would set at around 7pm.

In the past, admirals had tended to avoid fighting at night. True, Admiral Rodney had attacked the Spanish off Gibraltar in a famous 'Moonlight Battle' in 1780, but that was regarded as the exception rather than the rule and the Spanish navy was considered too unskilled to put up serious resistance. Admirals saw the dangers of running aground in strange waters and of firing into one's own side by mistake. Certainly these things happened at the Battle of the Nile.

Nelson had no hesitation in deciding to attack right away and it is doubtful if he considered any other option. Overhearing the conversation of his seamen, he commented, 'I knew what stuff I had under me, so I went into the attack with only a few ships, perfectly sure that the others would follow me, although it was nearly dark.'[10] As his last visit to Alexandria had shown, he was not temperamentally suited to waiting around and he knew that his officers and men were at a peak of fighting efficiency, ready to go into action at a moment's notice. With the French at anchor, the battle was clearly going to be a static one so the dangers of 'friendly fire' were much less than they would have been in the open sea. He had not yet had a chance to find the weaknesses in the French position but he had no intention of allowing them 10 hours to get themselves ready for battle, or perhaps to slip their cables and try to escape yet again. Perhaps the most decisive factor for a seamen, however, was the wind, which was very favourable. There was no guarantee that it would last until next morning. Land breezes during the night, for example, might blow off the shore and make his approach more difficult. Events were to justify this decision fully.

Having come to this resolution, there was no question of waiting for the fleet to gather itself together and then form a line of battle. If that were done it would be nightfall before they could reach the enemy, through dangerous and poorly charted shoals and rocks. An immediate attack would allow the first ships to find their position in daylight and that would be a great advantage to the attackers.

Just before 3pm Nelson made the signal for the fleet to 'Haul on the wind on the larboard tack' – to turn to port so that the wind was no longer behind the ships and head towards Aboukir Bay. Five minutes later he signalled for the *Culloden* to abandon her tow and he had already recalled the *Alexander* and *Swiftsure*. Among the main body the *Goliath* and *Zealous* were still closest to the enemy, followed by the *Vanguard* and then, according to Miller, 'the *Theseus* followed close to her stern, having the *Bellerophon* close on her weather quarter and the *Minotaur* equally so on her lee quarter.'[11] At about 3.50pm, as the ships passed round the end of the shoal at the western end of Aboukir Bay and came within about 3 miles of the enemy, Nelson hailed the *Zealous*, on his port side, to ask Hood if he thought it was safe to come so close to the shore. Hood replied 'We have now eleven fathoms water and if the Admiral will give me leave I will lead in, making known my soundings by signal and bring the van ship of the enemy to action.'[12] According to another report he said, 'I would bear up and try with the lead, which I would be very attentive to, and lead him as close as I could with safety.'[13]

A few minutes later the flagship dropped out of the race. She signalled the *Mutine* to pass within hail and hove to in order to wait for her. In the *Theseus* Miller was ready to forge ahead but he was hailed by Berry as he passed the flagship; he was to stay with the admiral and act as his second in battle, keeping just ahead of him. This was a post of honour, which must have been some compensation when he was overtaken by the *Orion* and *Audacious*.

At 5.30pm Nelson hoisted the signal to form line of battle 'as convenient'. The *Goliath* and *Zealous* were still jockeying for the lead. Hood then shortened sail to

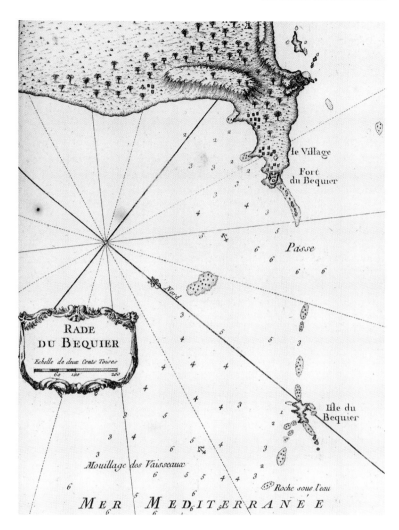

A chart of the western end of Aboukir Bay, from Bellin's *Petit Atlas Maritime* of 1764. This was possibly the French chart used by Foley during his approach. (National Maritime Museum, London: D8803)

stay in contact with the admiral but was ordered to go on. But he had lost the race and said to his first lieutenant, 'I see Foley does not like to give up the lead; let him take it, he is very welcome to it; therefore shorten sail, and let him place himself. I suppose he will take the van ship.'[14] According to George Elliot it was very fortunate that the *Goliath* was first to round the spit of land of Aboukir Island. 'Captain Foley had a French atlas, which proved quite correct and we passed the long shoal. Captain Hood of the *Zealous* had an English atlas, which proved very incorrect.'[15] Foley's *Goliath* was now only about 200 yards from the head of the enemy line. This delighted her captain, who had vied for the most important post of honour all afternoon and had got his staysails and studding sails on deck, ready to set them in case more speed was needed.

The approach to battle was the most dangerous period for Nelson's fleet. Ships of the line had very little forward-firing gunpower, and the structure at the bows was weak. They were approaching the French at an angle of almost 90 degrees and the enemy would be able to deploy the full force of his broadsides against one of Nelson's weakest points. However, the wind was favourable, so the period in the danger zone would be quite short; guns had an accurate range of about 200 yards and a ship doing 5 knots would pass through that in a minute and a half, having to resist one or at most two broadsides. Most important of all, Nelson judged that French gunnery and confidence were poor and no serious damage would be done to his fleet in the approach.

★

For the sailors of Brueys's squadron 1 August, or 14 Thermidor in the Revolutionary calendar, had dawned as a fine day with light breezes from the north-north-west and a slightly turbulent sea. Because of the shortage of water and the danger of disease from old supplies, working parties from the Second Squadron were sent ashore to sink bore-holes. Because of the hostility of the local Bedouin, each ship in the fleet also sent twenty-five well-armed men for protection.[16] Since the ships were already somewhat short-handed, this was a dangerous reduction in their complements.

At 2pm the look-outs on the *Heureux* were the first to spot any sign of trouble, though the ship was ninth in the line of battle and some distance away from the head of the fleet. She hoisted flags to indicate twelve sail to the east-north-east. It took an hour for the admiral to make certain that the ships were hostile and he ordered the men's hammocks to be stowed for action. Signals were hoisted to recall the shore parties but it is doubtful if they were obeyed, if only because many of the boats which had ferried the parties ashore had since gone on to other duties. In the case of the *Guerrier*, one boat had gone to Aboukir, another was at the *Tonnant* to transfer some victuals and the longboat had gone to Rosetta to get hold of spare rigging. The *Conquérant* also had boats at Aboukir and Rosetta, and two more collecting firewood in the anchorage; only the last two could be recalled in time.[17]

The admiral sent two small brigs, the *Alert* and *Railleur*, to reconnoitre and to carry out a pre-arranged plan. As the British began to round the shoal off the island of Aboukir, the *Alert* tried to lure them into shallower waters where they might go aground while the shallow-draughted brig could escape. Nelson's ships paid no attention and indeed only the *Theseus* even mentioned the *Alert*'s activities in her log. The French believed, incorrectly, that the ruse failed because Nelson had experienced pilots on board but it seems rather naive to expect that Nelson's captains would fall for such an obvious trick.

Despite the determination of the British approach, it was 5pm before Brueys became convinced that they intended to attack that night. He ordered some of the frigates to send their best gun crews on board the ships of the line and the frigates

Sérieuse and *Artemise* put 150 men on board the *Orient, Tonnant* and *Franklin*.[18] Brueys clearly intended to strengthen his centre, where two of his 80-gun ships protected the bows and stern of the flagship. He signalled for the ships to set their topgallant yards in case they needed to make sail but almost immediately he made another signal, to fight the battle at anchor, much to the disgust of Captain Etienne of the *Heureux* who longed for a more mobile action.[19] Apart from the three in the centre, each ship was on average about 200 men short of complement unless the shore parties returned. Such tactics would allow his men to concentrate on fighting, without worrying about sail handling or trimming. With this in mind, he signalled for his ships to take steps to increase their manoeuvrability at anchor. Each was to fit a spring to its cable – a hawser passed out of the ship though an after gunport on the opposite side from the anchor cable and attached to it 30ft from the ship. By hauling on this the ship could be turned round to meet the enemy fire if necessary. In addition each ship was to drop an extra anchor from her bows and to send a cable out to the ship astern to stop the enemy passing through the gaps. But the enemy was now only an hour away and the French crews were inexperienced and short-handed. Very few of these complicated evolutions were actually carried out, though it seems that most ships were linked by cable, except perhaps the *Tonnant* and *Heureux*, because the former failed to pass a cable out to the latter.[20] Certainly the *Heureux* and *Mercure* towards the rear of the line, were linked by cable and this had a slight effect on the action.[21]

Though some of the senior officers had reason to doubt the wisdom of Brueys's dispositions, no account of the battle shows any sign of fear among the French crews; they did not 'shudder at the attempt' as Thomas Trotter had claimed they would. The French fleet was superior to Nelson's in numbers of guns and men, if not in ships. The French had 13 ships of the line with a nominal armament of 1026 guns, though not all of these were actually mounted. Nelson had the same number of ships of the line plus the 50-gun *Leander*, nominally carrying 938 guns between them, all mounted and ready for action. The situation was slightly complicated by the presence of carronades on some of the British ships. These were lighter and shorter than ordinary guns and fired an extraordinarily great weight of shot for the size of the gun. At this stage they were only issued at the request of individual captains and it is not clear how many were used at the Nile. Certainly the *Goliath* had carried two 12-pounder carronades on her forecastle in 1782 plus six 18-pounders on the poop,[22] while the *Leander* had been equipped with two 24-pounders and six 18-pounders in 1793, bringing her total armament up to 58 guns;[23] the *Bellerophon* had at least two carronades on her poop, one of which was 'broke to pieces' in the battle[24] and the *Vanguard* had ten 24-pounders on her quarterdeck and four on her forecastle; but there is no evidence that the carronade had any decisive effect on the action. The *Goliath* certainly had extra guns, of an unconventional nature. During an attack on Cadiz in June 1797 she had captured several Spanish gunboats and taken four very large cannon, 68-pounders, out of them. They were fitted on *Goliath*'s poop but not regularly manned and had no supply of ammunition except what had been captured with them. They were

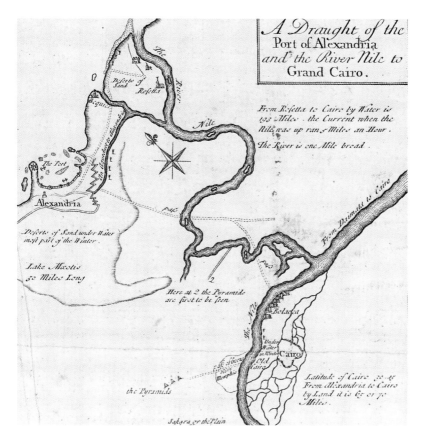

It is not clear what British chart Hood could have been using. The chart from Sayer and
Bennet's *East India Pilot* of 1775–81, shown here, gave virtually no detail of Aboukir Bay
(called Bequier) which is in the top left. (National Maritime Museum, London: D8883)

operated by the midshipmen of the quarterdeck when they could be spared from
other duties.[25]

The French lower decks were equipped with 36-pounder guns, equivalent to
39lbs English weight and, apart from the Spanish guns on the *Goliath*, Nelson's ships
had nothing larger than 32-pounders. However, the extra weight of the French ball
was not necessarily an advantage. British First Rates had once carried 42-pounders
but these had been replaced because the shot was too heavy for a man to handle in
action and it is possible that the 36-pounders slowed down the rate of the French
fire. At the time, many captains maintained that French ships had better sailing
qualities than British ones. Even if that was true (and it is certainly open to dispute)
it was irrelevant, because the French essentially fought the battle at anchor. Against
this, the French ships were of slightly lighter construction than the British and less
able to take punishment. That would prove more relevant in the battle that was
now beginning.

Brueys's force had all the trappings of a full fleet, rather than a squadron. It was commanded by a vice-admiral with a Captain of the Fleet under him as chief -of-staff and three rear-admirals, two with the ships of the line and one in command of the frigates and smaller vessels. The fleet had a great 120-gun three-decker, *L'Orient*, as flagship as well as three powerful 80-gun ships, two serving as flagships for the subordinate admirals. These ships had only six guns more than the commoner 74, but a considerably heavier broadside, with 24-pounders on the upper deck instead of 18-pounders. The bulk of the French force was made up of nine 74-gun ships, similar in principle to Nelson's ships but different in most of the details. There was no equivalent of the 50-gun *Leander*, for the French had abandoned such under-gunned ships 20 years ago. But Brueys had what Nelson yearned for, a full force of frigates – two of 40-guns and two 36s, as well as two brigs, three bomb vessels for shore bombardment and a flotilla of small gunboats. In his line of battle alone he should have commanded over 11,000 men. In practice, as a result of undermanning and the absence of many men on shore duty, it seems likely that he had considerably less, perhaps about 8000 or 9000.

The French had a long-standing tendency to fire at the rigging rather than the hulls of the enemy. This was partly to disable the opposition and prevent it from pressing the attack home, and partly as a consequence of their gunnery techniques. To a certain extent every gun aimer had to rely on the movement of the ship to point his piece and French gunners tended to fire as the gun was moving slowly upward with the roll of the vessel. They used slow match rather than gun-locks and this caused a slight delay while the powder burned down the touch-hole. The ship might thus roll further than expected and the shot go high. Of his own advance into the battle, Miller of the *Theseus* wrote, 'I observed their shot sweep just over us.'[26] However, the French were quite competent in holding their fire at the beginning of the action and did not shoot wildly at too long a range. As Willyams of the *Swiftsure* observed, 'The French received us with cool, deliberate courage and did not open their fire till we were within half shot distance of them.'[27]

★

Not every officer was a student of naval history but most had some awareness of the development of naval tactics over the last century and a half. Because a warship fired the great majority of her guns from the sides, it had become clear that the most effective way to deploy a fleet was to put all the ships in a single line of battle. This had first been discovered by General Monck against the Dutch in 1653 but the other side soon learned the technique. The tactic was essentially defensive in that a line of battle could not advance rapidly on the enemy without losing its advantages, so in the early eighteenth century battles tended to be indecisive unless one side was seriously inferior in numbers, quality or skill, or made a mistake. The ships on each side would exchange fire at relatively long range, doing little damage, until the action was broken off. Tacticians evolved two ways of avoiding this stalemate.

The first was by breaking the line. With a favourable wind, the more aggressive fleet could turn and pass through the enemy line, either as single ships or as a group. As each ship passed through it would deploy its full gunpower on both sides against the weak bows and sterns of the enemy, causing carnage as she went. This was known as 'raking' fire. At the Battle of the Saintes in 1782 the British fleet had done this as a group, and at the Glorious First of June in 1794 it had been done by individual ships. Both led to victories which were tactically decisive, though not overwhelming.

The second was to concentrate one's force on one part of the enemy – usually the leading ships, the 'van', as that would make it more difficult for those behind to escape. It was possible to do this on one only side of the enemy, by simply having one's own line more dense than his. With the French at anchor but somewhat spread out, for example, it would have been possible for a British ship to station itself near the bow of each of the first six Frenchmen, and another to station herself opposite the stern. There is some evidence that this is what Nelson had originally intended. The other possibility was to 'double' the enemy: to place a ship to both port and starboard of each enemy vessel, crushing her in the crossfire. This was devastating, but not without its disadvantages. In a mobile battle it would take time to get the ships in position on both sides. In the early stages at least, the enemy would be deploying his gunpower more effectively as he was using his guns on both sides, though this advantage would soon decline as his over-stretched gun crews became tired. There was also a danger that the ships of the doubling fleet would miss the enemy and fire on one another, especially in a night action.

In wars against the French, the British navy faced one other problem. In the seventeenth century, the Anglo-Dutch wars had been fought in the narrow waters of the southern North Sea, against an enemy who could only achieve his strategic purposes by active, aggressive fighting. The French wars were fought in much wider waters, and often the simple presence of a naval force was all that was required. The French tended to avoid battle, knowing that their total fleet was numerically inferior Britain's and likely to remain so. Each squadron which left port was charged with a specific task, to support rebels in Scotland or Ireland, to attack commerce, to reinforce an overseas army or to invade a distant colony. In the circumstances it was better to avoid the British fleet and press on with the mission. Taken in this context, Brueys's mission, was to form a 'fleet in being' which would, by its very existence, prevent Nelson from controlling the Mediterranean and cutting Bonaparte off. He did not have to fight a battle to achieve this and clearly regarded his position as well defended, strong enough to deter an attack from the British.

★

Nelson was not a theorist of naval tactics. Any ideas he had on the subject were expressed in the form of discussions among his officers, signals planned in advance or hoisted on the eve of battle, and in his actual deeds. He had added only two orders to the standard signal book during the campaign but one was to prove highly relevant to the battle which was about to take place:

> As the wind may probably blow along shore when the enemy at their anchorage, it is recommended each line of battle ship of the squadron to prepare to anchor with the sheet cable in abaft and springs etc.[28]

In other words, each ship was to be ready to drop an anchor with its cable led through a stern port, with a spring attached to give the ship some manoeuvrability at anchor. Nelson hoisted this signal at 4.22pm, after the ships had rounded into the Bay.

He also ordered the ships to 'clear for action'. The marine drummers 'beat to quarters' calling the men to their action stations but in the circumstances it is not likely that many men were skulking below. The officers' furniture was taken out of the cabins to clear space round the guns there – if they were lucky it would be stowed in the hold or put into a boat towed behind the ship but over-enthusiastic seamen had been known to throw it overboard. The bulkheads of all the cabins above the waterline were taken down. The seamen's hammocks were lashed up and stowed in rails round the decks, if this had not already been done. The decks were wetted to prevent fire, while buckets of water and boxes of sand were put in strategic places for the same reason. Surplus equipment was thrown over the side. Below decks the surgeon and his mates prepared the cockpit as an operating theatre and laid out their instruments beside them. On each deck the gun crews assembled and they began to open the gunports. The guns were already loaded but their crews cast off the muzzle lashings, drove in quoins under the breech to level the barrels and there was a great rumble as they hauled on the gun tackles to run them out through the ports.

Half an hour later he hoisted another signal, ordering the attack to concentrate on the enemy van and centre.[29] This too was an important decision, which has been rather neglected by historians. Brueys had clearly assumed that Nelson would attack his centre and rear and had deliberately strengthened those parts of his line. Nelson saw the matter differently. He must have been aware of the strength of the centre, with the three decks of *L'Orient* clearly visible. He might have been able to spot the 80-gun ships on either side of her and perhaps even the *Guillaume Tell* towards the rear of the line. What he could not know was the chronic weakness of the van ships. He did not know that they all had reduced crews, at the expense of the three in the centre centre: that the *Conquérant*, second in line, was more than 50 years old and armed only with 18-pounders, or that the *Guerrier*, the leading vessel, had been built in 1753 and the *Peuple Souverain*, fifth in line, in 1757. Nelson was probably motivated by the direction of the wind, which was blowing along the French line, from van to rear. His ships could approach the head of the line with a very favourable wind, on the beam, allowing his ships to make maximum speed through the most dangerous part of the approach. After that they could move down the line at will with the wind behind them, even if their rigging was damaged. The French rear, on the other hand, would find it difficult to move up in support of their van.

At some stage he also instructed each ship to hoist four lanterns hung vertically in line from the mizzen mast. These were to identify his ships in battle, for Nelson was fully aware of the dangers of night action. As the leading ships passed Aboukir Island, they came under fire from the French fort, equipped with guns and mortars. At a range of about a mile, few hits were scored and no damage was recorded in any of the British logs.

A miniature of Thomas Foley in later life, attributed to William Grimaldi. (National Maritime Museum, London: 4314)

What was Foley's state of mind in the *Goliath* as he approached the French fleet at the head of the British line? George Elliot, his signal midshipman, describes the situation.

> When we were nearly within gun-shot, standing as aide-de-camp close to the captain, I heard him say to the master that he wished he could get inside of the leading ship of the enemy's line. I immediately looked for the buoy on her anchor, and saw it apparently at the usual distance of a cable's length [240 yards], which I reported; they both looked at it, and agreed there was room to pass between the ship and her anchor (the danger was, the ship being close up to the edge of the shoal), and it was decided to do it . . . I heard Foley say, that he should not be surprised to find the Frenchman *unprepared* for action *on the inner side*.[30]

Had Foley done this on his own initiative as Elliot suggested or had he discussed this during the one occasion, on 7 July when he, with Troubridge and Ball, had been signalled to come on board the *Vanguard*? Had there really been time then to discuss every possible circumstance that might have arisen in meeting the enemy – at sea or at anchor, with or without the troop transports, in good or bad weather, with the squadron together or divided, with or without a favourable wind? If so, what would have happened if Miller or Westcott had chanced to be in the lead at this moment, for evidently neither of these officers had been on board the flagship during the campaign?

Berry was quite convinced that the plan was pre-conceived.

It is almost unnecessary to explain his projected mode of attack at anchor, as that was minutely and precisely executed in the action. These plans were formed two months before an opportunity presented itself of executing any of them, and the advantage now was, that they were familiar to the understanding of every officer in the fleet.[31]

Nicolas, the Victorian editor of Nelson's letters, agrees with this. However, he did not have access to Elliot's memoirs, nor had he examined the question of how much time the captains had really had for discussion, so the balance of the argument tips in favour of Foley acting on his own initiative, aided, ironically, by his possession of the best French charts. Certainly this was always maintained by his family. It is difficult to see how Berry's 'two months before an opportunity presented itself' could apply literally; that would take it back to 1 June, but the full squadron was nor formed until the 10th.

On the *Zealous*, immediately behind the *Goliath*, Hood was not prepared for Foley's manoeuvre. 'The van ship of the enemy being in five fathoms water [we] expected the *Goliath* and *Zealous* to stick on the shoal every moment and did not imagine we should attempt to pass within her.'[32] This too tends to suggest that the manoeuvre was not pre-planned.

The general outline of the attack had been given in Nelson's orders to prepare the anchors and to concentrate on the enemy van and centre. It seems that Foley was adding

The French position at Aboukir Bay, with the British attacking from the right and Foley's *Goliath* rounding the head of the enemy line, painted by Nicolas Pocock. (National Maritime Museum, London: BHC0513)

another touch, fully confident that Nelson would approve, but without prior discussion. According to Berry, Nelson saw the opportunity at almost the same moment as Foley, exclaiming 'that where there was room for an enemy's ship to swing, there was room for one of ours to anchor.'[33] There was no chance to signal this to Foley and no suggestion from any quarter that he attempted it. However, Nelson must take full credit for his tactical instinct and more important, for the initiative he gave to his captains, the leadership which made them aware that they would be backed up and encouraged to find any weakness in the enemy position. In a navy where many admirals were too old to absorb new ideas, or were bound by the cautious tactics and practices of an earlier generation, Nelson was a truly innovative figure.

★

As she passed round the bow of the *Guerrier*, the *Goliath* fired a broadside into her, doing great damage at short range against one of the weakest parts of the French ship. On reaching the inshore side of the enemy line, the men of the *Goliath* were gratified to find the French unprepared – 'her lower deck guns were not run out, there was lumber such as bags and boxes on the upper deck ports, which I reported with no small pleasure.'[34] Foley planned to anchor alongside the *Guerrier* and had duly prepared his cable, with springs out of the stern port. The anchoring was fumbled. The ship still had many of her sails set and enemy fire during the approach had done some damage, destroying part of the sail gear and making furling difficult. The anchor was dropped, perhaps a little late, but more important the crew failed to control the cable. Only about 20 or 30 fathoms of the 120-fathom cable would be needed in such shallow waters but it was allowed to run out to the end, leaving the *Goliath* between the second and third ship in the French line, not against the first as Foley had planned.

The *Zealous* was only a few hundred yards behind the *Goliath* and Hood was able to benefit from Foley's experience. She too fired into the hull of the *Guerrier* as she rounded her bows. The French ship was already seriously damaged and her foremast fell. Hood took up the position Foley had intended opposite her port bow, though some distance off. He then began to bombard the *Guerrier*, which was already half beaten by that time. She was fired on by more British ships as they rounded the head of the line and about 7pm, as darkness fell, her main and mizzen masts went by the board; but her crew was still fighting.

Gould's *Audacious* came next, about 15 minutes behind the two leaders. Passing the *Guerrier*, she fired three broadsides into her and claimed the credit for the fall of her mainmast, though that was disputed by others.[35] Gould took the first completely free space and anchored between the *Guerrier* and the second ship, the *Conquérant*. He claimed that 'I brought my ship to an anchor so very near him [the *Conquérant*], and on the opposite side from what he expected.'[36] Midshipman Elliot regarded this as a 'useless berth between the first and second ships of the enemy's line, both of them being utterly beaten and dismasted.'[37]

Saumarez's *Orion* rounded the French line by passing outside the *Zealous* and getting yet further into shoal water. She passed the third French ship, the *Spartiate*, and Samaurez planned to take up position against the fourth, the *Aquilon*. However, the captain of the frigate *Sérieuse*, anchored well inshore, thought differently. So great was the difference in firepower between a frigate and a ship of the line that, in a fleet battle, courtesy demanded that the larger ship would not fire on the smaller unless attacked first. There can be no doubt about Captain Martin's courage, then, in firing a broadside of about 296lbs of shot towards the *Orion*, wounding two men on deck. There was nothing to stop Saumarez from firing now, for unlike the French his ship was prepared for battle on both sides, with double-shotted guns and a broadside weight of 781lbs, even if the guns had been single-shotted. However, he told his officers, 'Let her alone, she will get courage and come nearer. Shorten sail.' Sure enough the *Sérieuse* came closer, when Saumarez ordered the helmsman to yaw the ship to starboard and he fired a broadside.[38] 'Got the starboard guns to bear on her which totally dismasted her, and some little time after [she] sunk in shoal water, with her upper works above water.'[39] Captain Martin had achieved little for the loss of his ship, but at least he caused the *Orion* to go a little out of her way. She was now too far downwind and to the east to get into the position she wanted alongside the fourth ship, the *Aquilon*. She came to rest instead off the bows of the *Peuple Souverain*, the fifth ship.

Captain Miller from New York brought the *Theseus* into the battle with yet another devastating blow to the *Guerrier* as he passed the head of the French line. 'I closed them suddenly, and, running under the arch of their shot, reserved my fire, every gun being loaded with two and some with three round shot, until I had the *Guerrier*'s masts in a line, and her jib-boom about six feet clear of our rigging; we then opened with such effect that a second breath could not be drawn before her main and mizzen mast were also gone.'[40] Miller believed that Saumarez had come close to grounding by going in too wide, so he now sailed through the gap between the *Zealous* and the *Guerrier*, trusting that Hood's gun crews would hold their fire while they passed within 10ft of them. Miller's men cheered loudly as they passed and this was returned by the crew of the *Zealous*. The French officers tried to rally their men with a counter-cheer but, according to Elliot, 'they made such a lamentable mess of it that the laughter in our ships was distinctly heard in theirs – and one of their captains told me that they could never get their men to stand to their guns afterwards.'[41] The *Theseus* passed down the line outside the *Goliath* but very close to her. She anchored near the bow of the *Spartiate*, in what seemed like a perfect position.

★

By now Nelson in the *Vanguard* was coming close to the action and another decision had to be made. The Admiral must have known of the success of Foley's manoeuvre as he watched the French masts come tumbling down but he was also aware that the waters between the French line and the shoals of the bay were becoming increasingly crowded and that night was falling fast. Moreover, he tended to favour doubling the enemy and his signal had demanded an attack on the enemy's van and centre. He decided to attack on the outside of the French line, expecting that the other ships would follow him. He could see that the two leading Frenchmen, the *Guerrier* and the *Conquérant*, were beaten by the *Goliath*, *Zealous* and *Audacious* and an attack on them would be pointless. He also considered the possibility that some of the rearmost French ships might weigh anchor and try to tack up the outside to the head to the line, to support their friends and he decided to block such a move. He headed for the third ship, the *Spartiate*, but got there a few minutes after the *Theseus* had already anchored and opened fire on her. Miller in the *Theseus* therefore 'desisted firing on her, that I might not do mischief to our friends and directed every gun before the main mast on the *Aquilon* and all abaft it on the *Conquérant*, and giving my proper bird to the admiral.'[42] This must have caused some difficulty, for the guns had only a limited amount of lateral movement and the ship was evidently anchored quite close to the *Spartiate*. There was also a danger from the fire of the *Vanguard*. Miller's statement, however, is evidence that he was not fully clear as to the Admiral's intentions and is further proof that details of the attack were not preconceived.

The *Minotaur*, *Defence* and *Bellerophon* followed the *Vanguard* and passed close to her on the way down the outside of the French line. The *Minotaur* anchored opposite the fourth ship, the *Aquilon*, which was now being engaged by the forward guns of the *Theseus*. The *Defence*, captained by the ailing John Peyton, took station opposite the next ship, the *Peuple Souverain*, already fully engaged on the other side by the *Orion*. Peyton did not share Miller's concern about the dangers of crossfire and had no inhibitions about attacking a ship which was already engaged. The *Bellerophon* intended to anchor alongside the next ship, the 80-gun *Franklin*, but like other ships her anchor ran out further than intended and she found herself alongside the bows of the French flagship, the mighty 120-gun *L'Orient*. She was to suffer heavily for this.

The *Majestic* was the last ship of the main group to reach the action. Just before 7pm, less than half an hour after the *Goliath* had first opened fire, she sailed past the *Vanguard* in darkness and thick smoke. Possibly Captain Westcott, the 53-year-old baker's son from Devon, had intended to anchor opposite *L'Orient* to give support to the *Bellerophon*, or perhaps opposite the 80-gun *Tonnant*, the next unengaged ship. But yet again there was trouble with the anchor cable and she ran on, and into the next ship, the 74-gun *Heureux*. Her bowsprit became entangled with the rigging of her opponent and she found herself in a dangerous position, with her main guns unable to bear and subject to musket fire from the enemy. Captain Westcott was killed before the ship could extricate herself.

The *Culloden*, having cast off her prize just after 3pm, had done well in catching up with the rest of the fleet and reached the bay ahead of the *Swiftsure* and *Alexander*, which had been looking into Alexandria. As the *Goliath* and *Zealous* were coming into action she was rounding Aboukir Island and Troubridge's natural impatience caused him to come in closer than even Hood had done. He misjudged the situation

The British deployment. The numbers give the order in which the ships engaged. ▶

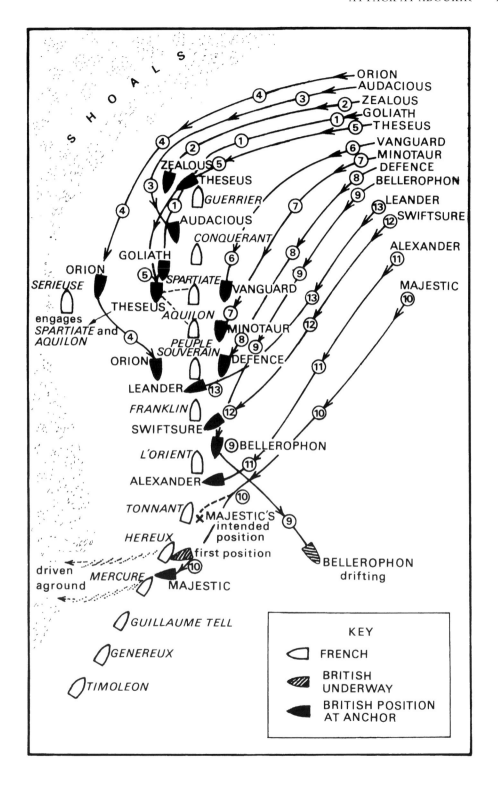

The *Culloden*, in the right middle distance, has just gone aground and is being attended by the *Leander* to the left and the *Mutine* behind her, while a boat in the foreground lays out an anchor. To the far right, the *Alexander* and *Swiftsure* are approaching, while the main battle begins to the left. From a print after William Anderson, apparently based on information by Captain Thompson of the *Leander*. (National Maritime Museum, London: PAG8968)

and at 6.40pm the ship struck heavily on a rock. As the Master of the *Majestic* noted rather complacently in his log, 'From this sandy island runs out a reef to the eastward . . . In coming into this bay from the westward you must give this island a berth of at least a mile, as the reef seems to run that distance to the eastward'.[43] Troubridge immediately made signal No. 43, that his ship was 'striking and sticking on a shoal', and the two following ships were able to veer away and avoid grounding.

Troubridge was the most thrusting, dynamic and abrasive of all Nelson's captains and his frustration can easily be imagined. He sent the ship's launch over to the *Mutine* and Hardy anchored 700 yards to the north. Two anchor cables were rowed across to the *Culloden* and passed through her wardroom window in the stern. Men at capstans hauled the cables taut in the hope of getting the ship off, while casks were taken out of the hold and thrown overboard to lighten her, but to no avail. She was stuck fast by her stern and slightly less heavily by her bows.[44]

The *Alexander* and *Swiftsure* steered round the reef and headed towards the outside of the French line. It was nearly 8pm before they reached the battle and 'total darkness had enveloped the combatants for some time, which was dispelled only by the frequent flashes from the guns. The volumes of smoke now rolling down the line from the fierce fire of those engaged to windward rendered it extremely difficult for the rest of the British ships who came in last to take their station.'[45] Captain Ball brought the *Alexander* to anchor alongside the stern quarter of *L'Orient*, which was already being engaged, albeit unintentionally, by the *Bellerophon*. Hallowell, the Canadian captain of the *Swiftsure*, had decided not to let his men's taste for action interfere with seamanship in the approach to battle. He was 'determined not to suffer a shot to be fired on board the *Swiftsure* till the sails were all cleared up and the ship anchored in her station.'[46] As he approached the line he saw a ship coming out under her foresail and foretopsail alone, showing no lights. Assuming she was French the crew got ready to fire but Hallowell forbade it because 'that would have broken the plan he had laid down for his conduct': perhaps he felt that attacking an already beaten ship would contribute nothing to the battle and gain him no glory. In any case the decision was fortunate, for the ship was the *Bellerophon*, already savaged by *L'Orient*. According to her log the *Swiftsure* dropped anchor at 8.03pm and began firing 2 minutes later. Despite the smoke and darkness her position was a carefully chosen one, where she could fire into the stern of the *Franklin*, which was unengaged, and the bow of *L'Orient*.

Only the 50-gun *Leander* was still to deploy but her captain had something of an identity crisis: the ship was too large to be a frigate but too small for a ship of the line, so it was not clear what she was expected to do in a fleet action. In the first instance Captain Thompson treated his ship as a frigate and went to the aid of the grounded *Culloden*, already receiving assistance from the *Mutine*. At 7pm he sent a boat to Troubridge with an offer of help and to ask 'if it was advisable for him to proceed towards the enemy. The officer was directed to go back to the *Mutine* and direct her to drop anchor astern of the *Culloden* and then return to the *Leander*, addressing Captain Thompson to lose no time in joining the fleet.'[47] According to Miller of the *Theseus* it was 9 or 9.30pm before the *Leander* reached the battle, by which time 'the five headmost ships of the enemy were completely subdued.'[48] However, his conduct at this point was exemplary. Berry wrote, 'Captain Thompson of the *Leander* of 50 guns, with a degree of skill and intrepidity highly honourable to his professional character, advanced towards the enemy line on the outside and most judiciously dropped his anchor athwart [the] hawse of *Le Franklin*, raking her with great success, the shot from the *Leander*'s broadside which passed that ship all striking *L'Orient*, the flagship of the French commander in chief.'[49] Nelson's fleet had completed its deployment.

CHAPTER 12

'A crashing sound that deafened all around her'

As Nelson's ships came into action one by one, each settled down to a rhythm of combat. Having brought his ship to battle and anchored alongside the enemy, there was little for a captain to do until his opponent looked ready to surrender, a boarding was likely to be attempted by one side or the other, or danger threatened from some other source. He had to stay on deck and set an example of fortitude in the face of danger, for his position on the quarterdeck was fully exposed to fire from both great guns and small arms and enemy sharpshooters might well take advantage of this. It was a highly dangerous position and in the battle as a whole on both sides, one admiral and three captains were killed and two admirals and nine captains wounded.

The captain was accompanied by the first lieutenant, who would take over if he was disabled and therefore had to know what was going on. The master was there to advise on the sailing of the ship and supervise the navigation. The captain's clerk stood by to take notes and record the times and progress of the action – a job which was badly done at the Nile, for the times recorded for the different events vary enormously from ship to ship. Two or three midshipmen were available to carry messages to the various gundecks and read signals from the flagship. In the *Swiftsure*, 10-year-old Theophilus Lee had this duty and was sent down to the gundecks on occasion with the captain's orders to concentrate fire on a particular ship or area. At other times he fetched ginger-beer from the cabin locker for the refreshment of the captain and officers.[1]

Four seamen stood by the wheel under the command of a quartermaster. Though the ships were now at anchor, someone had to be ready to take the helm if the situation demanded it. Two or three men were in each of the tops to help with the rigging in case of a sudden manoeuvre and a dozen or so stood by on deck to help in case trimming sail was required, when they would haul and let go the appropriate ropes, perhaps with the help of the men at the forecastle and quarter-deck guns, or with one man taken from each gun crew throughout the ship. But in a major manoeuvre like tacking or wearing, firing would have to cease while all the men were called from their gun crews.

Below decks and on the quarterdeck and forecastle, the bulk of the crew fought at the great guns. On the lower deck of a 74, completely under cover from the deck above, were twenty-eight 32-pounders which formed the main armament of the ship, fourteen on each side. Each cast-iron gun barrel was bored out to a diameter of 6.4in, about a fifth of an inch more than the diameter of the solid iron ball which would fit into it.[2] This was to allow for inaccuracies in the casting of the shot, or boring of the barrel. Because of this gap, known as windage, because the guns were entirely smooth-bored and because of variations in the size of the shot and the strength of the powder, accuracy was poor at more than about 200 yards range. British captains preferred to take their ships close in and Nelson would later say 'No captain can go far wrong if he places his ship alongside that of an enemy'.

Each gun barrel was mounted on a wooden carriage, which ran backwards and forwards on four wooden wheels, known as trucks. It was difficult to turn the guns from side to side, or 'traverse' them, though this could be done by using the tackles to slew the carriages, to some extent aided by levers known as 'handcrows'. Even then, the effects of all this heavy labour were limited by the sides of the gunports but the *Theseus* nevertheless managed to keep up a fire on both the *Aquilon* and the *Conquérant* at the same time during the early stages of the battle, so a traverse of about 45 degrees both fore and aft must have been possible.

Each 32-pounder was allocated seven men headed by a gun captain, if the ship was at full strength. If she had to fight on one side only (which was the case for the British ships for most of the action), then two crews could combine. The senior captain from the two gun crews would take charge of aiming, adjusting the elevation to suit the expected range. He had to be alert to possible changes of range and Miller of the *Theseus* noted that the French had neglected to take care of this. 'Knowing well that at such a moment the French would not have coolness enough to change their elevation, I closed with them suddenly . . . running under the arch of their shot.'[3]

Since aiming was difficult and accuracy was poor, it was rate of fire which distinguished one gun crew or one ship from another and which made the British navy superior to the French. The gun having fired, it was allowed to recoil back into the ship, where its movement was restrained by the breech rope. This was 7in in circumference, with each end attached to rings to the sides of the gunports and the centre running through a ring at the rear of the gun barrel. Even so the recoil could be dangerous and men could suffer serious injury if they failed to keep out of the way of 3 tons of wood and metal. To prevent the gun from running back out of its own accord with the heel or rolling of the ship, a rope known as the train tackle was attached to the rear of the carriage and a ring in the deck. A seamen hauled this tight before the gun could react and run itself out prematurely.

It was now time to begin reloading. The crews had been constantly trained in this so that it became second nature even in the heat of battle. The first task was to sponge the inside of the gun, to put out any burning embers which might detonate the new cartridge prematurely. A sponge was attached to the end of a large, stiff but flexible rope was thrust down the barrel. This needed less space in front of the gun than a solid wooden rammer, an important consideration on a crowded gundeck. Next the cartridge was put in. This was a measured quantity of gunpowder enclosed in canvas or paper. It had to be pushed home to the breech of the gun using a rammer; sometimes the other end of the rope already used for the sponge, known as a 'flexible rammer' might be used; but this must have been very difficult against the air pressure behind the cartridge and it is possible that a wooden-handled rammer would have been necessary. Next a wad made of pieces of old rope was put in and rammed home. It was followed by the cannonball and then another wad to stop the ball from rolling out.

Meanwhile the men at the rear of the gun were making it ready to fire. A quill tube was pushed into the touch hole, piercing the cartridge. A flint-lock, a larger version of those used in ordinary muskets, was fitted above it. It was cocked and a lanyard was attached, ready for firing. Now the heavy work began. The gun had to be run out, perhaps uphill against the heel of the ship. The members of the gun crew, apart from the captain, distributed themselves on the blocks and tackle fitted on each side of the gun and hauled as directed. This was the most labour-intensive part of the whole operation, the one which made it necessary to have such a large crew. When the gun was in position and pointed at a suitable target, the captain pulled on the lanyard and a great crashing noise came from the gun, along with a large cloud of smoke and a ball headed in the direction of the enemy. Then the process could begin all over again.

Solid shot were stored in holes drilled along the sides of the hatch coamings on each deck, for they posed no flammability problems. Powder was very different, so it was brought up from below in small quantities and only as needed. A ship's boy was allocated to each gun and collected cartridges one by one from a hatch in the magazine and put each into a wooden cylinder known as a cartouche box, to carry it to the gun. One such boy in the *Goliath* was thought to be unusually still, sitting on top of a box. 'One of the men gave him a push; he fell all his length on the deck. There was not a blemish on his body, yet he was quite dead and was thrown overboard.'[4]

A midshipman took charge of each group of guns, with a lieutenant in charge of half a deck, urging his men into action. 'Load and fire, we are too close to miss, warm work my boys,' cried Lieutenant Wilkes of the *Goliath*.[5] He would convey orders from the captain, or take some decisions on his own initiative, changing the amount of powder for each discharge, or the number and type of shot. Chain shot, for example, could be used against rigging instead of conventional round shot, or two or even three balls could be inserted to do extra damage in close-range action.

British seamen were well-trained in gunnery at sea and the long hours of practice began to pay off, for they were certainly faster than the gunners of the French ships, even allowing for the latter's difficulties of preparedness and manpower. Precisely how fast is difficult to say. The figure of one round per minute has been suggested for around 1812 but that is optimistic even for then and it is likely that the crews of Nelson's ships were slower – perhaps a minute and a half or two minutes for each round, where the tactical situation permitted.

The decks of a ship of the line in action were a scene of noise, smoke, sweat, exhaustion and carnage. The sound of a single gun firing in a open space is almost deafening and the discharge of several, together or one after another, in a confined area must have done serious damage to the eardrums. Most but not all of the smoke left the gun outside the hull of the ship. With 200 men toiling on each deck, the heat soon became unbearable and men stripped to the waist, perhaps with a head-band to keep sweat and hair out of their eyes. The lower deck was slightly safer than the forecastle and quarterdeck, in that enemy musket shot would not reach there: but cannonballs crashed into or through the sides, sometimes sending huge jagged splinters among the gun crews. Men worked in the very space where in happier moments they sat round a mess table drinking their beer and wine and telling stories, or hung their hammocks for a well-earned sleep. Conditions were crowded in battle, for the distance between adjacent guns was only about 6 or 7ft, excluding the tackle. In this space, about 10ft long when the gun was run in for loading, fourteen men from two different gun crews might be working. They would be hauling at ropes, pushing on rammers, levering on handcrows and putting powder and shot down the barrel. Sometimes the two crews would be at different stages in the operation, creating further confusion. Vertically, there was no area between decks that had headroom of more than about 6ft 6in. Deck beams were fitted every few feet, reducing the height to about 5ft 6in; seamen crouched low in action, or risked head injuries from hitting the beams. Often mistakes were made and too many powder charges were put in, risking the bursting of the gun. Yet the gun crews were soon caught up the excitement of battle. Captain Hallowell of the *Swiftsure* was 'aware of the difficulty of breaking the men off from their guns once they have begun to use them'.[6]

★

Yet further below decks, men and women toiled away in the magazines and in the cockpit. In the *Goliath* 7 years later at the Battle of Trafalgar, the space near the main magazine contained the gunner's mate and several members of the gunner's crew making up cartridges, along with miscellaneous crew members such as the cooper, the sentinel at the bitts and the gunner's yeoman's assistant, to hand powder cartridges along the passageway and up to the decks above. The schoolmaster, the barber, the ship's corporal and several others were stationed in the after magazine for the same task. Working in the same magazine in 1798, John Nicol was 'much indebted to the gunner's wife, who gave her husband and me a drink of water every now and then, which lessened our fatigue much'.[7] Some of the carpenter's mates were stationed down there, in the vulnerable area 'between wind and water', ready to plug shot holes near the waterline which might endanger the ship. One such hit was received on the *Goliath* and penetrated the magazine, fortunately without causing an explosion; it was quickly stopped up by the carpenters.

The cockpit below decks was a scene of horror. There is no eye-witness description of one during the Battle of the Nile but one by a surgeon at the Battle of Camperdown, less than a year earlier, gives much of the awful picture.

> Ninety wounded were brought down during the action. The whole cockpit, deck, cabins, wing berths and part of the cable tier, together with my platform and my preparations for dressing were covered with them. So that for a time they were laid on each other at the foot of the ladder where they were brought down . . .
>
> Joseph Bonheur had his right leg taken off by a cannon shot close to the pelvis, so that it was impossible to apply a tourniquet; his right arm was also shot to pieces. The stump of the thigh, which was very fleshy, presented a dreadful and large surface of mangled flesh. In this state he lived near two hours, perfectly sensible and incessantly calling out in a strong voice to me to assist him . . .
>
> Melancholy cries for assistance were addressed to me from every side by wounded and dying, and piteous moans and bewailing from pain and despair. In the midst of these agonizing scenes, I was able to preserve myself firm and collected, and embracing in my mind the whole of the situation, to direct my attention where the greatest and most essential services could be performed. Some with wounds, bad indeed and painful, but slight in comparison with the dreadful condition of others, were most vociferous for my assistance.[8]

In the *Theseus*, where Nelson's right arm had been cut off a year ago, Robert Tainsh now presided as surgeon and amputation was still the most common method of treatment. William Williams, aged 24, had his elbow joint shattered by a musket ball so the arm was amputated above the elbow; Joseph Oliver, a marine, had a similar wound below the ankle and the surgeon took off his leg below the knee. The next man, seaman John Smith, was luckier. His leg was fractured and the surgeon 'applied splints with a roller in the usual way'. Twenty-five more men would arrive in the cockpit before midnight, mostly helped down the steep ladder by mates from their own gun crew.

In the cockpit of the *Vanguard* the first casualty to be carried below was Richard Crader, a young ordinary seaman with a compound fracture of his left leg. Many more arrived over the next few hours: Phillip Murphy with horrific injuries which removed his right eye and laid bare his skull; many with wounds to arms and legs which required amputation, beginning with John Triff, a 25-year-old able seaman. Michael Auster, the boatswain who had been recommended to Captain Berry 9 months earlier, 'received a gunshot wound on the right arm' which obliged Michael Jefferson to cut it off. By mid-evening twenty-eight men had been treated, before the most important casualty of all came down to the cockpit.

★

A little before 8.30 that evening, Nelson was with Berry on the quarterdeck of the *Vanguard*. Amid the flashes of gunfire, noise and danger of shot he was looking over a sketch of the bay which had been taken from a French ship captured a few days earlier. While he was doing this a piece of langridge shot ('formed of bolts, nails, bars and other pieces of iron tied together and forming a sort of cylinder'[9]) fired from the *Spartiate* struck him on the forehead causing a 'wound on the forehead over the right eye. The cranium bared for more than an inch, the wound three

The British attacking the French in Aboukir Bay from the right. A few moments into the battle the masts of the *Guerrier* are already falling. From Cooper Willyams's *Voyage*. (National Maritime Museum, London: D8132D)

The night battle with *L'Orient* on fire and some of the other ships setting sail to move away from her. From Cooper Willyams's *Voyage*. (National Maritime Museum, London: D8132C)

Nelson wounded in the cockpit of the *Vanguard*, with a man on the right about to have his leg treated rather painfully. As always, the artist has greatly exaggerated the height between decks. (National Maritime Museum, London: 9583)

inches long'.[10] Nelson fell into Berry's arms, his blood staining the sketch in his hands. He could see nothing with his good eye because a flap of skin had fallen over it and he was convinced that such a wound to the head must be fatal. With his typical morbidity he called out 'I am killed; remember me to my wife.' Strong seamen helped him down three ladder-ways into the cockpit, where Jefferson and his mates were at work. Nelson insisted on waiting his turn for treatment but the surgeon got to him without much delay.[11] He took off the dressing hastily applied on deck, brought the edges of the wound together and applied linaments to it. He dressed it again with sticking plaster and lint.[12] Jefferson made light of the injury but Nelson continued pessimistic. Mr Comyn the chaplain was asked to convey his last remembrance to Lady Nelson. Jefferson asked Nelson to rest in the bread-room nearby, where he would be safe from danger but out of the way of the surgeon's activities. However, the admiral called his secretary, John Campbell, who had himself been wounded, though evidently not seriously enough to be treated by the surgeon – this was not unusual and in the *Goliath* sixty-eight men were eventually found to have been hurt, over and above those treated in the cockpit.[13] Nelson began to dictate a letter to the Admiralty, presuming it might be his last. Campbell saw his leader blind and in severe pain and was unable to go on. Comyn, the chaplain, was summoned to continue the letter but Nelson's sight was evidently beginning to recover, for even in the darkness of the bread-room he was able to trace out a few characters. Perhaps this was a first draft of the letter he eventually sent. In any case, he was soon left alone to rest.

★

The *Majestic* was the only ship to attack the rear of the French line and only after her assault on *L'Orient* and the *Tonnant* had miscarried. With her bowsprit jammed in the fore shrouds of the *Heureux*, Captain Westcott was killed within half an hour and she suffered terrible casualties from French musketry and from double-shotted cannon. Her jib-boom, the foremost part of her bowsprit, broke and she managed to shake herself free, running alongside her opponent and fighting her yardarm to yardarm for a brief moment.[14] She tried to slip astern of the *Heureux*, where she fell foul of the cable run out between that ship and the *Mercure*. Nevertheless she found herself a good position between the two French ships, being held in place by an anchor out of one of her stern gunports. She was able to fire on the port bow of the *Mercure* and the stern of the *Heureux*, having revenge on her former tormentor and wounding Captain Etienne.

Along the forward end of the French line the battle had developed into a series of duels between two, three or four ships. The *Guerrier* took the brunt of the early attack, for the *Goliath*, *Audacious*, *Orion* and *Theseus* all fired well-directed broadsides into her as they rounded the line. The *Zealous* anchored opposite her bows and kept up a sustained onslaught. Her crew abandoned the upper guns on the quarterdeck and forecastle; Hood of the *Zealous* thought they had been driven away by

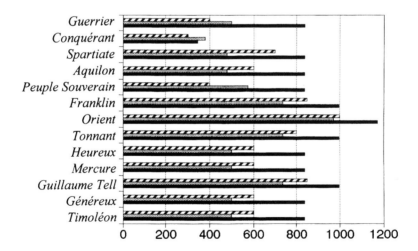

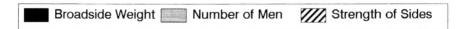

The relative strengths of the ships in the French line, based on broadside weight, numbers of men and an estimate of the strength of their timbers. The weakness of the van and strength of the centre round the flagship is immediately apparent.

canister shot fired from his guns and musketry of his marines[15] but her captain recorded that he withdrew them to help man the lower deck guns on the port side, neglected before the attack.[16] Her three masts fell very early in the action, before any ships but the *Goliath* and *Zealous* were engaged. But not all the fire was directed at her masts and decks. Hood records that 'from her bow to her larboard gangway, the ports of the main deck are entirely in one, and her gunwale in that part entirely cut away, two of the main deck beams fallen upon the guns in consequence'. The *Guerrier*'s captain was slightly more moderate, only claiming that 'three gunports were made into one' and that by this time his gun crews had been forced to abandon the 18-pounders on the upper deck.[17] All the same this was an enormous amount of damage for any ship to sustain and Hood, he claimed, hailed her captain twenty times to suggest surrender. After 3 hours of punishment and resistance, Hood decided that he was 'tired firing and killing people in that way'. He sent a lieutenant on board the French ship and she agreed to surrender. By pre-arranged signal, the *Zealous*'s lieutenant hoisted and lowered a light from the rigging, to show that this particular fight was over.[18] The *Zealous* had suffered only seven men wounded: the *Guerrier*'s losses are unknown but must have been in the hundreds.

The *Conquérant*, second in line, was in a particularly weak condition and should not have been placed in such a vulnerable spot. Her ancient timbers were easily penetrated by British shot. Her lower deck guns should have been 36-pounders but she had only 18-pounders and her crew had been reduced to less than 400 men, instead of 700. She was under fire from the *Goliath* and the *Audacious*, both on her port side, and her captain was soon wounded. Before being carried down to the steerage for treatment he called his first lieutenant and ordered him continue to defend the ship. However, the gun crews were driven away from the 12-pounder guns on the upper works, so only the 18-pounders were still firing. A gunner's mate, Laugier, lost his life in preventing boxes of grenades in the magazine from catching fire but around him 125 or 130 men were killed and 80 or 90 wounded. She surrendered to the *Audacious* and Captain Gould of that ship noted that the slaughter had been 'so dreadful in the ship that the French officers declared it was impossible to make the men stand at their guns'.[19]

The *Spartiate* was the first ship to be doubled. While she had only the *Theseus* on her port side her guns fired 'with great quickness' but when Nelson's *Vanguard* arrived to starboard her gun crews were stretched and the fire became slow and irregular.[20] She was 200 men under strength but put up a fairly strong resistance, causing most of the 105 casualties on board the *Vanguard* and 35 in the *Theseus*. Her main and mizzen masts were soon knocked down but both her opponents seem to have fired into her hull as well as the rigging. She suffered forty-nine damaging hits on the *Vanguard*'s side and twenty-seven from the *Theseus*, some passing through the ship from one side to the other. With holes below the waterline she began to leak alarmingly and soon had 9ft of water in her hold. She had more then 200 killed and wounded and the majority of the rest had to be withdrawn from the guns to work at the pumps.[21] After about 2 hours of resistance she was one of the first to haul down her flag and surrender. Berry sent Lieutenant Galwey over in a boat with a party of marines and the French captain's sword was handed over to him as a token of surrender. He returned to the *Vanguard* and Berry took it below to show it to Nelson, now wounded in the cockpit.[22]

The *Aquilon*, fourth in line, was unscathed in the early stages, after the *Orion* failed to anchor on her inside. Later she was attacked on the outside by Thomas Louis's *Minotaur* and received some of the fire of Miller in the *Theseus*. Her officers claimed to be under fire from three vessels but it is difficult to see what the third one was, except for stray shots. However, her men were driven from the quarterdeck and forecastle and then abandoned the 18-pounder guns on the upper deck to concentrate on the 36-pounders below – a cost-effective way of fighting with a reduced crew and opponents on both sides. After two hours of battle her three masts fell in quick succession and half an hour later virtually all her guns had been dismounted. She had 87 men killed and 213 wounded when she surrendered to the *Minotaur*.[23]

The *Peuple Souverain* was another ship to be doubled, with Saumarez's *Orion* firing into her port bow and the *Defence* anchored alongside her starboard side. She was quite well manned, with a total complement of 573, including 60 boys but there is no sign that her resistance was particularly effective. Neither of her opponents suffered particularly heavy casualties and the *Defence* lost only her fore-topmast.

Meanwhile the crew of the *Orion* spotted a blazing raft drifting down towards them, presumably released from one of the enemy ships at the head of the line. A boat was kept hanging over the stern ready for a quick launch but that had been shot to pieces. Men got booms and poles ready to push the raft away but it drifted clear, 25 yards from the ship's bows.[24] Action resumed against the *Peuple Souverain* and her masts fell one by one. Captain Saumarez was wounded in the thigh by a splinter from one of the ship's own spare topmasts. Captain Savage of the marines took him under the half-deck for safety but he refused to go below for treatment. Mr Baird, the captain's clerk, was killed and Charles Meills, one of the captain's favourite midshipmen, was seriously hurt by the same splinter. Eventually his arm and shoulder had to be amputated.[25] But soon the French ship's cable was cut, whether by accident or design, and she drifted out between the *Orion* and the *Franklin*, creating a fatal gap in the French line.

In this way the French van, disgracefully and tragically weak in the first place, had been swept away by Nelson's assault. The retreat of the *Peuple Souverain* was particularly important because it exposed the bows of the *Franklin*, the powerful 80-gun ship anchored just ahead of the flagship *L'Orient*. Thus the three ships forming the central stronghold of the line came under attack from several directions. The *Franklin* had had a relatively easy time in the first phase of the battle, for she was attacked only by the after guns of the *Swiftsure*, which was also engaging the flagship with her forward guns. Rear-Admiral Blanquet was soon wounded in the head and carried below, unconscious. When the *Peuple Souverain* was driven out of the line the *Franklin* was exposed, having no friendly ship immediately ahead of her, and several unengaged enemies. The *Leander*, finally joining the battle after trying to help the grounded *Culloden*, moved into the vacant space. At first the men of the

Orion were confused, thinking she might be an enemy fireship. They hoisted a signal of four horizontal lights, which was returned, confirming the *Leander*'s identity. She opened fire on the bows of the *Franklin* but in doing so she masked the more powerful guns of the *Orion*, which was forced to cease firing. Meanwhile the *Defence*, having helped dispose of the *Peuple Souverain*, moved to attack the next ship in line and fired into the *Franklin*'s bows. The French captain, Gilet, was wounded and soon afterwards an arms chest filled with musket cartridges, placed on deck to supply the marines with ammunition, blew up and spread flames to several parts of the poop and quarterdeck. These were extinguished but the onslaught continued. The main and mizzen masts fell and all the guns on the main deck were dismounted. As firing ceased from the ships ahead the crew became demoralised, while the situation of the flagship, only 160 yards away, caused even greater concern.[26]

★

The battle had begun well for the mighty 120-gun *L'Orient*. The *Majestic* had failed to attack her and had run up against the *Heureux* instead, much her disadvantage. The *Bellerophon* was the next to attack but she suffered heavily for her daring. Within an hour she had lost her mizzen mast, soon followed by her mainmast. By the end of the battle 16 of her guns had been put out of action and she suffered nearly 200 casualties – almost a quarter of the total British losses. Unconsciously echoing the language of Hood about the *Guerrier*, one of the officers of *L'Orient* reported that her gunports were almost 'reunited into one'.[27]

The *Bellerophon* had only three men in her sick berth at the beginning of the action, recovering from pleurisy, jaundice and fever. Her list of dead and wounded during the battle is a catalogue of horror. Men were brought down into the cockpit but several had died before the surgeon could look at them. Lieutenant David died after suffering 'loss of leg, many small shot wounds of body, thighs etc'. One seaman lost both his arms, another had 'half head off' before he died. Lawrence Curren had his 'bowels exposed, whole of abdomen'. In all twenty-six men died in the cockpit, apart from those killed on deck. Some of the wounded had equally horrific wounds. John O'Hare had a 'blown up face', Robert Williams had a 'splintered wound of thorax, behind' and many more lost arms and legs. A few were luckier; Isaac Whitfield lost only his little toe, others had only slight wounds and bruises.[28]

Soon the *Swiftsure* arrived to take position off the French flagship's bows, while the *Alexander* placed herself in a devastating position aft, able to fire shot through her weak stern, where it passed along the full length of the decks causing 'horrible carnage' according to one of the French officers.[29] Admiral Brueys was wounded in the head and arm early in the action and then took a shot in the belly which 'nearly cut him in two'. He demanded to stay on deck but died 15 minutes later. The crew were deeply affected by this and it 'added to their ardour for revenge'. However, their spirits began to flag as the ships ahead surrendered one by one and the gunfire from that quarter died down.[30]

Soon after, the *Alexander*'s raking shots started a fire in the stern cabin of the French flagship. It spread rapidly to the poop and was soon out of control. Rumour suggested that tins of paint had been left about the decks and Elliot considered this an example of 'true French carelessness'.[31] The field of battle was soon bathed in an eerie light, allowing Captain Berry to assess the progress of the contest. In the tower at Rosetta 12 miles away, Poussielgue saw 'an immense flame which announced to us that some ship was on fire'.[32] In the *Swiftsure* Captain Hallowell perceived the flames as coming from the chains of the mizzen mast. He ordered his guns pointed towards the spot, along with the muskets of the marines, to prevent the enemy from putting the fire out. It was done 'with such effective results that all their efforts to subdue it were rendered unavailing by the slaughter which the concentrated fire of the *Swiftsure* produced.'[33]

In the days of wooden ships, seamen would laugh at storms, scorn wind and waves and despise enemy gunfire but they were terrified of one thing – fire. Over the last 50 years or so, captains had attempted to find ways to control the blind panic that generally ensued on a burning ship and set disciplined teams to fight the flames, using pump-water, man-powered fire hoses and leather buckets. This had had some effect but the threat was still a very real one, as everyone knew. The captains of the ships close to *L'Orient* saw the danger of the fire itself and an even more serious risk if the flames were to reach *L'Orient*'s powder magazines. They began to move away, using all the means at their disposal. For the *Bellerophon*, with her main and mizzen masts down and the foremast fouled by the wreckage, this meant cutting her cable and setting a minimum of sail, a spritsail hung from under the bowsprit. Even this put too much indirect strain on the damaged foremast and it too went by the board over the port bow. Seamen hastened to clear the wreckage and sails were set on the stumps of the masts to carry the ship further away.[34]

Midshipman Elliot was in the *Goliath*, near the head of the line and about half a mile away from the burning ship. On seeing the flames he was in great suspense about her identity but admits to relief on discovering that she had three decks and was therefore a Frenchman.[35] Saumarez in the *Orion*, only about 300 yards from *L'Orient* and having very little room for manoeuvre with a damaged ship in crowded waters, felt much more threatened. The guns were run in and the ports shut to prevent the ingress of air. The magazine was closed down and the sails, among the most inflammable items aboard a ship, were hurriedly taken off the masts and sent below.[36] The *Theseus* put hawsers into her boats to send to the *Orion*, in a belated attempt to tow her further away from the burning ship.[37]

Ball's *Alexander* was relatively undamaged so far but within 5 minutes of seeing the fire on *L'Orient* Ball ordered the cutting of her stern cable. An anchor was quite a valuable item and could not be sacrificed lightly but it would take perhaps an hour to raise it, using about half the crew. In battle it was often necessary to cut cables to save the ship, perhaps attaching a buoy to the end of the cable so that it could be recovered later. The *Alexander* drifted down again and anchored again by her bows, swinging round in the process, and came alongside another ship, perhaps the *Tonnant*. But within a few minutes it seemed likely that the burning French flagship might drift down too, so the bow cable was cut again.

The *Swiftsure*, engaging both *L'Orient* and the *Franklin*, was upwind of the

The explosion of *L'Orient*, painted by George Arnald. Just as the event itself was the most universal image of the battle to those present, this painting has become perhaps the image best known to the public. (National Maritime Museum, London: BHC0509)

French flagship and felt less danger, and even though the heat was beginning to melt the tar between her planks, her crew merely 'hove in the cable and spring occasionally'.[38] According to young Theophilus Lee, 'Hallowell saw, with the eye of judgement, that her present station was the best calculated to secure her from danger. The explosion would naturally throw all up in the air and the *Swiftsure* being, as may be supposed, near the centre thereof, consequently the greater part of the fragments would naturally be projected over and beyond her.'[39] Hallowell ordered sentries to be posted on the cables to prevent anyone trying to cut them. As in the *Orion* the gunports and magazine were closed and the men went under cover, taking wet swabs and buckets of water to put out any fires.[40]

The French ships too saw the danger and the *Tonnant* cut her cables, to be followed by the *Heureux* and *Mercure*, perhaps pleased to find an excuse to get away from their punishing fight with the *Majestic*. The *Tonnant* drifted down the line and managed to anchor near the *Guillaume Tell* but the *Heureux* had some difficulty. Lieutenant Foucaud, in command after Captain Etienne fell wounded, tried to lay

The lightning conductor from the masthead of *L'Orient*, kept by Nelson as a souvenir. (National Maritime Museum, London: D4721)

out an anchor and to set topsails and topgallants but she was still under fire and the officers had difficulty in getting the men to go on deck to man the rigging. The *Heureux* thus went aground on the shoals of the bay, knocking off her rudder[41] and the *Mercure* followed her onto the shoal. These two ships were still engaged by the *Majestic* and *Alexander*. The *Timoléon*, *Guillaume Tell* and *Généreux* were slightly further away from *L'Orient* and so far undamaged. They simply let out more cable and allowed the wind and current to take them a few hundred yards further away from the great conflagration.[42]

In the *Goliath*, Purser Samuel Grant was released from his medical duties in the cockpit and from the poop he saw 'the French three decker in a blaze to the water's edge very near to us. It was the most melancholy but at the same time the most beautiful sight I ever beheld.'[43] Despite his wounds, Nelson insisted on coming on deck to see the fire. He ordered the *Vanguard's* last remaining boat to be sent over to save as many lives as possible.[44] Some men were already trying to swim away from *L'Orient* and fourteen of them, including the first lieutenant and purser, reached the lower deck ports of the *Swiftsure* and were helped aboard by the seamen.[45] By this time Nelson was convinced that *L'Orient* had ceased firing and had hauled down her flag to surrender. This was disputed by some and the *Swiftsure* was still feeling the effects of *L'Orient*'s guns even to the last: 'Yet the enemy on the lower deck, either insensible of the danger that surrounded them, or impelled by paroxysms of despair and vengeance, continued to fire upon us.'[46] Even so, some of the senior officers were abandoning ship as the fire reached the middle deck. Admiral Ganteaume, the chief of staff, found a boat to take him to the frigate *Salamine* and thence ashore at Aboukir. Adjutant-General Motard swam to the nearest ship, which turned out to be the *Swiftsure*. Commodore Casabianca, the captain, took to the water with his 10-year-old son, a cadet on the ship. They climbed onto a floating mast but soon perished.[47]

At some time between 9.37 and 11.30pm, but probably nearer the latter, the flames reached the magazine of the French flagship and she blew up with a noise that was heard many miles away. It was a moment of great shock for everyone, far and near. Close by, in the *Swiftsure*, Chaplain Willyams wrote that the ship 'blew up with a crashing sound that deafened all around her. The tremendous motion, felt to the very bottom of each ship, was like that of an earthquake. The fragments were driven such a vast height into the air that some moments elapsed before they could descend.'[48] In the magazines below the waterline of the *Goliath*, half a mile from the blast, seaman John Nicol thought that part of his own ship had exploded.[49] In Alexandria 9 miles away the staff of General Kléber saw 'a bright flame rising rapidly through the air. The flame became thicker and in a moment it turned into a black smoke, across which, for several minutes, sparks of light were visible.'[50]

The *Swiftsure* was one of the closest British ships when *L'Orient* exploded but evidently Hallowell had been right in his suppositions about the effects. Two large pieces of timber, fortunately not on fire, dropped on the main- and fore-tops of the ship but all men had been withdrawn from these positions and she was otherwise undamaged.[51] The *Alexander* was almost as close and was at considerable risk herself. As the burning embers fell to the water, some landed on her decks and among her sails. Her jib, a sail well forward in the ship over the bowsprit, was set on fire and the jib-boom, along with the spritsail and spritsail topsail yards, had to be hacked away to let the blazing sail fall into the water. The main royal, the highest sail on the mainmast, also caught fire and had to be cut from its position and dropped over the side. One can only imagine the risks to the men who cut it down and the tension in the ship as it fell past the rigging and into the water. The *Franklin*, the only survivor of the French vanguard, was showered with burning debris. 'red-hot pincers, pieces of timber, and rope, on fire.'[52] She was set on fire for the fourth time during the battle but the crew soon put it out. Thus the last embers from the burning *L'Orient* were extinguished.

CHAPTER 13

'No longer an enemy to contend with'

ALL ACCOUNTS AGREE that firing ceased for a while after the great explosion, but everyone had lost his sense of time in the heat of battle. Berry says there was deathly silence for 3 minutes while the debris of *L'Orient* fell into the water and onto the surrounding ships. The log of the *Vanguard* suggests 10 minutes, as did the distant observers in Rosetta and Alexandria.[1] According to Blanquet it was 15 minutes before the gun crews recovered from their stupor and resumed the action. Elliot suggests half an hour, if not an hour. In the *Theseus*, however, the men were denied even this brief respite from their labours. Captain Miller ordered that the ship should be sluiced down completely, to prevent her catching fire.[2]

The blowing-up of the French flagship caused mixed feelings among the British crews. The men of the *Theseus* cheered raggedly, rather against the wishes of Captain Miller, whose own feelings of pity were nevertheless 'stifled by a remembrance of the numerous and horrid atrocities their unprincipled and bloodthirsty nation were committing'.[3] To seaman John Jup of the *Orion* it was 'a most glorious scene to us, though would have been terrible to people which had never seen the like.' The explosion 'made the whole element shake'.[4]

Despite this apparent callousness, the officers and the lower deck showed true compassion in the rescue of survivors. Fourteen men were picked up by the *Orion* and according to John Jup, 'the French come swimming from their ships that was on fire and our brave spirited Englishmen threw them rope and took them in and stripped of their own clothes and gave them to cover their nakedness and went without themselves, as our bags were stowed away and we could not get them for a day or two afterwards.'[5] This is confirmed by Saumarez's biographer. 'The generous, warm-hearted sailors stripped off their jackets to cover these unfortunate men, and treated them with kindness, proving that humanity is compatible with bravery.'[6] The *Swiftsure* picked up two officers and nine seamen, while the dismasted *Bellerophon*, drifting close to the scene, rescued two men. In the *Goliath* the French survivors huddled under the forecastle until Foley took pity on them and ordered them taken down to the steward's room for provisions and clothing.[7] In the *Alexander* the survivors had come on board naked and were issued with 'shirts 28, trousers 28 pairs'.[8]

At this stage damage to the British ships was confined mainly to the *Majestic*, which had mishandled her attack on the *Heureux*, and the *Bellerophon* which had begun the attack on *L'Orient*. The *Majestic* had lost her main and mizzen mast and her fore rigging was much damaged but she still had a part to play. The *Bellerophon* was completely dismasted except for her bowsprit and was out of the action. Of the five ships which had rounded the head of the French line, none had suffered any great damage. Those which had attacked on the outside had suffered worse. The *Vanguard*, which of course was already under jury rig from the storm in May, had taken more punishment in her fight with the *Spartiate*. The *Minotaur*, which had come to her assistance, had lost a good deal of her rigging but her masts were intact. The *Defence* had lost her fore-topmast in the fight with the *Peuple Souverain* and the *Swiftsure* her main topmast (a relatively minor loss) to *L'Orient*. The *Alexander* had suffered some damage from the explosion and had lost her main yard and some sails but was still mobile. But often the real damage was much greater than was apparent from a distance. The *Orion*'s masts, for example, were still standing but seriously weakened by shot.

The French, of course, were in a far worse state. The first four ships in the line had already surrendered, as had the sixth, the *Peuple Souverain*, and most were completely dismasted. Only the *Franklin* still had her tricolour flying in that part of the line and she had lost her main and mizzen masts. *L'Orient* of course had gone and astern of her the *Tonnant* was dismasted with only her bowsprit standing. The fire of the *Majestic* had seriously wounded her captain, Dupetit-Thouars, who had lost both arms and a leg. He insisted on being propped up in a bran tub, until he died from loss of blood. The frigate *Sérieuse* was on shore and dismasted and the *Heureux* and *Mercure* had run aground. Three ships of the line and three frigates were still relatively undamaged as they awaited further attack.[9]

Pierre-Charles de Villeneuve, a rear-admiral at the time of the Battle of the Nile and the most senior French officer to escape. (Bridgeman Art Library)

At the rear of the line, Rear-Admiral Villeneuve had a dilemma. So far he had only fired his guns when the dismasted *Bellerophon* had drifted harmlessly past. Brueys had left no orders on what to do in the circumstances and Villeneuve, despite his youth, was an admiral of the old school, trained to obey orders rather than use his initiative. Thirty-four years old, he had entered the *Marine Royale* at the age of 15 and his zeal had attracted notice but it took the Revolution to get him to the rank of full captain (*Capitaine de Vaisseau*) in 1793. He rose rapidly in a navy which was starved of experienced sea officers, becoming a *Chef de Division* and then a rear-admiral in 1796. He had been intended to take part in the invasion of Ireland in 1798 but contrary winds delayed his ship in the Mediterranean, leaving him free to take charge of the rearguard of Brueys's fleet.[10]

Because the wind was against him, Villeneuve was unwilling to sail forward to help the ships at the head of the line. His ships were apparently moored far better than those ahead of *L'Orient*, because he had more time to get out extra anchors. It would take hours to get them up and he was unwilling to cut the cables and lose irreplaceable ground tackle. Furthermore Brueys's instructions, issued before the battle, had been based on the premise of an attack on the rear of the line and he had issued signals to be used in the event of having to call the leading ships back to support the rearguard. He had given no instructions for the reverse, that is for the rear ships to move up in support of the van. How could Villeneuve know whether the advanced ships would cut their cables under Nelson's attack and fall back to the protection of the rearguard? When *L'Orient* blew up, this was exactly what seemed to be happening, as the *Tonnant*, *Heureux* and *Mercure* moved down the line. Villeneuve believed that he had been ordered to stay in position and any other action would be a dereliction of duty. For the rest of his life he was haunted with vague accusations of failing to take the initiative, which hurt him deeply as a loyal and disciplined naval officer. Nelson, or for that matter Napoleon, would have behaved differently but such men were rare in any armed force.

★

It was the *Franklin*, the last French survivor forward of *L'Orient*, which resumed the firing after the great explosion. Since the death of Brueys could be presumed, Blanquet was now in command of the fleet, though himself wounded. His ship began to cannonade the *Defence* and *Swiftsure*, 'to preserve the trust confided in her' and presumably setting an example to the less damaged ships in the rear of the line. But the fire of the *Swiftsure* was no longer divided and the concentrated guns of two ships were far more than a match for the *Franklin*. Many of her guns had already been dismounted and two-thirds of her crew killed or wounded. With only three lower deck guns left in action it was decided to give up. The colours were struck on the orders of *Capitaine de Frégate* Martinet, the most senior unwounded officer.[11] The *Defence* was hailed to inform her of the surrender and her first lieutenant was rowed across to take possession. The *Swiftsure* was also hailed and sent Lieutenant Cowan over; he returned 15 minutes later, finding that the officer from the *Defence* had already taken possession.[12]

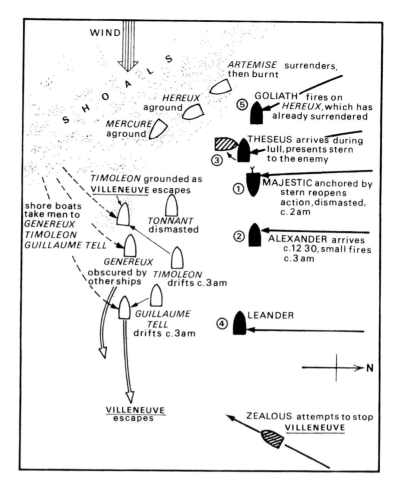

The southern battle during the night of 1 to 2 August.

However, the *Franklin* had some success in causing the rest of the French ships to resume the action. At what had once been the southern end of Brueys's line of battle, a new French position was beginning to establish itself. The *Heureux* and *Mercure* were inshore, aground but still fighting. The *Tonnant* and *Timoléon* were east of the *Guillaume Tell*, the flagship of Rear-Admiral Villeneuve, and the *Généreux* was behind her, with a restricted arc of fire towards the British position. Villeneuve was obliged to hail her several times as her shot passed dangerously low over the *Guillaume Tell's* masts.[13]

The *Alexander* and *Majestic* were still the most advanced ships of the British fleet and they were the only ones in action in the middle of the night. The exact nature of the fight is not clear. A 'very heavy cannonade' was observed from the *Goliath*,[14] but to Miller of the *Theseus* it seemed 'broken and disconnected'.[15] The *Majestic*, now commanded by Lieutenant Cuthbert after the death of Captain Westcott, was engaged with her old opponents the grounded *Heureux* and *Mercure*, and perhaps with the *Tonnant* as well. One of these ships dismasted her at 2am.[16]

Ball's *Alexander* had apparently drifted for 2 hours after the explosion, dealing with her burning sails and putting herself in order. According to her log (which was probably no more accurate in its timekeeping than any other) it was after midnight when she 'came to with the sheet anchor and commenced firing upon three of the enemy's ships',[17] presumably the *Tonnant, Guillaume Tell* and *Timoléon*. It was the last of these three, perhaps a little further forward than the rest, which took the brunt of the fire.[18] The fight in the south developed rather like a land battle, helped by the fact that ships were at anchor for most of the time and were close to the shore. Positions were held and abandoned, ships advanced while others retreated, reinforcements arrived, units were cut off and eventually the losers fled from the field.

★

Nelson was still effectively out of the action, exhausted and dazed after his excursion on deck to see the burning *L'Orient*. The rest of the British ships concentrated on patching up their damage, securing prizes and tending to their wounded. From the *Vanguard*, Lieutenant Vassal went out to take possession of a ship which seemed to have surrendered, perhaps the *Heureux* or *Généreux*. He returned unsuccessful more than 3 hours later, for the ship had got under way before he had been able to board her.[19] Meanwhile the *Defence* had sent her first lieutenant to take charge of the *Franklin*,[20] while later in the morning a lieutenant, a petty officer and 8 seamen from the *Orion* took possession of the *Peuple Souverain* – a small enough party to guard 477 survivors of the French crew, even if 150 were wounded.[21]

In Foley's *Goliath*, the men worked at the damaged masts, trying to save as much as possible. Midshipman Elliot succumbed to fatigue at 3am when he 'actually fell asleep in the act of hauling up a shroud hawser'. The boatswain took him down to his cabin where he got some rest.[22] By moonlight, Captain Miller of the *Theseus* spotted the dismasted, grounded hulk of the frigate *Sérieuse*, put out of action by the broadsides of the *Orion*. He sent Lieutenant Brodie over to take possession, with instructions to raise some lights, known as 'false fires' from his boat if the French still refused to surrender. He hailed the ship and was allowed to come on board. He found thirty survivors, including Captain Martin and three officers, huddled to-gether on the forecastle and more than ready to be taken prisoner. Miller also saw several enemy ships inshore of him, possibly the French brigs and bomb vessels. He ordered a master's mate to take a boat and sound the depth of water between the *Theseus* and the enemy, with a view to making an attack. Then, exhausted like all his crew, he took the chance to snatch some sleep.[23]

The *Swiftsure* had suffered damage below the waterline as she entered the action, by a shot striking her port bow. The pumps were kept constantly in use but she made several feet of water in her hold.[24] The carpenters evidently did a good job in repairing the hole for the ship was prominent in action later in the morning.

The crippled *Bellerophon* drifted for more than 3 hours after cutting her cable to get away from the burning French flagship. Early in the morning of the 2nd she set some jury sails on the stumps of her masts and with a favourable wind she was able to get clear of the French fleet. On reaching shallow water in the south of the bay, it was found that both the anchor cables in use had been damaged by enemy shot, so a smaller one, the stream cable, had to be fitted to a spare anchor and used instead. She anchored in 7 fathoms, 6 miles to the east of the main fleet. Her seamen hacked away at the mainmast which was still hanging over the side and got rid of the debris of the ship's boats. They also found time to 'bury' the forty-nine officers, marines and seamen who had been killed by the guns of *L'Orient*.[25]

Around 3am[26] there was another complete lull as both sides in the southern battle suffered damage. The rigging of the *Alexander* was hit by French shot, perhaps from the *Timoléon*. Three of her sails caught fire and yet again, as in the aftermath of the explosion of *L'Orient*, she had to cut them away and drop them over the side.[27] The *Majestic* had already been dismasted by the combined fire of several opponents. But unknown to the British officers the cables of two of the French ships, the *Timoléon* and the *Guillaume Tell*, had been cut by the persistent gunfire and they began to drift out of their positions.

★

At 4am the first signs of dawn began to break after the short but violent summer night and Nelson began to recover from the shock of his wound and take an interest in the action. There was no doubt that he had already won a great victory but it was not yet the one of annihilation he had planned. Perhaps he remembered what he had said to Admiral Hotham 3 years earlier and how he had written, 'had we taken ten sail and allowed the eleventh to escape when it had been possible to have got at her, I could never call it well done.' He sent his flag lieutenant, the young Thomas Bladen Capel, in a boat to urge the captains of the least damaged ships to move down the line to assist against some of the enemy ships which still held out.

Even before Nelson's message went out, Miller of the *Theseus* was wakened from his nap by Captain Hood, who hailed him to propose that the two ships should move down the line. The *Zealous* was slow in getting under way for some reason but the *Theseus* was already heaving up her anchor when Nelson's suggestion was received.[28] Miller says he was then contacted by an officer of the *Alexander* but this seems unlikely in view of the position of that ship in the thick of the southern battle and perhaps he meant Capel of the *Vanguard*.[29] The *Theseus* was the first British ship to go to the support the *Alexander* and *Majestic*.[30]

Gould of the *Audacious* was satisfied that he had already done his duty. Before midnight he had written to Nelson, evidently the only captain who found time to put pen to paper in the heat of battle. 'I have the satisfaction to tell you the French ship *Le Conquérant* has struck to the *Audacious* and I have her in possession . . . I give you joy of this glorious victory.'[31] The *Audacious* was not seriously damaged, as Gould admitted. 'We have but one killed and no great many wounded. Our fore and mizzen topmast are wounded, but I hope not very bad.' However, Gould declined to move, apparently on the grounds that Foley's *Goliath* was in the way. Capel was rowed to the *Goliath*, grinning at Gould's well-known caution. He approached Foley, who asked 'if he was specially sent to the *Goliath* to order him on that duty.' Capel replied no, that 'he was sent to the ships that were not disabled and he saw that we were completely so.'[32] Foley was aware of the damage to his ship, especially to the rigging of the main and mizzen masts, which seemed about to fall; all the seamen had been 'employed stoppering and repairing the same as fast as possible' ever since the *Conquérant* had surrendered many hours earlier.[33]

According to Elliot:

> Captain Foley, in his quiet way, said, 'not so much disabled that we cannot go down with the wind'; and immediately ordered the master to go down and cut the cable. We had not a sail to set, but the fore topsail was let fall, and hung down on each side of the stay, which, directly before the wind, kept her steering.[34]

It was 6am, according to her log, when the *Goliath* cut her cable and began to sail down to join the battle in the south. A few hours later Foley apologised to Nelson for his tardiness.

> I would not have waited the message you sent me to give assistance to the *Theseus* could I have secured my mainmast sooner. The dread of losing it and the appearance of so little defence on the side of the enemy this morning induced me to be so late in leaving my anchor. The rigging more than the mast is the damaged part.[35]

Thompson of the *Leander* was much more reluctant to move down. At 5.25am Nelson hoisted signal No. 55 'assist ships in battle' bearing the *Leander's* number. It was answered 10 minutes later but Nelson felt it necessary to repeat it at 5.30, 5.42 and 5.46am.[36] Because the *Leander's* log was later lost in battle, it is not possible to establish the reasons for the delay but in any case the *Leander* eventually joined the fray.

★

On reaching the firing line near the *Alexander* and *Majestic*, Miller anchored the *Theseus* in line with these two ships, inshore of both, directly opposite the frigate *Artemise* and to the north of the grounded *Mercure* and *Heureux*. At first he anchored by the stern but soon had a change of plan. Since the wind was now westerly, he dropped his bow anchor so that the ship would swing with her bows to the east, allowing his broadside to bear south towards the enemy. He had the stern anchor hauled in but the bow anchor failed to hold at first and in light and variable winds the ship was soon presenting her stern to the enemy. Miller saw most of the remaining strength of the French fleet concentrated on his weakest part. As well as the two grounded ships there was a powerful 80, the *Tonnant*, within range, plus the 74s *Généreux* and *Timoléon* further to the west. The *Alexander* and *Majestic* were still silent and Miller had no wish to attract attention to himself. As the ship settled down in her position he held his fire while the *Goliath*, *Zealous* and *Leander* moved down in his support. He sent an officer in a boat to ask the other three ships to hurry. His crew, who had not enjoyed the respite of other ships after *L'Orient* blew up, fell asleep over capstan bars and in 'every sort of posture'.[37]

They did not rest for long, for Miller saw the *Guillaume Tell* under way, after her anchor cable had been cut by gunfire. Believing the French ship was trying to escape, Miller opened fire on her and the *Tonnant* precisely at sunrise. The men of the *Majestic* opened up too, for they had succeeded in clearing the debris from over their guns. The *Alexander* had dealt with her burning sail and she too fired a broadside. At this point the *Leander* arrived to join the fight, anchoring east of the *Alexander*, forming the end of an impromptu line of four ships. Meanwhile the *Guillaume Tell* re-anchored further south and the *Timoléon* took up a position inshore of the undamaged *Généreux*. The French position was still coherent but they were at the limit of the range of the British guns. The *Heureux* and *Mercure* could not move and were left to bear the brunt of the attack by three British ships, though the *Theseus* was the only one with a clear field of fire. The *Heureux* was the most exposed and struck her colours. Lieutenant Brodie was sent out to take possession but there was much confusion as the *Goliath* arrived on the scene and anchored inshore of the *Theseus*. 'In half an hour,' wrote Elliot, 'we were again in action with some already very much disabled French ships, which went on shore, and too far off to do much execution. We were just touching the sandbanks ourselves.'[38] Not knowing of the surrender, Foley continued firing until Miller hailed him and told him to stop. Soon the *Mercure* surrendered as well, having lost 105 men killed and 148 wounded.

This left the frigate *Artemise* completely exposed to the broadsides of the *Goliath* and the *Theseus*.[39] She was seriously short-handed, as she was one of the vessels called upon to send men on board the flagship and her consorts at the beginning of the action. She lowered her flag and Miller sent Lieutenant Hoste to take charge. On meeting a lieutenant from the *Alexander* also on his way to board the prize, Hoste gave way and returned to the *Theseus*. But before the *Alexander*'s officer reached her, the *Artemise* was set on fire by orders of her captain, Standelet, and he and his crew made for the shore in boats. The British officers were outraged by this and regarded it as a serious breach of the etiquette of war, even by the standards of the French Revolutionaries. Miller wrote to his wife, 'This dishonourable action was not out of character for a modern Frenchman: the devil is beyond blacken-ing.'[40] The frigate burned for about half an hour and then blew up.

Hood missed this battle. He had cut his cable and was proceeding southwards in the *Zealous* when Nelson noticed the frigate *Justice* setting sail and trying to escape. He signalled the *Zealous* to 'chase east' and the frigate, which Hood mistakenly believed to be the *Diane*, turned back and anchored again. Perhaps realising that the southern battle was now taken care of, Nelson recalled Hood and ordered him to go to the aid of the crippled *Bellerophon*, anchored about 6 miles to the eastward of the battle.

The battle with the remaining French ships continued for nearly 5 hours after the surrender of the *Mercure*. Had Nelson been well and in an undamaged ship, he might have led a spirited attack on the enemy and brought a quicker conclusion, probably with complete destruction of the enemy but counterbalanced by further loss of life on his own side. As it was, both his senior captains, Saumarez and Troubridge, were out of action and there was no-one to take the lead. Ball in the *Alexander* was the most senior officer in the rather random collection of ships present on the scene but there is no sign that he attempted to assert any authority over them. Ball had already begun the second phase of the battle, after the

French van had crumbled, by doing decisive damage which ultimately caused the destruction of the French flagship. He had been at the forefront of the attack during the third phase, against the ships in the south of Aboukir Bay. It would have been unfair to expect him to do any more, given the general fatigue from which everyone was suffering. It would have been difficult to organise his forces in any case, for the ships were at anchor, the distances were probably too great for hailing, most of the ships' boats were out of action and relatively junior captains (Ball was sixth in line out of thirteen) were not issued with a full set of signal flags.

★

All night Troubridge had struggled to keep the *Culloden* afloat. Wine, bread and shot were thrown over the side, and some of the balls, which might be needed urgently in action, were transferred to the *Mutine*. In the middle of the night the swell increased and the stern struck heavily on the reef, breaking off the rudder. The hull was beginning to leak and 5ft of water was entering the hold every hour. By the early morning all hands were taking turns at operating the chain pumps. The rotary motion of the pump handles was demanding on the seamen's muscles and it was said, 'Few officers of any experience must not have known the difficulty with which men are almost drove to return to the pumps of leaking ships, when obliged to keep them going. It strains their loins, affects the muscular parts of their arms like violent rheumatic pains, and galls their hands.'[41] At 2.30am one of the cables parted and the ship's head swung round, causing her to strike against the rocks yet again.

As dawn approached some of the *Mutine*'s men came on board to take a turn at the pumps while the *Culloden*'s crew had breakfast. The carpenters cut up a spare topmast and were nailing its pieces together to make a new rudder. The sailmakers, meanwhile were 'thrumming' a sail. Tiny holes were pierced in it and short pieces of yarn passed through them. Eventually it would be passed over the side and manoeuvred against one of the holes in the bottom, in the hope that the sail would be sucked into it and stop the leak.[42]

As the sun rose, the exhausted men of the *Culloden* had the frustrating sight of their comrades' triumph. 'Observed six of the enemy's ships had struck and one to leeward totally dismasted. Observed the *Bellerophon* to an anchor east 8 or 9 miles, totally dismasted, also the *Majestic* with only her foremast standing. *Alexander*, *Defence* and *Swiftsure* very much disabled in the rigging and hulls but *Alexander*, *Majestic* and *Goliath* in action.'[43]

★

As the morning wore on, the French succeeded in getting several local boats out of Alexandria, carrying 300 seamen hastily recruited from the merchant ships in the harbour. They reached the remaining ships of the line, the *Guillaume Tell*, *Généreux* and *Timoléon*. In the *Theseus*, Miller saw the boats and was convinced that the men were being taken off, before the ships were set on fire. He concentrated his men on the lower deck guns, which had greater range and ordered Lieutenant England, in charge of that deck, to keep up a 'cool and steady fire' in an attempt to drive the boats away.[44]

Villeneuve was still racked with indecision, this time about whether to escape with what ships he could.

> I had hesitated long about setting sail. I counted the cost of abandoning the *Timoléon*, the *Tonnant* as well as the *Mercure* and the *Heureux*. It was probable that the enemy would cut me off at the exit from the bay, with the five or six ships I could see with their rigging intact and I would be obliged to succumb and run aground on a beach, where it would be difficult to save my crews. The frigate *Justice*, which had set sail, had been obliged to re-anchor by an enemy ship of the line which cut off her route. However, this was the only means which offered any hope of saving the remains of the squadron, seeing the *Mercure* and *Heureux* given up and taken as prizes, and the enemy ships directing their fire on me.[45]

The importance of Villeneuve's indecision is difficult to overestimate. Leaving aside his failure to move up to the head of the line in the earlier stages, an earlier retreat could yet have salvaged something from the defeat. With the *Timoléon* added to the *Guillaume Tell* and the *Généreux*, he would have had three ships of the line to dispute the sovereignty of the eastern Mediterranean. In view of the damage to most of Nelson's ships in battle, this would have been a significant force, perhaps enough to counter-attack the British ships one by one and minimise or even reverse Nelson's victory.

The *Timoléon* was clearly in a bad way, having suffered most from the fire, however desultory, of the *Alexander* and *Majestic* during the night, from the *Leander* after she joined the battle and later from Lieutenant England's 'cool and steady fire' from the *Theseus*. By this time she was disabled, with her rigging cut in many places, her masts peppered with shot and her rudder broken. Villeneuve managed to hail her captain, Trullet. He told him that he intended to try to escape, asking Trullet what he would do. The latter replied that he would fight as long as he could and then set his ship on fire. Villeneuve answered 'Bravo!'.[46]

The *Zealous*, in the centre of the picture, moves into position to try to stop the escape of the *Généreux*, *Guillaume Tell* and two frigates. (National Maritime Museum, London: PW4700)

Just before midday Villeneuve realised that to delay any longer would be to risk losing his last chance. He signalled to his ships to cut their cables and sail out of the Bay. He headed to the north east, followed by the *Généreux* and the frigates *Diane* and *Justice*.

True to his word, Trullet had the *Timoléon*'s cable cut and the ship drifted onto the shore, running aground 1000 yards from where she had been anchored. As she struck, her mizzen mast finally collapsed from the impact. Trullet sent an officer ashore to the fort at Aboukir to ask for boats to take off the wounded. He then settled down to await the British attack.[47]

Villeneuve's escape was quickly noticed from the British ships. Nelson signalled for his least damaged ships – the *Goliath*, *Audacious*, *Theseus* and *Zealous* – to go in pursuit. The *Theseus* and *Goliath* set some sail and fired several broadsides, doing little damage at long range. The *Zealous*, already under sail and on her way to help the wounded *Bellerophon*, was in easily the best position and went in chase. Sailing as close to the wind as he could, Hood took the *Zealous* within 80 yards of the *Guillaume Tell*, sailing in the opposite direction. He forced her to alter course to avoid being raked. The ships exchanged passing broadsides in which George Willis, a seaman of the *Zealous*, was killed and large parts of the ship's rigging were shot away. The *Guillaume Tell* suffered some damage but escaped. One of the French frigates came up behind her and Hood attempted to cut her off, hoping to board, but having lost so much rigging he was not able to bring his ship round in time and the frigate escaped undamaged.

At this point Nelson realised that the attempt was futile. The four French ships were all good sailers and relatively unhurt, while all of his ships had suffered severe damage in their rigging. Such ships as could still sail were needed to maintain a blockade of Alexandria and to prevent a French counter-attack. He hoisted signal No. 9, to 'leave off chasing' and called Hood over to the flagship, where he 'thanked me most kindly for my conduct, on the opportunity I had of distinguishing myself, particularly on that occasion.'[48]

The men of Nelson's fleet could only watch as the four escaping enemy ships ran parallel to the shore for three-quarters of an hour and then rounded Rosetta Point to the east. That night, sailing close to the wind on the starboard tack, they made good progress in the direction of Malta.[49]

★

The *Tonnant* and *Timoléon* continued to hold out for the rest of the day. In the afternoon the *Theseus* sent a boat out to ask if the *Tonnant* had surrendered but it was menaced by the French guns and had to return. She was no immediate threat and the British ships were too damaged, and their crews too exhausted to take any further action that day. Next morning Nelson, still lying wounded in his cot in the *Vanguard*, was 'naturally anxious to secure the *Tonnant* and *Timoléon*'.[50] He signalled the *Leander* to deal with the *Tonnant*, with help from the *Theseus*. The *Swiftsure* sent Lieutenant Davies to the *Tonnant* in a boat but her commander replied that he had 1600 men on board and that they would fight to the last unless he was given a ship

A French view the resistance of the *Tonnant*. Painted much later, it seems to be reasonably accurate and shows Captain Du Petit-Thouars gravely wounded on the quarterdeck. (National Maritime Museum, London: PAG9875)

to take them to Toulon.[51] At this the *Theseus* and *Leander* raised their anchors and moved into the attack. The *Theseus* sent the master ahead in a boat, taking soundings in the shallowing waters. She anchored 120 yards from the *Tonnant*, in 25½ft of

In the morning of 3 August, the *Theseus* and *Leander* move to attack the *Tonnant*, which is hauling down her flag to surrender. (National Maritime Museum, London: PAG8967)

water, leaving only about a foot under her keel, and used springs to bring her broadside to bear on the stubborn Frenchman. The *Leander* followed a few hundred yards behind and also sent a boat out to the *Tonnant*. The French commander, finally seeing the hopelessness of his position, agreed to surrender. Meanwhile the remaining crew of the *Timoléon* set the ship on fire, still with her colours flying, and made for the shore. She blew up late in the morning of the 3rd and Captain Miller wrote to his wife, 'There being no longer an enemy to contend with, we beat the retreat and solemnly return thanks to Almighty God through whose mercy we had been instrumental in obtaining so great and glorious a victory to His Majesty's arms.'[52]

CHAPTER 14

'An awful sight it was'

As the sound of the last shots died away on the morning of 2 August, the remains of the French fleet littered the waters of Aboukir Bay. Commissary Poussielgue of the French army had watched the battle from a tower in Rosetta, 12 miles to the east of Aboukir. Sweeping round the bay with his telescope he saw ships 'in good state', dismasted ships, ships aground, ships flying the British flag and various wrecks. Four ships formed 'a group with only four masts between them and those without topgallant masts'. Three more were said to 'form a group having only seven masts between them'. Poussielgue was still awaiting the results of the battle, though a boat had arrived that morning had brought news 'little tending to our comfort'. At first he thought 'the two squadrons so mingled among each other that it was impossible to distinguish French from English, nor on whose side the advantage was.' A little later he commented, 'Though the English have the advantage, they have been roughly handled since they could not follow the vessels who went away on the 15th [ie 2 August]'.[1] Perhaps this was the origin of a rumour which eventually spread to France, that the fleets had fought a drawn battle.

★

Probably no victorious fleet has ever been so isolated as Nelson's was on the afternoon of 2 August. The enemy was still dominant on land despite the guerrilla campaign of the Bedouin and a great army was only a few miles distant. The nearest British warship, apart from a few stray frigates, was 2000 miles away at Gibraltar or with St Vincent off Cadiz. At the most optimistic estimate, it would take about 3 weeks even to get a message home and in practice it was to take much longer. Even if St Vincent could be informed, it was not likely that he could afford to detach any more ships from his over-stretched fleet. Nelson had no frigates to spread the news to friendly lands and was almost completely out of contact with the world. Of his fifteen ships, the *Leander*, the nearest thing he had to a frigate, had to be sent home with dispatches and most of the rest were too damaged to be of any military value for the moment. With no dockyard nearer than Naples that was likely to be even grudgingly friendly, Nelson and his crews had to tend their wounded, repair their ships themselves and take them to sea.

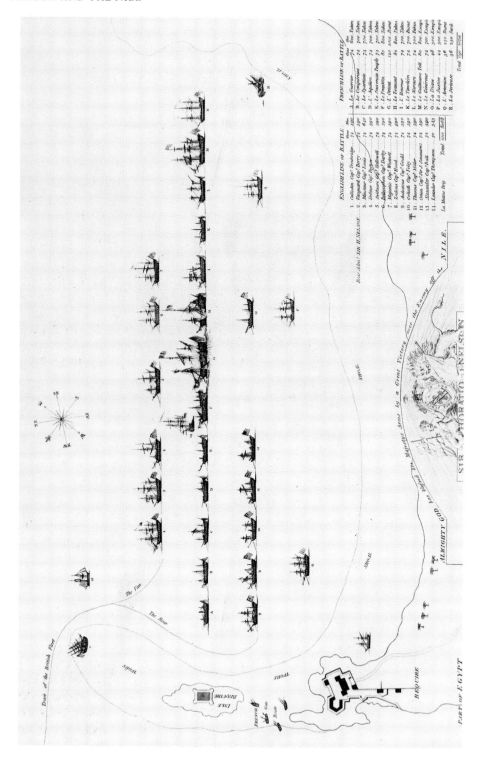

Nelson now knew that his wound was not mortal and his sight was not in danger. Michael Jefferson continued to see him every night, when he applied a compress. It was the end of the August before he was judged to be 'perfectly healed', though Jefferson continued treatment for yet another month as a precaution.[2] Miller visited him on the 6th and found him 'much better'.[3]

Saumarez was aware of the magnitude of the triumph and wrote to his wife, 'Happy am I in being enabled, through the mercy of divine providence, to acquaint you with our having obtained the most glorious and complete victory ever yet recorded in the annals of the world.'[4] But Sir James, almost unique among seamen, strategists, biographers and historians, believed that even more could have been done and that the doubling of the enemy fleet was actually a waste of resources. Going on board the flagship on 3 August, he got into a discussion with some of Nelson's officers. When they regretted that two ships of the line had escaped, Saumarez began to suggest that it might have been better if all had anchored on the same side. Nelson was in no mood to listen to criticism and interrupted, 'Thank God there was no order!' but perhaps Saumarez had a point. He believed that 'it never required two ships to capture one French', and that each British ship should have taken on one of the enemy, with perhaps two to each French three-decker, both on the same side. This would have avoided the 'friendly fire' which was inevitable when the line was doubled.

Perhaps, in the abstract, Saumarez was right but it is difficult to see how his plan might have been implemented. Foley's attack from the inside was a master-stroke, taking the French by surprise and shattering their defences. To have missed such an opportunity by going outside would have been a great waste. However much influence Nelson had on that part of the attack, it was the admiral himself who later decided on the doubling, by taking the *Vanguard* down the outside of the line. Since the waters inshore of the French line were already crowded with ships, it is doubtful if many more could have passed round and headed down the French line without risking grounding. In the circumstances there was probably no other option to attacking on the outside, though perhaps Nelson could have led an attack further down the line, so that each ship had only one opponent.

With hindsight, it is clear that St Vincent's original, small detachment had not been a success. Its only results had been the dismasting of the *Vanguard* and loss of contact with the frigates. It was the stronger fleet, sent under direct orders from the Admiralty, which had done the trick.

There was a little time for celebration. On the 2nd, before the last ships had surrendered, Nelson wrote to his captains that he intended to hold a public thanksgiving at 2pm and recommended other ships to do the same. Nelson also wrote congratulating the 'captains, officers, seamen, marines of the squadron he has the honour to command on the event of the late action . . . It must strike forcibly every British seaman how superior their conduct is when in discipline and good order, to

◄ A print published in England in 1798, showing the damage to the various ships, with *L'Orient* on fire. (National Maritime Museum, London: PAG8982)

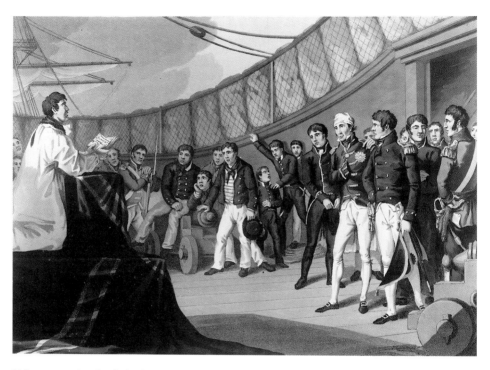

Nelson at a service after the battle with some of his officers and crew, with the Chaplain giving
thanks for the victory. The overcrowding aboard a ship of the line is greatly underestimated.
(National Maritime Museum, London: A769)

the riotous behaviour of lawless Frenchmen.'[5] In return, most of the captains met
on board the *Orion* on the 3rd and agreed to set up a fund to buy a sword for the
admiral, to commission a portrait of him and to set up an Egyptian Club where it
would hang.[6] In the *Theseus* the men were given 36 gallons extra allowance of wine
as a reward.[7] Perhaps the most bizarre commemoration of the action was provided
by Hallowell of the *Swiftsure*, who rescued the mainmast of the wrecked *L'Orient*;
he had it made into a coffin and presented it to Nelson. The crew of the *Vanguard*
were horrified but Nelson welcomed it with his usual morbidity.

★

As the Duke of Wellington was to say some years later, 'Next to a battle lost, the
greatest misery is a battle gained.' The British were in no position to feel the joys of
victory. John Nicol went on deck after hours in the magazine of the *Goliath* and
looked round the scene. 'An awful sight it was. The whole bay was covered with
dead bodies, mangled, wounded and scorched, not a bit of clothes on them except
their trousers.'[8]

   In every ship, whether victorious or defeated, there was grieving for the dead.
The crew was mustered on each ship and the survivors were counted. On the
Majestic Lieutenant Cuthbert found '50 of them killed and 143 had been

wounded'.[9] In the *Bellerophon* after her encounter with *L'Orient*, the figures were just as bad. 'Found we had three lieutenants, one master's mate, 32 seamen, 13 marines killed, the Captain, Master, Captain of Marines, one midshipman, 126 seamen and 17 marines wounded – in all 49 killed, 147 wounded.' But there was no time to grieve and the log went on 'got up a fore topmast for a jury mainmast and part of the main yard for a foremast.'[10] Naturally the casualties were unevenly spread through the ships and none had suffered as badly as the *Majestic* and *Bellerophon*. The *Vanguard* was the next worst, almost entirely because of the gunfire of the *Spartiate*. Of the officers, William Faddy, the captain of marines, had been killed and Nelson later tried to get a commission in the marines for his son, serving as a midshipman on the *Vanguard*, though the lad was only 14.[11] Two lieutenants, Vassal and Adye, had been wounded, along with Campbell, the admiral's secretary, and Auster the Boatswain who had lost an arm. In addition to the officers, 27 seamen and marines had been killed and 68 wounded, making a total casualty list of 105.

The *Minotaur* had also suffered badly, with 23 killed and 64 wounded in her fight with the *Aquilon*, while the *Alexander*, which had fought longer than most of the British ships, had lost 14 killed and 58 wounded. The *Goliath* had suffered 62 casualties but all the others had less than 50. Some ships had got off very lightly, either because they had mainly engaged soft targets (*Audacious*, 14 seamen wounded) or had taken advantage of the defects of French gunnery (*Zealous*, 1 seamen killed, 7 wounded). By the afternoon of 2 August, as the battle finally ended with the capture of the *Tonnant* and the burning of the *Timoléon*, Nelson had collected returns from all his ships and put the total figure at 16 officers, 156 seamen and 46 marines killed, 37 officers (including three captains), 562 seamen and 78 marines wounded – a total of 895, or about 10 per cent of those engaged.

Men continued to die from their wounds for weeks after the battle. On 5 August in the *Majestic*, 'Departed this life in consequence of their wounds, John Sutherland (Mid) Robert Smith, John Gonnion (seamen). Committed their bodies to the deep.'[12] In the heat of battle bodies were sometimes dropped over the side, like the powder boy in the *Goliath* mentioned by John Nicol. Only the *Bellerophon*, dismasted and out of the action, seems to have found time for any kind of ceremony during the battle itself.[13] But when time permitted, each dead man was sewn up in his own hammock, with the final stitch through his nose – seamen believed that this was to make sure that he was really dead. The ceremony is described by a chaplain of 1812;

> The body was brought up at 10 o'clock in the morning, to the starboard gangway, sewed in a hammock with a couple of 32 pound shots at the feet, extended on a grating and covered with a ship's ensign. The crew and officers, bare-headed, surrounded it and I read the funeral service. When I pronounced the words 'we commit his body to the deep' a seaman standing by took off the colours and, turning the grating, launched poor Tom into the bosom of the German Ocean, into which he sunk sullenly and for ever.[14]

The small island of Aboukir was captured a few days after the battle and used to bury some of the men who died later from their wounds. It also served as a recreation ground, according to Cooper Willyams. 'The island Aboukir . . . now served as a place of relaxation and exercise, and our seamen were allowed to go there without danger of hurting their constitutions in ale houses.'[15]

A burial on Aboukir Island, from Cooper Willyams' *Voyage*. (National Maritime Museum, London: D8806B)

In the *Orion* Sir James Saumarez was recovering from his wounds but to his great grief Midshipman Charles Miell finally died on the 7th, having expired in a fit of coughing after surviving an operation to remove his arm and shoulder.[16] In the crippled *Bellerophon* burial ceremonies took place almost daily for more than a week after the battle, as more men succumbed.[17]

Since the women were not officially there, no record was kept of any casualties they might have suffered. John Nicol records that several were wounded in the *Goliath* and one, from Leith, died of her wounds. She was buried on Aboukir Island.[18] Captain Foley took the unusual step of rewarding four of the women on board. Ann Taylor, Elizabeth Moore, Sarah Bates and Mary French were all widows of seamen or marines killed in the battle, or who died in the month following it. Foley had their names inserted in the ship's muster book and allowed them to receive victuals at two-thirds of the men's allowance, 'in consideration of their assistance in dressing and tending the wounded, being widows of men slain in fight with the enemy on the first day of August 1798.'[19]

The battle was good news for some, for there was no quicker way to promotion in the navy. Robert Cuthbert, the first lieutenant of the *Majestic*, was ordered to take the place of the late Captain Westcott, who was buried at sea with a 20-gun salute on the afternoon of the 2nd. Cuthbert had done well in getting the ship out of a difficult position in the battle and Hood remarked rather callously that the loss of Captain Westcott was 'not felt'. Her first lieutenant had 'fought the *Majestic* most gallantly during the remainder of the action as she had commenced.'[20] The following morning Cuthbert assembled the ship's company and read his orders from Nelson to command the *Majestic* until further notice.[21] Hardy, a mere commander, was given a captain's post in command of the *Vanguard* after Berry was sent home with the dispatches, becoming Nelson's flag-captain for the first time, but not the last. Thomas Bladen Capel, not the most senior lieutenant in the *Vanguard* but perhaps the best connected, took Hardy's place in the *Mutine*. Nelson had no authority to promote these officers but no-one doubted that his wishes would eventually by confirmed by a grateful Admiralty, after such a crushing victory.

★

To Poussielgue, 12 miles away at Rosetta on the morning after the battle, the damage to the rigging looked the most serious and those at the scene might have agreed with this. All the British ships except the *Culloden* were damaged in their masts and rigging. Of course the *Majestic* and *Bellerophon* were much the worst, being completely dismasted. The *Alexander* had lost her topmasts. The *Vanguard*, despite her heavy casualties, had suffered remarkably little above the decks and all her masts were still standing, although damaged. Because her fight with the *Spartiate* had been fought at close range in true Nelsonian fashion, few of the enemy's shot had been able to reach her rigging.

In the *Vanguard* the men began to repair the damaged rigging on 3 August. The flagship was of course in a particularly difficult position, since having already repaired herself after the storm in May, she had very little left in the way of spare rigging and stores. However, the men set to work, adopting the old principles of replacing damaged masts and sails with smaller ones, of patching up everything that could be saved and of transferring spares from other, less damaged ships. Thus the mizzen topmast was used as a main topmast, the main topgallant was made into a fore topmast and a fore topsail was used as a foresail. The mainmast was still standing but damaged. It was 'fished' by lashing and nailing stout pieces of wood to its sides over the damaged part. The mizzen mast needed similar treatment, while studding sail booms, which would only be used in very light winds, were lashed to the sides of the foremast to make it stronger. A jury mizzen topmast was made by the carpenters, while the *Culloden*, which of course had suffered in her hull rather than her rigging, sent a new mainsail. Spares parts for the rigging and guns were taken out of the captured *Guerrier* and adapted to British use. The work had roughly the same combination of skill and back-breaking labour as in May but it was done with a reduced and exhausted crew. The rigging itself was reasonably complete by the 14th but the carpenters toiled for another 5 days, repairing boats and gun carriages.[22]

The fact that a mast was still standing was no guarantee that it was usable. In the *Goliath*, Elliot reported 'we were in a most crippled state, our main mast had 24 large shot through it, besides quantities of grape shot, all above the quarterdeck – the mizzen mast was even more damaged, being cut more than half way through in one place; we had, however, a good carpenter and plenty of spars and other timber and iron from the French wrecks . . . We made such a good job of our masts and yards (which indeed we had nearly re-made) that they lasted for above 18 months, when we reached England.'[23]

The *Bellerophon* was aided by the *Audacious*, which had come alongside her on the morning of the 2nd after the *Zealous* was sent in an abortive chase of

Villeneuve's retreating ships. Her main capstan had been shot to pieces and the fore capstan was fitted in its place. She used her own fore-topmast for a jury mainmast and part of her main yard for a foremast while the *Audacious* supplied a jib-boom for a mizzen. She used topsail yards for lower ones and fitted topgallant masts for topmasts. This was a very weak rig, for a fore-topmast was not much more than half the diameter of a mainmast and therefore had less than a third of the strength.[24] However, it was enough to allow the *Bellerophon* to sail back to the main fleet on the afternoon of the 5th and Captain Darby noted that 'the ship behaved well under her jury masts'. She anchored a mile from the flagship, using a cable supplied by the *Audacious*. The next morning work began on a new rig, with materials supplied from the less damaged ships. The *Culloden* sent her spare fore-topmast and various sails and ropes, the *Swiftsure* a topgallant mast. Remains of the old mizzen mast were lifted out of their partners in the decks and some of the quarterdeck guns were sent down into the hold to increase stability. By the evening of the 12th the men were clearing her for sea, to sail home with some of the other damaged ships.[25] The *Majestic* had a similarly improvised rig, though it was set up without help from any other ship.

The *Culloden* was of course in a very different position: her rigging was intact but her underwater hull was seriously damaged by the force of running aground. The first task was to get the ship afloat and in the afternoon of the 2nd the sail which had been 'thrummed' by the sailmakers was carefully manoeuvred over the bows, with men pulling on ropes attached to the corners. Once it was in position the ropes were hauled tight and it began to have some effect. The leak decreased from 4 to 2½ft per hour and then to 1½ft. Three days later the ship could be floated off and she sailed down under her staysails, without a rudder, to anchor half a mile from the *Vanguard*. But the leak was still active and another sail was thrummed and placed under the hull. The carpenters finished the jury rudder on the 6th and it was fitted the next day, making the ship mobile though highly vulnerable.[26]

The prize ships also needed much repair. There was no prospect of rerigging them but their hulls at least had to be put in order so that they could be towed to St Vincent's fleet more than 2000 miles away. The *Theseus* laid out a cable to the *Tonnant* and hauled the French ship a mile and three-quarters towards her. Lieutenant England, in charge of the prize crew, got the French carpenters to do most of the work for the first day but then sent most of the seamen of the *Theseus* over to clear away the wreckage of the *Tonnant*'s masts. He encouraged his men by issuing meat every day, instead of only 4 days a week, and gave them an extra half allowance of wine. He sent over spare spars and sailmakers to make canvas for them and two anchors from captured ships. 'By these means, seconded by the indefatigable exertions of the officers and men in both ships, I was enabled to say to the admiral we were both ready to sail as early as he pleased on the 10th and I had the pleasure to find *Tonnant* the first prize ready.'[27]

By the 3rd or 4th Nelson had a clear idea of which ships, both captors and prizes, would be easiest to repair and send to sea. The *Swiftsure* had been the last of the 74s to reach the battle and was one of the least damaged in the rigging. Though several shots had struck her hull, these were repaired by the carpenters on the 2nd and 3rd. Nelson needed at least one mobile ship and after the *Leander* sailed with dispatches on the 5th, the *Swiftsure* carried out the duties of a frigate. On the 10th a sail was sighted in the north-east and she set off in chase. Eventually she caught up with a French polacre, *La Fortune*, which Brueys had sent to patrol off Damietta at the end of June. The French ship threw eight of her eighteen guns overboard during the chase but soon surrendered. She was brought back to Aboukir where Hallowell reported that she would be fit for immediate service once she had been watered.[28]

One of the biggest problems in the aftermath of the battle was the shortage of ships' boats. In the *Theseus*, Miller was thankful that he had insisted on carvel-built boats when the ship was fitted out, because they were much easier to repair than clinker-built ones. Three had been stowed out of the way in action, it is not clear where; two more were destroyed and the launch was damaged. 'I turned all the carpenters to patch her up for present use, merely while the people were dining.'[29] Elliot in the *Goliath* had to get his ship's jolly-boat repaired up before he could go over to the wreck of the *Sérieuse*.[30]

Victorious or not, the ships of Nelson's fleet could not regard themselves as free of danger. Though Bedouin tribesmen came out to cheer the British victory and lit bonfires in its honour, a great enemy army still held the land. The ships were mostly immobile with damaged rigging, wounded men, exhausted crews and prizes to guard and repair. There were plenty of native craft along the coast, not to mention the boats of the men, often first-class seamen, who had been on shore before the battle, or escaped during it. A determined counter-attack, launched in the dead of night while Nelson's crews were still weary from the battle, might have diminished or reversed the victory. Yet the resources to guard against this were not easily available and it was the night of 7 August, 4 days after the last shots of the battle, before boats were sent out every night to row guard round the fleet.[31]

★

It is estimated that 3305 prisoners were held on board the prizes, 1000 of them wounded.[32] They were not wanted, not least because it was necessary to guard them. When the *Theseus* took responsibility for the *Tonnant*, Captain Oldfield of the marines volunteered to take charge of the ship with his whole company and only Lieutenant England to represent the navy. He was given orders 'to secure the magazines, store rooms etc immediately, and having examined below to see every person and every light from them, and to have sentinels to prevent any one going on any pretence below the lower deck, and to render it unnecessary I would send provisions and water daily from the *Theseus*; I was thus cautious from knowing some of the other ships had been on shore [*ie* aground] since their capture.'[33] The *Tonnant* contained some of the most recalcitrant of the prisoners.

John Nicol noticed the French prisoners were very different from those he had seen in a previous war. 'In the American War when we took a ship, the *Duc de Chartres*, the prisoners were as merry as if they had taken us, only saying "*Fortune de guerre*" – you may take me today, I take you tomorrow. Those we now had on board were thankful for our kindness, but were sullen, and as downcast as if each had lost a ship of his own.'[34]

Until the French Revolutionary War it had been quite normal for prisoners to be exchanged as soon as possible after an action, for neither side wanted to take on the expense of feeding and guarding them. If there was an imbalance in the numbers, then some gave their parole that they would not serve until a prisoner of equal status had been sent back by the other side. If there was a long-term imbalance, as when large numbers of Frenchmen were captured in the Seven Years War, the system might break down. Nevertheless officers, even if they had to be retained as prisoners, were trusted with a different kind of parole. They were allowed to live in civilian lodgings without guards, provided they gave their word not to escape.

Much of this broke down after 1793, because the mistrust between the two sides was simply too great. A French official wrote in 1796, 'the mode in which the present war is carried on, has for a long time prevented the most necessary communication, such as had not ceased to exist between hostile nations at any preceding period. The persons whose lot it has been to suffer most from this interruption, are the prisoners of war on either side.'[35]

Nelson had no love for the French, especially the Revolutionaries, but he had little choice. It was simply impossible for his battered ships and exhausted crews to feed and guard 3000 men and tend 1000 wounded. When Saumarez suggested taking some of the Maltese volunteers into the navy, Nelson replied, 'I am not very anxious to receive any persons of the description you mention; they will all eat our meat and drink.'[36]

On the 3rd Nelson issued his first orders about prisoners. Ball was to negotiate their release and none were to leave the prize ships without his orders. The sick and wounded of all ranks were to be sent ashore first, followed by the common seamen and soldiers. No unwounded officers were to be released for the moment. No ship's carpenters were to be released, for they could be made to repair the prizes. Maltese and Italian seamen, who had no loyalty to the French state, would be invited to help in fitting out the prizes.[37] On the morning of the 4th, French boats came from the shore bearing flags of truce, offering to take the wounded ashore.[38]

Troubridge took charge of the negotiations and his abrasive style contrasted with Ball's liberalism. When Barre, the French negotiator, asked that non-combatants such as surgeons and pursers should be sent ashore immediately, Troubridge replied that this had been the case in past wars, until the French Revolution had distorted the laws of war. Troubridge's own purser and surgeon had been 'detained prisoners of war upwards of two years after being captured in the Castor'. Unwounded officers could not be landed on parole because 'Many officers now prisoners have been now serving without being regularly exchanged. Of course this parole cannot be taken again.' The French asked for the muster books of captured ships so that they could calculate who had been killed and eventually inform their families. Troubridge was inflexible and refused, for the books were needed as evidence in London, where the officers and men of the victorious fleet would claim 'head money' for each man in the enemy force. If duplicate books were found the French could have the second

The Harbour of Malta, with the New City of La Valette.

Two Mediterranean views from Serres' *Little Sea Torch*. The top scene is of ships off Palermo in 1801; the walled town is to the left of Monte Pellegrino. The bottom illustration shows the harbour at Malta.
(National Maritime Museum, London: D8805)

The British landing in Egypt in March 1801. Artist unknown. (National Maritime Museum, London: PAG9695)

one. He did agree that the wounded should continue to be sent on shore but even that was causing suspicion, According to Troubridge, French boats had carried a flag of truce on the pretext of ferrying wounded but in fact were supplying provisions to the scattered French garrisons.[39]

But Troubridge's hand was not very strong, because there was really no way of keeping the prisoners. The great majority of the officers were soon paroled, taking an oath;

> This [we] day give our word of honour separately as we sign in the most solemn manner that we will not serve either civilly or in arms against Great Britain or any of her allies until duly exchanged and liberated from our word of honour.[40]

The officers of the *Tonnant*, which had fought the longest fight of all the French ships and who had refused to surrender until the very last, would not sign their paroles.[41] They were sent away in Saumarez's ships when he sailed with the prizes and two of them, including the second captain, were held in the *Orion* where they lived in the wardroom and were invited to the captain's table.[42] Another went on board the *Theseus*. He spoke good English and her officers were able to compare notes with him about the events of the battle.[43]

★

Across the crowded bay there was much intercourse between the prize ships and their captors. On the 3rd, Midshipman Elliot went out with the *Goliath*'s patched-up jolly-boat to the sunken *Sérieuse*. He dived underwater, hoping to find gunners' stores and came up in an air pocket below decks. 'The first thing I met was a dead marine, swelled up and floating like a cork; he was by no means a pleasant companion where fresh air was scarce.'[44] Thomas Davies, an ordinary seaman from the *Goliath*, was part of a group sent to salvage goods from the *Sérieuse*. He found an enemy musket and amused himself in the boat back by cocking it and pulling the trigger. Back on the lower deck of his ship he continued the game and pointed it at his shipmate Jackson, assuming that days underwater must have made it inoperable. He pulled the trigger, there was a flash and Jackson was killed.[45] For many seamen, supplies of French wine and brandy on board the prizes were too much of a temptation. On 9 August Hood flogged seven of his seamen for drunkenness aboard a prize.[46] On the 10th, a seaman and marine were flogged on board the *Majestic* 'for breaking into the *Spartiate*'s spirit room'.[47] Some of the seamen of the *Theseus* suffered in a different way. On the 4th James Kettle, a 33-year-old quartermaster, reported sick with 'headache, nausea, cold chills with alternate heat. White tongue, much thirst with a painful back'. Surgeon Tainsh decided that this was caused by 'fatigue assisted by drinking a bad wine on board one of the prizes'. Eight more men would come down with the same complaint in the next few days. All would be cured by the middle of the month but parallel cases began to appear. Thomas Hanger, aged 29, was 'very irregular, much given to drunkenness, affected with the fatigue in action and fitting out our prizes', while many more of the crew were stricken with diarrhoea and nausea.[48]

It was fortunate that Nelson's ships had taken on supplies at Syracuse only 8 days before the battle, for the coast of Egypt could afford them nothing: even with an army on shore, Brueys had found it difficult to supply his ships. Not all ships were equally provided for, especially in those items which had suffered damage in battle. In the *Zealous*, the log noted that a cask containing 144 gallons of wine, brought on deck to serve the men before the battle, was lost in action when it 'received a shot by which it was stove and the contents lost'.[49] On the 8th, Nelson ordered each ship to send a boat to the *Culloden* to receive fresh fowls, in proportion to the sick aboard the ships. She had purchased them from a Turkish boat on the 4th, along with onions and eggs.[50]

★

On the 12th Nelson issued orders to Saumarez in the *Orion*;

> You are hereby required and directed to take the ships named in the margin [*Bellerophon, Minotaur, Defence, Audacious, Theseus, Majestic, Peuple Souverain, Spartiate, Aquilon, Franklin, Tonnant*] under your command, their captains having my orders for that purpose, and proceed with all possible dispatch down the Mediterranean. On your arrival near Europa Point [Gibraltar] you will send a boat on shore to the Commissioner's Office, to receive any orders which may be lodged there for your further proceedings. In case you find no orders at Gibraltar and learn that the Commander in Chief is off Cadiz or Lisbon, you will join him at either place with all possible expedition.[51]

He had chosen five relatively intact ships to go with the severely damaged *Bellerophon* and *Majestic*, for there were at least two serviceable French ships of the line loose in the Mediterranean, along with eight or nine former Venetian ships under French control. He kept the *Zealous*, *Goliath*, *Alexander* and *Swiftsure* with three frigates to maintain a presence off Alexandria and to help repair the crippled *Culloden*. In addition, Saumarez's ships were to take charge of some of the French prizes, sending men on board them as prize crews and towing them where necessary. In the *Orion*, Saumarez had the *Peuple Souverain* 'to drag after me'.[52] He sent his first lieutenant, Mr Barker, on board the prize where he was 'happier than a prince'.[53] The *Majestic* and *Bellerophon* took the *Spartiate* between them. The *Bellerophon* sent supplies over to feed the prize crew but it was the slightly less damaged *Majestic* which provided the prize crew of a lieutenant, two petty officers, forty seamen and ten marines and which took the dismasted ship in tow, hauling her close under her captor's stern on the afternoon of the 15th.[54] The *Minotaur* took the *Aquilon*, the *Defence* the *Franklin*, the *Audacious* the *Conquérant* and the *Theseus* the *Tonnant*. Each of the captured ships had a prize crew of 112 to 134 men, commanded by a lieutenant with 1 to 3 mates or midshipmen and usually including 10 or 12 marines under a sergeant or corporal.[55]

Saumarez's ships raised their anchors after breakfast on the 14th but there was not enough wind for the ships with their reduced rigs to make way while towing prizes, so they re-anchored at noon, 5 miles from the fleet. According to Saumarez, this 'gave the ships an opportunity to get completed for sea and afforded a night's repose for the men.' At 11pm the captain was wakened from a sound sleep with

A British 74-gun ship under jury rig, typical of the damage sustained by ships at the Nile, by the French artist Baugean. (Musée de la Marine, Paris)

news from Nelson, that a brig had arrived carrying mail for the ships. 'I soon had them sorted,' he wrote to his wife, 'and out of about twenty for myself I selected four from you which were read with an avidity you will better conceive than I can describe . . . Never were letters more welcome – never did any yield greater joy and comfort.'[56]

The ships weighed anchor again at noon next day and despite a contrary wind they were able to clear the land, though it was the following day before they lost sight of Nelson's ships still at anchor. Saumarez felt the effects of his wound again. 'Too great exertion for two or three days after being under sail certainly retarded my perfect recovery and, added to the excessive heat of the weather, threw me into a sort of languor that required three days rest and composure to shake off.'[57] Progress was slow. 'Sheep and poultry in abundance; but the fear of a long passage down the Mediterranean obliges to be frugal, wishing if possible to avoid putting into any place before we reach the fleet at Cadiz – a thing scarcely possible and rendered still more improbable from our little progress in the last five days: however, *Patience!*'[58]

Saumarez followed much of the route which the fleet had taken a month earlier, when they had sailed back from Alexandria in bitter disappointment. They encountered the same unfavourable westerly winds until the 22nd, off Crete, when a fair wind sprang up from the south. But Saumarez was not to be placated and complained that it produced 'such a close, sultry and damp air that it is scarcely bearable'.[59] Two days later a fleet was sighted astern but it was not too difficult to make out Nelson and two more ships of his squadron, with their jury masts and damaged hulls. Saumarez went on board the flagship to exchange whatever news there was with the admiral.[60]

★

Back in Aboukir Bay, the grounded *Culloden* had been one of Nelson's main concerns. Perhaps it would have been simpler to take everything out of the damaged ship and burn her, as was done with many of the prizes. But that would be a slight to Troubridge, one of Nelson's favourite officers, whose reputation was already vulnerable because he had failed to enter the action. Furthermore it would then be counted as a loss in battle, slightly tarnishing the glorious victory. Meanwhile the missing frigates were beginning to turn up – the *Alcmene*, *Emerald* and *Bonne Citoyenne* on the 16th, the *Seahorse* on the 17th and the *Thalia* on the 24th. Each had its own story to tell.

Originally Nelson had hoped to repair the grounded *Mercure* and *Heureux* and the battle-damaged *Guerrier*. However, when Saumarez sailed on the 14th he was already convinced that Nelson would destroy them after taking out any serviceable stores.[61] The next day Nelson described the three ships as being 'in the act of repairing' but he was aware of the scale of the task. It would take at least a month, and the service of the crews of at least two ships of the line, to get the ships ready to sail to Gibraltar. After that they would need a great deal of repair in the home dockyards. But to destroy them would be to give a certain amount of satisfaction to the French and, more important, it would deny his men the prize money from their capture. Reluctantly Nelson decided that he had to destroy them and he wrote to the Secretary of the Admiralty expressing the hope that the government would 'direct that a fair value shall be paid for these ships', making a 'liberal allowance' of compensation for the loss of prize money.[62]

At 7.30pm on 16 August his men set fire to the *Heureux* where she had gone aground more than 2 weeks earlier to avoid the explosion of *L'Orient*; the *Heureux* herself blew up an hour later and her companion the *Mercure* was destroyed the following day. On the 18th it was the turn of the *Guerrier*, which had borne the brunt of the first attack on 1 August; an hour later the sunken, dismasted frigate *Sérieuse*, which had taken on the might of Saumarez's *Orion*, was finally disposed of. Lieutenant Cathcart of the *Alcmene* wrote 'I never saw so awful and magnificent a spectacle in my life. You could count her ports through the flames and her masts seemed to be illuminated.'[63] At 8 o'clock the next morning the *Vanguard* weighed anchor with Ball's *Alexander*, Troubridge's crippled *Culloden* and the sloop *Bonne Citoyenne*.[64] Nelson left Samuel Hood in charge of the blockade of Alexandria, with the *Swiftsure*, *Goliath* and the frigates *Alcmene*, *Seahorse* and *Emerald*. Over the next few months Hood would form links with Turkish officials in Acre and succeeded in raiding enemy and neutral transports, destroying more than thirty, before he was replaced in February 1799.[65]

Nelson's progress was slow. At noon on the 20th the log shows the *Vanguard* 239 miles from the south-east point of Crete. Five days later she was 211 miles from the same point, having progressed only 28 miles. The winds were light and variable, the *Vanguard* had a reduced rig and the *Culloden* could only make slow progress at the best of times. Nelson and Saumarez, having met on 24 August, parted on the 26th, though they remained in sight of one another for several days and were in sight again at the end of the month when letters were exchanged by frigate. Saumarez's journey was as slow as he had feared but he began to put his cabin in good repair for his long-delayed reunion with his wife. On 16 September he was obliged to put into Augusta in Sicily, having failed to reach Syracuse. Becalmed on the way past Malta, he sent arms to the Maltese and invited the French garrison to surrender. At last, on 18 October he completed a two-month passage to Gibraltar, where a ball was given in honour of the victory. On 25 November he reached Spithead but was kept in quarantine and it was January 1799 before he paid off the *Orion* and made his way to Bath to meet his wife.[66]

★

Nelson's squadron passed through the Straits of Messina. At 7am on 15 September, within sight of Stromboli, the ships were struck by another storm. The *Vanguard* lost her foremast, part of the main topmast and the jib-boom. Four seamen who were up the foremast were also lost and several more injured. The frigate *Thalia* took her in tow while the ship's third jury rig of the campaign was set up.[67] Nelson called her the 'poor wretched *Vanguard*' when she arrived at Naples on 22 September.[68]

Even before that, Nelson had some indication of the reception he was likely to get, for he had a latter from Lady Hamilton which told him 'The Kingdom of the Two Sicilies is mad with joy; from the throne to the peasant, all are alike.'[69] Even that did not give the full extent of the euphoria, or the events which were to follow it. A new phase of Nelson's life was about to begin.

CHAPTER 15

'We are the most unfortunate in the world'

THROUGHOUT A SUMMER of searching the Mediterranean, the greatest single weakness of Nelson's force was its lack of frigates. St Vincent could not be blamed for that; he believed that Nelson was equipped with three or four and it was several weeks before he knew about the separation during the storm. After that he continued to send out ships to look for Nelson as far as his own resources allowed.

During the great storm which began on the night of 20 May, the *Bonne Citoyenne* took down her topgallant yards and cast off her prize, a French merchant brig captured that afternoon. Early next morning she struck down her topgallant masts, which must have been a considerable task in the storm.[1] Meanwhile the *Terpsichore* lost three of her foremast shrouds, putting the mast in danger. An anchor hawser was set up to support the lower mast, while the topmasts were got down. The force of the waves had also knocked some of the copper off her bottom. She was alone for 2 days but found the *Bonne Citoyenne* again in the afternoon of the 22nd.[2]

The *Emerald* had been driven south by the gale. At daylight on the 21st she 'saw the *Vanguard* with her fore mast, main and mizzen topmasts gone' – information that, by chance, was to prove vital in the campaign. At 6am on the morning of the 22nd she wore ship and headed back to the north-east, setting the reefed main topsail at 8am, followed by the foresail at 10.30am as the winds moderated. In the afternoon, having set yet more sail, she wore again and headed west, to begin a small, single-handed campaign against enemy shipping. On the 26th she had an unsuccessful chase and on the 29th she boarded a Ragusan brig, then captured a Spanish settee (a two-masted, lateen rigged vessel) from Mahon bound for Malaga with a cargo of sardines. She took some stores out and then scuttled her. In the afternoon of the 31st she sighted and identified another British frigate and Captain Waller went on board to make contact.[3]

★

On 12 May St Vincent had issued orders to the *Alcmene*, under Captain George Hope, to join Nelson. On the 23rd, 3 days after the storm, he reached the rendezvous off Toulon to find no sign of the squadron. He had been told to cruise along the latitude 41 degrees 20 minutes north and did so for 6 days until the 29th, when he sighted three strange sail to the south-east. These turned out to be the *Terpsichore, Bonne*

Citoyenne and a French prize. They brought news of the storm off Toulon. Two days later they fell in with the *Emerald*. She was the only ship that had seen the full extent of the flagship's damage and Captain Waller told the sorry tale to Hope.

Hope was the senior officer and took command of the force. He had to choose between two contradictory tasks – to find Nelson and his fleet, or to search for the enemy on his own. Nelson had given instructions, in an envelope marked 'Rendezvous – most private'. It was sealed and round the edge was written 'not to be opened but in the case of separation'. If that happened, the frigates were to cruise on the same line that had been given to Captain Hope – 'In the direct tract [sic] between Cape St Sebastians and Toulon in latitude 42 degrees 20 minutes north, from 20 to 30 leagues from the Cape and not having heard from me within ten days, to return to Gibraltar.'[4] The language is somewhat obscure but it means that the ships were to cruise back and forward along the line of latitude specified, turning when due south of Toulon or 60 or 90 miles east of Cape San Sebastian on the east coast of Spain, north of Barcelona.

This he did, making several passes over the whole range but on 31 May he began to make other plans. Knowing of the damage to the flagship from the

The position at noon on 1 June.

Emerald's report, it seemed likely that she would have gone to either Gibraltar or Naples for repairs. He sent the *Emerald* and *Bonne Citoyenne* to the Spanish island of Minorca where they landed the prisoners from the French prize. After that they had orders to cruise between Sardinia and the North African coast, looking for any information on Nelson's movements. Meanwhile the other two ships, the *Alcmene* and *Terpsichore*, would head east towards Cape San Sebastian, still on the rendezvous line but beyond its western limit, also seeking any information on Nelson. Reaching the Spanish coast, Hope had another diversion when he sent some boats inshore to take possession of two enemy vessels.[5]

At this point there were five different British forces in the area, all in pursuit of the same aim and, indeed, looking for one another. At noon on 1 June Nelson's three ships of the line were 90 miles south of Toulon, heading north. Troubridge, with ten more ships of the line, was just south of Minorca, 190 miles away, also heading north towards the same spot. The *Mutine* was off the Spanish coast heading north-east towards the rendezvous, while the *Alcmene* and *Terpsichore* were preparing to head down that coast in the opposite direction. The *Emerald* and *Bonne Citoyenne* were steering south towards Minorca, in the opposite direction to Troubridge's force and with a track that would take the two groups within 50 miles of each other. It was the events of the next few days that would determine the exact composition of Nelson's force, which ships would join him for the Battle of the Nile and which would not.

Nelson was within striking distance of Toulon by 1 June and was on station by the 3rd. But by that time Hope had abandoned the fruitless patrol off the port and was heading towards the Spanish coast. When he was 13 miles off Barcelona on 2 June, he sighted the British brig *Mutine*, also seeking Nelson with orders to tell him of the approach of the squadron under Troubridge. Hardy went on board the *Alcmene* and the captains conferred for 2 hours but no record survives of their discussion. The obvious thing to do was to follow the *Mutine* and join Troubridge's force. Even if Nelson was not found, the frigates would be attached to the strongest British force the Mediterranean and would be of invaluable assistance for scouting. However, Hope had apparently decided to find Nelson his own way. Having done his duty on the rendezvous line, he evidently wanted to re-establish contact with his other frigates, the *Emerald* and *Bonne Citoyenne*, to make the force even stronger. This decision was to prove unfortunate.

★

On 5 June the *Terpsichore* parted company, for Hope had ordered her to search some of the seven rendezvous that Nelson had appointed for the fleet, all in the eastern Mediterranean. She stayed off Minorca for 9 days landing her prisoners and headed for Cape Sicie off Toulon, then Leghorn Roads, where she waited at anchor until the 23rd. She went on to Naples, taking under her wing a Neapolitan polacre that had asked for an escort. Outside the harbour she met her three former companions, the *Alcmene*, *Emerald* and *Bonne Citoyenne*. On receiving news of the French being at Malta, the *Terpsichore* did not wait for long at Naples but headed south through the Straits of Messina, where Nelson had passed a few days earlier. She overtook a large convoy of Neapolitan merchant ships under the escort of a frigate, then spoke with the British consul, James Tough, at Messina. Over the next few days she stopped several ships, including a Tuscan brig headed from Alexandria to Venice. This ship must have left some time before the French landed, as no news was gained. With no means of knowing that Nelson had gone to the east, she headed for Malta, where she captured a tiny French ship, the *Assaillante*, with one mast, four guns and sixty men. Captain Gage was less obsessed with prize money than some. He threw the prize's guns overboard, took items he was short of such as cordage and gave the ship back to the prisoners. The following day, 13 July, he met the frigate *Seahorse*, under Captain Foote, with vital information.[6]

★

On 2 June St Vincent issued orders to Captain Edward Foote of the 38-gun *Seahorse*, to find Nelson and deliver stores for his squadron. Foote was 31 years old and a captain of 4 years seniority. He was an experienced and humane seaman, as events would show; perhaps too humane in the circumstances. The *Seahorse* eventually sailed from Gibraltar on the evening of the 12th, beating off an attack by Spanish gunboats on the way out. On the 18th she boarded a Danish brig from Tripoli and was informed, accurately, that a French fleet of fourteen sail had been seen off Sicily on the 6th, with several frigates and a convoy of merchant ships with troops on board. The Dane could not find out their destination. On the 10th however, he had been boarded by the *Emerald* between Sardinia and Tunisia and Captain Waller had given him 'a very handsome certificate' to prove his neutrality. He had been boarded by another frigate near the Tunisian coast and the captain had told him that he too was looking for the British fleet.[7] The *Seahorse* continued her voyage to the east.

On 26 June, south of Sicily, she sighted the French 36-gun frigate *Sensible*, on the way from Malta carrying dispatches, General Baraguay D'Hilliers and his staff and some valuables looted from the island, including a silver model of a galley. Foote hoisted a Spanish flag but the French were not fooled. They felt it necessary to complete their mission rather than engage in combat, so the *Sensible* crowded on sail to try to escape. A running fight developed throughout the night of the 26th to 27th. At 4am, after 12 hours, the *Seahorse* caught up with the *Sensible*. The British ship had a considerable superiority in gun power. Although rated as a 38, she actually had forty-six guns, including a main deck of 18-pounders and fourteen 32-pounder carronades on the quarterdeck and forecastle. The *Sensible* had only thirty-six guns, the largest being 12-pounders. There was a short but intense action in which the French ship was damaged in her masts and rigging, received thirty-six shot 'between wind and water' and many more in other parts of the hull; her first and second captain were wounded and she had 25 men killed and 55 wounded, according to French sources, out of 300 crew and passengers on board.[8] The ex-galley slaves who made up part of her crew refused to stand by their guns and the ship surrendered after an action lasting only 8 minutes. The *Seahorse*, carrying a complement of 292, lost 2 men and had 16

A model of the frigate *Seahorse*, made from the mainmast of *L'Orient*. (National Maritime Museum, London: 7408)

wounded. The loss of the *Sensible* was the first real setback to Bonaparte's campaign, which hitherto had enjoyed very good luck.[9]

Captain Foote showed much concern for the welfare of his prisoners. On 2 July seaman John Stapples and three other men were flogged severely with forty lashes each, for stealing from them. Stapples was a thoroughly bad character, for the day before the battle he had been given sixteen lashes for 'taking a plank in the wing for his private use'. Captain Foote paid no attention to the Admiralty regulation which specified twelve as the maximum number of lashes a captain could award, nor did he follow the usual custom of using multiples of twelve.[10] Perhaps Foote's protection from ill-treatment created an easy-going relationship with the captives, for according to later reports Foote's officers overheard some of the prisoners discussing the plans to head for Egypt. Foote sent the prize into Messina and landed the prisoners at Cagliari in Sardinia.

He resumed his journey towards Malta and arrived there on the 12th, passing within 2½ miles of the harbour, where he came close enough to see a ship of the line and a frigate inside and to exchange shots with several ships which were passing close inshore. At 6 o'clock the following morning he sighted the *Terpsichore* and the two captains got together and decided to head for Alexandria. On 21 July they arrived off Egypt, 3 weeks after the French had landed. Eight ships of the line were spotted, wearing the French tricolour, along with numerous transports. Eighteen more warships were to be seen at the mouth of the Nile. To check that they were not Nelson's squadron, the *Seahorse* made the private identification signal captured in the *Sensible*, while the *Terpsichore* hoisted French colours over British to imitate a prize, but the French were evidently not fooled. This was the first clear sighting of the French fleet by any British squadron and was information of the greatest importance. To get it to Nelson, they sailed towards Cyprus and then along the south side of Crete. On the 29th, in yet another irony of the campaign, they were only 30 miles away from the Admiral, sailing in opposite directions, with Nelson on his way to Alexandria for the second time. Although Nelson was already aware of the French presence in Egypt, the *Seahorse* and *Terpsichore* would have been able to give him vital information about their exact position and would have gained great honour by being the first to report a definite sighting of the enemy fleet.

★

On 12 June the *Alcmene* found the *Bonne Citoyenne* and *Emerald* on their station, halfway between Sardinia and the North African coast. The three ships went to the western end of Sicily where Hope judged, correctly, that a friendly or enemy fleet was likely to pass. They waited there for a week. Such a force would have done enormous damage to Bonaparte's strung-out, ill-disciplined convoys of transports but unfortunately the Armament had passed that way 10 days before they arrived. The *Bonne Citoyenne* then went off to search the southern end of Sardinia, another of Nelson's rendezvous. She rejoined the other two on the 24th and the three ships made sail for Naples, arriving on 27 June. On the way in they found the *Terpsichore*.

Sir William Hamilton soon came alongside with Nelson's letter saying 'my want of frigates is extreme'. But the ships needed to replenish, especially with water. This was still not as easy as it might have been, though Hamilton's diplomacy was beginning to gain support in Naples. The Neapolitans could not openly support Britain yet, because a treaty with Austria, guaranteeing support against the French, had not yet been ratified. Until then the Neapolitan government could not 'throw off the mask', as Hamilton put it. The treaty was not signed until 16 July and it was not until the 31st that Hamilton was informed officially of it and of 'His Sicilian Majesty's ports now being open to the King's ships without any limitation'.[11] But in the meantime the ports of Naples and Sicily in fact provided invaluable help to the various British frigates in the Mediterranean in the matter of water and supplies and giving them a channel of communication with St Vincent and one another, though not, as it turned out, with Nelson.

The *Bonne Citoyenne* took on 273 gallons of brandy, 240 gallons of red wine, as well as beef, flour and water. Despite the delays, Hamilton had to acknowledge the crews' efforts and wrote to Nelson, 'I must do justice to Captain Hope and the rest of the captains, that not a moment was lost and that their desire to join you was certainly equal to your desire of seeing them.'[12] They set off at 3pm on 30 June, passing through the Straits of Messina and then heading for the south coast of Crete,

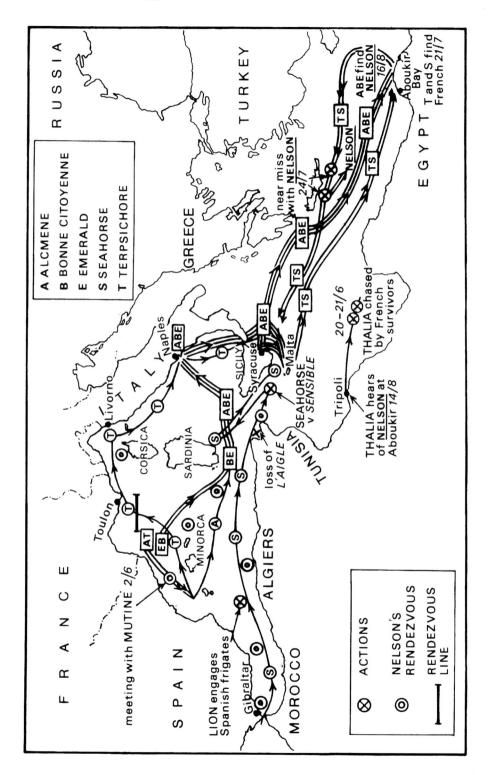

where they picked up information that Nelson's ships had been seen heading in the opposite direction some days ago. They headed for Malta but saw no signs of Nelson. They examined the Sicilian coast and on the last day of July, just as Nelson was heading towards his encounter with the French, they dropped anchor off Messina to seek more information. They soon found that Nelson had left Syracuse 4 days earlier.

On 2 August they headed east again. Knowing that from Syracuse Nelson had intended to look towards the south of Greece and then the islands, they sailed past Cape Matapan and were off Rhodes on 8 August. They evidently found some information there, for they set sail for Alexandria and like Nelson they made good progress, covering 282 miles in 2 days. They sighted the city from more than 30 miles away at 3.30pm on the 10th, with 'two strange fleets at anchor'[13] – presumably the visibility was clear and the lookouts had good eyesight or powerful telescopes. The wind dropped and it was eight in the afternoon of the 12th before they made contact with Hallowell's *Swiftsure*. At 10am on 16 August, 2 weeks after the conclusion of the Battle of the Nile, they anchored in 7 fathoms of water in Aboukir Bay. At last Nelson had found his missing frigates. Lieutenant William Cathcart of the *Alcmene* wrote, 'We are the most unfortunate in the world.'[14]

★

The *Seahorse* and *Terpsichore* arrived at Syracuse at sunset on 8 August, after a voyage in which they had found the French at Aboukir but failed to link up with Nelson. Foote ordered Gage in the *Terpsichore* to go to Naples and then resume the search, 'being guided by the information you may receive from Sir William Hamilton or the letters which may be left for you at Messina, or at this place.'[15]

The *Terpsichore* was delayed by a bizarre and tragic accident off Messina at 9pm on in the evening of 11 August. Some captured French and Spanish signal rockets were being tested when a marine accidentally fired his musket, igniting them on deck. Various powder horns were lying about and there was an explosion which destroyed the captain's cabin. The magazines were soon secured to prevent the fire spreading there but the marine died of burns and twenty-two men were 'dreadfully scorched'. The captain, first lieutenant, master and surgeon were wounded and the *Terpsichore* put into Messina for repairs.[16]

On 9 August, Foote issued orders to Bowen of the brig *Transfer*, whom he had met on arrival at Syracuse. Clearly he was running out of ideas.

> In answer to your letter of yesterday's date in which you mention not finding Sir Horatio Nelson at this anchorage you were to follow him, I have only to direct you that the instant you are acquainted with the Rear-Admiral's rendezvous or the route he has taken, by means of the letter hourly expected from Messina, or any other authoritative information you will proceed in quest of him without a moment's loss of time.

The letter from Messina was indeed received that day. It was from Nelson, written

◀ The voyages of the frigates.

on 22 July before the departure from Syracuse, addressed to 'the commanders of any of His Majesty's Ships' and concluding. 'Having received some vague information of the enemy, I shall steer north for Candia and probably send a ship to Milo and if the enemy are not in those seas I shall pass on for Cyprus, Syria and Egypt.'[17] Bowen was ordered to follow its directions but Foote, putting the information about Nelson heading east together with his own knowledge of French movements, added a postscript,

> I think you will most probably find Sir Horatio Nelson off Alexandria in Aboukir Bay, the western entrance of the Nile. I saw the whole of the French forces at these places on the 20th of last month.[18]

At 7am on the 10th, the *Seahorse* raised her anchor and sailed from Syracuse, heading back towards Alexandria. She arrived there a week later, to find the *Swiftsure* cruising off the port. Foote hailed Hallowell and asked 'What news of the French fleet?' On being told of Nelson's great victory the men climbed the shrouds in traditional fashion and gave three cheers, which were returned by the *Swiftsure*.[19]

★

Yet another frigate, the 36-gun *Thalia*, was ordered out on 13 June. This ship had problems of her own. Her popular captain, Lord Harry Powlett, had just been court-martialled for striking his lieutenant and was on his way home to launch an appeal to the King. Lieutenant John Newhouse was hurriedly promoted to commander and took acting command on 13 June. The ship was sent immediately to Gibraltar and then into the Mediterranean with dispatches from St Vincent to Nelson. Her orders were to seek Nelson off Toulon and then between there and Genoa, unless he could gain intelligence that he had gone elsewhere. Failing that, he was to go to Majorca, Leghorn or Naples, for St Vincent still had no inkling that he might have gone any further east.[20]

Off Toulon on the 25th, she found only three enemy frigates in the harbour. She headed for Corsica on a report of the French fleet being in San Fiorenzo Bay. She went to Leghorn to hear that the French had indeed sailed 16 days ago, with 15 ships of the line and 300 transports, for Malta. Nelson, according to the report, was 6 days behind them. On 8 July they heard from an Algerian privateer that the French had been seen off Sicily on the 7th and the British at Naples. The *Thalia* passed through the Straits of Messina on 13 July, more than 3 weeks behind Nelson. The next day she was off Malta and Newhouse 'determined on cruising off the island until an opportunity offered of procuring intelligence from neutral vessels.'[21] On the 15th a Greek merchantman informed them that the French had been in possession of the island for 15 days; they had already sailed, with Nelson 4 days behind them.

Receiving some 'dubious information' that Nelson was now going to Syracuse, they headed there, where seaman Richard Johnson was appalled rather than excited by the scenery. 'Made the grand bourning mountain caled Mount Eatna, see it bourning and throughing out fire and sulfer most hidiously to the beholder.'[22] Food was purchased but there was no intelligence of either the French or Nelson so the *Thalia* went on her way. On the 17th a Danish ship informed her that the British squadron had been seen off the Turkish coast and on the 20th she met the *Earl of St Vincent* cutter, who delivered more dispatches from Nelson and informed her of the *Seahorse* taking the French frigate off Malta. By the 24th she was off Crete, 'counted the plentifullest island in the Mediterranean, being the island that Jupiter was born upon.'[23]

She cruised in the eastern Mediterranean for almost 3 weeks, taking prizes, speaking to several ships and calling at Tripoli where the Grand Bashaw was honoured and the ship dressed overall; but 'he did not come on board on account of too much sea running for him'. However, he did visit the ship the following day, 13 August, with seventy-five guards and attendants, and was saluted with thirty-six guns. He presented the ship's company with 4 bullocks, 8 sheep, 4 bags of bread and 200 watermelons, along with 'all sorts of vegetables that the country would afford'. On the 14th they heard news of Nelson being at Alexandria. They set sail immediately and on the 20th sighted two French ships of the line and a frigate – the survivors of the Battle of the Nile making their escape. Four days later they encountered the *Seahorse*, which informed them of Nelson's victory. Meeting the *Zealous* off Alexandria, the *Thalia* was ordered to deliver some of her stores and water to the crippled *Goliath*. As with the other ships, her intelligence had generally been good and her captain's actions sensible; but she had always been a few steps behind the main fleet.[24]

★

On 20 June St Vincent decided to send the 64-gun ship of the line *Lion* to increase Nelson's fighting force. She was to complete her stores and provisions at Gibraltar and also to take on a spare fore and main topmast for the repair of the *Vanguard*, as well as a new surgeon, boatswain and several midshipmen and volunteers for the *Alexander*.[25] She sailed from Gibraltar for Naples on 1 July but chased several warships and merchant ships on the way. On the 3rd she stopped a Danish brig who informed her that a month ago she had seen a convoy of 6 warships and 200 transports on the north coast of Malta. On 15 July, sailing east with a good following wind, she sighted four Spanish frigates approaching from the south-east. Dixon ordered some of his sails taken in, so that he would not sail past the enemy and allow them to have the wind behind them – the 'weather gage' which gave the initiative to the ship possessing it and was vital in all naval battles.

The ship was cleared for action, which according to her captain was 'effected in the shortest time I ever recollect.' He told the officers and men of his intentions and noted 'the cheerfulness with which it was received.'[26] He set course towards them, hoping to cut off one, the *Santa Dorothea*, which he could see had lost her fore topmast. 'It immediately occurred to me that the crippled ship was my object, in order to secure a general action, supposing that a Spaniard (from the nobleness of his character) would never, with so superior a force, forsake a friend in need.'[27] He succeeded in this and the other three tacked and formed line of battle to attack him. But the Spanish kept their ships too far apart. As each attacked it was damaged by

The battle between the *Lion* and four Spanish frigates, showing the *Santa Dorothea* cut off and the other three ships engaging. An engraving after Thomas Whitcombe from Jenkins's *Naval Achievements*. (National Maritime Museum, London: PAD5602)

the superior broadside of the 64-gun *Lion*, which had time to reload before the next one came along. Dixon closed with the crippled *Santa Dorothea* while her comrades made a second and a third attack and were beaten off. The Spanish decided to abandon the attempt, leaving the *Santa Dorothea* to be captured.

The *Lion* had not escaped unscathed and suffered much in her sails and rigging. 'I found the *Lion* totally ungovernable, having all her braces, bowlines, clew-garnets shot away, the foresail nearly rendered useless and the other sails much torn.' However, the ship was easily repaired and only one man had been lost, after having his leg amputated.[28] The *Dorothea* was taken in tow and fifty seamen and ten marines sent over to navigate her and guard the prisoners.

She reached Naples on 28 July, by which time Nelson had almost reached Alexandria. There she met a Portuguese squadron sent to the assistance of Nelson and such a collection of allied ships in a neutral port inspired the French Charge d'Affaires to complain about this, as well as Nelson's ships being supplied in Syracuse.[29] The agreement opening Neapolitan ports to the British, however, was just coming into operation. The *Lion* left on 12 August, met the *Terpsichore* 3 days later, now repaired from her fire off Messina and the two ships sailed in company to the south-east. They found the Portuguese squadron again on the 23rd, with news of Nelson's victory. On 26 August, nearly a month after the battle, the *Lion* finally delivered the spare topmasts to the fleet in Aboukir Bay. By this time, with the massive damage to rigging in action, they were a drop in the ocean.

★

St Vincent continued to send ships out to Nelson, either with dispatches or to join his fleet. On 5 July he ordered the sloop *L'Aigle* to look for him. She was to deliver dispatches, take some officers and men belonging to Nelson's ships (including his stepson Captain Nisbet) and then return to Gibraltar. According to St Vincent's latest information, Nelson was 'in pursuit of the French Armada, which was spoke of with neutral vessels 8 or 10 leagues short of the Faro of Messina on the 8th of June.'[30] Off the coast of Tunis Captain Tyler of *L'Aigle* was overconfident in his knowledge of the area. He mistook Cape Farino for Cape Bon and at 9.30am on the 18th the ship ran aground, making several holes in her hull. It was impossible to save her. Tyler had her burnt and the crew were taken ashore by a passing Ragusan. brig. They made contact with the British consul who got 'every assistance' from the Bey, in the form of accommodation for the sick and two transports to return the men to Gibraltar.[31]

★

By 2 June, the British government had persuaded the Portuguese that they should send a small squadron of ships of the line to the aid of Nelson. The Portuguese were still at war with France, though negotiating for peace. There was a risk that a force of this sort would cause the French to take further aggressive action and indeed when the news reached Paris, Talleyrand asked the Spaniards (who were at war with Britain but not Portugal) to allow the French to send 60,000 men through their territory to invade Portugal. The Spaniards discouraged this request, suggesting that the Portuguese were doing nothing beyond the normal activities of a belligerent nation.[32]

The Portuguese navy was small, with a dozen ships of the line and about fifteen frigates.[33] A squadron of four 74-gun ships was selected, with a brig. Rear-Admiral the Marquis of Niza was in command with his flag in the *Principe Real*. On 2 July he went out to St Vincent's flagship off Cadiz, travelling incognito in a vessel called the *Alfonso Albuquerque* and the two admirals had a discussion. He returned to Lagos Bay in the Algarve bearing orders from St Vincent to consider himself as head of an auxiliary force under Nelson. He was technically senior to Sir Horatio but under a long-standing treaty between Britain and Portugal, when a combined force was operating, the admiral commanding the fleet whose navy contributed the larger number of ships was in command. Niza was 'hereby authorised and required' to proceed up the Mediterranean as soon as possible, taking the British fireship *Incendiary* with him and avoiding any communication with the Barbary states, Spain or Gibraltar. He was to look for Nelson off the coast of the Two Sicilies, where the latest intelligence suggested he might be. Failing that, he was to go to the rendezvous off Majorca and Leghorn.[34]

The squadron sailed in the evening of 13 July and headed round the Balearics and past the north end of Corsica. It had some problems with its seamanship, for on the 25th the *Falcon* brig was run down and sunk by the flagship, which lost her bowsprit in the collision. In the morning of 5 August, the squadron anchored off Naples.[35]

Sir William Hamilton knew that his duty was to get these reinforcements to Nelson as quickly as possible. The Neapolitans, however, tried to persuade the

Portuguese to linger at Naples, where they would offer some protection against any French invasion. According to Hamilton, 'This government has also been underhand, tampering with me to persuade him [the Portugese admiral] that it would be more use to the King's service for him to remain cruising in these seas than to go and join Admiral Nelson.'[36] Hamilton, an old soldier himself, pointed out that Niza's orders were not discretionary and had to be obeyed.

As far as Niza knew, Nelson had gone towards the Greek islands, which were Turkish possessions. This caused him some difficulty, because as he remarked to Hamilton, he was 'much embarrassed about going into the Archipelago, as he said the Portuguese were not at peace with the Porte and until he should have joined Admiral Nelson might be under many difficulties among those islands!'.[37] Hamilton was informed that the squadron intended to go round the western end of Sicily, not through the Straits of Messina. He suggested that the Messina passage was much better, being quicker and leading close to Syracuse, where more information might be obtained. Furthermore, if the longer route might lead to any delay in the British fireship *Incendiary* joining Nelson, then it should be detached to go its own way.[38] Eventually Niza was persuaded to make the slightly more difficult Messina passage. He finally sailed on 11 August. Perhaps he was hastened by desertions from his ships in the congenial city of Naples. Hamilton believed he had lost 170 men and that 'he would have been without a man on board his ship' had he stayed any longer.[39]

On the 23rd, heading towards Crete, they came upon the *Mutine* which gave them news of the battle. They steered for Alexandria and arrived on the 27th, to find that Nelson had already sailed with the bulk of his fleet. On eventually meeting the Portuguese squadron, Nelson wrote to Niza, 'It is a matter of regret to me and I am sure it must be to your Excellency, that your squadron did not join me before the 1st of August, when not a single French ship could have escaped us.' More candidly he wrote to Hamilton, 'I never expect any real service from that squadron.'[40] The latter also lacked faith in the Portugese commander and wrote that Niza was 'sensible that the command he has is much above his ability'.[41]

★

Essentially Nelson, having lost his frigates in the first place, was caught in a vicious circle. It was difficult to send regular messages to either St Vincent or Hamilton by which he might be traced. Without a frigate screen, his force was much more compact than it might have been and therefore more difficult to find.

The frigates, however, had conducted their own war on French and Spanish control of the Mediterranean, capturing two major warships in exchange for the loss of *L'Aigle*, damaging several others and harassing enemy commerce. Like Nelson they had learned to survive for several months in a hostile sea, without any regular shore bases. None of the frigate captains were as single-minded as Nelson in pursuit of his object and most spent considerable time pursuing merchant ships and warships. Some found quite rich pickings in a sea which had been almost free of British warships for a year and a half.

CHAPTER 16

'The Satisfaction of Receiving your Letters'

DESPITE HIS WOUND and general weakness in the days after the battle, Nelson knew that he had to send out official reports. He had already started one during the night of the battle but it was 3 August before the main report to St Vincent was concluded. It began:

My Lord,
Almighty God has blessed His Majesty's arms in the late battle by a great victory over the fleet of the enemy, who I attacked at sunset on the 1st of August off the mouth of the Nile.[1]

He did not describe the course of the battle in any detail but gave a full list of officer casualties, with the numbers of seamen and marines killed and wounded on each ship. He gave special mention to Hood for offering to chase the French survivors and to Berry for taking command of the *Vanguard* after the admiral was wounded. He said nothing of Foley leading the attack, or of Saumarez as second-in-command. This was perhaps because of a conversation on the 2nd. Ball suggested that having been the second-in-command, Saumarez would undoubtedly receive some mark of distinction. According to his biographer the latter replied, 'in the enthusiasm of the moment' that 'We all did our duty – there was no second-in-command!'. This was evidently conveyed to Nelson, for Ball came on deck the next day and said, 'Nelson says there is to be no second-in-command; we are all to be alike in his dispatches.'[2] But Saumarez always resented Nelson's failure to give him special mention.

Nelson chose Berry to go home with the dispatches in the *Leander* with Thompson, believing 'it requisite that an officer of your rank should have charge of my dispatches to the Earl of St Vincent.' As flag captain he would be able to fill in any details missing from the dispatch from his personal knowledge. As the bearer of good tidings he could expect to be sent on with the message to the King and government and perhaps to be rewarded with a knighthood and a cash sum, as was Robert Calder, Jervis's Captain of the Fleet, for bringing home the news of the Battle of Cape St Vincent in 1797.

Thompson and Berry sailed at 7pm on 6 August. On the 12th the *Leander* was 40 miles from the eastern end of Crete and took advantage of a passing ship to send a note to Nelson. At 6.30am on 18 August, a few miles south of Crete, the sails of a ship were spotted in the south-east, heading directly for them. She was soon identified as a large ship of the line and Thompson decided that it was more prudent to retreat as she could almost certainly outfight a 50-gun ship, particularly one which was eighty men short of her complement and carrying about forty sick and wounded. Had the *Leander* been a frigate she might have used her superior sailing qualities to escape, despite being trapped within a bay. With the poor performance of a 50-gun ship, this was not easy.

The strange ship tried to confuse the officers of the *Leander*. She hoisted Neapolitan colours and then Turkish, suggesting she was a neutral but 'this deception was of no avail and plainly made him to be French'. The enemy had the wind behind him and the *Leander* was restricted by the coast of Crete. Although he did not want to seek action in the circumstances, Thompson saw there was no escape and decided to turn and face the enemy. At 8am he altered course and fired a broadside at long range, which was quickly returned. As the ships approached one another it became clear that the enemy intended to come alongside. Thompson could do nothing to prevent it, for the winds were light and his rigging and sails were already suffering damage. The port bow of the enemy ship rammed into the *Leander* and the Frenchmen prepared to board but a small party of the *Leander*'s marines under their sergeant kept up an accurate fire on the enemy decks and held them at bay. The wind got up again and the *Leander* was able to break free. Thompson luffed the ship up into the wind and seized the chance to pass behind the stern of the Frenchman, raking her with each gun as he did so and causing great damage on the enemy decks.

The wind dropped again and the two ships fought 'at pistol shot', at a range of about 25 yards. The battle of attrition continued until 3.30pm, by which time the *Leander* had only the shattered remains of her fore and main mast and bowsprit standing, her hull full of shot-holes and her decks strewn with killed and wounded: thirty-six died on board the ship and fifty-seven were treated for wounds. Her starboard guns were largely disabled by debris falling from the masts and rigging above while the Frenchman had lost only her mizzen topmast. As another breeze sprung up, the enemy rammed the *Leander* on the disabled starboard side and invited her to surrender, as she was no longer firing her guns. The French ship was clearly moving to place herself across the *Leander*'s stern, where she could wreak the same kind of havoc as the *Leander* had done a few hours earlier. Thompson hastily consulted with Berry, who agreed that 'we could do no more, he coinciding with me that further resistance was vain and impracticable and indeed all hope of success had for some time vanished.' Thompson shouted his surrender to the French. Nelson's dispatch would never reach its destination. The enemy proved to be the *Généreux* of 74 guns, one of the ships which had escaped from Aboukir on the morning of 2 August.

The officers and crew of the *Leander* soon found that Captain Lejoille of the *Généreux* did not respect the conventions of war as understood by the *ancien régime*. The men were plundered of their belongings and even the captain had most of his

The *Leander* dismasted by the *Généreux*, from a drawing in a letter by the marine artist W G Anderson. (National Maritime Museum, London: PAF5593)

shirts taken from him. The prisoners were set to work preparing jury rigs for both the *Leander* and her captor. The surgeon too had his troubles.

> A vast number of Frenchmen came down into the cockpit after they had swarmed on board and stole one of my cases of instruments and the greatest part of the dressings. I was just then preparing an operation of taking off an arm when at the same time one of them gave two or three blows.[3]

The prisoners were eventually exchanged and reached home in December. As custom demanded, Thompson and his officers and crew faced a court martial for the loss of the ship. This concluded that they had conducted a 'gallant and almost unprecedented defence . . . against so superior a force as that of the *Généreux*' which was 'deserving of every praise his country and this court can give'.[4]

The loss of the *Leander* had an unusually profound effect on history. Because of his shortage of frigates and the damage to his ships of the line, Nelson sent only one copy of his dispatch in the first instance, rather then duplicating it as was usual. As a result the news was disseminated throughout Europe by various means, initially by rumours and the haphazard pattern of its spread was to have some effect on policy-making. Historiography too suffered from the loss of the *Leander*. There are comparatively few personal accounts of the Battle of the Nile, largely because many of them were lost with the ship. Three bags of mail were loaded with shot and jettisoned when capture was imminent.

Because of the mishap to the *Leander*, the first news was spread by a French transport bark which arrived off Egypt as the battle was in progress. Staying long enough to see the flagship *L'Orient* in flames, her captain decided to flee and fetched up at the Turkish-held island of Rhodes. The governor of the island interrogated the captain and found that on 1 August a British squadron of fourteen ships of the line, a frigate and a corvette had attacked in the French in Aboukir Bay. He sent a report to his government in Constantinople. It arrived there by 22 August and was soon picked up by the British ambassador, Spencer Smith, who sent a message to London and another to the ambassador in Vienna. The Turkish reaction was decisive: they declared war on France on 9 September and gave permission for the Russian fleet to pass through the Dardanelles to operate against the French. The report of the battle remained unconfirmed for nearly 2 weeks, however, and Smith was still anxious as he did not know how reliable the report from Rhodes was, or even the final outcome of the action.

★

In view of the threat to India, Nelson took steps to send the news eastwards. On 9 August he ordered Lieutenant Duval of the *Zealous* to take dispatches and proceed to Alexandretta in the Gulf of Scandaroon (Iskenderun) in the extreme north-east corner of the Mediterranean. At 4pm on the 11th he left in a three-masted local craft carrying a cargo of beans and armed with two tiny swivel guns. He was instructed to make contact with British diplomatic or commercial officials at Alex-andretta, who would help him overland towards India. Duval arrived there on the 15th but discovered it to be 'a paltry little place' and found no British representative. Instead he made contact with the Turkish governor who was delighted with the news of the battle. Duval's crew were sent on to Cyprus to spread the news further, while the lieutenant was dressed in Arab clothes and given a servant and two guards for the journey to Aleppo, some miles inland. There he was supplied with a horse, nineteen camels and an escort of twenty-four Arabs for the journey across the desert. On 4 September they arrived at the Euphrates and on the 7th at Baghdad. The local Bashaw, as pleased with the news as every other Turkish official, feted Duval and had him appear at his apartments dressed in naval uniform. He was offered a boat to take him down the Tigris and on the 19th he arrived at Basra. There he found the *Fly*, packet boat, and was taken to Bombay, arriving on 21 October after a journey of 10 weeks by land and sea.

On the 31st, less than 2 weeks after he had first received news of Bonaparte's invasion of Egypt, Lord Mornington, the Governor-General of India, was informed of Nelson's victory. It was wonderful news but he did not relax his military and naval preparations, 'being still uncertain of the fate of the French army in Egypt and ignorant whether and additional force might not have been intended to co-operate with it in India, by the ordinary passage round the Cape of Good Hope.'[5]

The spread of the news of Nelson's victory, by rumour and official report. ▶

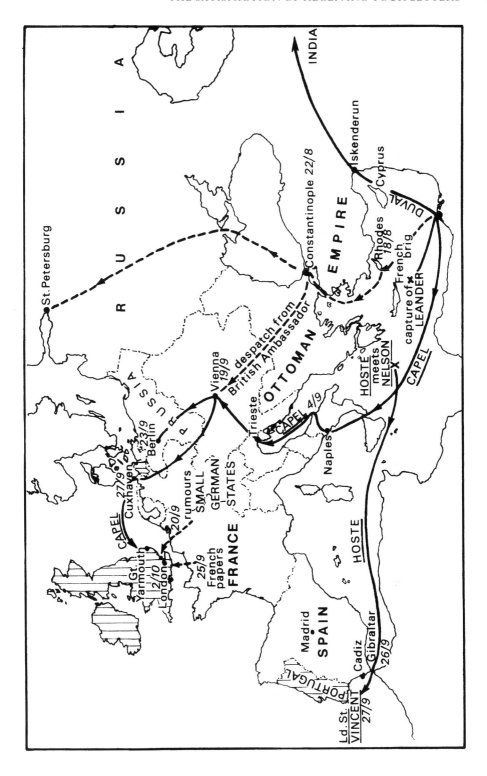

With the arrival of the *Emerald*, *Alcmene* and *Bonne Citoyenne* on 12 August, Nelson at last had an effective frigate force. He was aware that there was a certain risk in sending only one copy of his dispatches and he decided to order the *Mutine* to Naples to inform Hamilton and perhaps stimulate some support from the Neapolitans. He promoted his flag-lieutenant, Thomas Bladen Capel and put him in charge of the brig, with orders to 'proceed with all possible dispatch to some place in the continent of Europe, in the Neapolitan territories.'[6] Capel sailed on the 13th. On the 23rd he was off Crete, not far from the position where, unknown to him, the *Leander* had been captured 5 days earlier. A fleet of several ships was sighted and the *Mutine* had no private signals to confirm her identity to allied forces. She fled and was chased for several hours by the strange vessels. Eventually some ordinary signals were exchanged between the ships and Capel realised they were not hostile; they belonged to the Portuguese squadron under the Marquis of Niza. Capel passed on the news of the victory and went on his way.

Five days later, approaching the southern tip of Italy, the *Mutine* sighted two ships of the line, presumed to be French, both damaged and one towing the other. Capel believed they were the *Guillaume Tell* and *Généreux*, damaged at the Nile and heading for safety in Corfu. He approached closely to identify them, causing some consternation in the enemy ships, but the *Mutine* was far too small and weak to engage. Despite his bold curiosity, his identification was seriously amiss. He had actually seen the *Leander* with her captor the *Généreux*.

Passing through the Straits of Messina, he arrived at Naples on 4 September.[7] From her window in the city, Miss Cornelia Knight saw the *Mutine* approach.

> Our telescope was constantly directed towards the entrance of the beautiful bay, the prospect of which we so perfectly enjoyed from our windows. At length one morning while I was reading to my mother, I happened to turn my eyes towards the sea, and thought I discerned a sloop of war in the offing. I consulted the glass and found that I was not mistaken . . . My attention was instantly distracted from my book and my dear mother was rather displeased with my evident preoccupation . . . She rose from her seat and went to the telescope. The sloop was now approaching nearer and nearer to the land. The book was laid aside and we alternately put an eye to the glass. Presently we saw a boat pull off from the shore and pull out to the ship. Two officers were on deck and drew near the side. We clearly distinguished a gold epaulette on the shoulder and this was quite sufficient to convince us that one was the commander of the sloop and the other a captain going home with despatches [presumably a misidentification, as Capel was the only officer on board entitled to wear an epaulette]. News of a victory no doubt. We observed the gestures of the officers while they were conversing with the persons in the boat, Englishmen resident at Naples. We fancied we could see them, with the commotion natural to sailors, and particularly on such an occasion, depict by their action the blowing up of some ships and the sinking of others.[8]

★

Until this moment the Neapolitan government had been having serious doubts about Nelson. On the very day when the battle was being fought, Acton wrote to Hamilton expressing fears that their support of Nelson at Syracuse had tended to provoke a French attack, while the British squadron had neither destroyed the French at sea nor stayed on the scene to protect the Kingdom. The situation was 'disagreeable but not desperate'. In the meantime, however, the Austrians, in support of their demand for a British fleet in the Mediterranean, had insisted that the ports of the Two Sicilies should be open to British warships and a treaty had been signed to that effect. Any British fleet would be 'most heartily welcome'.[9]

Throughout August and most of September, Hamilton had agonized about Nelson's fleet. On 10 August he heard a report that the French were in Tunis but discounted it because he had recently had a communication from the British consul there. On the 21st he heard rumours that Bonaparte had landed at Alexandria on 10 July but commented, 'It is incomprehensible that we should still be without positive news of General Bonaparte and his fleet.' On the 27th he received Captain Foote's report that he had seen the French fleet in Aboukir Bay. [10]

Capel's arrival on 4 September ended all speculation and he was left in no doubt about Neapolitan feelings. 'I am totally unable to express the joy that appeared in everybody's countenance and the bursts of applause and acclamation we received.'[11] Miss Knight rushed into the apartment of her neighbour, General Di Pietra, who was entertaining a party of officers. 'Never shall I forget the shouts, the bursts of applause, the toasts drank, the glasses broken one after another.'[12] Hamilton wrote to Nelson, 'It is impossible, my dear Sir Horatio, for any words to express, in any degree, the joy that the account of the glorious and complete victory you gained . . . occasioned in this court and city.'[13] Sir John Acton wrote that the 'stupendous news' had 'filled their Sicilian Majesties, and all their faithful subjects, with the most sensible joy, gratitude and extensive admiration.'[14] The Queen wrote to the Marquis of Circello, 'The brave and gallant Admiral Nelson has gained a most complete victory . . . Italy is saved on the part of the sea, and that is only due to the gallant English. This action, or better-named, total defeat of the regicide fleet, is owing to the valour and courage of this brave admiral, seconded by a marine which is the terror of its enemies.'[15]

Hamilton took Capel to see the King and Queen. On the way from the palace he met Cardinal York, Jacobite pretender to the throne of Britain and now a refugee from the French. He told him the news but the cardinal asked, 'But may we depend on the truth of this great affair? There are so many false reports.' Hamilton then introduced Capel as a nephew of the Earl of Essex who had been in the action.[16] After that, Hamilton wasted no time in sending Capel on to Austria. Acton gave permission for one of his diplomatic messengers to go with him to ease his passage as far as Vienna. He was sent to Manfredonia on the Adriatic coast from where he went to Trieste in a Sicilian warship, and then on to Vienna by land.[17]

Vienna, second only to Paris as the cultural centre of Europe, was regarded as the key to any new alliance against the French and the first report of the battle, from Smith in Constantinople, was received there on 8 September. The British ambassador, Sir Morton Eden, was sceptical of the news until the 15th, when a messenger arrived via Trieste, bearing the substance of Capel's dispatch and it was now 'no longer doubted'. By the 19th Capel himself had arrived and Eden took him to

Baron Thugut, the Chancellor, who 'manifested the greatest pleasure at this memorable event'. But this was not enough to override the ongoing dispute over subsidies to assist the Austrian war effort and Eden noted that he 'in vain endeavoured to engage him to abandon his temporising system and take advantage of the consternation that must reign in France'.[18]

At Eisenstadt, south of Vienna, the great composer Joseph Haydn had been working at a mass since 10 July and completed it on 31 August. He could not have heard the news of the Battle of the Nile for at least a week after the completion but the work included a flourish of trumpets which was appropriate to the great victory and it soon became known as the Nelson Mass. His only mass in minor key, it is regarded as 'the most exciting and dramatic work of its kind Haydn wrote'.[19]

★

Berlin was the only major court where the official news arrived before the rumours. The British *chargé d'affaires*, Benjamin Garlicke, received a dispatch from Eden in Vienna on 23 September, the first account to reach the city. He went to the military manoeuvres at Potsdam and passed the news to the King via the Prince of Orange. The joy was 'marked and universal' and Garlicke noted an increased friendliness in the court. 'From everything which I have been able to collect at Potsdam, I am obliged to give more and more credit to the opinion that a material change is taking place in the politics of this cabinet . . . The language of the king is less reserved than it was. That of Count Haugwitz [the Prime Minister of Prussia] continues to be violent against France and favourable to a good understanding with Austria. General Wallendorf is avowedly for war, if Austria be engaged.'[20]

After Vienna, Capel passed through several of the smaller states of western Germany, following a well-established diplomatic route and arrived at Cuxhaven on the German North Sea coast. On 27 September he made contact with Captain Rotherham of HM ship *Good Design*, charged with the protection of trade hwith Britain. Realising that the dispatches were more important than the ordinary convoys, Rotherham ordered Captain Brown of the sloop *Kite* to take Capel to England.

★

The whole campaign was dogged by poor communications and the government in London was usually about 2 months behind what was happening in the Mediterranean. In the middle of July St Vincent received five letters from Nelson, sent by the *Transfer* from Naples, taking the story up to 15 June and reporting his decision to steer through the Straits of Messina. He sent copies to London, where they were received on 16 August.[21]

Meanwhile, Nelson had sent out another set of dispatches. With Capel gone to Vienna, Lieutenant William Hoste sailed again from Alexandria in the *Mutine* and on the way he met Nelson with the *Vanguard*, six other British 74s and six prizes on the way to the Naples. He was ordered to take Nelson's latest dispatch to the commander-in-chief at Cadiz. Hoste arrived at Gibraltar on 26 September and the Governor, General O'Hara, ordered a 21-gun salute in the middle of the night. He

William Hoste.
(National Maritime Museum, London: BHC2784)

sent a messenger down to the border to tell the Spanish, so that the salute would not be seen as a provocative attack on them. Gibraltar went 'mad with joy'.[22]

St Vincent had had no contact with Nelson since his letter of 22 July, reporting his presence in Syracuse, had been received more than a month after it was written. He had set up regular communications with Hamilton in Naples, mainly using the sloop *Transfer*. This worked quite well while Nelson was in Neapolitan territories, for Hamilton had ways of getting messages from all parts of the kingdom, including Sicily. But when Nelson went east, contact was severed and St Vincent was already looking at a different plan to reoccupy the Mediterranean. Spencer had written to him on 27 July:

> Upon a full consideration of the situation of the war in the Mediterranean and the immense advantages which may be derived by enabling Lord St Vincent to keep a squadron within the straits both with a view of checking operations of the enemy in that part of the world and of encouraging and assisting those powers who may be disposed to withstand his further progress in the overthrow of Europe and consequent extension of his power in Africa and Asia, it has occurred to H M's confidential servants that the occupation of the Island of Minorca will be of the most essential use at the present moment, and Lord St Vincent as well as General Stuart having been consulted on the subject, and having given their opinion that the attempt is practicable, it is intended that the latter officer shall be immediately sent out. . .[23]

In many ways Minorca was the most suitable base for the British navy in the Mediterranean. It was only 220 miles from the main French naval base at Toulon, whereas Gibraltar was more than 750. It was quite a small island, 230 square miles compared with the 3380 of Corsica, so it could be held by a fleet with naval superiority in the area. It was much closer to Gibraltar than the old base in Corsica, so the supply line was less likely to be cut. It had a fine harbour at Port

Mahon and some dockyard facilities, built by the British during their previous occupations of 1708-56 and 1763-82. Although there was no reason to be sure that Nelson would destroy the French fleet, at least it was out of the way and committed to protecting Bonaparte in Egypt, so Minorca was not covered. The Spanish fleet was no longer seen as a threat and the planning of the expedition went ahead, the naval side being headed by Rear-Admiral John Duckworth and the army by Lieutenant-General Charles Stuart.

On 27 September Hoste arrived at St Vincent's fleet off Cadiz and passed the dispatch to the delighted admiral. St Vincent wrote immediately to Nelson, 'God be praised! and you and your gallant band rewarded by a grateful country! for the greatest achievement the history of the world can produce.'[24] To Spencer he wrote of 'The almost incredible and stupendous victory . . . which Rear-Admiral Sir Horatio Nelson and his gallant train of heroes has under the blessing of God obtained over the Toulon squadron.'[25] The Minorca expedition could go ahead with increased confidence.

★

As early as 10 August, William Pitt had been shown copies of French newspapers of the 7th and 8th, 'containing vague reports of an action between Nelson and Bonaparte, and some pretending that the latter had been victorious'.[26] It is unlikely that any true report had reached Paris less than a week after the action and this may have been another version of a rumour which Hamilton had picked up in Naples at the very moment when the actual battle was being fought. 'Reports have been current of your having defeated the French fleet in the Bay of Alexandretta [off Syria] on the 30th of June, and taken Bonaparte prisoner.'[27]

On 21 August Grenville, the Foreign Secretary, heard, via a Turkish official sent from Constantinople, that Bonaparte had arrived in Alexandria and succeeded in landing an army. Windham, the Secretary at War, was pessimistic. 'Not more than an even chance even that there is some exaggeration in the news. Certain that some part of the army must have arrived and that the enemy are in possession.'[28] With his constant fear for India, Henry Dundas, the Secretary of War, was the worst affected by the news.

> Although the accounts from Constantinople are confused, I take it for granted ithere is no just ground of doubt that Bonaparte has made good his landing with a large force in Egypt . . . I am always in hopes we shall hear of Nelson doing something brilliant with regard to the fleet, as it is so far good and will gratify the feeling of the country, but neither that nor any other success will compensate to the country in reality for the misfortune it has undergone by the French with a large army getting possession of Egypt. The circumstance haunts me night and day . . .[29]

But Count Woronzow, the Russian ambassador, was far more optimistic. He treated the report with 'the incredulity of St Thomas' and was confident that even if it was true, Nelson would find them in the end.[30]

By 8 September the news was even worse. It was known that Nelson 'had totally failed in his search for Bonaparte and had returned on 19th July to Sicily', having been at Alexandria on 28 June.[31] Admiral Samuel Goodall noted a current of criticism of Nelson at this stage though he claimed that he himself had never lost faith in him.

> I have been obliged to stand in the breech against senseless criticism of the noble and ignoble of this country . . . How often have I been questioned, 'What is your favourite hero about? The French fleet has passed under his nose etc etc,' from which I have answered 'I know him well, if fortune has not befriended his labours and anxieties in this event, yet something capital will be done.'[32]

On 14 September Pitt wrote to Spencer Smith in Constantinople. 'The many concurrent accounts which have been received here of the landing of at least a considerable part of the French expedition under General Bonaparte in Egypt make it no longer possible to doubt the fact.' Smith was instructed to urge the Turks towards war with France.[33]

At the Admiralty, Spencer had heard rumours which put the matter in a very different light. 'Extravagant reports' had been circulated all over Europe about a 'decisive victory said to have been obtained by Sir Horatio Nelson over Bonaparte'. He was sceptical of them, for 'the present situation . . . of the two fleets in the Mediterranean leaves but little hope that anything very decisive can take place.' Having taken Alexandria the French would obviously take their ships into port where they would be unassailable. The news of Nelson missing the French seemed to discredit the rumours totally and Spencer had 'seldom experienced a more severe disappointment'.[34] On 23 September he commented 'I hope he will have a pretty good story to tell at least. His missing the French fleet both going and returning was certainly very unfortunate; but we must not be too ready to censure him for leaving Alexandria when he was there, till we know the exact state of his intelligence which he received on his arrival there.'[35] On the 30th he wrote to the Admiral in desperation.

> You may easily conceive the anxiety we have been under about you and your operations and the distance at which you are really placed from us increased as it is by the present very inconvenient situation of Europe for communication make it impossible almost to know what to write.

Nelson's letters of 25 May and 15 June had been received along with a few reports from Hamilton but nothing further. He was urged to write more often and send duplicate copies of all his letters.[36]

In Norfolk, Lady Nelson was also aware of the rumours. By 11 September, the last letter she had received from her husband was dated 24 May and described the storm. She also had a note that he was well on 22 July. Reading the reports of battle, she would have understood the feelings of the close relatives of modern celebrities. 'The newspapers have tormented and almost killed me in regard to the desperate action you have fought with the French fleet. How human faculties can be brought to make others intentionally miserable I cannot conceive. In my opinion a newspaper writer, or a fabricator for them, is a despicable creature bearing human shape.'[37]

Yet even at the height of Spencer's despair the reports of Nelson's victory were strengthened. On 20 September the artist Joseph Farington was in Dover when a neutral Swedish ship came in from Gravelines with reports from the French press of an action near Alexandria in which both sides had lost ships but the French flagship had blown up. The Collector of Customs was informed and sent a message to London via the Admiralty telegraph at Deal.[38] By the 25th Spencer was again receiving reports, via the French newspapers, of 'an action in the Bay of Bequieres', though the source was suspect.[39] On the 26th Farington in Dover heard a report via Constantinople which had obviously originated with the French ship which had escaped to Rhodes; 'the French admiral's ship was on fire when the French brig which carried the account got off.' George Canning, the Under Secretary for Foreign Affairs, accepted this as the truth and wrote officially to announce it to the City of London.[40] On the 27th Windham heard a report from one Pocock concerning 'Aboukir or Bequieres, the place where Nelson is supposed to have had his victory.'[41] On 28 September William Gartshere of Wimbledon wrote: 'There is no certain confirmation of Nelson's victory. There can be no doubt I think of this and this seems to be the general opinion.'[42] In the same week Lady Nelson read newspapers which 'positively asserted you have gained some advantages over the French fleet assuring the public you arrived safe with your prizes in Naples.'[43] On 2 October *The Times* reported that a dispatch from Sir Morton Eden in Vienna, giving details of the victory, had been brought over by Captain Sutton of the *Prince of Wales* packet ship.

Capel's arrival at the Admiralty in London, at 11.15am on 2 October, finally settled the matter. Lady Spencer, living with her husband in Admiralty House, was one of the first to hear the news and had no inhibitions in expressing her emotions. 'Captain Capel just arrived! Joy, joy, joy to you, brave, gallant, immortalised Nelson . . . My heart is absolutely bursting with different sensations of joy, of gratitude, of pride, of every emotion that ever warmed the bosom of a British woman on hearing of her country's glory . . . I am half mad and I have written a strange letter, but you will excuse it.'[44] Her husband was more formal. 'Since my last letter of the 30th ultimo, I have had the satisfaction of receiving your letters by Captain Capel and most sincerely and cordially do I congratulate you on the very brilliant and signal service you have performed to your country in the glorious action of the 1st of August last.'[45]

The news was all over London by the evening and in Bolton Row Betsy Wynne was saddened to hear of the death of a friend, one Jollife. That night the town was illuminated.[46] At Richmond near London, the Prime Minister's mother celebrated in her own way. 'Last night I had a great N in brilliant lamps adorning the front my mansion and all our royal village was illuminated. My walks have been rendered pleasant by the continual sound of people ringing bells all around, the fire of cannon without ceasing.'[47] At Bury the Admiral's 10-year-old nephew, also Horatio Nelson, attended a *feu de joie* fired by soldiers.[48] In Bradford the local volunteer companies fired a similar volley after their regular parade, after which the town was illuminated. In the village of Chew Magna near Bristol, 'a sheep was

A popular print published in November 1798 and used for Christmas greetings. The message of 'peace on Earth' conflicts with the warlike images round the edges, which of course are crude and rather ignorant. Poussielgue's letters to his wife were captured and published in England and he is shown here expressing his horror in the Aboukir Fort, not the tower at Rosetta from which he in fact witnessed the battle. (National Maritime Museum, London: PAG8973)

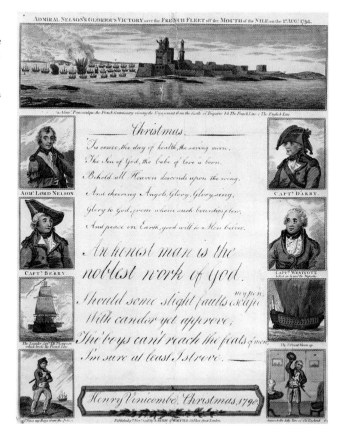

roasted whole and given, with plenty of beer, to the populace'.[49] The Admiralty messenger was sent to Weymouth, where the King was taking the waters. His Majesty attended the theatre where a song was sung in honour of the victory. Back in London, a subscription was opened for the relief of those widowed and orphaned in the battle and had raised £1165 by the 6th.[50] The front of a hotel in Oxford Street was decorated with 'festoons of variegated lamps. The initials of the Admiral suspended from a knot, a beautiful star and large anchor. The whole had a pleasing effect.' At Drury Lane Theatre, a new verse was added to *Rule Britannia*, linking Nelson with Britannia as the mistress of the seas.[51] The victory inspired many to take up the pen, though no great poetry was written to rival Haydn's contribution to music. The *Bath Chronicle* published a work on the reception of the news in the town, beginning,

> Permit, O ye Britons, a patriot Muse
> To record the effect of the glorious news
> Of brave Nelson's vict'ry, obtained on the main
> Who has taken and burnt nine French ships of the line.

But this was surpassed, one way or another, by a poem by 'Peter Pindar' published in the new magazine, the *Naval Chronicle*, in the following year;

Keel up lies France! long may she keep that posture!
Her knav'ry, policy, on the rocks have tost her.

Amid the general rejoicing, Dundas could find a pessimistic note.

I hate to indulge retrospective melancholy, but in this instance I cannot relieve my mind from it. If we had not been too incredulous as to the object of Bonaparte's armament, I think such instructions would have been given to Sir Horatio Nelson as would have prevented him from leaving Alexandria, after he had once reached it in the auspicious and promising way he did. What a change that circumstance would have made on the state of the country? I must close the subject, for it almost drives me mad to think of it.[52]

More recent writers have echoed this view. Of the failure to find the French after they left Malta, A B Rodger wrote, with the First and Second World Wars fresh in his mind 'Europe might have been saved fifteen years of vulgar caesarism and bloodshed and a civil war which, like all European civil wars of modern times, merely increased the relative power of the Slav.'[53]

There is no doubt that in the long term an earlier attack on the French at sea would have altered history. Nelson's ships would certainly have attacked the flagship and probably captured it, with Napoleon Bonaparte. But how far would they have gone in destroying the ships of the line, not to mention the merchant-men? It is unlikely that the warships would have been beaten as comprehensively as they were as at Aboukir Bay, for Nelson's forces would have been divided between the transports and ships of the line, while beaten warships would have stood some chance of escaping from the battle in the open sea. As to the trans-ports, 13 ships of the line could not have taken all 350, even without interference from the French warships. There can be little doubt that the majority would have escaped, because there was no frigate force at hand to chase them, nor sufficient seamen to man captured vessels. The expedition would have been dispersed but many of the troops would have made it to neutral or friendly ports, to rejoin the war in due course. Conversely, the effect of Aboukir Bay was to cut off more than 30,000 French troops in Egypt until the end of the French Revolutionary War in 1801. Furthermore, the diplomatic effects of an early battle might have been different. Would Turkey have been persuaded into a coalition if the attack had been stopped before reaching Egypt? As Spencer wrote a few months after the Nile,

I have long since felt very confident that the Battle of the Nile will prove to have as effectually beat the land part as it did the naval part of the French armament, with the additional advantage of giving them room enough to visit the hatred and detestation of a Frenchman in the minds of all the inhabitants of that part of the world as firmly as it is now fixed in those of Europeans.[54]

What might have happened, and with what consequence, had Nelson met the French Armament before its landing at Alexandria are intriguing but ultimately unanswerable questions. Given what did happen, it could be argued that, by luck as much as judgement, he had won the best victory possible to build a coalition, and at the best possible moment.

CHAPTER 17

Bonaparte Isolated

As THE FRENCH soldiers and sailors on shore looked out over the wreckage of their fleet in Aboukir Bay on the morning of 2 August, their first thought was for the safety of their own position. They were not to know of the complete exhaustion of the British crews and they put themselves in a state of defence, both against the British and the Bedouins who were clearly encouraged by the destruction of the French fleet. General Kléber organised the defences of Alexandria and Rosetta and also on the Aboukir peninsula. Even by 15 August, as the bulk of the British fleet prepared to sail from the bay, the movement of two ships to the mouth of Alexandria harbour caused some concern.[1]

Also on the 15 August, in the small town of Es Saliya on the eastern boundary of Egypt where he had gone in pursuit of a Mameluke leader, Bonaparte received the news of the defeat in Aboukir Bay. He took it calmly and according to his own account told his companions,

> Well Gentlemen, now we are obliged to accomplish great things; we shall accomplish them. We must found a great empire, and we shall found it. The sea of course, of which we are no longer master, separates us from our homeland, but no sea separates us from either Africa or Asia. We are numerous; we have enough men to form our cadres. We have no lack of munitions.[2]

Bonaparte was quite consistent in his understatement of sea power. Ironically his view was similar to that of Henry Dundas in London, who still feared for an attack on India and regretted that the French had ever been allowed to land in Egypt. Bonaparte had a certain amount of truth on his side. His army was still dangerous and undefeated and no-one doubted the resourcefulness of its commander. As one of his *savants* wrote,

> . . . we first heard the melancholy news of our naval action, in which we lost a great number of vessels, and amongst the rest *L'Orient*; and had Admiral Brueys killed by a cannon shot. You may easily conceive how embarrassing this event must render our situation in this country. It would deprive the army of every hope, if they were not acquainted with the genius of the Commander-in-Chief. It is entirely on him, therefore, that we rely for the care of extricating us from the perilous step in which we are engaged.

But his conclusion was far more pessimistic. 'May the measures he may take bring us nearer to our country! EGYPT IS NOT MADE FOR US.'³

In a letter to the widow of Admiral Brueys, Bonaparte was lavish in his praise of the deceased, but in his report to the Directory in Paris he put the blame squarely on him. He had ordered the admiral to take his ships into Alexandria harbour, to discharge the remaining supplies and armaments and then to sail for the safe anchorage of Corfu. He said nothing about the other choice he had offered and Brueys had in fact taken, to anchor the fleet at Aboukir Bay.⁴

Bonaparte suggested that, apart for the insecure anchorage at Aboukir, the defeat had been due to three factors: ineptness by the captains of the *Guerrier* and *Conquérant* at the head of the line, the blowing-up of *L'Orient* and the failure of Villeneuve to take the initiative. None of these claims is fully justified. Both ships at the head of the line had behaved well, given the limits of their position and the *Conquérant*, in particular, was far too weak to stand any chance in battle. The blowing-up of *L'Orient* was the climax of the battle but it was not the turning point. The French were already defeated, perhaps from the moment when Foley turned their line. Criticism of Villeneuve is valid on a certain level but he was able to justify himself and indeed Bonaparte was to employ him again, fatally, as commander-in-chief in 1803-05. Defeated at Trafalgar and captured, he was returned to France where he committed suicide in 1806, amid unproved suggestions that he was in fact murdered on the orders of Napoleon.

★

Apart from the difficulties in communication and reconnaissance, one of the outstanding features of the Egyptian campaign is the way in which the leaders of both sides failed to understand each other's psychology and situation. General Montgomery had a picture of Rommel in his caravan during campaigns in the desert in the Second World War, in the hope that he might see into the mind of the enemy. Such an approach might have done much to assist Bonaparte, Brueys and Nelson in the Mediterranean.

If Nelson could have envisaged how slow and disorganised the French convoy was, he would have had no qualms about splitting his force. A convoy spread over 12 miles would have been impossible to defend and the warships would not have been able to flee while the convoy was under threat. Brueys, on the other hand, failed to appreciate how an aggressive admiral like Nelson would seek out the weak points in his line of battle in Aboukir Bay.

Perhaps Bonaparte's greatest mistake was to misunderstand the nature of sea-power. The unspoken assumption of the Egyptian campaign was that the Mediterranean was essentially French territory, that the British had been driven from the sea and the French had effectively conquered it. But seas cannot be conquered in the way that land can. While the British still had a fleet, there was always the chance that a force might enter the Mediterranean, even at the expense of dispositions elsewhere. Nelson's squadron was not the only card to be played here. French communications with Egypt could be disrupted by other means, including isolated cruisers. The frigates searching for Nelson incidentally captured two major warships during June and July, the taking of the *Sensible* disrupting the communication between France and Malta. On a much larger scale, plans for a British attack on Minorca had already been drawn up before the news of the Nile was known.

Nelson and Bonaparte had much in common. Both had immense charm and constantly used it to advantage. Each was a supreme tactician on his own element. Both had fathers from the provincial professional classes and unsuccessful marriages with women from the West Indies. But the Nile campaign illustrated the most striking difference between the two. While Bonaparte dreamed of enormous horizons, political reform, debated the age of the earth with his scientists and even dreamed of creating new religions, Nelson was tightly and indeed obsessively focused. He thought of virtually nothing for 3 months, except finding the French fleet and destroying it.

★

Despite Bonaparte's apparent confidence after his defeat at the Nile, the position of the French army was becoming more and more difficult. Bonaparte's propaganda claimed his sympathy with Islam, as an opponent of the Pope and vanquisher of the Knights of Malta. But in fact his soldiers and administrators had no more feel for the susceptibilities of the Egyptian people than they had shown in Malta or elsewhere. As a Turkish chronicler wrote,

> The presence of the French in Cairo was intolerable, especially when Egyptians saw their wives and daughters walking in the streets unveiled and appearing to be the property of the French, with whom they were seen in public and with whom they cohabited. Before these facts, the Moslems died of shame. It was bad enough for them to see the taverns that had been established in bazaars of Cairo and even in several mosques . . . All told, the scum of the populace was doing well, because it benefited from the new freedom. But the élite and the middle classes experienced all sorts of vexations, because imports and exports had come to a standstill.[5]

Apart from guerrilla warfare by the Bedouin and passive resistance by the urban population, the French faced two main enemies within Egypt – Murad Bey and Ibrahim Bey, the *de facto* leaders of the Mamelukes. Ibrahim was defeated by Bonaparte near the boundaries of Syria in August 1798, just before the news of the Nile was received. Murad operated in the Nile valley above Cairo and was opposed by General Desaix. With a relatively small force Desaix chased the Mamelukes up and down the river, defeating them in a series of battles up to May 1799, when he finally broke their resistance. In the meantime, more potent enemies were preparing to attack.

As part of the conditions for the expedition to Egypt, Talleyrand, the French Foreign Minister, had promised to go to Constantinople in person, to negotiate with the Porte and persuade the Sultan that he had no reason to fight the French in Egypt. But Talleyrand showed no sign of going on such a mission, which would remove him from the centre of power in Paris and put him in danger from British cruisers on the way, or from Turkish anger should his diplomatic skills fail him. Nor did he rush to find anyone else. Bonaparte constantly asked the Directory for news of his activities in Turkey but none came. On 9 September the Turks declared war on France, having received practical support in the form of a fleet sent by their traditional enemies, the Russians, and having heard of Nelson's victory at the Nile. Talleyrand had at last appointed an ambassador to go to Constantinople but news of the declaration of war was received before he could leave France.

At this stage in history, no European nation had experience of conquest on the scale of Bonaparte's in Egypt. The Portuguese, British and French had ruled parts of India but this came about through trade, sporadic military action and the gradual filling of a power vacuum among the native rulers, rather than by sudden conquest. In North America and the West Indies, the Europeans had operated very differently, creating their own populations, whether slave or free, and ignoring or exterminating the native peoples. But the Egyptians, despite their appearance of degradation, had their own history and culture and knew the benefits and horrors of strong government. The Europeans were certainly better organised and disciplined than the native peoples of Egypt and India, which gave them an advantage in politics and in battle. They had a lead in the organisation of their industry, agriculture and government at home but this was not obvious to the conquered. Later in the nineteenth century steam power, the railway, the electric telegraph and the repeating rifle, combined with enormous self-confidence, allowed the European powers to take over almost all of the world, for they could either buy submission with the lure of material goods or intimidate the people with military might. In Egypt in 1798 however, there was only French self-confidence and a belief in their Revolutionary superiority which almost mounted to religious fervour. This was not an advantage in the circumstances, for it conflicted with the religious beliefs of the population. The deeply conservative Moslems had not yet reconciled themselves to rule by the Infidel and opposition to the French took on the status of a holy war.

Even so, Bonaparte might have done better in ruling Egypt had he understood more about the feelings of the people. His *savants* did a marvellous job in opening up the culture of its distant past but little about the present day. Bonaparte himself made several naive and transparent attempts to win the Moslems over, but this had little effect on a people who, for better or worse, regarded all Europeans as infidels.

None of this prevented Bonaparte from carrying out reforms with his usual superhuman energy. A postal service was set up, a hospital founded and local leaders were co-opted into the government. He called a 'General Divan' to represent the various sections of the people, such as the merchants, mayors of towns, peasants and Bedouin but each member was chosen by the French military governors. Islam was of course tolerated, because there was no prospect of repressing it with a mere 35,000 men, and Bonaparte was not entirely insincere when he tried to win over the religious and civil leaders. He had read the Koran during the voyage across the Mediterranean and found it 'sublime'.

Cairo, with a population of 300,000, was much larger than Alexandria but no less of a disappointment to the French. Major Detroye wrote,

Once you enter Cairo, what do you find? Narrow, unpaved and dirty streets, dark houses that are falling to pieces, public buildings that look like dungeons, shops that look like stables, an atmosphere redolent of dust and garbage, blind men, half-blind men, bearded men, people dressed in rags, pressed together in the streets or squatting, smoking their pipes, like monkeys at the entrance of their cave; few women of the people, hideous, disgusting, hiding their fleshless faces under stinking rags, and displaying their pendulous breasts through their torn gowns; yellow, skinny children covered with suppuration, devoured by flies; an unbearable stench, due to dirt in the houses, dust in the air, and the smell of food being fried in bad oil in the unventilated bazaars.[6]

In August 1798 Bonaparte set up the Institute of Egypt, with three aims;

1. The progress of knowledge and its propagation in Egypt.
2. Research, study and publication of the natural, industrial and historical facts about Egypt.
3. To give advice on the various questions upon which it may be consulted by the government.

But at its first meeting the following day, he confined himself to very practical questions. Could native bread baking facilities be improved? Were wind or water mills the most efficient? Was it possible to manufacture gunpowder from Egyptian resources?[7] A week after hearing news of the Battle of the Nile, Bonaparte knew that his army would have to develop self-sufficiency.

The work of the *savants* was the most successful feature of the expedition. The mathematicians, astronomers and engineers did their best but it was the historians and archaeologists who really gripped the imagination and exposed the wonders of the world of the Pharaohs to the intellectuals of Europe. The soldiers who saw the impoverished people and the decrepit cites of modern Egypt had little conception of the glories of the past, even as they prepared to fight in the shadow of the Pyramids and Bonaparte addressed them with the words 'Forty centuries look down on you.' Dominique Vivant Denon, like many of the *savants*, was subjected to the hardships of campaigning when he was with Desaix's division in Upper Egypt. Drawing some ruins on the banks of the Nile, he was interrupted by a shot from an Arab, which passed close to his piece of paper. He picked up his own gun and killed the Arab, then resumed his drawing. When General Desaix commented that the horizon was not straight, Denon commented, 'Ah, that's the fault of the Arab. He fired too soon.'[8]

In July 1799, Denon reported to Bonaparte on his findings and two commissions were set up. One eventually resulted in Denon's massive work, the *Description de l'Egypte*, published between 1808 and 1828, consisting of ten volumes of text and fourteen of beautifully engraved plates. Pyramids were measured, drawn and entered, isolated ruins were sketched. The Sphinx was drawn, though only the head was apparent in those days, the rest remaining buried in sand until 1816. However, the legend that its nose was blown off by French gunfire does not bear examination. The publication of Denon's *opus* had a great effect in Europe, comparable with that of the discovery of Tutankhamun's tomb a century later.

Meanwhile, Bonaparte's private life was under strain. Letters from Paris told him that his wife, Josephine, was having an affair with an officer by the name of

Hippolyte Charles. He was shocked by the news and by the public nature of the affair, which he felt was making him a laughing-stock. He threatened divorce, which would be relatively easy under the laws of the Republic but would bring yet more publicity. Instead he found consolation with Pauline Fourès, the wife of an officer in the dragoons serving in Egypt. Lieutenant Fourès was sent home to clear the field for the General-in-Chief but his ship was captured and he was sent back to Egypt, to the embarrassment of all concerned.

★

Bonaparte heard of the Turkish declaration of war by the beginning of October and the news spread among the Egyptian population, despite French attempts to suppress and ignore it. Bonaparte's efforts to open diplomatic relations with the Turkish-appointed governors of Syria, Tunis and Damascus were rebuffed and he decided to take the initiative.

As always, it is not easy to be sure of Bonaparte's reasons for the campaign northwards into Syria. Did he intend to turn eastwards through what is now Iraq, renewing the threat to British India? Would he go west instead, capturing and looting Constantinople and eventually linking up with French armies in northern Italy? The Napoleonic legend requires such grandiose aims and indeed he adopted them, retrospectively at least. But at the time his letter to the Directory suggested a much more modest plan. His attack to the north would create an extra line of defence, cause 'the establishment of a strong point beyond the desert which will hold armies, of whatever nation, so far from Egypt that they cannot combine with a European army landing on the coast.' It would create a rather vague threat to the Porte, helping the Directory in negotiations which, Bonaparte believed, they had 'no doubt begun'; and it would remove potential bases for British cruisers operating against his forces in Egypt.[9]

On 6 February 1799, the advance guard under General Reynier marched out from Kateeh, on the Mediterranean just east of where the Suez Canal was later built, and headed along the coast. It was delayed at El Arish, near the Egyptian frontier, where a force of Mamelukes and Albanians held out for 11 days. It was the 23rd of the month before the full army, consisting of 13,000 troops with Bonaparte at the head, entered the province of Syria. The fortress at Gaza was taken without any difficulty and Jaffa was assaulted on 7 March. The Turkish garrison surrendered to Bonaparte's aides, believing that they would be granted mercy, but the Commander-in-Chief felt that he did not have the resources to feed and guard them. He ordered their mass execution, to the horror of many of his battle-hardened troops.

> The next morning, all the Moroccans were taken down to the sea-shore, and two battalions began to shoot them down. Their only hope of saving their lives was to throw themselves into the sea; they did not hesitate and all tried to escape by swimming. They were shot at leisure and in an instant the sea was red with blood and covered with corpses. Soldiers were ordered to follow them in boats and finish them off.[10]

Sir Sidney Smith at the siege of Acre, engraved after a portrait by John Eckstein. (National Maritime Museum, London: B112)

The French army resumed its march north but in the meantime Bonaparte's enemies began to make their preparations. Under two great but somewhat erratic leaders, the Turks and the British combined at the fortress of Acre, where more than 600 years before, Richard the Lionheart had fought against the Saracens.

The Turkish leader was Djezzar Pasha, over 60 years old, who had been born in the Turkish province of Bosnia and had once been the slave of a Mameluke. His drive and ruthlessness as both a tax-collector and an assassin furthered his rise to become governor of the province of Acre, on behalf of the Sultan of Turkey. His nickname 'Djezzar' meant 'butcher' and it was given because of a well-justified reputation for cruelty: he was said, for example, to have buried a great number of Greek Christians alive when he rebuilt the walls of Beirut. He also had a kindly side in that he helped the poor of his province, even the widows created by his own activities. A large and irascible man, he had picked up a good deal of political skill in his rise to power and as a military commander he was aggressive and resourceful.

At the head of the British forces was Captain Sir Sidney Smith, whose appointment had caused considerable annoyance to Nelson (see Chapter 18). He was a relatively junior captain in the Royal Navy and used the title of Commodore without authority from his admiral. His knighthood came from 3 years of service in the Swedish Navy but his use of it outside that country was regarded as a breach of etiquette and Nelson habitually referred to him as 'the Swedish knight'. He was described by Midshipman Parsons as 'of middling stature, good-looking, with tremendous moustachioes, a pair of penetrating black eyes, an intelligent countenance with a gentlemanly air, expressive of good nature had kindness of heart'.[11] In 1796 he had been captured off Le Havre during a raid and locked up in the Temple prison in Paris. Accused of espionage, he narrowly escaped being shot and later made a daring escape with the help of his gaoler's daughter.

Smith might be seen as a rival to Nelson in the quest for naval glory. He had the charisma and the tactical daring and he was not afraid of disobeying orders when he felt the situation demanded it. Like Nelson he could win the loyalty of his men but his undoubted charm did not melt St Vincent's heart, as Nelson's did. Nelson did not always enchant his superiors but Smith almost invariably annoyed them. In later years Admiral Lord Keith wrote, 'I am so perfectly acquainted with that restless spirit and ungovernable vanity which renders it irksome to him to feel any superior.'[12] But Smith enjoyed the favour of the government, for political as well as naval reasons. For his brother was Spencer Smith, the British ambassador in Constantinople, who had sent the first news of the Battle of the Nile to London. The government was determined to stiffen the Turkish resistance against the French in Egypt and with orders direct from Spencer at the Admiralty and Grenville at the Foreign Office, Sir Sidney was to have both naval and diplomatic authority to operate in the Levant.

The Anglo-Turkish campaign was assisted by Louis-Edmond de Phélippeaux, a French Royalist officer who had been a schoolboy rival of Bonaparte and had helped Smith to escape from Paris. An artillery officer, his knowledge, of gunnery and fortification was to prove invaluable.

The town of Acre (or Akko) was situated on the coast of historical Syria, though now in Israel. It took up a small triangle of land, not quite a peninsula, and had stout though ancient walls, with a small harbour which could be used by the forces holding the town. It stood at the northern end of a six-mile wide bay, where British warships could anchor out of the range of enemy artillery. Djezzar Pasha was able to muster 4000 men of various nationalities for the defence, while Smith eventually landed 800 sailors and marines from his squadron. Smith arrived on 15 March and rapidly prepared the town for the expected assault. Bonaparte arrived on the 18th, so the delay of 11 days at El Arish turned out to be vital.

The forces at Acre put Bonaparte in a difficult position. He could not afford to march on, leaving Smith and the Turks in possession, for a large army might be landed in his rear. Yet he could not divide his army, leaving part at Acre and proceeding northwards with the rest, for neither part would be strong enough for the task it was to do. His only choice was to besiege Acre and try to capture it before the plans for the campaign were disrupted too seriously. It was an unpleasant situation for the General-in-Chief, who preferred a strategy of rapid movement and hated siege warfare. Smith on the other hand relished it, as a seaman ashore making the best of his short time on land. Like many a British officer in a tight corner, he delighted in improvisation and invention, carrying out psychological warfare on the enemy by sending him copies of intercepted French newspapers with news of the

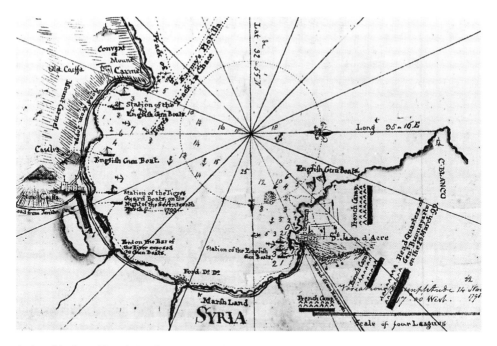

A plan of the Bay of Acre during the siege, signed by Sir Sidney Smith. The town (St Jean d'Acre) is on the north or right side of the bay. (National Maritime Museum, London: D554)

Directory's defeats in northern Italy. The siege was packed with incident, the most celebrated being when Daniel Bryan, captain of the foretop of Smith's ship the *Tigre*, insisted in burying a dead French general in no-man's-land, in full view of both armies and to the cheers of both sides.

The usual rules of siege warfare did not apply, however. The British and Turkish forces were not truly cut off, because they could be supplied by sea. The French had little in the way of heavy artillery, while the forces inside Acre had 240 guns, including the French siege train, which had been captured at sea by the Royal Navy on 18 March. The besieged could afford to wait indefinitely, it was the French who were in a hurry. Too long spent investing Acre would allow Bonaparte's enemies to gain in strength elsewhere and the main Turkish army was approaching.

Even more serious for Bonaparte's men, signs of bubonic plague had begun to appear among the troops. Disease had always been a problem for the army and as early as October 1798, 15 per cent of the men were on the sick list. By the end of the year, plague had spread among the troops in Cairo, Alexandria and Damietta and 2000 men had died. The outbreak in Syria was never quite so serious and only affected about 3 per cent of the force in a fortnight. Moreover the doctors, such as Desgenettes who thrust his lancet into the revolting pus of one of the patients in order to 'calm the fears and restore the spirit of the army', were increasingly confident of saving the majority of those infected. Bonaparte showed great personal courage and did much to restore flagging morale by visiting the hospital at Jaffa.

> The General walked through the hospital and its annexe, spoke to almost all the soldiers who were conscious enough to hear him, and for one hour and a half, with the greatest calm, busied himself with the details of the administration. While in a very small and crowded ward, he helped to lift, or rather carry, the hideous corpse of a soldier whose torn uniform was soiled by the spontaneous bursting of an enormous abscessed bubo.[13]

The French did their best to bombard the walls of Acre and on 26 March they made a small breach. General Kléber, already finding it difficult to work under Bonaparte, told the General, 'Of course the breach is practicable, a cat could get through.' Nearly 6 feet tall himself, he said of the trenches, 'They are all right for you, General, but as for me, they hardly reach up to my belly.'[14] The breach was soon blocked up with wood and stones but the following day it was bombarded again and widened. When Bonaparte ordered an assault, it was the crisis of the battle and, indeed, of the campaign. The Turks were intimidated by the massive attack but the French were stopped when they reached a dry moat. One general wrote, 'This was the day when Acre should have fallen.'[15]

Meanwhile, a Turkish army was assembling in Galilee. Bonaparte reacted by sending troops against it and on 11 April Kléber routed a large force of Turks near Canaan. But his 2000 men were then attacked by up to 35,000 of the enemy near Mount Tabor and risked being cut off. They put up a very effective defence over 2 days, until Bonaparte marched north with one division from Acre and surprised the enemy, dispersing the Turkish Army of Damascus.

More siege artillery arrived at the French lines towards the end of April and more assaults were made on Acre, but still the walls could not be penetrated against the stout defence by the Turks and British. Bonaparte began to see that morale was sinking, plague was taking a slow but regular toll on his troops and the city was still being supplied by sea. On 17 May, after 63 days of failure, he raised the siege. Smith announced this in a letter to Nelson, using terms which the Admiral himself might have employed.

> My Lord, the providence of Almighty God has been wonderfully manifested in the defeat and precipitate retreat of the French army, the means we had of opposing its gigantic efforts against us being totally inadequate of themselves to the production of such a result.[16]

Bonaparte's proclamation to his troops also smacked of triumphalism, with much less justification.

> Soldiers, you have crossed the desert dividing Africa from Asia faster than an Arab army. The army that was marching to invade Egypt has been destroyed; you have captured its general, its field equipment, its waterskins, its camels. You have taken the forts defending the desert wells. On the field of Mount Tabor you dispersed that horde of men who had run from every corner of Asia in the hopes of looting Egypt . . .
> . . . having razed to the ground the fortifications of Gaza, Jaffa, Haifa, Acre and all with a handful of men, we are going back to Egypt. The season for landings calls me there. In a few days you might have hoped to capture the Pasha himself in his palace; but at this time of year the capture of the castle of Acre is not worth the loss of a few days and besides, the brave men I should lose there are needed for more essential operations.[17]

In a foretaste of the retreat from Moscow 13 years later, the army had to withdraw over some of the most hostile territory in the world, short of supplies, carrying more than 2000 sick and wounded and harassed by a skilled and ruthless enemy. They crossed the Sinai Desert in four days, while mutiny was narrowly averted. Back in Egyptian territory with a third of his force dead, wounded or sick, Bonaparte continued to put a brave face on his defeat. He held a triumphal parade through Cairo which was enough to fool those who had not been at Acre.

★

Smith decided to follow up his success by an offensive in Egypt itself. Using a Turkish fleet of 7 ships of the line, 5 frigates and 58 smaller vessels and a force of 20,000 assorted troops based in Rhodes, he planned a landing in Egypt. The force arrived off Alexandria on 11 July, where the French sighted it from the signal post and sent out men to oppose the attack, which they knew could only take place in Aboukir Bay. Before they could get there, 3000 men had been landed and the fort on the Aboukir peninsula was attacked. However, the tiny garrison of the fort resisted for a week, after which the rest of the Turkish force was able to disembark on the beach. They did not move inland but dug entrenchments in the bay.

Bonaparte was in the interior when he received news of this and he went straight to Aboukir at the head of 10,000 men. He arrived on the 24th and battle began the next day. Small gunboats were placed in the Bay to help disrupt any landing by

Defeat of the Turks at Aboukir, painted by Le Jeune. Bonaparte is on the dark horse, centre left, with the town and Aboukir Fort and promontory in the background. (Musée de Versailles)

Turkish reinforcements. The French cavalry charged while the infantry fought its way through the entrenchments and the Turks were routed. Smith could only watch in dismay from the *Tigre*, anchored in deep water in the bay, as 2000 Turks were killed by the French or drowned in the sea, while 2500 more were besieged in the fort of Aboukir and eventually starved out. The rest retreated to the boats.

Thus Bonaparte had defeated two Turkish armies, at Mount Tabor and at Aboukir, but he was still cut off from France and unable to progress in any direction, with a depleted and demoralised army and a rebellious local population. Even before his victory at Aboukir he had decided to risk the British blockade and

Bonaparte just after his seizure of power. His speech to the former rulers, the Council of Five Hundred, has been badly received and soldiers are moving in to escort him from the hall. (Mansell Collection)

go home. Command would devolve on General Kléber, though his relations with the General-in-Chief were already strained.

On 22 August 1799, almost exactly a year after he had heard the news of the Battle of the Nile, he issued another proclamation.

> In view of the news from Europe I have decided to leave for France. I leave General Kléber in command of the army.
>
> The army will soon have news of me; I can say no more. It is hard for me to leave the soldiers to whom I am most attached; but it be only for a time, and the new commander-in-chief has the confidence of the government and myself.[18]

Half an hour after sunset that night, Bonaparte emerged from among the dunes of Aboukir Bay and after a tense wait boarded a boat from the frigate *Muiron* and was rowed out to the ship. Taking advantage of darkness and the relative weakness of the blockading force, in the absence of Sidney Smith on a mission to Cyprus, the frigate set sail in company with another, the *Carrère*, and two smaller vessels. By sunrise on the morning of the 23rd they were west of Alexandria and beyond the visual range of the British and Turkish cruisers. The winds were from the north-west, forcing the ships to sail close-hauled along the coast of Africa but eventually on 11 September they found an easterly wind which carried them as far as Sardinia. After that the *mistral* blowing from the north-west forced them to take refuge in Bonaparte's home town of Ajaccio. Finally on 7 October the coast of France was sighted and Bonaparte stepped ashore at Frejus at 10am the following morning, after an absence of nearly 17 months. He left immediately for Paris.

As Napoleon Bonaparte crept away from his demoralised army on 23 August, few could have predicted that his greatest days were still ahead of him: that he would have an incalculable effect on European history, giving his name to a regime, to the most extensive war that had ever been fought and to the age itself. The Egyptian campaign, however, removed his aura of invincibility. Even if he could evade responsibility for Nelson's defeat of Brueys, he would have to admit to a personal defeat by another British sailor, Sir Sidney Smith, in alliance with Djezzar Pasha. He had failed as a colonial administrator, losing the support of both the Maltese and the Egyptians. His reputation for loyalty to his troops had also been damaged by his flight from Egypt. What had he gained from the experience? The occupation of Malta and Egypt provided Bonaparte with his first taste of government. He never learned to cope with the cut-and-thrust of real politics, not to mention the delays and compromises caused by the need to debate everything openly. He was to be much more successful as an administrator and his experience in ruling Egypt may have helped him see a solution for France, in the exercise of his own personal power.

CHAPTER 18

The Rise of the Hero

ON 19 SEPTEMBER the city of Naples had a rehearsal for Nelson's arrival when the *Culloden* and *Alexander* were sighted off the port and King Ferdinand went out at the head of a long procession of boats, including one carrying the Hamiltons and their companion Miss Cornelia Knight. On the way the boats passed the two ships of the line, close enough for Hamilton to speak to some of the crew through the gunports. He called out to the seamen, 'My lads! That is the king, whom you have saved, with his family and kingdom.' With bemused deference the men replied, 'Very glad of it, sir – very glad of it.'[1]

The real celebration began 3 days later, when the crippled *Vanguard* finally appeared over the horizon and headed in painfully slowly, in light winds and with a thrice-damaged rig. The King, perhaps misjudging the speed of Nelson's flagship, was rowed out 9 miles to sea, followed by an even larger gathering of barges and boats, while thousands of less privileged spectators lined the shore. At 9am the Hamiltons came on board and Emma, always ready with a dramatic gesture, collapsed in front of Nelson, exclaiming 'Oh God! Is it possible?'.[2] The Royal barge eventually reached the *Vanguard* an hour later and the King came on board. Nelson paid his respects, the King took him by the hand and addressed him as 'deliverer and preserver' and Nelson showed him round the ship, during which tour he paid much attention to the wounded seamen. His Majesty sat down to breakfast in the Admiral's quarters, along with a little bird which had settled in the cabin the day before and was regarded as a good omen by the superstitious seamen. Less auspicious was the arrival of Francesco Caracciolo, Duke of Brienza and commander of the Neapolitan navy. He was already jealous of Nelson, it was said, because he felt he had been slighted by him during Hotham's action in 1795.[3]

Nelson was rowed ashore and was feted by the common people of Naples, who shouted out 'viva Nelson' every time he appeared in the streets. The local bands has hastily learned *Rule Britannia* and *See the Conquering Hero Comes* to add to their usual repertoire of *God Save the King*. Count Esterhazy hosted a ball for the admiral and then on Nelson's 40th birthday on 29 September, Hamilton organised a great fete in a ballroom dominated by a rostral column inscribed with the names of Nelson and his captains.[4]

Nelson arriving at Naples. A later drawing by Giacomo Guardi, which seems to underestimate the amount of interest shown by the local population. (National Maritime Museum, London: PAG9746)

He went to stay with the Hamiltons in their city home, the Palazzo Sessa. Visited by the great men of Europe over the 34 years since Sir William had first lived there, it was described by one of the most famous, Goethe.

> The rooms he has decorated in the English taste are charming, and the view from the corner room is perhaps unique. Below us the sea, Capri facing us, Posillipo to the right, the Villa Reale promenade nearer by, to the left an old Jesuit building, in the distance the coast from Sorrento to Capo Minerva. There may well be nothing in Europe to match this, at any rate not in the middle of a large populous city.[5]

But there is no sign that Nelson ever appreciated such scenic beauty, unlike his former second-in-command, Saumarez.

Nelson could find no rest and he wrote to his wife, 'Our time here is actively employed; and between business and what is called pleasure, I am not my master for five minutes.'[6] The crippled ships had to be repaired, especially the *Culloden*, which was sent to the Neapolitan arsenal at Castellamare, 20 miles across Naples Bay. The Mediterranean had few dry-docks as such, except for the French ones at Toulon, for in the days before steam power it was difficult to empty them in a tideless sea. The only way to repair the bottom of a ship was to 'careen' her, or 'heave her down'. She was brought alongside a jetty and emptied of everything – stores, rigging, upper masts and guns. Her gunports on one side were closed and sealed, and strong tackles were attached to the heads of her lower masts. The ship was heeled over until one side of her bottom was exposed, allowing repairs to take place. It was a dangerous and tiresome procedure with a large ship, only used when there was no alternative. Neapolitan carpenters did 849 man-days of work on the hull of the *Culloden*, replacing her damaged keel and stem post, while hundreds of pounds worth of rope and rigging equipment were bought for the *Vanguard*, *Minotaur* and *Goliath*.[7] Meanwhile the *Alexander* was given new masts from stocks which had been sent out by St Vincent when he heard of the damage to the *Vanguard*, while the flagship's own masts were 'fished' yet again. Nelson believed they would 'hold fast until I can send her to Gibraltar, some months hence.' There were deficiencies in other stores and Nelson wrote to St Vincent of the 'great distress for slops [seamen's clothing] and beds.'[8]

Nelson also began to catch up on home news. He had received three of his wife's letters before he got to Naples but still had no turn for domestic affairs and, among many pages on his own activities, he wrote only a few lines in direct reply to her. 'As to Round Wood if the place or neighbourhood is not to your satisfaction, I hope the country will put me in a situation of choosing another, but my dear Fanny, unless you can game, and talk scandal, that is lies, most probably your company will never be coveted by country town tabbies.'[9]

Nelson was already beginning to appreciate the charms of Lady Hamilton, who fed him with asses' milk and brought him back to health as his wife had done last year. But as yet Nelson's loyalty to Fanny was not under test. In his first letter after his arrival back in Naples, he wrote to Lady Nelson, 'I hope one day to have the pleasure of introducing you to Lady Hamilton. She is one of the very best women in the world. How few could ever have made the turn she has. She is an honour to her sex and a proof that even reputation may be regained, but I own it requires a great soul.'[10] At the same time he wrote a rather formal letter to Lady Hamilton, addressing her as 'My Dear Madam' and concluding 'Your Ladyship will, I beg, receive this letter as a preparative for Sir William Hamilton, to whom I am writing.'[11] Soon after, he was asked if the Battle of the Nile was the happiest day of his life. He replied, apparently sincerely, 'No; the happiest was that on which I married Lady Nelson.'[12] In December Emma Hamilton herself wrote to Lady Nelson, in terms which suggest she had nothing to be ashamed of.[13]

By 9 October Nelson had seen enough of Naples. It was 'a country of fiddlers and poets, whores and scoundrels.'[14] The harbour was too open and his ships had been subjected to a heavy swell during their repairs.[15] He was unimpressed with the city which, he wrote, 'sees this squadron no more' after they departed on the 15th.[16] He intended to devote his attention to the blockade and reduction of Malta, where he expected the French occupiers to surrender soon. He planned to use Syracuse as his base, for it was much closer to Malta and Nelson had fond memories of his visit in July. 'Syracuse in future, whilst my operations lie on the eastern side of Sicily, is my port, where every refreshment may be had for a fleet.'[17]

★

The people of Malta had become increasingly unhappy since the beginning of the French occupation, especially with the Republican policy of looting the treasures of their churches. On 26 August Regnaud, the civil governor, reported 'a fanatical agitation having shown itself amongst the people.'[18] Two days later Admiral Villeneuve arrived in his flagship the *Guillaume Tell*, following his escape from Nile, and the French began to get ready for a British blockade. News of the French defeat began to spread among the islanders and on 2 September French officials, attempting to put church treasures on public auction throughout the island, were confronted in the ancient capital of Mdina and forced to retreat to Valletta. The revolt had begun and within a few days the French forces were besieged within the walls of the city.

It was essential for the rebels to make contact with the British fleet, to get supplies of arms and to blockade the French in Valletta. On 25 September a deputation of Maltese managed to find Saumarez's ships, sailing past on their way to Gibraltar with the prizes of the Nile. Saumarez suggested sending a message to the French demanding a surrender, to which General Vaubois quickly replied;

> You have without doubt forgotten that Frenchmen are now at Malta. The future of its inhabitants is a matter which does not concern you. With regard to your summons to surrender, Frenchmen do not understand such style.[19]

Saumarez landed more than 1000 muskets with 18,000 cartridges for the support of the rebellion and went on his way, sending a message to Nelson in Naples by the frigate *Terpsichore*. On 6 October Captain Alexander Ball left there for the island in the *Alexander* with two frigates, a sloop and a fireship, beginning an association between Ball and Malta which would last until his death.

Vaubois's 3000 French troops had supplies for less than a year but found it was still possible to circumvent the blockade. 'One can come from the coasts of Italy and France and enter easily when the north-westerly wind forces our enemies to steer under the wind.'[20] According to Nelson's information they had 'Corn for eighteen months, and mills, plenty of oil, very little cheese; scarce the smallest taste of anything else. The aqueduct is cut off, but they have wells not likely to fail but in summer.' Nelson arrived on 24 October and the next day he again summoned Vaubois to surrender, to meet another refusal. More supplies were sent to the rebels but on the 31st Nelson set sail back to Naples with the *Minotaur* and *Vanguard*, leaving Ball in command. The French were isolated in Malta but they were not fully blockaded and the siege was to last far longer than anyone expected. Though the blockading forces were under Nelson's command, he payed less and less attention to the island, for his interests were diverted elsewhere.

★

On 5 November Nelson arrived back in Naples in the *Minotaur* – a visit which was to have momentous consequences. He was soon to become involved in several episodes which would seriously damage his reputation and credibility. What was the Admiral's state of health and mind over these crucial months? He was still suffering from the effects of his wound and endured headaches which made him unusually bad-tempered. However, medical opinion is not clear on the full effects of the wound. Surgeon Michael Jefferson had made light of it at the time and medical histories do not suggest that it had any long-term consequences, though some of Nelson's biographers have implied that it does much to explain his actions in the 2 years following the battle. He was not unconscious for any length of time, so the injury was probably not serious enough to cause a major and permanent change in his personality.

Perhaps the effects of prolonged stress were more serious. He had been through many extreme ups and downs throughout the campaign but his eventual triumph attracted extravagant praise, perhaps best illustrated by the historical perspectives of

Sir William Hamilton. It was 'A battle . . . of the greatest importance that was ever fought, and the expected good consequences, of which are incalculable. History, either ancient of modern, does not record an action that does more honour to the heroes that gained the victory.'[21] This sort of language, combined with his religious fervour, perhaps went to his head in a different way and gave him a feeling of invincibility.

The news from home was not entirely to Nelson's satisfaction. He received the thanks of both Houses of Parliament, a pension of £2000 per annum, letters from numerous dignitaries and was awarded the freedom of many cities. As the ultimate reward for his efforts, he was raised to the peerage as Baron Nelson of the Nile and Burnham Thorpe (his birthplace) in the County of Norfolk. The home government had discussed this intensively and regarded it as a fair and almost unprecedented reward for such a junior admiral, who was merely commanding a detachment from the main fleet. Nelson was not satisfied with this, the lowest of five ranks in the peerage. He had won a far more decisive victory than St Vincent's 18 months earlier and even that had relied heavily on Nelson's unauthorised initiative; but Jervis, as commander-in-chief, had been created an earl, two stages higher than Nelson's barony. Lady Hamilton commented, 'If I was King of England I would make you the most noble puissant Duke Nelson, Marquis Nile, Earl Alexandria, Viscount Pyramid, Baron Crocodile and Prince Victory, that posterity might have you in all forms.'[22]

He was further dissatisfied with the recognition of Troubridge, his favourite among the captains. Because the *Culloden* had not actually been engaged in the battle, the promotion of her first lieutenant was not confirmed by the Admiralty, which Nelson regarded as a slight both to himself and to Troubridge. He wrote to St Vincent, 'For Heaven's sake, for my sake, if it be so, get it altered. Our dear friend Troubridge has endured enough . . . he deserves every word which a grateful country can bestow.'[23] Among other irritants was the behaviour of his stepson Josiah Nisbet, now captain of the frigate *Thalia*. He had constant disputes with his officers and had to be rebuked by his mother. 'My dear Josiah take yourself to account every day. Don't excuse any foibles. I do assure you your first lieutenant has always wrote of you in a handsome manner. I have seen his letters to his mother. Silence on this subject.'[24] But late in September Josiah was one of the first to see the burgeoning relationship between Nelson and Emma Hamilton, perhaps before the participants themselves were aware of their own feelings. At the ball to celebrate Nelson's birthday, he accused Lady Hamilton of having supplanted his mother and was hustled out of the room by Troubridge.[25]

Another slight came in December, when Nelson received news that Captain Sir Sidney Smith was to command the forces operating off the coast of Egypt, apparently without any reference to Nelson, his senior officer. Since Smith had been given diplomatic as well as military status, his orders were addressed to 'All admirals, generals and officers, military as well as civil, of His Britannic Majesty' and enjoined them to give every assistance.[26] This was highly offensive to Nelson and he wrote 'I do feel, for I am a man, that it is impossible for me to serve in these seas with the squadron under a junior officer – who could have thought it? – and from Earl Spencer! Never, never was I so astonished as your letter made me.'[27] St Vincent had to placate him by writing, 'On the subject of Sir Sidney Smith, there must certainly have been some very great misunderstanding, as it was never our intention here that he should consider himself as a Commander-in-Chief, or that he should be authorised to take a single gunboat even from your command without your orders.'[28] Nelson wrote to Spencer Smith, Sidney's brother in Constantinople, 'I could not like to have any junior in some measure placed, if not over my head, at least taking from my conse-quence. I did not think it was necessary for any sea officer to be joined in signing a treaty which you had brought to such a happy issue; but if it was, I shall ever think that sea officer should have been *Nelson*.'[29] Much of the trouble was eventually cleared up and put down to Nelson's misreading of the situation; but one suspects that the basic problem was that there was no room for two Nelsons in the same fleet. In any case, his attitude to Smith began to improve after the siege of Acre.

All this seemed to contrast with his reception in Naples, where in December he was made Duke of Bronte in Sicily and given an estate there, though by convention he was not expected to use a foreign title in British territory. From the Sultan of Turkey he received the most striking of all his decorations – the chelengk, a spray of Brazilian diamonds to be worn in the hat, with a cluster in the centre which glittered as it slowly rotated, powered by clockwork.

Nelson was new to political influence but he was emerging as part of a British triumvirate which had reached pre-eminence in the Two Sicilies. Sir William

Nelson's chelengk; a plume of Brazilian diamonds and a central star which turned clockwise to glitter in the light. This photograph is the only one known of it, since it was stolen and broken up in 1951. (National Maritime Museum, London: 3969)

Hamilton provided the diplomatic and political skills, his wife supplied the charm and Nelson, with the air of a conqueror, contributed the military and naval backing. As he wrote to his wife, 'Good Sir William, Lady Hamilton and myself, are the mainsprings of the machine, which manage what is going on in this country.'[30] After his desperate loneliness during the chase of the French, the appeal of such a co-operative effort was irresistible to Nelson. He was always deferential to royalty, even when he had had Prince William under his command more than a decade earlier. In the face of real or imagined slights from home, the adulation of the Neapolitans, from the King to the meanest peasant, was intoxicating. After all he was a Duke there but a mere Baron anywhere else in the world. The victory at the Nile, after so many vicissitudes, made him feel he was blessed by fortune. In the period from November 1798 to July 1799 he can be accused of three major errors of judgment in his professional capacity, all brought on by his obsession with the Kingdom of Naples.

★

In the first place, he interfered in military-political affairs, of which, as events were soon to show, he had little real understanding. His participation in land campaigns was often disastrous. At Calvi in Corsica in 1794 he had been reasonably successful despite the loss of the sight of his eye, though he always felt that his work had never been fully recognised. At Tenerife in 1797, as well as the loss of his arm, he had jeopardized a force of 1000 men against 8000. A few years later he would lead an attack on Boulogne in which he would suffer heavy losses and gain nothing. His advocacy of the attack on Rome, however, had far more serious consequences than any of his other misjudgments.

Miniature of Ferdinand of Naples by Biaggio di
Costanza. (National Maritime Museum, London:
B3173B)

An amphibious attack on Livorno was decided on first, in order to disrupt French communications in northern Italy. This was well within an admiral's usual duties to attack the enemy and his allies on his coasts. But at 6am on 13 November, on the eve of sailing, he went to the King. His Majesty was in some distress, fearful of the French forces which intelligence reports showed were massing in Rome, ready for an attack on Naples. Nelson urged him to have courage, for he had confidence in the Neapolitan army, confirming the judgement of its commander General Mack, that it was 'La plus belle armee d'Europe'. Nelson told the King that he had two choices; 'Either to advance, trusting to God for his blessing on a just cause, to die with "l'épée a la main", or to remain quiet and be kicked out of your kingdoms.'[31] This advice was in contradiction of Nelson's own opinion of himself, as expressed to St Vincent in April 1799. 'I own myself, My dear Lord, myself much fitter to be the actor, than the counsellor of proper measures to be pursued.'[32] But the King was convinced and agreed with Nelson's plan. The army was mobilised and General Mack was given orders to march on Rome.

The attack was also in contradiction of British government policy. Austria was still seen as the centre of a potential alliance and was not yet ready for war. It was important that any conflict be seen as a reaction to French aggression, not something clearly provoked by the British. When the Austrians heard of the attack they assumed that it had been set up to cause their entry to the war, a suggestion which infuriated Lord Grenville, the British Foreign Secretary.[33]

The move on Livorno was a complete success. Nelson arrived off the port on 29 November, with three British ships of the line, three smaller vessels and the Portuguese squadron. The British and Neapolitan ambassadors came on board. The governor of the town agreed to surrender and troops and cannon were landed. Nelson

Queen Maria–Carolina of Naples. (National Maritime Museum, London: 4933)

left Troubridge in command on the 30th and was back in Naples by 5 December.

The attack on Rome seemed equally successful. The Neapolitan army was commanded by General Mack, lent by Austria, and it outnumbered the enemy forces by two to one. The French prudently withdrew and on 29 November King Ferdinand entered the Eternal City in triumph. But his success lasted little more than a week. The French troops, far more experienced than the Neapolitans, quickly regrouped and counter-attacked, forcing Ferdinand to retreat in haste. The Neapolitan troops panicked, leaving their own capital open to attack and the French had a perfect excuse to invade Neapolitan territory. Nelson's ships, now arrived back from Livorno, provided the only hope of salvation for Ferdinand and his court. They decided to abandon mainland Italy and flee to their Sicilian capital, Palermo.

Getting the Royal family on board Nelson's ships was a very tricky business, for any hint of their desertion would cause riots and panic in the city. According to Miss Knight, 'The populace had become very riotous, crowding about the King's place, beseeching His Majesty not to leave them. It was even unsafe for strangers to be in the streets, unless well known; for all foreigners were liable to be mistaken for Frenchmen.'[34] Despite the haste and secrecy, Nelson did everything possible to make the *Vanguard* comfortable for the Royal party. Sailmakers were set to work making canvas cots for them, the wardroom and the cabins under the poop were painted and the log records the unusual activity (for a naval officer at least) of 'smuggling on board the Queen's diamonds etc.'[35] In the cold, dark night of 21 December, boats were loaded for a long row to the ships, which were anchored well offshore for fear that the Neapolitan forts might be betrayed and fire on them. Miss Knight's party could not be accommodated in the *Vanguard* so was sent on to one of the Portuguese ships, where high-ranking refugees of several countries were gathered in the great cabin, to the distress of her commodore whose manners were 'by no means prepossessing'.[36]

The squadron sailed at 7pm on 23 December. On Christmas Eve, the *Vanguard* found herself in danger once again, when a storm blew up. Nelson had clearly learnt the lessons of the gales off Toulon 7 months earlier. All sails were furled except the three topsails, which were reefed; nevertheless they were torn apart by the wind. One sail on the mizzen mast was blown to pieces, though it was furled at the time. Even Nelson was impressed with the force of the wind – 'It blew harder than I ever experienced since I have been at sea,' he wrote to St Vincent.[37] On Christmas Day, when the *Vanguard* was already in sight of Palermo, Prince Albert, the youngest child of Ferdinand and Caroline, died in the arms of Lady Hamilton, who did her best to comfort the distraught mother. Showing the heroic side of her character, she tended to the needs of the Royal family and never slept during the 3-day voyage. The *Vanguard* discharged most of her passengers in the morning of the 26th, the Queen going ashore in the early morning darkness to avoid being seen in her tearful condition. After sharing such a voyage, the five principals – the King, Queen, Nelson and the Hamiltons – had become bonded together in a way which would affect the judgement of all of them.

As well as the death of her son, the Queen grieved for the loss of most of her

Kingdom. Ferdinand was less concerned, for the hunting at Palermo was at least as good as that at Naples. Sir William Hamilton was distressed because many of his private treasures had been left behind in the flight from Naples. Others he had already sent home in the *Colossus* with wounded from the Nile and he would have been considerably more distressed had he known then that the ship had been lost by grounding on the Isles of Scilly on 10 December.

The city of Palermo had a striking situation, on a fine bay under the north-western mountains of Sicily. It formed a square, enclosed within high walls. On the north side, 'the walls are surmounted with noble palaces belonging to the powerful people of the island, at one of which Sir William Hamilton . . . resided, and at his house Lord Nelson took up his abode, where often the officers of the Navy were received with great hospitality.'[38] The King and his family were able to occupy the Royal palaces but some of their followers had to had to find accommodation in the town's single inn, a disreputable place once run by 'a noisy troublesome Frenchwoman . . . fat as a pig, as ugly as the devil, and lays on a quantity of paint that looks like a great plaister of red morocco.'[39]

Meanwhile the long-term effects of an exhausting campaign began to catch up with Nelson. One of his staunchest defenders describes his state as one of 'despondency and listlessness'.[40] His *amour propre* was obvious, as when he spoke to Pryse Lockhart Gordon, an English visitor to Palermo. 'Pray sir, have you ever heard of the Battle of the Nile? . . . that, sir, was the most extraordinary one ever fought, and it is unique, sir, for three reasons; first, for its having been fought at night; secondly, for its having been fought at anchor; and thirdly been gained by an admiral with one arm.' Nelson bowed with each of these assertions (only the third of which was absolutely true) causing Gordon to think that 'had the speech been made *after* dinner, I should have imagined the hero had imbibed an extra dose of champagne'.[41]

After 3 months of intense loneliness in pursuit of the French fleet, Nelson began to find all the things he had lacked for so long – love, political influence, public adulation and relative comfort. He had tired of life on board, of the plain cooking of Anthony Leary, the insolence and incompetence of his servant Thomas Allen, the laziness of his secretary John Campbell and the confines of his ship. When he went back on board the flagship in May his cabin, where he had lived and worked for 3 vital months leading up to the battle, seemed like 'a solitary cell', the ship itself 'dreary and uncomfortable', a striking contrast to the society of Palermo and the love of Lady Hamilton.[42]

It was probably at this time that Nelson's relationship with Emma Hamilton became a physical one. She was much maligned because of her vulgarity, her exhibitionism and her clear influence on Britain's greatest naval hero. Her attractions were equally obvious to any who cared to look for them. To a young officer under Nelson's command, 'Her generosity and good nature were unbounded – her talents and spirit unequalled; and to my knowledge, her heart was of softer materials than to rejoice in the sufferings of the enemies of the court [of Naples].'[43] She was of course an actress at heart. She had a beautiful and expressive face, which shows a different aspect in each of the numerous portraits of her. At private parties she never

Lady Hamilton performing one of her
'Attitudes', from a series of prints
published in 1799 by George Townly
Stubbs. (National Maritime Museum,
London: C1399)

missed an excuse to perform her celebrated 'attitudes' in which she posed as figures
from the Classics. Her unrestrained admiration of Nelson was intoxicating to a man
emerging from the isolation of naval command. As Nelson wrote more than a year
later, 'I did remember well the 12th February and also the months afterwards. I shall
never be sorry for the consequences.'[44] It is not clear whether this refers to 1799 or
1800 but certainly there was more opportunity in the earlier year, when both were
settled in Palermo.

★

After their conquest of Naples and the rest of southern Italy, the French set up the
'Parthenopean (or Vesuvian) Republic', supported by many enlightened elements
of the professional and merchant classes but opposed by the peasantry and by the
lazzaroni, the fiery proletariat of the city of Naples. In February 1799, the Neapolitan court began to fight back against the Republicans. Cardinal Fabrizio Ruffo
was sent to lead a rising in the extreme south of the mainland and he was increasingly successful, especially after most of the French troops were withdrawn to
fight against Austria, which declared war on 12 March. Nelson sent Troubridge to
blockade Naples, though in May he had to concentrate his forces off Marittimo off
the western end of Sicily to meet the threat posed by Admiral Bruix's fleet (see
Chapter 19). As they advanced, Ruffo's ill-disciplined army committed many out-
rages on the conquered, using the cover of the Royal flag to settle private vendettas.
By mid-June they were on the outskirts of Naples and by the 16th, the Neapolitan
Republican forces were besieged in the forts of Uovo and Nuovo, with the French
in the Castle of St Elmo.

   In the Bay of Naples, Captain Edward Foote of the *Seahorse*, who had already
distinguished himself in the capture of the *Sensible* while looking for Nelson's fleet,
was in command of a force of frigates and Neapolitan galleys. He supported the

Royalists in their bombardments of the Republican-held forts and on 16 June a boat came out from the naval arsenal at Castellamare with a flag of truce. Foote agreed that the garrison should march out with full military honours, give up their arms and then disperse. He told them that 'relying on British generosity they trust you will receive such of them on board your ship as think proper to avail themselves of the protection of the British flag.'[45] The Union flag was hoisted on shore and 320 rebels came on board the *Seahorse*. Several gunboats were captured and used to bombard the forts in Naples from the sea. On 18 June an armistice was agreed between Foote and the rebels of Ouvo and Nuovo, with Foote offering 'an asylum under the flag of my sovereign.'[46] Eventually it was agreed, with the support of Ruffo, that the defeated rebels would be sent to Toulon.

Nelson took some time to get to Naples, because he had been diverted by orders to patrol off Cape Marittimo. Reaching the island of Ischia off the city on the 24th, with the Hamiltons on board, he made his second great error of judgement. Horrified on hearing the news from Foote, he wrote,

> That as to rebels and traitors, no power on earth has a right to stand between their Gracious King and them; they must instantly throw themselves on the clemency of their Sovereign, for no other terms will be allowed them.[47]

The Queen was even more outraged.

> To capitulate with one's rebel subjects, who were without force, without hope of succour, either by sea or land!!! . . . I feel it dishonourable to treat with rebels!! They ought to have been attacked in full force, or left alone till a more favourable opportunity presented itself.[48]

The rebel garrisons surrendered on the 27th, without any military honours. The leaders were taken on board ships of the naval squadron, others into small polaccas in the harbour, which at first they hoped would take them to Toulon. Instead, large numbers of them were executed under the authority of King Ferdinand, or as part of the revenge of the ill-disciplined *lazzoroni* against men and women, some of whom at least were no more than innocent victims of class hatred. Naples became for a while a bloodbath, amid scenes of daily savagery. Bishops, physicians and professors as well as workmen and peasants suffered degrading and humiliating deaths. Nelson personally discouraged many appeals for clemency, believing that loyalty to the throne was, or ought to be, absolute and that 'rebels, Jacobins and fools' deserved no mercy.

The tone of events can perhaps be gauged by a letter from Joseph Vitella, sending the head of a captured rebel to Thomas Troubridge. 'As a faithful subject of my King, Ferdinand IV (whom God preserve) I have the glory of presenting to your excellency the head of D. Charles Granozio di Giffoni . . . I beg your excellency would accept the said head, and consider this operation as proof of my attachment to the Royal Crown, and am with due respect a faithful subject of the King.' He apologised for not sending it to Nelson but the journey was longer and the heat would have caused it to decay.[49]

Caracciolo, the Neapolitan admiral, had ended up on the side of the rebels and was also captured. His trial and execution were separate from the persecution of the other rebels but also attracted revulsion. Nelson, however, was not afraid to have his name associated with it. Caracciolo was brought on board the *Foudroyant* as a prisoner on 29 June, escorted by British marines. He was tried by Neapolitan officers in the wardroom. By midday he had been condemned to hang and his requests to be shot as befitted his rank, rather than 'hung up like a felon and a dog' were adamantly refused by Nelson.[50] He asked for time to prepare himself but within 2 hours his corpse was dangling in chains from the yardarm of the Neapolitan frigate *Minerva*, before being dumped in the sea. Two days later the King, Sir John Acton and the Hamiltons arrived on board the flagship and Nelson gave up the great cabin to His Majesty. A few days later the body of Caracciolo, insufficiently weighted by his executioners, floated to the surface of Naples Bay alongside the *Foudroyant*, within sight of the King who 'turned pale, and, letting his spyglass fall on deck, uttered an exclamation of horror'.[51] The superstitious, numerous among the seamen and the Neapolitans, remembered this for a very long time.

The persecution of the 'Jacobins' did not attract the censure of Nelson's superiors. The most public criticism was made by Charles James Fox, the leader of the opposition, in the House of Commons in February 1800. Opposing a motion thanking the King for refusing to negotiate with the French, he claimed that not all the atrocities in the war had been carried out by the enemy. The recapture of Naples had, he asserted, been 'stained and polluted by murders so ferocious, and by cruelties of every kind so abhorrent, that the heart shudders at the recital.'[52] This part of the attack was ignored by the government and the vote was carried by 264 votes to 65. Indeed Fox was so discredited and isolated at this stage in his career that his censure did Nelson more good than harm. But it does not absolve him from blame for what happened.

There are two main parts to the criticism of Nelson: that in refusing to accept the terms guaranteed by Foote he degraded the honour of a British officer; and that he failed to use his influence to reduce the bloodshed after the surrender. Nelson's supporters have produced a convincing case that he was within the letter of the law in his actions.[53] As to his personal feelings, he was consistent in his hatred of republicanism, which he called Jacobinism, after the faction which had ruled France for 18 months during the most extreme phase of the Revolution. He was a strong disciplinarian himself, who believed in the 'carrot and stick' approach; 'I ever preach that rewards and punishments are the foundation of all good government.'[54] The strong suspicion remains, however, that he was too much involved in Neapolitan affairs to take an objective view and that he allowed this to override his normal humanitarian instincts. He was completely in thrall to the King and court of Naples and not likely to oppose the King's wishes. Yet again the stress of his months of lonely command, combined with the effect of his head wound, seem to have taken their toll.

★

Nelson's third great error was to disobey his orders to take a substantial part of his force to Minorca, in circumstances which did him little credit. When the French Admiral Bruix escaped from Brest and entered the Mediterranean with a large fleet (see Chapter 19), St Vincent and his new deputy, Vice-Admiral Lord Keith, saw the importance of concentrating forces to meet them. By this time there were four separate naval operations in the Mediterranean, only two of which were under Nelson. Minorca, captured by Admiral Duckworth and General Stuart in November 1798, was now a key base which had to be defended. Co-operation with the Turks and blockading the French in Egypt was now under the control of Sir Sydney Smith. Nelson, who had won the naval initiative off the coast of Egypt, was left with operations in the central Mediterranean – the blockade of Malta (which was rather neglected at this point) and support of the Kingdom of the Two Sicilies – a task which was to involve more and more of his energy and his personal commitment. Chasing Bruix and blockading Toulon now became the major operation, mainly under the control of Lord Keith.

Nelson, however, believed himself tied to Palermo by a promise to King Ferdinand that he would not desert him until the last rebels were crushed. At this stage the towns of Capua and Caserta were still holding out and Nelson sent seamen ashore to help in the siege of Capua. For this he was eventually rebuked by the Admiralty: 'although in operations on the sea-coast, it may frequently be highly expedient to land a part of the seamen of the squadron to co-operate with and assist the army, when the situation will admit of their being immediately re-embarked, if the squadron should be called away to act elsewhere, or if information of the approach of an enemy's fleet should be received – yet their lordships cannot approve of the seamen being landed to form part of an army at a distance from the coast.'[55]

Even more serious, he had no right to promise the services of a British fleet to a foreign sovereign. He wrote to St Vincent on 28 May, 'My reason for remaining in Sicily is the covering of the blockade of Naples, and the certainty of preserving Sicily in case of an attack, for if we were to withdraw our ships, it would throw such a damp on the people that I am sure there would be no resistance.'[56] On 13 July Nelson received direct orders from Keith, that he should send all the ships he could spare to Minorca unless he had definite information of Bruix's squadron being in the area. Nelson refused to do this, claiming that the withdrawal of any of his ships would be a severe blow to the morale of the Neapolitans. He explained his actions to Spencer. 'Lord Keith writes me, if certain events take place, it may be necessary to draw down this squadron for the protection of Minorca. Should such an order come at this moment, it would be a cause for some consideration whether Minorca should be risked, or the two kingdoms of Naples and Sicily? I rather think my decision would be to risk the former.'[57] Certainly Nelson had an arguable case in saying that Naples and Sicily were more important than Minorca, and that the loss of Sicily, in particular, to the French would destroy Britain's position in the Mediterranean. But whether he was right or not, Nelson was subverting discipline by writing to the First Lord questioning the orders of his commander-in-chief in such terms.

In the past Nelson's credit at the Admiralty had allowed him to make alterations to the great cabin of his flagship and to change the order of seniority of his lieutenants. He was allowed to ignore orders in battle when this brought success, as at Cape St Vincent. Now his disobedience was on a different scale. He was interfering in matters of politics, strategy and diplomacy, though he had no great qualifications in any of these fields. His rebuke, written by the Secretary of the Admiralty on 20 August, was severe.

> Although the co-operation of a British naval force with the army of His Sicilian Majesty might be, and it appears to have been necessary, yet . . . it does not appear to their Lordships to have been necessary that the whole of the squadron under your command should have been kept for such co-operation, but that a part of it would have been sufficient . . . and that their Lordships do not, therefore, from any information now before them, see sufficient reason to justify your having disobeyed the orders you had received from your commanding officer, or having left Minorca exposed to the risk of being attacked, without having naval force to protect it.[58]

In his personal letter Spencer was more conciliatory, as always. Keith was 'certainly right' in sending Nelson's orders and 'nothing but the strongest necessity could justify you in disobeying them . . . I trust however that you will have sufficiently considered the extreme importance of providing for the security of Minorca . . . to have induced you to have taken the first opportunity of calling the seamen and marines to their ships and of detaching such parts of your squadron as may have appeared requisite.'[59]

Keith's aim in all this was to use Nelson's fleet to protect Minorca from an invasion from Majorca, which seemed an imminent possibility at that moment. He wanted to free his own fleet for a chase of Bruix leading, he hoped, to a decisive fleet battle – an eminently Nelsonian aim and one which should have found favour with his supporters through the ages, such as Captain Alfred Thayer Mahan, the great naval apostle of the late nineteenth century, who in his *Influence of Sea Power upon History* quoted Napoleon to the effect that dividing one's fleet in the face of a strong enemy was 'a glaring piece of stupidity. The lesson is the same in all ages.'[60] Now it was Nelson who, completely contrary to his attitude before the Nile, was dispersing his resources in land warfare and in small detachments, even as an enemy fleet was at sea.

This was of a different order from Nelson's more celebrated disobediences, at Cape St Vincent and later at Copenhagen, when he turned a blind eye to his Admiral's signal. In both those cases Nelson was at the centre of the battle, better placed than the commander-in-chief to see the situation. In the real naval campaign of 1799, the neutralising of Bruix's fleet, Nelson was no nearer to the centre than Keith. The question of whether to protect Naples or Minorca (if that was really the issue) was not one for a rear-admiral to make, especially one whose judgement was clouded by personal involvement and whose private affairs were so deeply entangled with the politics of Naples.

In June 1799 Nelson was further hurt by news of St Vincent's intention to leave the fleet and begged, 'for the sake of our country, do not quit us at this serious moment.'[61] But the commander-in-chief was ill, worn out and increasingly aged. He was replaced by Lord Keith, who had already fallen out with Nelson over the reaction to Bruix's raid. Keith left briefly, leaving Nelson in acting command, but in November he was appointed permanently. Nelson was not considered for the post, probably because his dubious judgement and behaviour were being noticed in England. In any case, he was still only a rear-admiral, too junior for such a command. His health was in decline, his headaches were recurring and he was spending a large amount of time in his sickbed, even when at sea. He wrote: 'Greenwich Hospital seems a fit retreat to me, after being evidently thought unfit to command in the Mediterranean.'

In 1800 Nelson lost the official support of an even more important friend, when Sir William Hamilton read in the *Morning Chronicle* that he was to be replaced as ambassador by Sir Arthur Paget. On 24 April Nelson and the Hamiltons made a farewell cruise to Malta in the *Foudroyant*, to support Ball in the siege of Valletta. By the time they arrived back at Palermo on 1 June the new emissary had arrived but Hamilton was reluctant to give up his office. On 10 June the trio sailed for Leghorn, taking with them the Queen, a prince and three princesses, who intended to visit their relatives in Austria. On 13 July he struck his flag and began a slow journey home – overland because Keith refused Nelson the use of the *Foudroyant* and also because Lady Hamilton (who was pregnant), remembered her experiences in the *Vanguard* when fleeing from Naples and had no wish to go by in a smaller ship.

Travelling with Lady Hamilton's mother, Miss Cornelia Knight and their servants, they passed in triumphal progress through Vienna, Prague, Magdeburg and Hamburg, meeting such luminaries as Haydn, who had composed the Nelson Mass. There were many and varied descriptions of Lady Hamilton during the trip. In the progress through Europe, those who met her were alternately charmed or repelled by her. According to James Harris in Vienna, she was 'without exception the most coarse, ill-mannered disagreeable woman I ever met with.' Hugh Elliot in Dresden saw her as 'bold, forward, coarse, assuming and vain.' Perhaps the key to the contradiction was found by Mrs Trench in Dresden, who remarked, 'though coarse and ungraceful in common life, she becomes highly graceful and even beautiful during this performance [of her attitudes]'. But on the whole it was the English upper classes who despised her. Foreigners, including the King and Queen of Naples, were unaware of the commonness of her accent and manners and to a Hungarian newspaper she was a 'tall Englishwoman with a very handsome face, who knows how to demean herself.'[62]

On 6 November the party arrived at Great Yarmouth and Nelson set foot on his native soil for the first time in 2½ years. If his association with Lady Hamilton had lost him the respect of the upper-class Englishmen he had met in his travels, and of some elements in the navy and in politics, he soon to find out how much he was loved by the common people of England. Great crowds gathered to greet him and took the horses from the shafts of his carriage, dragging it through the streets to the Wrestlers Inn. The Mayor and Corporation presented him with the freedom of the city, while a local army regiment staged a *feu-de-joie* and artillery was fired well into the night. It was the kind of adulation which never tired Nelson, which was fortunate, for it was to become a regular feature of his life.

He arrived at Nerot's Hotel in St James's Street in London, to find his father and Lady Nelson. He was feted by the Admiralty and the Lord Mayor but all was not well with his marriage, for obvious reasons. At dinner parties and other social events, Nelson was seen to treat his wife with contempt, very different from his attitude before the Nile campaign. At the same time he was regularly seen in the company of the Hamiltons, though Emma still managed to conceal the fact that she was 6 months pregnant with Nelson's child. By November it was clear that the Nelson was going to live apart from his wife, although he accepted that she had given him no reason to complain during the whole of their married life.

Nelson's career might have sunk further, his private life might have attracted yet more ridicule in London society and the glory of the Nile might have been expunged or forgotten. But on New Year's Day 1801 the Admiralty promoted him to Vice-Admiral of the Blue and sent him to join the Channel Fleet under St Vincent, with his flag in the *San Josef*, which he himself had captured at the Battle of Cape St Vincent. In February he was appointed second-in-command of a special fleet for the Baltic and on 2 April he returned to the one activity at which he excelled when he defeated the Danes in the Battle of Copenhagen.

CHAPTER 19

The Second Coalition

IMMEDIATELY AFTER HEARING news of the Battle of the Nile in October 1798, Lord Spencer set out four immediate aims for the fleet in the Mediterranean: Naples and Sicily were to be protected and supported in any war against the French; communication between France and Egypt was to be cut off; Malta was to be blockaded; and there was to be co-operation with the Turkish and Russian fleets.

In the meantime, British forces gained a considerable success in the western Mediterranean. On 7 November 1798, Commodore John Duckworth arrived off Minorca with a force of two ships of the line, six smaller vessels and a number of transports carrying troops under General Charles Stuart. The operation had been conceived in July, before the Battle of the Nile had been fought, far less reported in England, but ships of the line were in short supply and the operation relied on the knowledge that the French Mediterranean fleet was distracted, wherever Bonaparte's Armament might be heading. Nelson's victory had been known for several weeks by the time Duckworth's force left St Vincent off Cadiz and the squadron sailed in full confidence, despite having only two large warships to cover it. The Spaniards put up little resistance and Minorca was taken without the loss of a single man.

The island had long been considered as a great acquisition to the British crown, by far the best naval base for watching Toulon. In 1756 it was so well regarded that Admiral Byng was shot for failing to prevent its loss. It was far easier to defend than Corsica but more difficult than Gibraltar or Malta. Unlike the last it needed the presence of a strong naval force for its defence, for its fortifications, though extensive, were far from impregnable and the coastline could not be held by the garrison alone. As Admiral Keith wrote,

> The harbour of Mahon in the island of Minorca . . . is sufficiently large to contain any fleet, and it is sufficiently deep too, but narrow at the entrance. There is convenience for careening three ships at a time, and as much more could be made of the port as might be required. There is plenty of water at St Johns . . . but it is absolutely impossible to fortify the ground so as to cover the arsenal and harbour; by this I mean that a superior force landed would drive the troops into garrison, when the arsenal would fall into the hands of the enemy and the ships go to sea.[1]

The harbour of Port Mahon in Spanish hands, with a ship of the line to the right and a sheer legs, for lifting masts into place, on the land behind. (National Maritime Museum, London: PAG9692)

With the port of Toulon empty of warships, Minorca was of no immediate use and might even prove a hostage to fortune, if the French and Spanish threatened its recapture. It had considerable long-term potential but that was never to be realised.

★

To achieve a real and final victory against French power, Britain's leaders were well aware that they still needed to build a coalition of European allies. The support of Russia and Turkey was already forthcoming, because of Bonaparte's Egyptian expedition and Nelson's victory. Formally, the Second Coalition against Revolutionary France came into existence on Christmas Eve 1798, when an alliance between Britain and Russia began. But to get at France, an Austrian alliance was essential. The Battle of the Nile had provided a triumphant response to the Austrian request for a British fleet in the Mediterranean to safeguard her southern flank. But the re-entry of Naples to the war, inspired by Nelson, had actually tended to retard Austria's re-entry to the war. Mistrust between Britain and Austria continued, especially over the question of subsidies. It was only in March 1799, after French troops had begun to move into threatening positions, that Austria declared war and the campaign against France began to look formidable. But the term 'coalition' is perhaps misleading here. There was no single alliance to which all France's enemies agreed and each had very different war aims and interpretations of its purposes. Moreover Prussia, one of the strongest military powers in Europe, was never persuaded to join it.

The most fundamental issue of all was the purpose of the war against France. Was it a crusade against the Revolution, which could only end with the overthrow of the government? If so, it was different from all the other wars of the eighteenth century, which had ended in compromise peace. Or was it merely to limit the danger, to confine France within her 'natural boundaries', forcing her to give up her possessions in the Netherlands and Italy and her alliance with Spain. In June 1799 Grenville, the Foreign Secretary, offered one definition of the alliance.

> It was a coalition of powers gloriously in arms to defend all just and legal governments, and the rights of every people, against the madness, the wickedness, the oppression, the tyranny and the injustice of the French Directory.[2]

It was decided that the attack on France should begin in Switzerland and in Holland, at the opposite ends of the French conquests. Presenting extremes of geography, both were difficult territories for military attack. Both created proud, independent people who had in the past been inclined mainly to republicanism and capitalism even when the rest of Europe was semi-feudal. Both had shown tendencies to rise against French rule and this was an important part of whole strategy, in a war where nationalism and ideology played a greater part than ever before. Even 'governments in exile' were set up in the form of agencies for the refugees from the occupied territories. This strategy would eventually be successful in Spain in the next decade but needed much caution and refinement, as the experience of the Second Coalition would show.

★

Before the new coalition could get its attacks under way, there was a naval diversion which threatened all the gains that Nelson made at the Nile. Admiral Bruix, the French Navy Minster, arrived in Brest to lead the main fleet in a grand expedition, planned by Paul Barras of the Directory. On 15 April his force of nineteen ships of the line and ten smaller vessels managed to evade Lord Bridport's blockading squadron in a fog. This was a serious matter for the British, for yet again he could have gone anywhere – to support a rebellion in Ireland, to the West Indies or India, or to attack British forces in the Channel – but British intelligence had no reports of troops being moved to Brest, as had happened more than a year earlier with the Toulon expedition. A rumour that they had 25,000 soldiers on board was clearly incredible, for the warships could not carry that number in addition to their crews and they had no fleet of transports with them. Nevertheless, all points had to be protected as well as possible.

In fact they were heading for the Mediterranean, as Admiral Keith found out when they confronted his blockading force of fifteen ships of the line off Cadiz. With a gale blowing onshore, Keith (who counted thirty-three ships in the enemy fleet) was unable to take the offensive and was satisfied to prevent a junction between the French and the Spaniards. In fact the French had no such intention and regarded the Spanish ships in Cadiz as a stagnant force, mere prison and hospital ships for their disgruntled and sickly crews.[3] Bruix took his force through the Straits of Gibraltar, where it was seen by St Vincent, who was sick on shore.

The move could not have come at a worse time for the British, for their fleet was dispersed. As with Bonaparte in 1798, it had been taken for granted that control of the Mediterranean was secure, that an enemy fleet would not come to dispute it. The British navy was busy exercising its command of the sea. Nelson was at

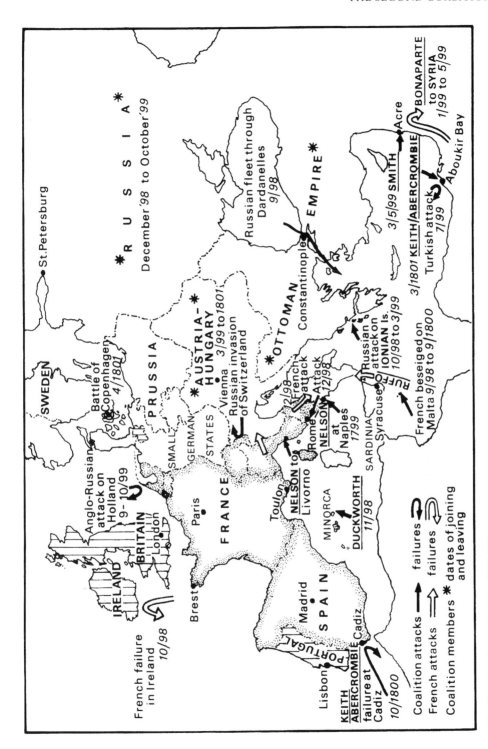

The War of the Second Coalition 1799-1801.

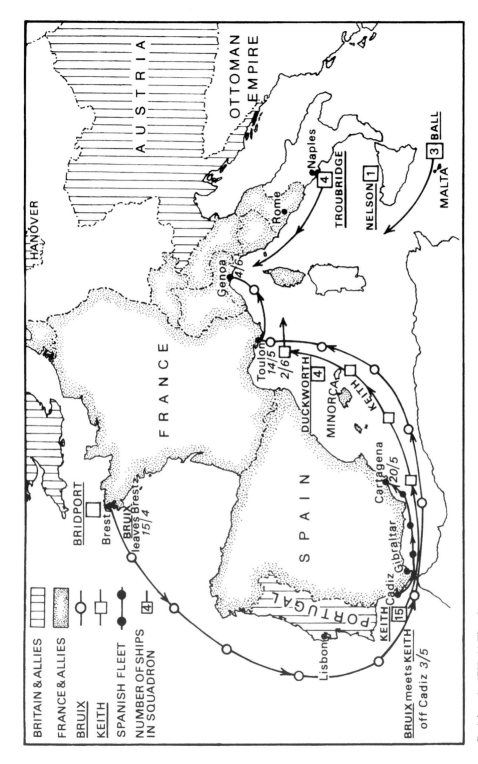

Bruix's cruise 1799. (a) The advance.

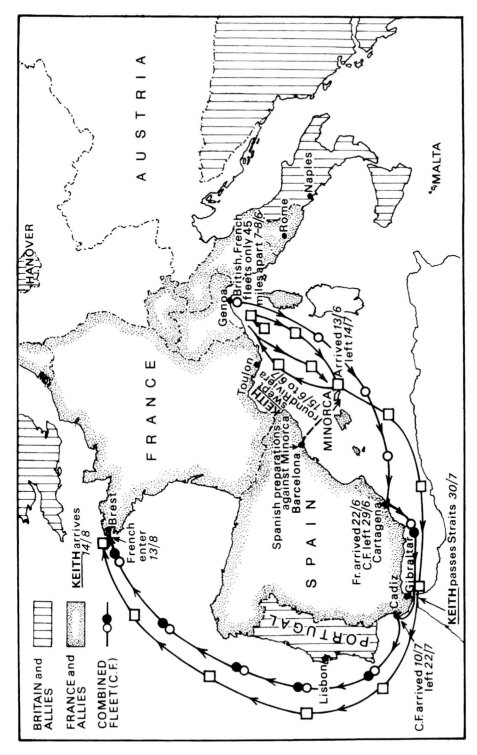

Bruix's cruise 1799. (b) The retreat.

Palermo with the *Vanguard*, Troubridge at Naples with four ships of the line and Ball was off Malta with three. Smith had two more ships at Acre and Duckworth had four at Minorca. The French force of nineteen, which was in fact intended to support the armies in northern Italy, could have overwhelmed any one of these dispositions, or driven it off station. Besides the potential loss of ships, Malta might be relieved, Nelson and Troubridge driven away from Naples, Minorca re-taken or Bonaparte rescued in Egypt. Each of the gains from the victory at the Nile was under threat.

Keith followed Bruix into the Mediterranean, though some distance behind. He in turn was followed by the Spanish fleet, which of course was no longer blockaded in Cadiz. Bruix reached Toulon on 14 May and a few days later the Spaniards, with their ships much damaged by bad weather, put into their base at Cartagena, in south-east Spain. Bruix was now ordered to Genoa to relieve the French troops there and had arrived on 4 June. On hearing that the Spaniards were in also the Mediterranean he decided to sail to join them at Cartagena, where they would form an enormous allied fleet of forty-three ships.

Because St Vincent was ill and increasingly feeble, command of the British force of nineteen ships of the line devolved on Vice-Admiral Lord Keith, a competent, puritanical and acerbic Scot who claimed (with perhaps some exaggeration) to have left home with £5 in his pocket but ended up the richest man in the navy from prize money. On 8 June the British and French forces passed within about 45 miles of each other in the Gulf of Genoa, heading in opposite directions. It was a repeat of the situation that Nelson had faced during the Nile campaign and averted a battle which might have been the greatest of the age of sail. Keith reached Minorca on 13 June, while Bruix arrived at Cartagena nine days later. Meanwhile Keith had sailed back, looking round the south of France and finding nothing. He concentrated his forces at Minorca, which was a likely object of the French fleet and of Spanish preparations at Barcelona, but which also provided a convenient rendezvous for a force to operate against the French in Toulon. In this of course, he was not assisted by Nelson's refusal to spare some of his ships from Naples.

By the end of June Bruix and the Spaniards had failed to agree where to attack next. The latter naturally put the recovery of Minorca at the top of their priorities but feared for the strength of the British fleet, which they believed, with considerable exaggeration, had sixty ships of the line in the Mediterranean. They had no way of knowing how difficult it was proving to unite what forces there were. The combined fleet left the Mediterranean for Cadiz, hoping to mislead the British and take control of the English Channel. Keith heard of this in the middle of July and went in pursuit. He had bad luck with the winds in the Straits of Gibraltar and meanwhile the French left Cadiz for Brest. He pursued, arriving off the French base a day after Bruix had re-entered it.

The campaign was a disappointment to both sides. The French had done little to support their troops in Italy and were now blockaded again in Brest, while the British had not succeeded in bringing the enemy to a battle in which they were confident of victory. The French had come out, as the navy had long hoped they would but the combined forces of Bridport and St Vincent had failed stop them, or to find them in time. The close blockade of Brest was shown to be fallible and the British command structure had not worked well. But the greatest problem, as in the Nile campaign, was to find the enemy in a world which provided many targets for his activities but no means of reconnaissance better than a lookout at a masthead. It was a problem endemic to this kind of warfare, in which fleets ranged over the seas of the world but there was no kind of telecommunication. Keith had done no better than Nelson in finding the French and perhaps he was less successful at second-guessing their intentions. He has been much criticised by supporters of Nelson, who find it difficult to forgive his disputes with their hero, but he was praised by St Vincent, who wrote, 'I approve of every part of your conduct, and most sincerely lament that it was not attended with merited success.'[4]

★

By the summer of 1799 Britain had the makings of an effective army, augmented by volunteers from the militia, who had initially been recruited through a form of selective conscription, so were of better quality than the 'scum of the earth' who formed a large part of the regular army. Various plans were made for an invasion of Holland, supported by a rising of the people against French rule and by a large force of Russian troops. In fact only 11,000 Russians were provided, along with 24,000 British. The first British force of 15,000 men landed in Northern Holland, near the naval base of Den Helder, on 27 August. There was an initial and rather unexpected success, when the Dutch fleet, including eleven ships of the line, was captured with the help of some of its own officers. After that the landing became bogged down, the expected rising did not materialise and the French began to rally. The weather was rainy and progress was slow over the dykes and marshes of Holland. More than 4000 men were lost and after 6 weeks the force was withdrawn. The new British army had proved a disappointment, perhaps because the same 'Grand Old Duke of York' was in command. But his second-in-command, Sir Ralph Abercrombie, gained invaluable experience which could be used in the future. Ironically it was British seapower which benefited, with the almost complete elimination of the Dutch navy.

In Switzerland, the plan was for the Russian army under their famous General Suvorov to drive through the country and then into central France, while the Austrians were engaged in northern Italy and the Danube basin. The reality was rather different, for the Austrians and Russians did not co-operate well, leaving the Russians exposed at Zurich. They prepared to withdraw but on 25 September they were attacked by the French General Massena and driven back, losing all their artillery and half their men. Combined with the failure in Holland and the lack of progress in Malta, Tsar Paul began to see no future in the coalition and a month after the battle he ordered the withdrawal of all his troops from western Europe.

★

Nelson visited Malta only twice after his trip in October 1798 and he was disparaging about the value of the island, regarding it as 'a useless and enormous expense'.

He became increasingly involved in the affairs of Naples and in July 1800 Keith was 'as much grieved as surprised' to hear that he had taken ships away from Malta to carry the Queen of Naples to Livorno.[5]

In the meantime the fortifications of Valletta proved their strength and General Vaubois remained determined in his defence. Like Acre, the siege of Valletta reversed many of the traditional rules of warfare. The French, isolated in the city, were better fed and armed than the Maltese besiegers, for the reserve supplies of the island were stored under Fort St Elmo. The wealthier inhabitants of the island were mainly in Valletta and most of their money was with them. The siege took place over an 8-mile front, for all the satellite fortifications of Valletta were in French hands, allowing them the use of both Marsamxett and Grand Harbours; only a tight naval blockade could prevent them supplying themselves. Both sides were under-manned for such a siege. The French had 3000 troops inside the walls while the Maltese had perhaps a hard core of 500 to 600 men, with 2000 or 3000 more armed peasants who could be called on when needed. For both sides, the siege was rather passive. The French made very few sorties into the countryside, for they were well supplied within the city. The Maltese had not the skills, numbers or equipment to mount an assault on the massive defences. At one stage there was a plan to attack the Cotonera Lines in support of a revolt inside the walls but this was discovered and ruthlessly put down by the French.

The Maltese besiegers also lacked direction, being led by priests and lawyers with no military experience. Local and personal feuds were opened up and threatened to destroy the campaign. In these circumstances, the diplomatic skills of Alexander Ball were essential. He was appointed governor of the island in the name of His Sicilian Majesty and granted leave by Nelson to be absent from the *Alexander* when his duty

Valletta during the siege, seen from the west. Manoel Island, with its fort, is in the middle ground, with the city of Valletta behind. Engraved form a drawing by Major J Weir. (National Maritime Museum, London: B4776)

on shore required it. As a British general wrote of him: 'For the management of the Maltese too much praise cannot be given to Governor Ball; he has devoted himself to listen to their complaints, to relieve their distresses, to settle their disputes, to redress their grievances and to administer equal justice to them with a degree of patience, address and judgement that very few men are capable of.'[6]

Everything depended on the naval blockade but there were other priorities. Few ships were available and even these were liable to recall in times of crisis. Thus, in mid-1799 even Ball and the *Alexander* were temporarily withdrawn to help in the recapture of Naples. When Bruix's fleet was in the Mediterranean, more ships were taken away for a time, allowing the French to restock their supplies in Valletta. Nelson paid little attention to the island for, despite his experiences in the Nile campaign, his interests were to remain firmly in the western Mediterranean and Malta was too far from Toulon to be useful. Ball on the other hand believed that,

> Malta, from its natural strength and its fortifications may be considered as the most secure possession we have next to Gibraltar. It has many advantages over Minorca, which is so vulnerable in many parts that it is not secure against a superior number to the garrison. The harbours of La Valette are equally capacious with and more secure than those of Port Mahon. The naval dockyard is small but complete. There are mast houses, and a great many store-houses. There are six watering places where water can be got without moving a cask out of the boat.[7]

Whatever its strategic importance, Malta was a microcosm of the difficulties of holding the coalition together. Initially Britain had little interest in the sovereignty of the island, accepting that it should revert to the Sicilian royal house which had held feudal suzerainty over it even under the Knights. Ball proved his worth in gaining the hearts of the Maltese with his wise and liberal policies, particularly his non-interference in religious affairs. In February 1799 he was handed a petition by three 'gentlemen of good character' from the island, asking to be put under a protectorate by Great Britain, for they realised that a small island could not maintain its independence in a predatory world. Having sampled French Revolutionary zealotry and avarice, they had no wish to go back to that. Nor would they welcome the Sicilians who had once ruled the island, and whose misgovernment was well known throughout the Mediterranean.

The Russians would have been even less welcome. Tsar Paul of Russia already claimed a protectorate over the Order of St John, based on the acquisition of some of the estates of the Knights during the Partitions of Poland from 1772 to 1795. The Russian advance into the Mediterranean began in March 1799, when Corfu and Zante were taken from the French. Tsar Paul accepted the title of Grand Master of the Knights of St John in the same year and as part of the campaign against France he was supposed to send a fleet and troops to help with the siege of Valletta. In an extraordinary document, which for a time was accepted by British diplomats, he claimed that Russian troops should occupy the city after its capture, leaving the British and Neapolitans only the outlying fortresses. British army troops arrived in Malta in December 1799 and Neapolitans early in 1800 but it was perhaps fortunate that the Russians never got there.

There were times when the islanders were in considerable distress for food and Troubridge, in temporary command in January 1800, showed his characteristic ruthlessness in illegally seizing neutral supply ships. He railed against King Ferdinand's government for its failure to supply an island over which they claimed sovereignty. 'If the Neapolitan government will not supply corn, I pray your lordship will recall us, we are of no use . . . Such is the fever of my brain at this minute, that I assure you on my honour, if the Palermo traitors were here, I would shoot themselves first and then myself.'[8]

The French attempts to relieve the island, however, led to two further skirmishes which put the final seal on the victory at the Nile. In February 1800, Keith visited Nelson in Palermo and the two admirals sailed to Malta in their flagships *Queen Charlotte* of 100 guns and the *Foudroyant* of 80, carrying 1200 troops. They arrived at Marsaxlokk in the east of the island on the 15th. Meanwhile Rear-Admiral Perree of the French navy had left Toulon on the 7th with his own relief force, consisting of 4000 troops, carried in his flagship (the Nile survivor *Généreux*), a storeship, two corvettes and a small frigate. They were sighted by the British frigate *Success* off Sicily and the news was brought to Malta. Keith kept his flagship close to Valletta harbour to prevent the French getting in, while three more ships of the line were spread out to windward to intercept, with another between Malta and Gozo and the *Alexander* (with Captain Ball on shore engaged in the siege) waiting to the south-east of Malta. It was that ship which first sighted the enemy and went in pursuit. The French storeship was soon taken while the *Généreux*, unable to tack without coming into action with the *Alexander*, fell foul of the frigate *Success* which was able to fire several broadsides through her bows, preventing her from escaping. The *Foudroyant* came up, accompanied by the 74-gun *Northumberland*, and the *Généreux* surrendered with no further resistance. It was Nelson's last sea action of the campaign and very gratifying to him; but perhaps even more so to Captain

The capture of the 80-gun *Guillaume Tell* off Malta. The frigate *Penelope* is raking the Frenchman through the stern, while the *Lion* and *Foudroyant* approach. (National Maritime Museum, London: 1095)

Berry, now in the *Foudroyant* with Nelson, for he still had bitter memories of his captivity in the *Généreux* in 1798.

The last French ship of the line from the Nile, Villeneuve's *Guillaume Tell*, had been in Valletta harbour since September 1798. It became clear that the French could not hold out much longer and at 11pm on 30 March Rear-Admiral Decrès took advantage of a southerly wind and headed for Toulon, hoping to persuade the government to send more support. Within an hour the fugitive ship of the line was sighted by the frigate *Penelope* stationed off the harbour mouth and she, like the *Success* a month ago, began a David-and-Goliath struggle, raking her opponent through the stern and doing considerable damage. Meanwhile the 64-gun *Lion*, guided by the *Penelope's* gunfire, arrived at 5am and ran alongside the enemy, with the yardarms almost touching. Yet again the *Foudroyant* arrived, though Nelson was no longer on board, and the *Guillaume Tell*, the last of Brueys's battle fleet, hauled down her flag and surrendered.

On 5 September 1800, almost exactly 2 years after the start of the Maltese revolt, the French forces capitulated to the British. The Maltese rebels were not recognised at the negotiations, despite their great efforts, because neither the British nor the French wanted to include them. The French forces were allowed to return to Toulon, without being treated as prisoners of war. It was generally assumed that the island would eventually revert to either Naples or the Knights but for now the British found it useful as a naval base. They continued to do so until the last forces were withdrawn in 1979.

★

Meanwhile off Brest, St Vincent took command of the Channel Fleet in April 1800, having recovered from his exhaustion and illness. He was a fanatical supporter of close blockade, determined to keep a force close to the French base in all possible weathers. The change in command did not make so much difference as it might have, since Bridport had already been urged to implement a close blockade but St Vincent used the anchorage in Douarnenez Bay in Britanny, long considered too close to the shore for a British fleet to anchor safely. He was aided by unusually good weather and the blockade of Brest was tighter than ever before. However, the port could never be completely sealed and in January 1801 Admiral Ganteaume, who had been Brueys's chief of staff at the Nile and had escaped from *L'Orient*, took command of a force of seven ships of the line, including three of 80 guns, plus two large frigates and a lugger. They carried 5000 troops for a final attempt to support the army in Egypt against a threatened British invasion. Diversions were created by ships at all the French other ports in the area and Ganteaume slipped out of Brest, only to be discovered and chased back. He waited for a westerly gale to blow the British squadron off station and escaped again in circumstances of great danger. Topmasts were lost in several ships and the admiral was separated for a time, until the squadron was reunited off Cape Spartel, near Tangier.

By then the French had already had several encounters with British ships and were sighted again as they passed through the Straits of Gibraltar. The only seagoing ship in the harbour at that moment, the 32-gun frigate *Success*, set off in pursuit, initially planning to go to Egypt and warn Keith and Abercrombie of the threat to their expedition, but she was eventually captured. Meanwhile a British force of seven ships of the line had been sent in pursuit but went to the West Indies in the mistaken belief that the French had gone there. Another British force, of six ships of the line, was off Cadiz when it received reports of the French movements and set off into the Mediterranean. It went to Minorca and Palermo where it met several more ships, including Ball in the *Alexander*. Eventually they found Ganteaume and gave chase. The French escaped and headed for Toulon, arriving on 5 April 1801.

In April, under orders from Bonaparte in Paris, Ganteaume made another attempt to get to Egypt. He evaded the British and on 9 May his most advanced frigate succeeded in entering Alexandria, thanks to the temporary absence of the blockading force. Meanwhile Ganteaume attempted to land his troops along the coast in Libya but was opposed by the inhabitants. At this point Admiral Keith's squadron caught up with them and the French made off. Benjamin Hallowell in the *Swiftsure* engaged three of them but they escaped, ending the last French attempt to relieve the Army of Egypt.[9] Ganteaume's force was much smaller than Bruix's of 2 years before and therefore less dangerous; but it threatened British operations in Egypt, which at that time were coming to a climax.

★

By the autumn of 1799 both the national heroes, Bonaparte and Nelson, had left Egypt, leaving the local leadership of the opposing sides to Kléber and Sidney Smith. These two had much in common. Both were overshadowed by much more famous superiors but might well have been equally famous had circumstances been slightly different. Both were mistrusted by their leaders and both had ambitions of their own. Kléber was almost as political as Bonaparte himself and might have proved a serious rival had he returned to France. He was bitter at being abandoned in Egypt when Bonaparte fled, leaving him isolated and with all the problems of administering the country, maintaining the crumbling morale of an army without any sense of purpose and dealing with internal rebels and external invasions.

During the Bruix expedition there was some hope of relief but by the end of 1799 Kléber was ready to open negotiations with the British and the Turks, as indeed Bonaparte had authorised him to do in the circumstances. Sir Sidney Smith looked favourably on this, believing that the troops left behind in Egypt, including Kléber himself, were only there to keep them out of French politics. They were 'liberal, gentleman-like men, it is not expected they will be reconciled to a more monstrous tyranny established in place of the Directory.'[10] On 24 January 1800, on board Smith's flagship the *Tigre* moored off Damietta at the mouth of the Nile, the Turks, French and Smith agreed that Kléber's forces would abandon Egypt, to be ferried back to France with their arms and baggage.

This agreement, the Convention of El Arish, horrified almost everyone in the Coalition who had not been a party to it. Smith had exceeded his authority, not for the first time. More important, he had allowed far too generous terms to the French. Kléber's men, although reduced to about 15,000 by battle and disease, were among the most experienced and seasoned troops in the world and could make a significant contribution to the war in northern Italy if they were allowed to go home. The Convention was quickly rejected by Keith, the Admiralty and the British government, and Kléber was obliged to remain in Egypt. In June he was assassinated by a Moslem fanatic and command devolved on General Menou, a very ineffective leader.

In September 1800, Dundas suggested to Spencer that a major British military expedition should be sent to Egypt. Peace negotiations with France were in progress and the conquest of the country might prove a useful bargaining counter. A force of 15,000 troops was embarked in 138 ships. Combined operations were often difficult for the British. There was then no legal way to put a general in command of an admiral or vice versa, so the command had to be joint and everything depended on co-operation between the land and sea officers. During the last century there had been several failures in such ventures owing to differences between the generals and admirals, such as Admiral Vernon and General Wentworth in the West Indies in the 1740s. Keith had already gained considerable experience of combined operations, with the capture of Charleston, North Carolina, in 1780 and the taking of the Cape of Good Hope in 1795. Admittedly the Keith-Abercrombie partnership had not performed well off Cadiz in October 1800, when a landing near the Spanish naval base had been called off at the last minute but Keith had never really believed in that operation. Unlike Nelson, Keith was able to learn from his mistakes in amphibious warfare and he brought a great deal of knowledge to the Egyptian operation in 1801. General Abercrombie had fought in the West Indies early in the war and served as second-in-command in the Holland expedition of 1799. The two had evidently made up their differences over Cadiz and Keith wrote in February 1801, 'We meet on terms of intimacy and the duty has gone on uninterruptedly well. I have laid my shoulder to it, the army has wanted nor been refused nothing.'[11] A rendezvous was fixed at Marmaris in southern Turkey and many difficulties of supply were overcome. On 1 March 1801, Keith anchored his fleet in almost the same place that Brueys had used in 1798; indeed the *Foudroyant* touched the wreck of *L'Orient* on the way in. There were several days of bad weather and the landing began a week late.

The landing was unusual for that age in that it was opposed on the beaches. The French were well aware of the British preparations and that Aboukir Bay was by far the best place to anchor a fleet and land troops, so the area was defended by 2000 Frenchmen. General Menou, however, remained at Cairo with the bulk of his forces and so lost an opportunity for a repetition of the French success against the Turkish landings at the same spot in 1799. In the first line, fifty-eight flat-bottomed boats carried fifty soldiers each. They were towed by the ships' barges and pinnaces of the squadron, followed by smaller craft such as jolly-boats and cutters to help disabled boats. The flanks were protected by naval cutters and the fort of Aboukir was attacked by bomb vessels. Five thousand five hundred British troops were landed in the first wave, almost as many as the boats could carry, and about 600 were killed or wounded. But the French were driven back and the beachhead was consolidated. The second and third waves were soon ashore and the army marched out to defeat the

French at the Battle of Lake Mareotis. Both sides suffered heavy casualties and Abercrombie, a promising general who might have rivalled Sir John Moore and the Duke of Wellington in later years, was fatally wounded. His successor, General Hutchinson, was no more effective than his opponent Menou but in alliance with the Turks he captured Cairo on 28 June. Indeed the French, demoralised after years in Egypt and terrified of falling into the hands of the Turks, were only too glad to surrender. In August Hutchinson turned his attention to Alexandria, where General Menou now had his headquarters. With naval support, he forced its surrender, but a peace treaty between Britain and France had already been signed, so the French soldiers were allowed to return home and the effort was largely wasted. Nonetheless the expedition had completed Nelson's work at Aboukir and it had restored the British army's self-confidence after two decades of defeat.

★

When Bonaparte arrived back in Paris in October 1799, the threat to France from the new coalition was over. On meeting Gohier, the President of the Directory, he told him 'The news that reached us in Egypt was so alarming that I did not hesitate to leave my army, but to set out at once to come and share your perils.' The President put him in his place when he answered, 'General, they were indeed great, but we have now gloriously overcome them. You have arrived in good time to help us celebrate the numerous triumphs of your comrades in arms.'[12]

The Directory was now seen to be weak and indecisive and the notionally democratic Revolution was brought to an end on the night of 9 November, the '18 Brumaire', when Bonaparte organised a successful coup and had himself installed as the first and most powerful of three Consuls, with quasi-dictatorial powers. Democracy had finally been sacrificed but the addiction to war and the need for a strong state had reached a logical conclusion. A soldier-statesman was on the way to absolute power and his creed of military conquest, modernisation and ruthless efficiency would soon take over from the more idealistic and radical doctrines of the 1790s. Political stability was welcome to the middle classes of France but his message had no appeal in the other countries of Europe. It had become less of an ideological war and more of a national one.

Though the First Consul was not allowed to take personal command of the army, Bonaparte went to Italy and defeated the Austrians at the Battle of Marengo in June 1800. General Moreau followed this up by a further defeat of the Austrians at Hohenlinden on 3 December, followed by an advance on Vienna which caused the Austrians to sue for peace. They left the war in February 1801 and Naples was again threatened by French power, as it had been early in 1798 during the Nile Campaign. By the Peace of Florence, agreed in March, Neapolitan ports were again closed to British vessels and the alliance with Britain was ended. It was the end of the Nelsonian dream for Ferdinand and his court.

Relations between Britain and Russia went from bad to worse, partly because the Tsar's ambitions in Malta had been thwarted. The Russians put an embargo on British shipping in November 1800 and went on to form the 'League of Armed Neutrality' with Sweden, Denmark and Prussia, threatening to exclude Britain from her vital supplies of timber and naval stores in the Baltic. In these circumstances, Nelson was sent to Copenhagen and won a crushing victory against the Danes. Ironically, it might not have been necessary had the news of Tsar Paul's assassination 9 days earlier reached the west, but the combination of both events ensured the League's collapse.

Thus the Second Coalition, the most important result of Nelson's victory at the Nile, came to nothing. The Turks had no aims beyond the recovery of their territory in Egypt. The Russians, in contrast, had very grandiose and unrealistic aims which conflicted with those of their allies. Their army, though large, was unused to western fighting and living conditions and only a small part of it could reach the places where it was needed. Tsar Paul was dangerously unstable. Austria was essentially a land power, with an army which was still inferior to that of the French and could not succeed without much reorganisation and a set of more reliable allies. Naples was a minor power, constantly under threat from French forces in the north and with the grave internal weaknesses of a corrupt *ancien régime*. Britain had wealth and sea power but the wealth was not unlimited and sea power, though greatly strengthened at the Battle of the Nile, could not defeat land power on its own. The British army was just beginning to recover from its low point in the mid 1790s, as was demonstrated by its success in Egypt. It had yet to advance the strategy which would eventually win the wars against France, that of co-operating with rebels against French rule, as it was finally to do with the Spanish guerrillas in the 1800s. Meanwhile, France, though she had political problems of her own, had at least settled her form of government for the moment and gained a certain amount of national and political unity. She had the interior lines of communication, the most effective army in the world and the greatest military leader in modern history at her head.

By March 1801, as had happened several times in the last hundred years or so, Britain was triumphant on sea and France on land. Largely but not entirely as a result of the Nile campaign, Britain had made great gains in the Mediterranean. She had been driven out of western Europe but controlled a chain of four Mediterranean bases – Gibraltar, Minorca, Malta and Alexandria. Nelson had captured none of them in person but Minorca had been gained because of the diversion caused by the Egyptian expedition, while Malta and Alexandria were a direct result of his victory at the Nile.

But all these bases, except the long-standing one at Gibraltar, were threatened with loss when peace negotiations began with the French in 1801. The Pitt government fell on 14 March, because the King refused to accept the Prime Minister's plans to give full political rights to the Roman Catholics in Ireland and elsewhere, regarding it as a breach of his coronation oath to defend the Protestant religion. The new government, with Henry Addington as Prime Minister and St Vincent as First Lord of the Admiralty, was prepared to make considerable concessions to secure peace. Nearly all the British conquests – the West Indian islands, the Cape of Good Hope, Malta and Minorca – were to be returned to their former owners. As the treaty was signed at Amiens on 1 October 1801, the French knew that their army in Egypt had surrendered but the British did not. As a result, the remnants of Bonaparte's Army of Egypt were sent home and the country was restored to Turkish rule. It was not a good deal for Britain, for France remained in control of Holland and northern Italy. The Peace of Amiens itself was destined to last only a year and a half.

On the British side, the agreement to withdraw from Malta was never implemented, providing part of the *causus belli* when war resumed in 1803. The island became a British possession for the next 164 years. It gained a place in the national heart with its brave defence in 1940-42 but its value in wartime still causes some controversy. Perhaps its greatest use was as a peacetime base, with far better facilities than Gibraltar. It allowed the British to keep a strong fleet in the Mediterranean in peacetime, so that they would not be taken by surprise when war was declared, particularly in 1803.

★

The short-term hopes raised by Nelson's victory were enormous, seeming to offer the isolation of France's greatest general, the makings of a new coalition and the basis of a British control of the Mediterranean equivalent to the one which France had enjoyed a few months before the battle. But none of these was to be fully realised in the medium term. Bonaparte soon escaped from Egypt, the coalition soon collapsed and the gains in the Mediterranean were negotiated away at the Peace of Amiens. Only Malta, a base which Nelson himself regarded as of dubious value, remained as a permanent possession.

In the medium term, then, the results of the Battle of the Nile were a great disappointment to the British. The long-term effects, spread over the next few decades, were less obvious and more complex but far more important. The science of Egyptology was born, initially fostered by the French, though the Rosetta Stone, which provided the key to decoding the ancient hieroglyphics, ended up in British hands. Turkish rule was restored to the country but the Mamelukes were no longer an important force. Mehemet Ali, who had fought against Bonaparte in 1798, came to power as Viceroy in 1805 and ruled for more than 40 years. He began to reform the country, creating a modern port at Alexandria among his other achievements.

For Britain the long-term results of the battle were of purely naval importance, though that is not to denigrate them. The captured ships of the line were taken into the British fleet, though only three of them saw active service. The *Tonnant* and *Spartiate* proved perfectly adequate ships. The *Franklin* was renamed the *Canopus* and served for more than 60 years, providing the model for ten new ships built between 1815 and 1832.

But the real effects were far more profound. The new French navy, rising from the ashes of the Brest mutinies and the Toulon occupation, was strangled at birth and never allowed to rise again. As two modern French historians have put it, 'The Battle of the Nile, as the English call it, was the first battle of annihilation in maritime history. It consecrated, whether you like it or not, the finish of the French Navy as a force capable of counterbalancing British power. It could not be put together again and Aboukir carried within itself the germ of Trafalgar.'[13] Britain's naval confidence was greatly strengthened and her new naval hero reached the take-off point in his career. His mistakes in the months following the battle were serious enough but like Bonaparte he survived these vicissitudes and won two more great battles, led an even greater chase of the French fleet and died gloriously as Britain's greatest national hero.

Yet despite its dramatic circumstances, Trafalgar was a less important battle than the Nile. Napoleon had in fact abandoned his invasion plans several weeks before, and the tactical supremacy of the British navy was undisputed by this time. Less than half the enemy fleet was destroyed or captured, compared with about 85 per cent at the Nile. However, far more men took part in the Battle of Trafalgar than the Nile and told tales about for decades afterwards. Trafalgar was the only one of Nelson's three great battles that was fought at sea rather than at anchor in sheltered waters. It was the last in a long series of battles between the British and French, and the last battle fought between sailing ships, apart from a very easy victory against the Turks at Navarino in 1827. Despite the legend, however, the Nile was the battle which first established the Nelson myth and created much of his character.

The Nelson cult, so created at Aboukir Bay, had an ambiguous effect on the British character and the Royal Navy, for in the nineteenth century it may have caused an exaggerated respect for the past and slowed technological progress. While virtues of courage, initiative and leadership are valid in any period, any illusion that fleet victories of annihilation could still be won against a determined foe in the age of steel, steam, long-range rifled guns disappeared in the grey waters off Jutland in 1916. Yet the next age of naval warfare, dominated by submarines and aircraft rather than surface ships, produced its own kind of heroes, in the form of successful pilots and submarine commanders. But fleet battles are a thing of the distant past and there will never by a repetition of the events 1 and 2 August 1798, when, amid the shoals of Aboukir Bay, the result of a contest between two modestly-sized sailing squadrons changed the balance of world power, literally overnight.

Principal Sources

(As cited in the Notes)

Berry	Berry, Edward, *An Authentic Narrative of the Proceedings of His Majesty's Squadron . . .* (London 1798).
Ehrmann	Ehrmann, John, *The Younger Pitt – The Consuming Struggle* (London 1996).
Elliot	Elliot, Sir George, *Memoir of Admiral the Honourable Sir George Elliot* (London 1863).
Fortescue	Royal Commission on Historic Manuscripts, *The Manuscripts of J B Fortescue of Dropmore* Vols 4 to 6 (1905-8).
Gloires	Loir, Maurice, *Gloires et Souvenirs Maritime* (Paris 1895).
Gutteridge	Navy Records Society (NRS) Vol 25, *Nelson and the Neapolitan Jacobins*, ed Gutteridge (1903).
Keith	NRS Vol 90, *The Keith Papers*, ed C Lloyd, Vol 2 (1950).
Hardman	Hardman, William, *A History of Malta during the Period of the French and British Occupations, 1798–1815* (London 1909, reprinted Valetta 1994).
Herold	Herold, J C, *Bonaparte in Egypt* (London 1963).
Health	NRS Vol 107, *The Health of Seamen*, ed C C Lloyd (1965).
Knight	Knight, Cornelia, *Autobiography*, 2 vols (London 1861).
La Jonquière	La Jonquière, Clement de, *L'Expedition D'Egypte, 1798–1801*, 5 vols (Paris 1900).
Lavery	Lavery, Brian, *Nelson's Navy, the Ships, Men and Organisation* (London 1989).
Lloyd	Lloyd, C C, *The Nile Campaign: Nelson and Napoleon in Egypt* (London 1973).
Logs	NRS Vol 16, *Logs of the Great Sea Fights*, ed T Sturges Jackson (1898).
Naish	NRS Vol 100, *Nelson's Letters to his Wife and Other Documents*, ed G P B Naish (1958).
Nicol	Nicol, John, *The Life and Adventures of John Nicol, Mariner*, ed. Gordon Grant, (Edinburgh 1822, reprinted London 1937).
Nicolas	Nicolas, Sir Nicholas Harris, ed, *The Dispatches and Letters of Vice Admiral Lord Viscount Nelson*, 7 vols (first edition London 1844).
Ralfe	Ralfe, J, *The Naval Biography of Great Britain*, 4 vols (London 1828).
Ross	Ross, John, *Memoirs and Correspondence of Admiral Lord de Saumarez*, 2 vols (London 1838).
Spencer	NRS Vols 46, 48, *The Private Papers of George, second Earl Spencer*, ed Julian S Corbett (1913–14).
Tucker	Tucker, J S, *Memoirs of Admiral the Right Honourable the Earl of St Vincent*, 2 vols (London 1844).
Willyams	Willyams, Rev Cooper, *A Voyage up the Mediterranean in His Majesty's Ship the Swiftsure* (London 1802).

Notes

Abbreviations

Addit	Additional Manuscripts, British Library
BL	British Library
HMC	Royal Commission on Historic Manuscripts
MM	*Mariners Mirror*, the Journal of the Society for Nautical Research, 1911 –
NMM	National Maritime Museum, Greenwich, London
NRS	Navy Records Society
PRO	Public Records Office, Kew, London

CHAPTER 1

1. PRO Logs, especially the *Savage* sloop, Adm 51/1307.
2. Bourrienne, Louis, *Memoirs of Napoleon Bonaparte* (London 1836), Vol 1, p115.
3. Desbrière, Edouard, *Projets et Tentatives de Débarquement aux Îles Britanniques 1793-1805* (Paris 1900), Vol 1, pp387-90.
4. Quoted in Vercoutter, J, *The Search for Ancient Egypt* (London 1992), p39.
5. Winter, M, *Egyptian Society under Ottoman Rule, 1517-1798* (London 1992).
6. La Jonquière, Vol 1, pp154-68.
7. Ibid, pp188-9.
8. Duffy, Michael, *Soldiers, Sugar and Seapower* (Oxford 1987), p11.
9. Lloyd, p12.
10. Chandler, D, *The Campaigns of Napoleon* (London 1967), pp44-52.
11. Brenton, E P, *The Naval History of Great Britain* (London 1837), Vol 1, pp96-8.
12. La Jonquière, Vol 1, p413.
13. Ibid, p303.
14. Ibid, p315.
15. Ibid, p333.
16. Ibid, pp443, 446.
17. Ibid, p449.
18. Ibid, p451.
19. Ibid, p379.
20. Ibid, p401.
21. Ibid, p418.
22. *Gloires*, p96.
23. La Jonquière, Vol 1, p260.
24. Ibid, p264.
25. Ibid, p221.
26. Ibid, pp274, 277, 331.
27. Ibid, p353.
28. Ibid, p486.
29. See Chapter 6.
30. La Jonquière, Vol 1, p281.
31. Ibid, p371.
32. Ibid, p277.
33. Acerra, M and Meyer, J, *Marines et Revolution* (Rennes 1988), p220.
34. La Jonquière, Vol 1, p511.
35. Ibid, p517.
36. Ibid, p275.
37. Lloyd, p15.

CHAPTER 2

1. This conclusion is disputed by Michael Duffy in *Soldiers, Sugar and Sea Power*, op cit, passim.
2. Windham papers, Vol 2, p246.
3. Fortescue, Vol 4ii, p893.
4. Quoted in Lavery, p121.
5. Ackerman's *Illustrated London* (reprinted London 1985), p166.
6. Ibid, p16.
7. Robinson, C N, *The British Tar in Fact and Fiction* (London 1911), pp239-41.
8. *The Times*, 16 March 1798.
9. *Oxford Dictionary of Quotations*, p568.
10. *Dictionary of National Biography*, Vol 53, p764.
11. Quoted in *History of Parliament, 1790 to 1820*, Vol 5, pp265-6.
12. PRO Adm 3/120.
13. Spencer, Vol 1, p13.
14. PRO Adm 1/6033, 16/2/98.
15. PRO Adm 1/6034.
16. Macpherson, D, *Annals of Commerce* (London 1805), Vol 4, p261.
17. PRO Adm 1/395, 10/8/1795.
18. Ibid, pp320-3.
19. Spencer, Vol 1, p327.
20. Order Book, NMM GRE/15.
21. Tucker, Vol 1, pp384-6.

22. NMM GRE/15.
23. Spencer, Vol 2, p401.
24. Ibid, p373.
25. Ibid, p380.
26. Ibid, p430.
27. PRO Adm 1/397.
28. Ibid.

Chapter 3

1. Nicolas, Vol 2, p26.
2. Ibid, pp434, 444-5.
3. Ibid, p455.
4. Quoted in Naish, p381.
5. Admiralty Progress Books no 5, f 97 in PRO Adm 180.
6. Nicolas, Vol 2, p449.
7. Ibid, Vol 3, p2.
8. Ibid, Vol 2, p456.
9. Elliot, p5.
10. BL Addit 34966, 27/9/1797.
11. Ibid, 22/11/97.
12. Nicolas, Vol 2, pp453-4.
13. Naish, p21.
14. BL Addit, Nelson in letters 34906.
15. Nicolas, Vol 2, p457.
16. BL Addit 34966, 25/2/1798.
17. Nicolas, Vol 3, pp3-4.
18. Ibid, pp18n, 20.
19. BL Addit 34966, 25/2/1798, PRO Adm 1/1518, 5/4/1798.
20. Ibid, 14/3/98.
21. Ibid, 25/2/98.
22. Nicolas, Vol 3, p5.
23. PRO Adm 1/1518.
24. BL Addit 34966, 25/2/98.
25. PRO Adm 106/1305.
26. Nicolas, Vol 2, p8.
27. NMM RUSI/35.
28. Nicol, p209.
29. Naish, pp421-2.
30. Trotter, T, *A Practical Plan for Manning the Royal Navy* (Newcastle 1819), pp15-16.
31. Ibid, pp30-1, 37-8.
32. Nicolas, Vol 2, p456.
33. BL Addit 34966, 25/2/98.
34. PRO Adm 35/1990.
35. BL Addit 34966, 8/3/98.
36. NMM RUSI/36.
37. PRO Adm 95/70.
38. Hasted, Edward, *The History of Topography of the Country of Kent* (Canterbury 1798) Vol IV, p192.
39. BL Addit 34966, 25/2/98.
40. Ibid, 8/3/98.
41. Ibid, 8/3/98, 12/3/98.
42. PRO Adm 95/70.
43. BL Addit 34966, 12/3/98.

Chapter 4

1. PRO Adm 36/15356.
2. BL Addit 34974.
3. Naish, p391.

4. BL Addit 34966, 8/3/1798.
5. Ibid, p389.
6. Naish, p389.
7. Spencer, Vol 2, p441.
8. Nicolas, Vol 3, p11.
9. Tucker, Vol 1, p439.
10. Ibid, p438.
11. PRO Adm 8/75.
12. MM, Vol 58, 1972, p282.
13. NRS Vol 20, *Naval Miscellany*, 1901, Vol 1, p272.
14. Naish, p395.
15. Nicolas, Vol 1, p86.
16. Ibid, Vol 3, p21n.
17. PRO Adm 51/1260.
18. Nicolas, Vol 3, pp15-16.
19. Ibid.
20. Berry in Nicolas, Vol 3, p18n.
21. NMM Logs, Adm/L/B/132.
22. Nicolas, Vol 3, pp17-18.
23. Ross, Vol 1, p195.
24. Nicolas, Vol 3, p18.
25. W H Smyth, *The Mediterranean* (London, 1854), p241.
26. Ibid, p242.
27. PRO Adm 52/3265.
28. Falconer, William, revised by Burney, William, *New Universal Dictionary of the Marine* (1815, reprinted New York 1970), p220.
29. Ross, Vol 1, p195.
30. Berry in Nicolas, Vol 3, p18.
31. PRO Adm 52/3265.
32. Nicolas, Vol 3, p19n.
33. Ibid, p19n.
34. Ross, Vol 1, p197.
35. Nicholas, Vol 3, p19n
36. Ibid, pp17-18.
37. Ibid, p21.
38. Ibid, p19.
39. Ibid, p20.
40. Ibid.
41. Ross, Vol 1, p196.
42. Nicolas, Vol 3, pp21-2.
43. Ross, Vol 1, p197.
44. BL Addit 34966, 27/5/98.
45. MM, Vol 58, p290.
46. Nicolas, Vol 3, p18.
47. Ibid, p19n.
48. Ibid, p19n.
49. Ibid, p22.
50. Ross, Vol 2, p199.
51. Ibid, p199.
52. Nicolas, Vol 3, p27n.

Chapter 5

1. La Jonquière, Vol 1, p539n.
2. Ibid, p564.
3. Ibid. p540.
4. Ibid, pp540-1n.
5. Bourrienne, Vol. 1, p127.
6. La Jonquière, Vol 1, p533.
7. Ibid, Vol 1, p547.

8. Ibid, Vol 1, p548.
9. Ibid, pp531-2.
10. Ibid, p548.
11. Ibid, pp552-3.
12. Ibid, pp554-5.
13. Ibid, p553.
14. Keith, Vol 3, p216.
15. La Jonquière, Vol 1, p591.
16. Hardman, pp11-12.
17. Ibid, p13.
18. Ibid, p46.
19. La Jonquière, Vol 1, pp606-7.
20. Ibid, Vol 1, p601.
21. Ibid, p607.
22. Ibid, p596.
23. Hardman, p51.
24. Lloyd, p17.
25. La Jonquière, Vol 1, p598.
26. Bourrienne, Vol 1, p125.
27. Hardman, pp65-6.
28. Glete, Jan, *Navies and Nations* (Stockholm 1993), Vol 2, p544.
29. Hardman, p74.
30. La Jonquière, Vol 1, pp642-50.

CHAPTER 6
1. Fortescue, Vol 4, p167.
2. Ibid, p153.
3. Ibid, p151.
4. Spencer, Vol 2, pp435-7.
5. Fortescue, Vol 4, p166.
6. Ibid.
7. Aspinall, A, ed, *The Later Correspondence of George III* (Cambridge 1967), Vol 3, p54.
8. Spencer, Vol 2, p240.
9. Fortescue, Vol 4, p178.
10. Windham, *Diary* (London 1866), ed Mrs H Baring, Vol 2, pp392-4.
11. Spencer, Vol 2, p438.
12. Ibid, pp438-9.
13. Tucker, Vol 1, pp348, 350.
14. PRO Adm 2/284, 8/1/98, 12/1/98, 17/2/98.
15. PRO Adm 8/75.
16. Ehrman, Vol 2, p126.
17. PRO Adm 8/75.
18. PRO Adm 2/1353.
19. PRO Adm 2/1353, 31/5/98.
20. Spencer, Vol 2, p439.
21. Nicolas, Vol 3, p24.
22. Tucker, Vol 1, p349.
23. Spencer, Vol 2, p437.
24. Fortescue, Vol 4, p178.
25. *Oxford English Dictionary*.
26. NRS Vol 98, *The Private Correspondence of Admiral Lord Collingwood* (1957), p90.
27. PRO Adm 50/93.
28. Disposition of the fleet is shown in PRO Adm 1/394, 29/9/1796.
29. Fortescue, Vol 4, p185.
30. Ibid, p193.
31. Wood, M, *The Importance of Malta Considered . . . also Remarks . . . During a Journey from England to India, through Egypt* (London 1803), pp11-12.
32. Spencer, Vol 2, pp448-9.
33. Ibid, p449.
34. PRO Adm 1/3552, 17/6/98.
35. Windham, *Diary*, op cit, Vol 2, p400.
36. HMC, *Report on the Laing Manuscripts* (1914), Vol 2, p661.
37. Naish, p379.
38. Ibid, pp420-450, passim.
39. Spencer, Vol 2, p451.
40. NRS *Collingwood*, op cit, p89.
41. Lloyd's, Corporation of, and Dawson, Warren, *The Nelson Collection at Lloyd's* (London 1932), p114.
42. PRO Adm 1/397.
43. PRO Adm 1/397.
44. MM, Vol 58 (1972), p287.

CHAPTER 7
1. Ross, Vol 1, p199.
2. Ibid, p200.
3. Nicolas, Vol 3, p27n.
4. PRO Adm 51/1253.
5. Ross, Vol 2, p200.
6. Ibid, p201.
7. PRO Adm 51/1253.
8. Stalkaart, Marmaduke, *Naval Architecture* (London 1781), pp135-6.
9. Sailing reports in PRO Adm 95/39.
10. MM Vol 4, pp266-74.
11. NRS Vol 32, *The Letters and Papers of Charles, Lord Barham* (1906), Vol 1, pp302-3.
12. PRO Adm 95/39.
13. PRO Adm 95/39.
14. NMM RUSI/36.
15. PRO Adm 101/124/1.
16. NMM ADM/L/V/28.
17. Berry, p9.
18. PRO Adm 101/124/1.
19. NMM RUSI/36.
20. Rodger, N A M, *The Wooden World* (London 1986), p346.
21. Spencer, Vol 2, p403.
22. Nicolas, Vol 2, p397.
23. NMM GRE/15 22/6/1798, 9/5/1798, 8/7/1797.
24. BL Addit 30360.
25. PRO Adm 51/1261.
26. PRO Adm 51/1253.
27. PRO Adm 51/1244.
28. NMM ADM/L/V/28.
29. BL Addit 34907.
30. Ross, Vol 1, p241.
31. Nicolas, Vol 3, p43.
32. PRO Adm 101/124/1.
33. PRO Adm 101/123/2.
34. Ibid.
35. PRO Adm 51/1244.
36. PRO Adm 36/14817.
37. Nicol, pp193-4.
38. MM, Vol 23, pp366-7.

39. Lloyd, C C, and Coulter, J L S, *Medicine and the Navy, 1200-1900* (Edinburgh and London 1961), Vol 3, p147.
40. NMM Prints and Drawings Collection, PAD 4287.
41. BL Addit 34966, 8/3/1798.
42. Phillip Patton, *Strictures on Naval Discipline* (Edinburgh c1807), p140.
43. BL Addit 30260, 1/6/98. Originally issued by Troubridge, but confirmed by Nelson.
44. BL Addit 34907 ff 113-6. The list does not include the Ragusan ship which gave the news of the French sailing from Malta, so it cannot be assumed to be complete.
45. BL Addit 36608.
46. Quoted in Ross, Vol 1, p212.
47. BL Addit 30260. It is dated 6 June but this is clearly wrong, as the ships were not together on that date.
48. Nelson Museum, Monmouth, log of the *Vanguard*.
49. Nicolas, Vol 3, p49n.
50. BL Addit 30260.
51. Stalkaart, op cit.

CHAPTER 8
1. Nicolas, Vol 3, p31.
2. Quoted in Fraser, Flora, *Beloved Emma* (London 1986), p94.
3. Ibid, p95.
4. PRO FO 70/11, 29/5/98.
5. Knight, Vol 1, pp106-7.
6. PRO Adm FO/70/11.
7. BL Addit Nelson in letters f 57, 30/6/98.
8. Nicolas, Vol 3, p35.
9. Ibid, p33.
10. Ibid.
11. Ross, Vol 1, p205.
12. Willyams, pp14, 16-7.
13. Ibid, pp14-5.
14. Berry, p11.
15. Nelson Museum, Monmouth, log of the *Vanguard*.
16. Nicolas, Vol 3, p45.
17. Spencer, Vol 2, pp448-9.
18. NMM AGC/W/2.
19. Nicolas, Vol 3, p40.
20. Naish, pp407-9.
21. Naish, pp408-8.
22. Ross, Vol 1, p207.
23. Nelson Museum, Monmouth, log of the *Vanguard*.
24. Ross, Vol 1, p207.
25. Nelson Museum, Monmouth, Nelson's signal log.
26. Nicolas, Vol 3, p42.
27. *Logs*, Vol 2, p19.
28. Quoted in Herold p57.
29. Berry, p13.
30. Ross, Vol 1, p208.
31. Nicolas, Vol 2, p43.
32. Ibid, p41n.

33. Eg Elliot, Nicol.
34. NRS AGC/W/2.
35. Broadley, A M and Bartelot, R G, *Nelson's Hardy* (London 1909), p 35.
36. PRO Adm 7/55, 8/6/98. He was disappointed in his hopes, and later complained 'the sum falls very short of what I expected' (28/9/98).
37. Ross, Vol 1, p205.
38. Naish, p398.
39. Ibid, p392.
40. Parsons, Lt G S, *Nelsonian Reminiscences* (London 1843, reprinted 1973), p241.
41. Nicolas, Vol 1, p13, Vol 2, pp346, 405n.
42. PRO Adm 35/1856.
43. Ross, Vol 1, p207.
44. Nicolas, Vol 1, p124n.
45. Ross, Vol 1, p196.
46. Berry, p13.
47. BL Addit 37077.
48. Nicolas, Vol 3, pp43-5.
49. BL Addit 34974.
50. Nicolas, Vol 3, p42.
51. Ibid.
52. Ibid, pp44-5.
53. Ibid, p43.
54. Ibid, pp42-3.
55. Willyams, p24.
56. Nicolas, Vol 3, p47.
57. Ibid, p46.
58. BL Addit 36608, passim.
59. Willyams, p25.
60. Ibid, p33.
61. Ibid, p37.
62. NMM AGC/W/2.
63. NMM GRT/6.
64. BL Addit 36608, 30260.
65. NMM HOO/4.
66. Nicolas, Vol 3, p47.

CHAPTER 9
1. La Jonquière, Vol 2, p9n.
2. Ibid, p8.
3. Ibid, p9.
4. Ibid, p18.
5. Lloyd, p58-9.
6. La Jonquière, Vol 2, p33.
7. Ibid, p57.
8. Ibid, p41.
9. Ibid, p44n.
10. Ibid, p41.
11. Ibid, p45n.
12. Ibid, p48n.
13. Ibid, pp45-6.
14. Ibid, pp58-9.
15. Lloyd, p60.
16. La Jonquière, Vol 2, p48n.
17. Lloyd, p59.
18. Lloyd, p60.
19. *Copies of Original Letters from the Army of General Bonaparte* (London 1798), No 16.
20. La Jonquière, Vol 2, p68n.
21. Wood, M, *Importance of Malta . . .*, op cit, p55.

22. La Jonquière, Vol 2, p85.
23. Ibid, p86.
24. Ibid, p89n.
25. Ibid, p89.
26. Ibid, p83.
27. Ibid, p91.
28. Ibid, p94.
29. Ibid, p243.
30. Ibid, p94.
31. Ibid, p96.
32. Ibid, p244.
33. Ibid, p248.
34. Ibid, p92.
35. Ibid, p94.
36. Ibid, p249.
37. Ibid, p252.
38. Willyams, p122n.
39. La Jonquière, Vol 2, p255.
40. Ibid, p252.
41. Ibid, pp254–5.

CHAPTER 10
1. Nicolas, Vol 3, p230.
2. Act IV scene III.
3. Nicolas, Vol 3, p129; Naish, pp355, 404.
4. BL Addit 30260.
5. Ross, Vol 1, p204.
6. Ibid, pp212-3.
7. Quoted in Nicolas, Vol 3, p49.
8. PRO Adm 52/2902.
9. Nelson Museum, Monmouth, log of the
   Vanguard.
10. Naish, pp406-7.
11. Ross, Vol 1, p201.
12. Ibid, pp204, 207, 211, 227-9.
13. Ibid, p207.
14. Naish, p363.
15. See Lavery, B, *The Ship of the Line* (London
    1983), Vol 1, p123.
16. Quoted in *History of Parliament, 1790-1820, The
    Commons* (London 1986), Vol 5, pp416-7.
17. Spencer, Vol 2, p472.
18. Nicolas, Vol 3, p30.
19. BL Addit 34907, 3/7/1798.
20. Nicolas, Vol 3, p41n.
21. Ralfe, Vol 4, pp70-1.
22. NMM RUSI/36.
23. Ralfe, Vol 2, pp485-6.
24. Herbert, J B, *The Life and Services of Sir Thomas
    Foley* (Cardiff 1994), p40.
25. Dictionary of National Biography, Vol 60,
    p350.
26. Nicolas, Vol 3, pp43-4.
27. PRO Adm 52/2902.
28. *Logs*, Vol 2, p20.
29. Ross, Vol 1, p215n.
30. NMM AGC/W/2.

CHAPTER 11
1. Nicolas, Vol 3, p49.
2. Ross, Vol 1, p215n.
3. Long, W H, *Naval Yarns* (London 1899,
   reprinted Wakefield 1973), p201.

4. Quoted in Lloyd, p55.
5. Trotter, T, *A Practical Plan for Manning the Navy*
   (Newcastle 1819), p266.
6. *Health*, p265.
7. Nicol, p188.
8. Ibid, p188.
9. The times in the logs of the different ships are so
   variable that it is difficult to know which to
   believe. For the approach to battle the signal log
   of the *Vanguard* is used as standard. (LGSF, Vol
   2, pp52-9).
10. Quoted in Lloyd, p55.
11. *Logs*, Vol 2, p40.
12. Ralf, Vol 4, p63.
13. *Logs*, Vol 2, p21.
14. Ibid, p27.
15. Elliot, p17.
16. La Jonquière, Vol 2, p392.
17. Ibid, p392n.
18. *Gloires*, p97.
19. Ibid, p97.
20. Ibid.
21. Based on Blanquet's account, in La Jonquière,
    Vol 2, p413.
22. Lavery, B, *Arming and Fitting the English Ship of
    War* (London 1987), p275.
23. James, W, *Naval History of Great Britain* (London
    1886), Vol 1, p423.
24. *Logs*, Vol 2, p63.
25. Elliot, pp15-16.
26. *Logs*, Vol 2, p41.
27. Willyams, p51n.
28. BL Addit 30260.
29. *Logs*, Vol 2, pp56-7.
30. Berry, p11.
31. Nicolas, Vol 3, p62.
32. *Logs*, Vol 2, p21.
33. Nicholas, Vol 3, p50.
34. Elliot, p11-12.
35. The accounts from the *Goliath* and *Zealous* (LGS
    10, 42) suggest that the *Audacious* broke through
    the line between the *Guerrier* and *Conquérant*.
    This is not born out by the log, which reads
    'engaged the van ship of the enemy, fired three
    broadsides (larboard guns)'. Futhermore, Gould
    makes no claim to have undertaken such a
    manoeuvre, still regarded as quite daring.
36. *Logs*, Vol 2, p30.
37. Elliot, p12.
38. Ross, Vol 1, p217.
39. *Logs*, Vol 2, p32.
40. Ibid, pp42-3.
41. Elliot, p12.
42. *Logs*, Vol 2, p42.
43. Ibid, p65.
44. Ibid, p73.
45. Willyams, p50.
46. Ibid, p51n.
47. *Logs*, Vol 2, p75.
48. *Logs*, Vol 2, p43.
49. Nicolas, Vol 3, p50.

CHAPTER 12

1. Lee, Sir J T, *Memoirs of the Life and Services* (London 1836), p52.
2. Burney, *Universal Dictionary of the Marine*, op cit, p69.
3. *Logs*, Vol 2, p41.
4. Nicol, p195.
5. NMM AGC/W/2.
6. Willyams, p51n.
7. Nicol, p194.
8. Quoted in *Medicine and the Navy*, op cit, Vol 3, pp58-9.
9. Burney, op cit, p214.
10. *Medicine and the Navy*, op cit, Vol 3, 147.
11. Nicolas, Vol 3, p55, based on Clarke and McArthur (*The Life of Lord Nelson*, 2 vols, London, 1809), who had some direct oral evidence.
12. *Medicine and the Navy*, op cit, Vol 3, p147.
13. NMM GRT/6.
14. *Gloire*, p98.
15. *Logs*, Vol 2, p22.
16. La Jonquière, Vol 2, p406.
17. Ibid, p408.
18. *Logs*, Vol 2, p22.
19. La Jonquière, Vol 2, p408; *Logs*, Vol 2, p30.
20. *Logs*, Vol 2, p43.
21. La Jonquière, Vol 2, p409.
22. Nicolas, Vol 3, p51.
23. La Jonquière, Vol 2, pp409-10.
24. *Logs*, Vol 2, p32.
25. Ross, Vol 1, p221.
26. *Logs*, Vol 2, p69.
27. La Jonquière, Vol 2, p412.
28. Manuscript, Surgeon Bellamy's *List of Killed and Wounded*, Michael Nash Archive.
29. La Jonquière, Vol 2, p412n.
30. Blanquet, quoted in Nicolas, Vol 3, p69.
31. Elliot, p19.
32. BL Addit 34907, 3/8/98.
33. Lee, op cit, p52.
34. *Logs*, Vol 2, p62.
35. Elliot, p19.
36. Ross, Vol 1, p220.
37. *Logs*, Vol 2, p37.
38. Ibid, p70.
39. Lee, Theophilus, (ed Garfield) *Child O' War* (London 1977), p53.
40. Ibid, p54.
41. La Jonquière, Vol 2, p414.
42. Miller in *Logs*, Vol 1, p52.
43. NMM GRT/6.
44. Nicolas, Vol 3, p51.
45. Lee, op cit, p53.
46. Willyams, pp54-5.
47. Nicolas, Vol 3, pp69-70.
48. Willyams, p55.
49. Nicol, p193.
50. La Jonquière, Vol 2, p421.
51. Willyams, p55.
52. Nicolas, Vol 3, p70.

CHAPTER 13

1. La Jonquière, Vol 1, p412.
2. *Logs*, Vol 2, p45.
3. Ibid, p44.
4. NRS Vol 131, *British Naval Documents, 1204-1960* (1993), p421.
5. Ibid, p422.
6. Ross, Vol 1, p221.
7. Nicol, p194.
8. *Logs*, Vol 2, p68.
9. MM Vol 4 (1914), pp271-2.
10. *Biographie Universelle, Ancienne et Moderne* (Paris and Leipzig 1856-8), Vol 43, p475.
11. Nicolas, Vol 2, p70.
12. Ibid, pp60, 70.
13. La Jonquière, Vol 2, p415.
14. *Logs*, Vol 2, p10.
15. Ibid, p44.
16. Ibid, p64.
17. Ibid, p67.
18. La Jonquière, Vol 2, p415.
19. *Logs*, Vol 2, p54.
20. Ibid, p60.
21. La Jonquière, Vol 2, p410; *Logs*, Vol 2, p33.
22. Elliot, p13.
23. *Logs*, Vol 2, p44.
24. Willyams, p51n.
25. *Logs*, Vol 2, p63.
26. Different times given: *Orion*, 3.30; *Vanguard*, 2.55; *Defence*, 2.30; *Alexander*, 3.15: *Logs* Vol 2, pp33, 54, 61, 67.
27. *Logs*, Vol 2, p67.
28. Ibid, p37.
29. *Logs*, p45.
30. Ibid, p33.
31. BL Addit 34907.
32. Elliot, pp13-14.
33. *Logs*, Vol 2, p10.
34. Elliot, p14.
35. BL Addit 34907.
36. *Logs*, Vol 2, p58.
37. Ibid, p45.
38. Elliot, p14.
39. *Logs*, Vol 2, pp45-6.
40. Ibid, p46.
41. Quoted in Lavery, p189.
42. *Logs*, Vol 1, pp73-4.
43. Ibid, p74.
44. Ibid, p47.
45. La Jonquière, Vol 2, p415.
46. Ibid, p417.
47. Ibid, p417.
48. *Logs*, Vol 2, p24.
49. La Jonquière, Vol 2, p416.
50. *Logs*, Vol 2, p48.
51. Ibid, p48.
52. Ibid, p49.

CHAPTER 14

1. BL Addit 34907.
2. PRO Adm 101/124/1.
3. *Logs*, Vol 2, p50.

4. Ross, Vol 1, p232.
5. Nicolas, Vol 3, p61.
6. Ross, Vol 1, p231.
7. *Logs*, Vol 2, p34.
8. Nicol, p194.
9. PRO Adm 51/1249.
10. PRO Adm 51/1288.
11. Nicolas, Vol 3, p127.
12. PRO Adm 51/1249.
13. *Logs*, Vol 2, pp62-3.
14. Edward Mangin, in NRS Vol 91 (1951), *Five Naval Journals*, ed Thursfield, H G, p35.
15. Willyams, p100.
16. PRO Adm 51/1253. Ross, Vol 1, p226 gives the impression that he died during the battle, but this is contradicted by the log.
17. PRO Adm 51/1288.
18. Nicol, p194.
19. PRO Adm 35/14817.
20. *Logs*, Vol 2, pp23-4.
21. PRO Adm 51/1249.
22. BL Addit 24974.
23. Elliot, p20.
24. Figures calculated from Lees, J, *The Masting and Rigging of English Ships of War* (London, 1979), p183.
25. PRO Adm 51/1288.
26. NMM ADM/L/C/246.
27. *Logs*, Vol 2, p51.
28. BL Addit 39407, 10/8/98.
29. *Logs*, Vol 2, p49. 'Carvel-built' is wrongly transcribed as 'carved-built'.
30. Elliot, p14.
31. PRO Adm 51/1288.
32. La Jonquière, Vol 2, p419.
33. *Logs*, Vol 2, p49.
34. Nicol, p194.
35. See Lavery, p318.
36. Nicolas, Vol 3, p103.
37. BL Addit 30260, 3/8/98.
38. BL Addit 34974.
39. BL Addit 34907, 16/8/98.
40. BL Addit 34907.
41. La Jonquière, Vol 2, p413.
42. Ross, Vol 1, p242.
43. *Logs*, Vol 2, p52.
44. Elliot, p15.
45. BL Addit 34907, 10/8/1798.
46. PRO Adm 51/1283.
47. PRO Adm 51/1249.
48. PRO Adm 101/123/2.
49. *Logs*, Vol 2, p14.
50. NMM/ADM/C/246.
51. Nicolas, Vol 3, p101.
52. Ross, Vol 1, p251.
53. Ibid, p241.
54. PRO Adm 51/1288, 1249.
55. PRO Adm 1/398.
56. Ross, Vol 1, p237.
57. Ibid, p240.
58. Ibid, p242.
59. Ibid, p244.

60. Ibid, p245-6.
61. Ibid, p236.
62. Nicolas, Vol 3, p105.
63. NRS Vol 20, *Naval Miscellany* (1901), Vol 1, p273.
64. PRO Adm 51/1288.
65. Ralfe, Vol 4, p63.
66. Ross, Vol 1, pp255-86.
67. Nicolas, Vol 3, p124n.
68. Ibid, p130.
69. Ibid, p98.

CHAPTER 15
1. NMM ADM/L/B/32.
2. PRO Adm 51/4507.
3. NMM ADM/L/E/105.
4. BL Addit 36608.
5. MM, Vol 58, p289.
6. PRO Adm 51/4507.
7. NMM ADM/L/S/224.
8. James, *Naval History* (London 1886), Vol 2, pp234-5.
9. La Jonquière, Vol 1, p649.
10. NMM ADM/L/S/224.
11. Naish, p414.
12. BL Addit 34907.
13. NMM ADM/L/A/86.
14. NRS *Naval Miscellany* Vol 1, p273.
15. BL Addit 34907.
16. PRO Adm 51/4507.
17. Nicolas, Vol 3, p46.
18. BL Addit 34907.
19. Willyams, p90.
20. MM Vol 58, p293.
21. BL Addit 34907.
22. NMM JOD/11.
23. Ibid.
24. PRO Adm 51/4507.
25. PRO Adm 50/93.
26. PRO Adm 1/398.
27. PRO Adm 1/398.
28. James, *Naval History*, Vol 2, pp254-5.
29. Nicolas, Vol 3, p46n.
30. PRO Adm 50/93.
31. BL Addit 34907, PRO FO 77/4.
32. PRO FO 63/79.
33. Glete, J, *Navies and Nations* (Stockholm 1993), Vol 2, p622.
34. PRO FO 63/78.
35. PRO Adm 51/1254, log of *Incendiary*.
36. Naish, p414.
37. Ibid, p414.
38. PRO Adm 1/398.
39. Naish, p415.
40. Nicolas, Vol 3, pp121, 120.
41. Naish, p415.

CHAPTER 16
1. Nicolas, Vol 3, p56.
2. Ross, Vol 1, p228n.
3. PRO Adm 1/5347.
4. PRO Adm 1/5347.

5. Quoted in Mill, J, *History of British India* (London 1840-8), Vol 6, pp101-2.
6. Nicolas, Vol 3, p103.
7. BL Addit 34908, 4/9/98.
8. Knight, Vol 1, pp109-110.
9. Nicolas, Vol 3, p94n.
10. PRO FO 70/11.
11. BL Addit 34908, 4/9/98.
12. Knight, Vol 1, p111.
13. Nicolas, Vol 3, p72.
14. Ibid, p72.
15. Ibid, p73.
16. Knight, Vol 1, pp112-3.
17. BL Addit 34908, 8/9/98.
18. PRO FO 7/53.
19. Karl Geiringer, *Haydn, a Creative Life in Music* (Sydney 1982), p347.
20. PRO FO 64/51, 23/9/1798.
21. Spencer, Vol 2, pp447-8.
22. BL Addit 34908.
23. Lloyd, p301.
24. Tucker, Vol 1, p452.
25. Spencer, Vol 2, p473.
26. *Diaries and Correspondence of the Right Hon. George Rose*, ed Harcourt, Rev L V, Vol I, London, 1860, p216.
27. Nicolas, Vol 3, p93n.
28. *The Diary of the Rt Hon William Windham, 1784-1810* ed Mrs H Barry (1866), p401.
29. Spencer, Vol 2, p454.
30. Fortescue, Vol 4, pp284-5.
31. Windham, *Diary*, op cit, p402.
32. BL Addit 34907.
33. PRO FO 78/20.
34. Spencer, Vol 2, pp459-60.
35. Spencer, Vol 3, pp468-70.
36. BL Addit 34908, 30/9/98.
37. Naish, p448.
38. Faringdon, J, *Diary* (New Haven, Conn, 1978–84), Vol 3, p1059.
39. Spencer, Vol 2, p470.
40. Faringdon, *Diary*, Vol 3, p1060.
41. Windham, *Diary*, p402.
42. Paget, Rt Hon Sir A, *The Paget Papers* (London 1896), edited by Mrs J R Green, Vol 1, p120.
43. Naish, p449.
44. Nicolas, Vol 3, p74.
45. Ibid, pp73-4.
46. *The Wynn Diaries*, ed Anne Fremantle (Oxford, 1940), Vol 3, p3.
47. HMSO, 'So Dearly Beloved, so Much Admired; Letters to Hester, Lady Chatham 1744-1801, ed. Vere Birdwood (London 1996) p174.
48. Naish, p450.
49. NMM Prints and Drawings Collection, PAD 4025.
50. *The Times*, 7 October 1798.
51. Naish, p387.
52. Fortescue, Vol 4, p328.
53. A B Rodger, *The War of the Second Coalition, 1798 to 1801* (Oxford 1964), pp52-3.
54. BL Addit 34908, 25/12/98.

CHAPTER 17
1. La Jonquière, Vol 2, pp433ff.
2. Quoted in Herold, p126.
3. Lloyd, p68.
4. La Jonquière, Vol 2, pp423-4.
5. Quoted in Lloyd, p72.
6. Ibid, p67.
7. Ibid, p70.
8. Quoted in Vercoutter, *The Search for Ancient Egypt*, op cit, p50.
9. Quoted in Lloyd, p76.
10. Quoted in Herold, p277.
11. Quoted in Pocock, T, *A Thirst for Glory* (London 1996), p144.
12. *Keith*, Vol 3, p23.
13. Quoted in Herold, p279.
14. Pocock, op cit, p95.
15. Ibid, p96.
16. Quoted in Lloyd, p91.
17. Ibid, pp87-8.
18. Ibid, p94.

CHAPTER 18
1. Knight, Vol 1, p115.
2. Ibid, pp115-6; Nicolas, Vol 3, p130.
3. Knight, Vol 1, pp116-7.
4. Ibid, pp117-9.
5. Goethe, J W, *Italian Journey* (Princeton 1989), p177.
6. Nicolas, Vol 3, p138.
7. BL Addit 34907.
8. Nicolas, Vol 3, pp132-3.
9. Naish, p400.
10. Ibid, p401.
11. Nicolas, Vol 3, p141.
12. Knight, Vol 1, p139.
13. Naish, p462.
14. Nicolas, Vol 3, p138.
15. Ibid, p146.
16. Ibid, p147.
17. Ibid, p128.
18. Hardman, p98.
19. Ibid, p109.
20. Ibid, p348.
21. Nicolas, Vol 3, p71.
22. Naish, p420.
23. Ralfe, Vol 4, p404.
24. Naish, p520.
25. Fraser, *Beloved Emma*, p224.
26. Nicolas, Vol 3, p336.
27. Nicolas, Vol 3, p215.
28. Ibid, p335n.
29. Ibid, p373.
30. Naish, p482.
31. Nicolas, Vol 3, pp170-1.
32. Nicolas, Vol 3, p344.
33. Mackesy, P, *Statesmen at War; The Strategy of Overthrow* (London 1974), pp54-6.
34. Knight, Vol 1, p126.
35. Nicolas, Vol 3, p209.

36. Knight, Vol 2, p127.
37. Nicolas, Vol 3, p212.
38. Willyams, p174.
39. Knight, Vol 1, p133n.
40. Gutteridge, pxxxviii.
41. Fraser, *Beloved Emma*, p238.
42. Nicolas, Vol 3, p361.
43. Parsons, *Nelsonian Reminiscences*, p11.
44. Fraser, *Beloved Emma*, p257.
45. Gutteridge, p92.
46. Ibid, p103.
47. Nicolas, Vol 3, pp385-6.
48. Gutteridge, p159.
49. Nicolas, Vol 3, p348 and n.
50. Parsons, *Nelsonian Reminiscences*, p5.
51. Ibid, p6.
52. Nicolas, Vol 3, p510.
53. Beginning with Gutteridge, 'Nelson and the Neapolitan Jacobins' NRS (1903).
54. Nicolas, Vol 3, p325.
55. Ibid, pp409-10.
56. Ibid, pp367.
57. Ibid, p407.
58. Ibid, p410n.

59. Spencer, Vol 3, pp99-100.
60. Mahan, Alfred Thayer, *Influence of Sea Power upon History 1660-1783* (Bester 1890, reprinted London 1965), p119.
61. Nicolas, Vol 3, p378.
62. Fraser, *Beloved Emma*, pp268-70.

CHAPTER 19
1. Keith, Vol 3, pp214-5.
2. Quoted in Ehrmann, p229.
3. *La Campagne de Bruix en Méditerranée, Mars-Aout 1798* (Paris 1923).
4. Keith, Vol 2, p34.
5. Ibid, p177.
6. Hardman, p326.
7. Ibid, p348.
8. Ibid, p254.
9. James, *Naval History*, Vol 3, pp69-76.
10. Quoted in Keith, Vol 2, p200.
11. Ibid, p231.
12. Monge, quoted in Chandler, *The Campaigns of Napoleon*, op cit, p253.
13. Acerra, M and Meyer, J, *Marines et Revolution* (Rennes 1988).

Index